A SHORT HISTORY OF
FRENCH LITERATURE

A SHORT HISTORY OF FRENCH LITERATURE

Sarah Kay, Terence Cave, Malcolm Bowie

OXFORD
UNIVERSITY PRESS

OXFORD
UNIVERSITY PRESS

Great Clarendon Street, Oxford OX2 6DP

Oxford University Press is a department of the University of Oxford.
It furthers the University's objective of excellence in research, scholarship,
and education by publishing worldwide in

Oxford New York

Auckland Bangkok Buenos Aires Cape Town Chennai
Dar es Salaam Delhi Hong Kong Istanbul Karachi Kolkata
Kuala Lumpur Madrid Melbourne Mexico City Mumbai Nairobi
São Paulo Shanghai Taipei Tokyo Toronto

Oxford is a registered trade mark of Oxford University Press
in the UK and in certain other countries

Published in the United States
by Oxford University Press Inc., New York

British Library Cataloguing in Publication Data

Data available

Library of Congress Cataloging in Publication Data

Data available

ISBN 0–19–815931–5

10 9 8 7 6 5 4 3 2 1

Typeset by Hope Services (Abingdon) Ltd
Printed in Great Britain
on acid-free paper by
Biddles Ltd,
Guildford and King's Lynn

PREFACE

This short history of French literature is not a beginner's manual, nor is it a reference work. It offers broad narratives of literary development that spotlight what we see as significant scenes and moments, provides a foretaste of at least some key literary works, and raises questions about the nature of French literature and its history. We hope that the book will be used by readers who want a first overview of this extraordinarily fertile cultural terrain; by those who already know something about individual authors or periods but would like to see them in context; and by those who want to get a sense of what from among its many and various riches they might like to read, whether it be famous classics or as yet relatively unknown works.

If students use this book, we suggest they do so as a preliminary to studying particular periods, writers, or works in more detail rather than as a source of ready-made information and critical perspectives. We have not debated with particular critical accounts or individual, named critics: the constraints on space made it essential to give priority throughout to the texts and their contexts. None of the materials of a literary history are timeless, but it is obvious that what are known as the 'primary' texts have a longer lifespan than 'secondary' ones. We include some suggestions for further reading at the end of the book but these are limited to works of broad coverage and to landmark studies of major issues. Similarly, although each of us has taken a professional interest in literary theory in the course of our careers, we have preferred not to engage explicitly with the issues raised by recent critical reflection, but rather to allow our awareness of it to inflect our way of presenting the materials and to question some of the commonplace assumptions of literary history.

We have also, for the same reasons, been resolutely selective. Inevitably, therefore, we say less about certain authors or movements than some readers might have expected. What we were aiming at was not a 'history' in the sense of an even sequence of literary events, but a series of stories told in a broadly historical perspective. It goes without saying that these stories could have been told in many different ways; what mattered to us was that, however we chose to tell them, we should give the reader a synoptic view of the vast, polymorphous cultural phenomenon we call 'French literature'.

Each of us has been primarily responsible for one third of the book: Malcolm Bowie for the modern period, Terence Cave for the early modern period, and Sarah Kay for the Middle Ages. But both the overall plan and the detail of individual sections have resulted from lengthy discussion among the three of us. The Introduction was written jointly, and we likewise assume joint responsibility for the volume in its final form, while also acknowledging differences of treatment between our various contributions. We have not attempted to iron these out because reading literature (and reading history) is not a purely objective activity, and we wanted each contributor to trust his or her personal judgement and vision. We hope that this will provide a stimulus to our readers, in their turn, to make their own judgements and undertake their own exploration of French literature, passing rapidly beyond the limits of the territory we have sketched out here.

ACKNOWLEDGEMENTS

We wish to thank Sophie Goldsworthy of Oxford University Press for her patience and persistence in overseeing this project, and the anonymous readers enlisted by the Press for their perspicacious and constructive comments. Parts of the book have also benefited from advice from Adrian Armstrong, Matthew Bardell, Alison Finch, Miranda Griffin, Sylvia Huot, and Angela Scholar, to all of whom we offer our warmest thanks. Lastly, we are grateful to those scholars and critics whose views have informed our own, and whose findings may appear, without further acknowledgement and in a simplified form, in the pages that follow.

CONTENTS

LIST OF ILLUSTRATIONS

INTRODUCTION: THE LONG VIEW

If you stand on the great Cour Napoléon of the Louvre in Paris, with Mitterrand's glass pyramids in the foreground, there are, more or less visible in the scene behind, signs of constructions going back to the Middle Ages. It was on this spot that King Philippe Auguste constructed a fortress in the late twelfth century; the foundations of the fourteenth-century castle which King Charles V built on the same site have now been excavated and opened to the public; the present palace was begun in the sixteenth century and was continued into the nineteenth. There has always been a palace at the Louvre and it has always monumentalized a view of French power and culture. The glass pyramids would not be here if Philippe Auguste had not built there, and conversely, if the pyramids had not been built, we would have known much less about the medieval fortresses beneath them. The transformations wrought on the site over successive centuries, the alterations of use to which buildings have been put, can thus be drawn into a narrative whose parts interconnect despite their radical disjunction. If you walk around this part of Paris, guidebook in hand, you can take in the great sweep of this history more or less at a glance. Or, of course, you can choose to dwell on one period or another, exploring it at your leisure.

In this book, we offer a guide to French literature which, like these great cultural monuments, goes back at least a millennium. Unlike architecture, however, literary texts do not have to be torn down for others to be built in their place. The literature of the past is easier of access than its buildings. While it is undoubtedly true that those early texts which hold our attention today do so because they chime in some way with modern interests, it is also true that modern texts would not have come to assume the form they have without the influence of those that precede them. Consequently, although what we may understand by 'French literature' has changed almost beyond recognition since the earliest texts emerged more than a thousand years ago, its various manifestations may none the less be viewed as forming a great single narrative. The purpose of this Introduction is to take a first view of this narrative, and of the foundations on which it might rest, as if from afar; and it will go on to indicate how this view will be supplemented from different perspectives, and increasing degrees of proximity to its subject matter, in the subsequent parts of the book. We end with the suggestion that the story of French literature is a many-stranded one that can be told in various ways, ways that are explored in the remainder of this book.

If one surveys the course of French literary history from the oldest surviving medieval examples to contemporary works, one is confronted by a series of radical transformations. Literature changes from being primarily based in oral performance to being mediated principally through reading. Its reception shifts from the ear to the eye, from verse to prose, and from being a group activity to becoming a solitary experience: one can see the shift in process in works like Boccaccio's *Decameron* and its French equivalents, the *Cent Nouvelles nouvelles* and Marguerite de Navarre's *Heptaméron*, where a manuscript or printed text represents the oral delivery and consumption of narrative by groups of story-addicts. Early literature, like other early cultural productions, is reproduced through technologies of the body, whether in performance or the laborious copying out of texts by hand—and on skin, in the case of most medieval manuscripts; but the invention of printing leads to its reproduction through ever more refined technologies, manufacturing, industrial, or electronic. The very conception of what material is suitable for literary expression is transformed, as the valuing by early texts of traditional themes and modes of expression gives way to prizing originality of invention, while at the same time the range of available genres shrinks from the multitude available in the Middle Ages to the emphasis on narrative that is to be found in so many modern novels and films. Initially produced under the auspices of patronage of some kind, and hence with some degree of collaboration by a person or group other than the author, literature later becomes an expression of individual sensibility and creativity, to be protected by laws of copyright and consumed by a mass market.

This account of the literary history of France, compressed as it is into a single paragraph, would hold true of most European literatures. Its value is that it highlights major changes that can easily get lost as the focus closes in on particular periods or moments; and it reminds us that the forms that literature adopts today are both contingent on past change and subject to further mutation. We shall now expand upon this account by asking a series of broad-based questions that are framed so as to address the terms of our title, and of our project. They will enable us to sketch the first outlines of this ever proliferating and open-ended story.

WHAT IS LITERATURE?

The domain of the literary encompasses different genres at different periods. Although today literature is usually understood in the restricted sense of 'literature of the imagination', it has traditionally formed part of the wider history of thought, and has included historical, didactic, devotional, and other kinds of writing. Most of the surviving vernacular texts of the Middle Ages, apart from some legal and other technical documents, would count as 'literature'; in the early modern period, historical, philosophical, and religious writings were similarly produced and read, for the most part, within what came to be known as the 'Republic of Letters'. Many works that we class as literary, such as the thirteenth-century *Roman de la rose* or the writings of Rabelais and Montaigne in the sixteenth century, were written by polymaths who drew on the whole range of their cultural knowledge and respected no precise boundaries of genre or subject matter. The interest shown by many critics of modern French literature in the conjunction of literature and philosophy in contemporary writing attests to a renewal of this vital role of literature as a medium of thought.

For most of the history of French literature, its status as a vehicle for serious reflection has been determined in part by the extent to which Latin was still in use as a language of learning and culture. The availability of Latin as an international cultural medium meant that texts written not in Latin but in the vernacular were perceived, broadly speaking, as less serious and authoritative. Doctoral theses in some French universities were still written in Latin as late as the twentieth century. The spread of the vernacular to learned works is a gradual process, continuing from the early Middle Ages to the threshold of the modern era, but gaining exceptional momentum between the fourteenth and the seventeenth centuries. Descartes favoured Latin for his more extended philosophical writings, yet his *Discours de la méthode*, intended only as a brief preliminary sketch, became one of the most famous French texts of early modern times.

Concomitantly, one way in which European literature is defined, in varying degrees, throughout its history is with reference to Latin and Greek models. Ideas of literary genre, composition, and style have, for virtually the whole period of French literature, reflected or engaged with the teachings of ancient authors on the art of writing. Such teachings, systematized in works of 'rhetoric' or 'poetics', commanded respect until the modern period. But beyond and regardless of these, many French writers have positioned themselves, more or less consciously, relative to the canon of ancient authors—not only for their content but also as models of good style. If we leave aside philosophical writings, in particular those of Aristotle, which had an enormous impact in other cultural spheres, the ancient canon comprises principally poetic works such as the epics of Homer and Virgil and the lyric poetry of Horace and Ovid, or the dramatic legacy of Sophocles and Terence; in addition, the prose writings of Cicero, Seneca, and historians such as Tacitus were widely read and studied. Until the sixteenth century, the canon was almost exclusively Latin; Greek works came to be known later and more slowly, mainly through translation. It is this corpus that defines and shapes the work of the scholars and writers who were called 'humanists' and that has led historians to speak of a series of 'Renaissances', from the twelfth century to the sixteenth, and the sense of what literature was and what it could do evolved in the shadow of this sometimes daunting heritage. As will become clear from the more detailed accounts of the Middle Ages and early modern period below, one of the most telling indicators of the vigour and fertility of French culture is the extraordinary variety of its rewritings of Latin and Greek models. And the reverberations continue even later: Chénier, Baudelaire, and Mallarmé still perceive Latin verse as a paradigm, Proust refers frequently to Homer and Virgil, while Cocteau, Giraudoux, Anouilh, and Sartre turn to the mythical themes exploited in the theatre of antiquity for their own dramatic and political ends.

The use of verse as a medium is another factor in the definition of the literary as a distinct domain. In earlier times, nearly everything we think of as literature was or at least could be written in verse: not only lyric poetry, but also narratives of all kinds, devotional works, cosmological speculations, philosophical reflections, and the whole range of theatrical forms and genres. Few plays were written in prose before the eighteenth century; Hugo's revolutionary *Hernani* (1830) was written in the same verse-form as Racine's tragedies, even though some of the hallowed conventions of the alexandrine couplet were notoriously broken, creating a furore on the first night. The shift to prose was prolonged and gradual, affecting first biblical translations and historical works, and—almost immediately after—the enormous romance narratives of the high Middle Ages. It is hard to imagine Montaigne's *Essais* in verse-form, although nearly two hundred years later Voltaire and others wrote extended philosophical poems. Hugo's *La Légende des siècles* is still a kind of verse epic, but a fragmentary one, and by the later nineteenth century, the great tide of prose has taken possession of the literary domain, leaving high lyricism as the main refuge for verse. And even that refuge was not secure: at about the same time, experiments in prose poetry began to multiply, with Baudelaire's *Spleen de Paris* as the model, and the metrical conventions of verse were increasingly challenged or disrupted.

Literature may of course also be defined in its relations with the other arts. Earlier lyric poetry is intimately connected with song, and the connection will continue through the Renaissance *chanson* and madrigal to resurface in nineteenth-century *mélodies* by Berlioz, Duparc, Fauré, and Debussy, then more recently in the popular songs of Charles Trenet and Georges Brassens, who, like the troubadours, both wrote their songs and performed them. Similar threads may be traced in the theatre. In the late sixteenth century, complex courtly entertainments involving dramatic scenarios, dance, and song form the nexus out of which opera will evolve in the seventeenth century. One of the ways in which late seventeenth- and eighteenth-century audiences most commonly enjoyed tragedy was through operatic versions of the myths that Racine and his contemporaries made famous; on the threshold of the twentieth, Debussy's *Pelléas et Mélisande* grew out of his interest in finding musical equivalents for the distinctive patterns of the spoken French language.

From the earliest times books have not only transmitted literary works, but also served as art objects in their own right; and so there has always been an intimate relationship between literature and the visual arts. The production of sumptuously bound and beautifully illustrated manuscripts reached a peak in the fifteenth century, just as printing was about to be introduced to France. Technologies were gradually developed that could combine comparably elaborate images with the printed word—woodcuts and engravings that were then often coloured by hand—so that illustrated books could continue to provide opportunities for collaboration between writers and artists, and furnish collectors' items for the luxury market. Many painters of the modern period have depicted the act of reading, while the works of real or imaginary painters have been described in novels by Balzac, Zola, and Proust. The rise of the French film industry, beginning in the inter-war years, sees numerous novels and plays reaching out to new audiences by way of adaptations for the screen. Even architecture, seemingly the least verbal of the visual arts, has a literary dimension. From the great Gothic cathedrals of the Middle Ages to the *très grande bibliothèque* recently unveiled at Tolbiac, buildings have been designed and erected in homage to the book.

Finally, and perhaps most obviously, literature is defined by the way it reflects on its own nature and status, and on the conventions that constitute its various genres. The history of French arts of poetry is both continuous and complex, extending from treatises on how to write troubadour poetry, or the later medieval *arts de seconde rhétorique*, via the Aristotelian poetics that dominated the neo-classical period, to the alternative poetics of Romanticism, Parnassianism, Symbolism, or Surrealism. Classical models, as we have already indicated, often nourish this process of reflection. Horace's *Ars poetica* plays a key role for Renaissance poeticians, generates a French equivalent in Boileau's *Art poétique*, and is later echoed in various nineteenth-century poems—by Gautier and Verlaine, among others—which sketch out a poetics in imaginative terms. Prefaces and dedicatory epistles regularly contain programmatic claims to a specific position in the literary typology, or defend the status of the accompanying works against potential accusations of frivolity or immorality: the preface to Racine's *Phèdre* provides one very striking example among many.

Questions concerning the truth-value of literary works, the way in which they should be read and interpreted, and the kinds of readers they are designed for, are raised not only in these textual adjuncts but also, albeit often less explicitly, within the works themselves. It would be a mistake to think that literary self-consciousness is a modern phenomenon: it has been a feature of French literary culture from the outset. Any literary work is the product of interaction with its (distant or immediate) forebears, and the process of rereading and rewriting them can take on many different colorations: reverential or combative, serious or comic, eagerly incorporating other texts or carefully assuming distance from them. A process of reflection on their own literary nature characterizes the more sophisticated works of all periods, from Chrétien de Troyes's self-conscious romances to Rabelais's comic fictions, and from Diderot's *Jacques le fataliste* to the twentieth-century *nouveau roman*. Read attentively, therefore, any individual work may be said to enclose in embryonic form its own account of the literary history of which it is a part.

WHAT DO WE MEAN BY 'FRENCH'?

In neither the early period nor the post-colonial world can France—and thus 'French'—be defined by the hexagon of modern France. Its boundaries, like those of other continental countries, are permeable and liable to shift: large tracts of 'France'—notably Aquitaine—were in English hands until the late Middle Ages, fifteenth-century Burgundy formed part of the imperial (that is, German) territories, and Alsace has notoriously changed hands more than once. Conversely, French was spoken in England throughout the early Middle Ages, and more recently in many other parts of Europe and the Middle East. France attempted to assert territorial claims in the Italian peninsula in the fifteenth and sixteenth centuries, while the colonies it acquired in the early modern period have in many instances retained a French culture of their own long after decolonization: Quebec provides a graphic illustration of this process. Internally, France still has a wide variety of regional cultures and languages, some of which are close relatives of standard French, some—like Breton—entirely different; before the rise of the nation state in the early modern period and the consequent centralization of government, what we now call 'France' was more like a cluster of loosely related provinces.

It is better, then, to use the plural when speaking of French languages and literary cultures over its thousand-year history. The differences to be found in earlier times between the literatures of 'langue d'oc' (in the south of France) and 'langue d'oïl' (in the north), or between the Burgundian and the French courts, are matched in the present day, although along a different axis: the ways of speaking and writing French cultivated in Martinique or Guadeloupe often define themselves in deliberate contradistinction to those of metropolitan France, while some regions of France itself are now seeking once again to assert their own political and linguistic identity. The prestige of Paris as a cultural centre has brought many writers to France from the former French colonies and from elsewhere in Europe, and these visitors have often injected new energy into the literary language of the hexagon.

Against this picture of plurality must be set a powerful tendency towards the central control and normalization of the French language. Beginning in the late Middle Ages with the triumph of the vernacular and the growing aspiration towards a standard national language, this tendency reached its high point in the seventeenth century with the founding of the Académie Française, which has ever since legislated for 'correct' French usage. In recent years, the Académie and other conservative sectors of French culture have exerted a good deal of pressure to inhibit the freewheeling innovations of the media and the importation of foreign words (mainly Anglo-American); only time will tell whether this new form of purism will prevent the French language from undergoing major mutations in the twenty-first century.

Questions of linguistic identity are of course closely related to the formation of a canon of literary works perceived as representing not only the history of the culture but also its most essential character. In France, this process of canon-formation, as a conscious enterprise, began in the eighteenth century and has continued ever since. It has various components, each embodying a myth of national identity. At one end of the scale is the popular myth of the 'gaulois' tradition, which arose originally from the notion of 'Gaul' as the ancient homeland of the French people: the Astérix series provides an amazingly successful modern example of this cultural 'memory', but there are perfectly serious earlier ones, like Jean Lemaire de Belges's enormous *Illustrations de Gaule* of the early sixteenth century. Reflected in the bawdy *fabliaux* of the Middle Ages, the seamy poetry of Villon and the comic fictions of Rabelais, this myth also carries with it the belief that the French have a special capacity to enjoy the earthier pleasures of life—good wine, good food, and of course good sex (smoking could be added to the list in the form of the *gauloise*, the quintessentially French cigarette).

Another quite different component epitomizing the 'Frenchness' of French culture is belief in 'la clarté française', a unique ability for clear and rational expression. Usually associated with Descartes, who made 'clarté' an essential criterion for recognizing the truth, it helps to ground the appeal to a rationally established linguistic norm. It is doubtless also a legacy of the unchallenged position that French occupied, over a period of two hundred years or more, as the international language of diplomacy: French is perceived as a language of order, an order which may be political, grammatical, or aesthetic *au choix*. The elasticity of this conception is shown by the fact that it draws into its net a broad range of very different works: the comedies of Molière and the tragedies of Racine, the writings of both Pascal and Voltaire, Benjamin Constant's *Adolphe* and the *récits* of André Gide, the poetry of La Fontaine and of Paul Valéry.

One could add many other identities to this list, each with its own literary monuments: the appropriation of the Troy myth by medieval authors to exalt the lineage of their patrons; the Catholic orthodoxy of Bossuet and its twentieth-century variants in Bernanos and Mauriac; the rebelliously Protestant vision of d'Aubigné; the rationalist zeal identified with Voltaire; the Napoleonic dreams of Stendhal's Julien Sorel; the post-romantic disillusionment of Flaubert's *L'Education sentimentale*; the intellectual and moral iconoclasm of Gide's characters; and the 'outsider' mindset of Camus's anti-hero Meursault. All these, and many more, have been thought of as 'typically French' at one time or another. Such fragments of a national identity are of course for the most part only stereotypes that prove, on closer inspection, to be a travesty of the texts towards which they gesture. Yet stereotypes have a powerful life of their own, generating their own successors and counter-images, and they need to be understood as part of the total myth-making activity of a national culture.

As some of these examples suggest, literature provides a medium of identity-formation and myth-making for disadvantaged or minority groups—such as women who, throughout most of French history, suffered legal and economic discrimination relative to men. Christine de Pizan established her authority as a writer by assimilating into her own works the writers most revered in her day, from Ovid to Dante. Modern feminists have often called for a new kind of writing, born of women's experience, that would serve as a counterblast to oppressive patriarchal attitudes. Gay and lesbian campaigners, similarly, have had recourse to literature, and to experiments with literary form and genre, in order to raise public awareness of sexualities lying outside the heterosexual mainstream.

WHAT KIND OF HISTORY?

Writing a literary history is a far from straightforward activity in an age when history and history-writing are open to challenge: narrative is liable to generate its own momentum, a dynamic closer to fiction than to the 'reality' of the past, which is of course irretrievably lost to us.

Besides, the literature written in French, or in France, is so long-standing and so abundant that a short history of it could never be more than partial and provisional. We have responded to these problems by indicating, in the design of the book itself, how the perception of historical developments changes in accordance with the time-frame in which they are viewed and the pace at which they are described. In addition, the structure of the book is intended to provide not only different levels of analysis but also different points of entry for the reader.

In this Introduction, we have taken stock of the sweep of French literature as if from a great distance. Hereafter the book is divided into three main sections which are linked together in a broad historical sequence: the Middle Ages (from the beginnings to the late fifteenth century), the Early Modern period (sixteenth to eighteenth centuries), and the Modern period (from the Revolution to the present day). But within each of these three parts the narrative unfolds on two different levels. Each opens with an overview of the period, which is then followed by a more detailed study of the period in close-up. In practical terms, this double structure will allow readers either to read the book in the sequence in which it is laid out, or else to select between a broader and a narrower focus for any particular period. So far as the question of history-writing is concerned, we want to show how different phenomena emerge as significant according to the view that is adopted. Our emphases, as between overview and close-up, diverge, although they do not contradict one another. We trust that this multi-layered approach will give depth and perspective to the volume and make it clear that no single story can in fact be complete, however much it may seem to be so.

Although each of us has written the overview to our period in his or her own way, we have all done so in response to a series of questions that were agreed upon at the start. We all touch on the social role of literature, and on its economic context, considering what it means to be a reader or writer in the period concerned. We say something about the nature of literature during the period, and how it relates to other art forms. The major genres, movements, and temporal divisions within each section are identified. And we allude to developments in the French language, and in 'Frenchness' more generally, and how they affect literature. Each of us adheres more or less faithfully to this agenda, though we also make our own decisions about what to emphasize and what to leave in the margins, guided partly, no doubt, by personal preference, but mainly by our understanding of the specific requirements of each period. Indeed, because we are all engaged in teaching and researching French literature, our own current preferences and preoccupations inevitably inform our writing. We hope that, as with the deliberate adoption of narratives that proceed at different speeds, the variety of our approaches will enhance the usefulness of this study.

Within the longer section of each part, where the literature of the period is discussed in close-up, we have similarly worked on a principle of conformity tempered with variety. Our chief concern here has been to get close to the texts: to convey the pleasure of reading the works of each period and to communicate the excitement we ourselves have experienced as researchers. We have not always chosen to follow a strictly chronological line. Where generic questions predominate, or where the history of a particular phenomenon needs to be dealt with in a connected way, we have allowed the organization to reflect those pressures. References backwards and forwards are also made with a certain freedom so that some sense is built up of a coherence that is not necessarily linear. The motif of retrospection recurs throughout our narratives and analyses: the awareness that a historical narrative, although apparently obeying a forward impetus, is necessarily constructed from the perspective of the present.

Writing our book at the turn of the millennium, we have been led to reflect on the permutations that the literary text has undergone. From orality to written record, from manuscript to print, *incunabula* to paperback, print to CD-Rom, texts have revolutionized both their material form and their cultural role. To what extent is a text to be identified as a performance, an act, an artefact, a commodity, or a momentary fluctuation in cyberspace? In the many-stranded story we are about to tell, the increasing identification of literature with the book goes in harness with a gradual extension of literacy, although now, after nearly 1100 years of French literature, some would claim that the age of the book is coming to an end.

So does literary history have a future? Will people continue to read histories such as this in an age that is increasingly preoccupied with the modern and the postmodern, with cultural studies and other interdisciplinary approaches? It is clear enough that the days of the standard, would-be authoritative history are over. Each generation will rewrite literary history, like other kinds of history, according to its needs, its ideologies, its preferences, and (no doubt) its prejudices. Yet the authors of this book are confident that, just as people still want to read biographies, which were so unfashionable in the later twentieth century, so too those who read and enjoy literature will continue to want to know how whole literatures were shaped over time.

And so we turn to look a little more closely at our subject, beginning long before the modern printed book was invented.

Part I

The Middle Ages: From the Earliest Texts to 1470

Overview of the Period

Time did not pass more slowly in the past than it does today. Although to the modern eye the centuries that make up the Middle Ages may blur together, to the people who lived in them one decade was as different from another then as it is now. Time may have been reckoned more by human activity than by instruments, just as distances were reckoned in journey times rather than in miles, but this made the experience of change central to people's concept of time rather than a consequence of measuring its passage. Life expectancy was low, which could only increase awareness that time was fleeting. Some communities, such as some monastic or rural ones, may have been slower to evolve than others. But cultural activity was concentrated in intellectual, courtly, and urban circles that were more responsive to change. In surveying French literature from the earliest surviving texts of the ninth century to the dawn of the Renaissance in the late fifteenth, we are going to encounter more innovation and diversity than unwavering adherence to tradition.

What are the major changes that take place during this period? The very fact of composing texts in the vernacular, and subsequently committing them to writing, is remarkable in itself. Some of the very earliest works to survive still convey the sense of being overwhelmed by their own novelty—as though their paint were still fresh. But these early texts are not 'literary' in the sense in which most people nowadays understand the term; they are historical or religious, like the intriguing life of Saint Faith composed in the south of France some time in the eleventh century. Probably the most important innovation of the French Middle Ages, from the perspective of French literary history, was the rediscovery of the concerns which characterize literature to this day. Twelfth-century literature canonizes themes such as selfhood, individual development, love, and adventure. Literature establishes itself as a secular diversion and a means to personal gratification; fiction, self-consciously deployed, takes a leading role, while the language that gives it shape is also relished as a substance to be enjoyed. Such a literature had existed in classical antiquity, but it disappeared with the decline of the Roman Empire. The new literature of Europe was created largely without reference to the classical past

by the lyric poets and romance writers of the twelfth century, the pio-
neers of 'courtly' poetry and 'courtly love'. Even though few of these
poets' names are familiar to modern readers (those of Jaufre Rudel or
Chrétien de Troyes may evoke a glimmer of recognition), and many
indeed were anonymous, the scenario of the love-struck troubadour
serenading his lady, or tales of lover-heroes such as Lancelot and
Tristan, remain well-known cultural reference-points. These innovative fictions are not only the forebears of much modern literature,
they have also enduringly shaped our experience of love, desire, and
gender.

Such 'courtly' compositions, however, are first produced and consumed by a restricted circle of aristocrats and their courtiers; indeed,
they serve (initially at least) as a hallmark of the refinement and sensibility of a leisured elite. The fantasy aspirations of this social group
find expression in the later twelfth century in the newly born genre of
romance, where the typical hero is a king's son seeking personal fulfilment in love and chivalric exploits until such time as his father's
death calls him to power and responsibility. Courtly writing continues
its gradually broadening course throughout the Middle Ages, from
the amorous sophistries of thirteenth-century poets like Richard de
Fournival (Figure 1) to the melancholy musings of Charles d'Orléans
in the fifteenth.

The thirteenth century witnesses another major innovation: the
emergence on a large scale of literature concerned with, and apparently addressed to, the inhabitants not of courts but of France's bur-
geoning cities. No doubt there always was a popular culture of jokes,
stories, or songs, but it is only from the thirteenth century that numerous such works survive in written form, in the racy, short narrative
genre of the *fabliau*, for example, or in the satirical poetry of Rutebeuf.
The prosperous city of Arras seems to have fostered an especially vital
culture. Gradually the urban bourgeoisie emerge as patrons of literature. As for the social background from which these seemingly
'urban' poets emanate, that is harder to judge. Most medieval authors
seem to have enjoyed some level of education which, throughout the
Middle Ages, fell within the orbit of the Church. Educated men thus
were, or had for a while been, 'clerks' (members of the clergy), a social
group unlike the aristocracy or the non-noble since it was exclusively
male and predominantly celibate. As a result, it was non-hereditary,
but instead recruited its members from backgrounds of all kinds.
Rutebeuf certainly, and the Arrageois poets and *fabliau*-writers probably, were clerks in this sense. Their social background prior to their
education is unknown—indeed the *fableors* are mainly anonymous—

1. Courtly authorship. Above, a scribe offers a book to a nobleman while a lady looks on; below, the nobleman and lady watch from the edges of the picture while a man shows the book to another lady. Richard de Fournival, *Bestiaire d'amours*, Bibliothèque Nationale fr. 15213, fo. 57.

but there are southern French troubadours of bourgeois origin from the late twelfth century onwards. The thirteenth century is also the period when prose first becomes widely used for narrative composition, whether history or fiction, although it continues to take second place to verse until the late fourteenth.

The end of the thirteenth century saw the composition of what is arguably the single most important text of the French Middle Ages and, indeed, one of the most influential works of all European literature. Surprisingly this landmark text is not a self-contained composition but the continuation by the writer and translator Jean de Meun of the *Roman de la rose* begun some forty years previously and apparently left unfinished by an otherwise unknown poet called Guillaume de Lorris. Expanding—or exploding—his 4,000-line model into a sprawling almost 22,000-line extravaganza, Jean de Meun showed the intellectual excitement to be derived by colliding together the traditions of courtly love, philosophical reflection, social satire, bawdy, theology, and classical literature, not necessarily in that (or indeed any) order. The repercussions of this symphonic—or cacophonous—achievement extend to Dante, Chaucer, and beyond.

Jean's *Rose* also inspired the principal literary innovation of the French fourteenth century, the *dit amoureux* in which a first-person narrator incorporates into a verse love-story miscellaneous material including dream visions, lyric poems, mythological narratives, personified abstractions, and even letters. Although they sometimes give the impression that they were paid by the yard for these compositions, their authors—like the famous poet-composer Guillaume de Machaut—exude awareness that they are just that: professional authors. The word *poëte*, formerly used to refer only to classical authors, is for the first time applied to contemporary poets who had previously been termed *trouvères* or *troubadours*, meaning 'finders', 'inventors'. French authors increasingly see themselves as continuing, and indeed as supplanting, the tradition of the great writers of antiquity; it becomes possible to make a living by writing whereas previously composition seems typically to have been either a rich man's hobby or else additional to some other, more 'valuable' activity (that of secretary or administrator, for example). Concomitantly anonymity (which had been widespread) becomes a rarity as poets hasten to lay claim to their works. At the end of the fourteenth century, Christine de Pizan, recently widowed and needing an income to support herself and her children, embraces a career as a writer in a way that, while exceptional in her day, would have been quite unthinkable earlier. She goes on to produce, in the early years of the fifteenth century, the most prolific *œuvre* of any medieval French writer. Since she also oversees the manuscript production of her own works, she can be hailed not only as the first fully professional author, but also as the first publisher, of French literature.

The *dits amoureux* offer a strange combination of *roman personnel* and anthology. They are orchestrated around a central 'I' which performs its personal deficiencies, moral hesitations, and intellectual reflections, attentively serving more refined and aristocratic sensibilities than the writer's own (typically embodied in the patron), yet also seeking out the first person's own fragile satisfactions in love, friendship, or poetry. Inherent to this performance is the composition, and inclusion, of lyric pieces. Lyric poetry is enjoying an exceptionally high status in this period. Its forms become codified in a series of *formes fixes* ('fixed forms'), among which the *ballade* and *rondeau* at least will have a long posterity. The most celebrated product of the *dit amoureux* tradition, although admittedly at some distance from it, is the mid-fifteenth-century 'Testament' of François Villon, the author-figure's half self-mocking, half self-pitying first-person reflections worked into the format of a will and studded with inset lyrics, mainly *ballades*.

Throughout the Middle Ages and beyond, Latin is the language of learning. Across Europe it is the default medium of expression, in speech as well as in writing, for schools, universities, professions such as law or medicine, and the Church. Gradually, however, its monopoly is challenged by the vernacular. In the late thirteenth century, Philippe de Beaumanoir writes the first legal treatise in French, and the official Latin history of the realm—the *Grandes Chroniques de France*—is translated from Latin into French. In the late fourteenth and early fifteenth centuries the prestige of French prose history-writing is consecrated by contributions from Froissart and Christine de Pizan; history goes hand in hand with lyric poetry as the major genre cultivated by court poets. In the fifteenth century the task of translating classical writers is energetically pursued. Increasingly, French is used for medical and other scientific or technical writing. And Italian literature, recently made prestigious by such authors as Dante, Boccaccio, and Petrarch, is likewise emulated in French, Boccaccio's *Decameron* (for example) giving rise, in the late fifteenth century, to the compendium of 100 stories called the *Cent Nouvelles nouvelles*.

Although previously instigating a literature of entertainment seemed a tremendous cultural achievement, French writing is now dignified by moral earnest, while its language assumes the status of a language of learning. The Middle Ages is a period of continual renaissance of one kind or another, the intense interest in classical literature in the twelfth century having led to this period being dubbed the 'Twelfth-century Renaissance'. But by the fifteenth century the aspiration to a national literature of a weight comparable with those of antiquity has fired French authors: what we know as *the* Renaissance is taking shape. Court chroniclers and poets are accepted as authoritative voices entrusted with shaping moral and political opinion, and humanist scholars, formerly gathered under the influence of Petrarch at the papal court in Avignon, install themselves in Paris, where their ambitions are served by the newly established printing press (1470).

This series of changes has been charted from the point of view of their success: these developments are ones whose repercussions are still felt beyond the Middle Ages. But clearly for every innovation which, for whatever reason, remained influential, there were others that were headed for oblivion. If these were the winners in the lottery of history what, then, were the losers? Certainly they were often just as magnificent and as interesting in their own right, and also more typical of their period, which provided their sole, but enthusiastic, audience.

For much of the twelfth and thirteenth centuries, courtly literature was composed alongside another genre that was just as prolific: that of the *chansons de geste*. These are long, usually anonymous narrative songs that use fictionalized or legendary episodes from French history to reflect on political conflict, human violence, and the strength or weakness of different kinds of social bond. They have been the object of controversy among medievalists, some vehemently maintaining that they arise from a tradition of popular, oral history stretching back to the events on which they are based (mostly eighth- or early ninth-century), others claiming them as literary compositions of the same order as historical romances. The *chansons de geste* were clearly widely appreciated by their contemporaries. Many of the troubadours, for example, cite heroes like Roland or Ogier as freely as they do Tristan, as figures epitomizing a certain kind of character or experience. These narrative songs are, indeed, closely akin to the lyric tradition: often intensely moving, they paint historical existence in heroic, tragic, or satirical terms. As the Middle Ages advance, however, they seem increasingly sidelined. The sense which they convey of history as traumatic evidently proves less appealing than the more decorous, mediated, and self-consciously artful representations offered by courtly romance. Eventually the stories narrated by the *chansons de geste* do find another home in medieval culture, but it is one where the impact of their original verse is neutralized and their apparent immediacy subordinated to authorial control. From the early fourteenth century onwards, they are recast in prose and fused with the tradition of vernacular chronicle. This process of *dérimage* ('unrhyming') continues late into the fifteenth century. The shock of confrontation with our past does not disappear from human experience, but in the post-medieval period it will find expression in quite different forms (in autobiography, for example).

A second aspect of medieval literature which seems to have been peculiar to the period is not generic but thematic. The sense that, alongside our familiar world, there lies an Other World of marvellous occurrences, enticing fairies, dark menace, or ineffable bliss, informs not only romance but also some *chansons de geste* and history- or travel-writing. Mortal men are often lured into this Other World by strange animals that they imagine themselves to be hunting, but which in fact are hunting them, drawing them away from their companions into the toils of a fairy mistress. Others are mysteriously transported to the Other World on an apparently empty ship. Sometimes the fairy herself irrupts into the everyday, challenging its norms. Whatever the means, the result is a life-changing encounter with the Other. The opening pages of Jean d'Arras's *Mélusine* describe a France where unimaginably beautiful ladies cluster round every spring. The men they choose to honour with their love enjoy untold prosperity so long as they obey their lady's dictates. Mélusine's mother, for instance, forbids her husband to see her during her lying in, while Mélusine herself must remain unseen by her husband on Saturdays, when she changes into a serpent from the waist down. These magical motifs are hauntingly uncanny, their mythic links with sexuality and death still perceptible even when the motifs themselves have been to some extent rationalized, moralized, or turned into metaphors of love and adventure. In the case of *Mélusine*, the *fée*'s interdiction is a caution about the potential for inhumanity in all of us; by breaking her taboo, her husband betrays his own love and fidelity to her, and the mark of his crime is her permanent transformation into a winged beast. Composed around 1395, *Mélusine* is a late flowering of the theme of Other World which had made many earlier narrative works internationally successful, such as the late twelfth-century romance of *Partonopeu de Blois*, translated into no fewer than nine languages (German, Dutch, English, Italian, Norwegian, Icelandic, Danish, Spanish, and Catalan). Although this sense that there is a parallel universe of marvels may be rekindled in subsequent literature, for example in nineteenth-century fascination with the 'Gothic', it is most often relegated to children's or so-called 'folk' literature. So far as prestige culture is concerned, the encounter with the impossible Other of the *fée* and her world is a great medieval theme sacrificed to the rationalism of the ages that followed.

A third casualty of literary history is religious drama. Most medieval works are in some degree dramatic; even the most 'written' literature was intended to be read aloud, as for example in 1388 Froissart read his romance *Meliador* in ten weeks of nightly instalments to the count of Foix. There must have been quantities of performed works in the repertoires of professional performers which were never written down, or were not intended to survive, and which have thus been lost. But while the Middle Ages bequeathed abundant narrative and lyric forms to the later European tradition, its strictly theatrical production, with the exception of farce, was swept away in the early modern period in favour of neo-classical revivals. The great

mystery plays dramatizing biblical narratives were prolifically composed in the fifteenth century and performed into the mid-sixteenth,
but to modern readers they can seem simultaneously gruesome and
pompous, and even their admirers sometimes have little to say about
their qualities except how long they are. These monumental French
dramas seem to have shared the fate of the dinosaurs, which is odd
given that many other forms of medieval religious literature in
French—such as religious lyrics, saints' lives, or other devotional
works—while they may not be every modern reader's favourite, have
nonetheless enjoyed a perennial appeal.

Time, then, wrought changes in literature throughout the French
Middle Ages. Not least of these were changes in what it meant to be
'French'. Indeed, ascribing *any* meaning to such a word is difficult
before the emergence of modern nation states in the early modern
period gives rise to the belief that different kinds of frontier (cultural,
political, and linguistic) should coincide. It used to be acceptable to
speak of the institutions prior to such states as 'feudal', but medieval
historians have now more or less renounced this term as a misleading
obfuscation. Perhaps the rise of the regions in contemporary Europe
will help us to find a model for the simultaneous regionalism and
internationalism of the Middle Ages, and the complex network of
overlapping jurisdictions which made up its governmental structures.

Medieval speakers were aware of the interrelation between
Romance languages (those of the former Roman Empire). From
Cordoba to Carlisle, a series of similar, related dialects were spoken.
Poets and writers whom we think of as 'French' composed in the
langue d'oc (*oc* being the southern French word for 'yes') and in the
langue d'oïl (*oïl* meaning 'yes' in Old French, modern *oui*). The *langue
d'oïl*, in turn, exhibits many variant forms ranging from Burgundian
to Anglo-Norman (the French spoken in Britain following the
Norman invasion). All these linguistic forms changed very significantly over the centuries. Although there was, apparently from early
on, some standardizing of literary usage, it remains the case that every
new medieval text presents the reader (and thus probably presented
its medieval audiences too) with a new linguistic experience.

There seems to have been a high degree of mutual intelligibility
between these linguistic variants. The troubadours, for example, composed in a literary language now called Occitan (in recognition of their
native *oc*), formerly referred to as 'Provençal', which seems to
be a standardized form of the Limoges dialect; but they enjoyed
careers in Spain, Portugal, northern Italy, northern France, and even

England. Either audiences over a remarkably wide geographical area could understand troubadour songs, or they didn't care if they couldn't follow the words, and merely drank in the music and the glamour. At the beginning of his *Le Joli buisson de Jonece*, probably composed in 1373, Froissart enumerates all his many patrons. He himself stems from Valenciennes, and his language is strongly marked by northern features, but he has had money showered upon him (he modestly records) by royalty and aristocracy in England, Scotland, Italy, Cyprus, the Low Countries, and all over what is now France.

'France' is, of course, as ambiguous a term as 'French', as already noted in the Introduction. In the mid-twelfth century, the French king had less direct control over land and resources than the count of Champagne, and far less than the English-based Henry Plantagenet. After marrying Eleanor of Aquitaine in 1152, Henry commanded not only his father's lands of Anjou and Maine, and the duchy of Normandy, which his father had conquered in 1144, but also immense estates in south-western France: Poitou, and the vast territory of Aquitaine. When he was then crowned King Henry II of England in 1154, he controlled an empire stretching from the Pyrenees to Scotland. To the north and east, in the same period, France (or 'France') was no less encroached upon by the 'Empire', a political mass centred on what is now Germany and which saw itself as heir to Charlemagne's christianized restoration of the Roman Empire. Throughout the Middle Ages the kings of France sat squeezed uncomfortably between these two powerful and heavily militarized neighbours, their vulnerability especially exposed by the humiliations of the Hundred Years War with England (1337–1453). Another source of their discomfort, in the later Middle Ages, was the rapid economic growth and successful urbanization of two more of their neighbours: the Low Countries to the north and the city states of northern Italy to the south. French kings made repeated efforts to consolidate their power within the modern hexagon, but successes depended heavily on the military, diplomatic, and administrative skills of individual kings. Philip Augustus (reigned 1180–1223) and Charles V (reigned 1364–80) were examples of astute kings who successfully extended royal power, in Charles's case with the aid of the formidable general Du Guesclin. But retaining such power was inherently problematic. No one could hope to exercise individual control over an extensive, relatively undeveloped country. Yet to delegate it in the hope of securing loyal supporters immediately ran the risk of empowering potential rivals. No one was so dangerous as one's friends, a truth bitterly confirmed when King John II ('le Bon', reigned 1350–64) entrusted the duchies of Burgundy, Anjou, Berry, and Bourbon to his younger sons. The duchy of Burgundy swelled its power base through alliance with Flanders, joined the English side in the Hundred Years War, and under Duke Charles ('le Téméraire') almost succeeded in establishing itself as a fully independent realm rivalling the might of France itself.

Literature, like other prestige crafts, followed centres of power as they rose and fell. Rich people commissioned texts in the same way as they did armour, furniture, and jewellery; they employed poets as they did diplomats and spiritual advisers, roles which may indeed often have coincided in the same individuals. In addition to the intellectual or artistic prestige to be obtained from retaining in one's service a sought-after poet, patrons benefited from the praises that a hireling could be relied on to pen. But throughout the Middle Ages, the royal court of France was regularly eclipsed and, on occasion, menaced by the richer, more glittering courts of provincial and other neighbouring rulers. Medieval 'French' literature was produced almost everywhere in greater abundance than it was in Paris. The ground-breakingly innovative courtly literature of the twelfth century was *all* composed outside the Île de France, most of it in Occitania and Britain. Most of the great literature—like the great art—of the later Middle Ages was produced under the patronage of lords of Flanders, Brabant, Luxemburg, Orleans, and above all Berry and Burgundy. It was only in the sixteenth century that the royal court became an undisputed centre of literary activity.

This kaleidoscope of regions and their courts did not favour ideological consistency. It is unwise to approach medieval literature with the assumption that this was an age where everyone thought alike. It was, of course, a Christian age, but anyone half alert to Christian doctrines and institutions knew that it was also an age of schism. The Eastern and Western churches had long been at loggerheads, in the thirteenth and fourteenth centuries Franciscans and Dominicans struggled for control of the universities, and for several brief periods there were even rival popes shoring up competing claims to the Holy See. It is true that the Church used accusations of heresy, or the threat of excommunication or interdiction, to police its members, but its persecutions tended to be inconsistent and inefficient. Only its own errant theologians were pursued with any rigour although the Inquisition, established in the early thirteenth century in order to combat the Cathar heresy, was active in Occitania for a period. Christian beliefs probably provided the bedrock of most people's personal convictions.

It seems, for instance, to have been the major reason for participation in the Crusades which began at the turn of the twelfth century and continued into the fourteenth, although young men's longing for land and glory, and the need for an outlet for military energies severely contained at home, were no doubt also important motives. Prejudice in favour of Christianity also accounts for the racist attitudes towards Jews and Muslims that are rife in medieval texts. 'Saracens', for instance, are slanderously depicted as pagan idolaters. In their daily attempts at self-enrichment at their neighbours' expense, and self-defence against their neighbours' attempts at self-enrichment at theirs, medieval people, however, were not noticeably more inhibited by religious scruple than the people of any other age. And the rich variety of beliefs held by ordinary people is vividly displayed by inquisitorial records such as those of Montaillou.

It is true, and has already been said, that the Church controlled education. The cathedral schools of the early Middle Ages, and the universities that dominated the educational system from the mid-thirteenth century onwards, were staffed by members of the clergy. Here too, however, we should not assume that they were all guided by uniform beliefs, still less that their students were. After all, these students had no choice but to pass through the Church system if they wanted to advance themselves. Their very familiarity with it bred scurrility, much of which was cloaked in the decent obscurity of Latin, but also spilled out into vernacular compositions such as the *fabliaux*, or the parodic recasting of the 'joys of the Virgin' in the virulently anti-feminist *Quinze Joies de mariage*. Graduates who failed to secure a living in the Church may have felt acutely resentful towards it. This is the likely background of many vernacular poets (Villon, for example) and it explains why, in medieval literature, ecclesiastical institutions come second only to women as a target for satire.

In the schools and universities, students first studied the Seven Liberal Arts, grouped into the *trivium* (grammar, rhetoric, logic) and *quadrivium* (mathematics, geometry, music, astronomy), for the degree of MA. As a higher degree they could study theology, law, or medicine. Although teachers of theology enjoyed the highest prestige, arts masters commonly had more *chic*. Their domain, after all, was the world of pagan antiquity, a world both racy (Ovid) and intellectu-ally challenging (Aristotle). The most successful arts masters were stars rather like today's literary theorists: virtuosi of a desirable, diffi-cult, yet also potentially subversive realm of thought. Aristotle's writ-ings on natural philosophy and metaphysics were periodically banned from university syllabi; in retaliation, academic philosophers appealed to the principle of 'double truth' whereby what was true according to the light of reason could be maintained even if it conflicted with what was true in the eyes of faith. Indeed masters of divinity, like the redoubtable Saint Thomas Aquinas, drew extensively on Aristotle in their exquisitely meticulous investigations of that faith.

Medieval vernacular poets had varying levels of exposure to this education, with its differing biases towards the various branches of antique or Christian thought. Some, of course, may have had no education at all and relied on oral composition, and the assistance of others, to commit their works to writing—if indeed their compositions ever were written down. But whatever education they had, it will not have been primarily pious, and will more likely, through its emphasis on persuasion, questioning, and debate, have nurtured intellectual virtuosity and scepticism more than submission to dogma.

There is one respect, however, in which medieval education may have generated cultural uniformity: its gendering. Although in some respects a social melting pot, the clerical order was a male preserve. The reason Christine de Pizan was a prolific writer and publisher was that, as a woman, she could not receive a clerical training and therefore, unlike her male contemporaries, could not draw an income from the Church. Women in magnates' families were usually educated by private tutors, but their influence on literature was more as patrons and audiences than as producers. The region which saw the greatest number of women writers was Occitania; thirty or so songs survive which can be attributed in whole or in part to some two dozen *trobairitz* (female troubadours) active between the mid-twelfth and the mid-thirteenth centuries. There seem also to have been some northern French women's songs. And there are isolated women writers like Clemence of Barking and Marie de France in the twelfth century (both writing in England) and Christine de Pizan in the fifteenth. But there is no tradition of women's writing in the sense of women writing in response to the writings of other women: women write on their own or else in response to men. Many medieval works are anonymous, especially in the earlier period, but it is generally assumed that, like virtually all the attributed ones, they are by men.

The masculine bias of literary culture in the Middle Ages does not just reflect access to education; it is also a question of who has the right to speak, or sing, in public. The role of orality in medieval literature is hotly debated, but minimally medievalists agree that in the earlier part of the period works were characteristically orally performed, and thus addressed in the first instance to an audience rather than a reader.

Some works may, additionally, have been orally composed, and orally transmitted for a long time before being written down. The genres to which the 'oralists' lay claim in this way are the *chansons de geste* and the lyric. Both genres go back at least to the late eleventh or early twelfth centuries and were sung, the musical setting providing mnemonic support for the text. Troubadour culture, in which the norm was for the poet to perform songs of which he himself had composed both words and music, flourished into the thirteenth century and inspired many imitators in northern France. Whether *chansons de geste* continued to be sung through the thirteenth century is uncertain. The genres intended to be read aloud rather than sung are verse narratives, including some saints' lives, chronicles, and romances. The fourteenth century was, however, a turning point. Music and lyric poetry, hitherto inseparable, now began to drift apart. Ironically, it seems that the cause of this lay in the very success of their union. Advances in music in the early fourteenth century, in particular the exploration of polyphony by Guillaume de Machaut, made music too technically demanding for composition and performance to lie within the range of any but professional musicians. From Machaut onwards, it became increasingly common to compose lyrics without any musical accompaniment. Whereas in the very early Middle Ages virtually all literature is sung, by the end almost none is.

The obverse of this process is the rise of the book which, as the performer reads from it, takes over the place of music as prop to the text. Successful writers of the later Middle Ages oversaw the copying, compilation, and illumination of their work. The expectation grows that such books will be read, as opposed to read from. Jakemes, author of the late thirteenth-century verse romance *Romans dou castelain de Couci*, devises an acrostic whereby the initial letters of the concluding lines spell out his name; Machaut and Froissart leave ingenious clues to where to find anagrams of their own and their lady's names. Sumptuous presentation copies are given to patrons; manuscript illuminations depicting the presentation by an author of a book to his patron, like the one in Figure 1, often form the frontispiece to a work. Such extravagantly produced books retain the performative dimension of oral literature, translating it into the medium of writing. The *dit amoureux* in particular appears as a kind of talking, singing book: the first person addresses us from pages which reproduce the anthology-like structure of most medieval manuscripts. (Most of the books compiled in the Middle Ages are compendia of a variety of works; single-work, and still more so single-author, manuscripts are the exception.)

Inevitably, the art form to which literature now appears most related is no longer music but painting. The fabulous *Très riches heures* of John, duke of Berry, or the radiant Van der Weiden altarpiece in the Hôtel-Dieu in Beaune, are just two of the better-known examples of works produced under the same princely patronage as literature. Through their alliance with Flanders, the dukes of Burgundy could command the painters and craftsmen of the Low Countries. The pincer movement with which they threatened the French crown was also an artists' highway that was paved with gold.

Although the book becomes the privileged way of enshrining literature relatively late in the Middle Ages, it is true, of course, that our only knowledge of medieval literature derives from books: hand-copied parchment volumes for the most part, with paper manuscripts, and eventually printed paper, appearing only in the fifteenth century. Parchment is relatively robust. Nonetheless very few manuscripts of vernacular texts survive from the twelfth century, and there is commonly a gap of up to a couple of hundred years between the putative date of composition of a text and the date of its earliest surviving copies. There is thus a major 'information deficit' about the earliest state of many important medieval works. At the same time, there is an 'information overload' about many of them as well, since what we may think of as the 'same' work may be transmitted in multiple copies which conflict one with another. The circumstances of performance and transmission clearly make medieval texts more unstable and mutable than most modern works. It is only in the latter part of the thirteenth century that manuscripts are overseen by authors (for instance, by the so-called 'last troubadour' Guiraut Riquier), while the earliest major French poet of whom we have an indisputably autograph manuscript is Charles d'Orléans (1394–1465).

Thus it is that much of the literary history of the early Middle Ages remains conjectural. We can have only an approximate knowledge of what early medieval texts were like. Not only are many of them unattributed, they are also undated and—to a considerable extent—undatable. Much effort has been devoted to narrowing the time-frames within which particular works may have been composed, by identifying possible allusions to contemporary events, or the influence of one text on another. But the findings of such research often remain open to dispute while, to some scholars, it is fruitless even to attempt to identify a determinate point of origin for texts that live and evolve in an at least partly oral tradition. Similarly it is difficult to gauge how popular particular works were. Even the wide diffusion of manuscripts is not a reliable guide, since a prestigious work may have been

widely copied without its being widely read; conversely a work surviving only in a single, fragmentary manuscript may have been so
well loved that all the other copies of it literally fell to pieces. There
are certainly medieval references to poets and works of which we now
have no trace, and many of the early medieval texts which modern
critics most admire survive in only single or lacunary manuscripts.

Although the usual shape of a history is that of a narrative that
advances *forwards* through time, the nature of the material in
medieval literary history exposes the extent to which that is a fiction,
since in composing it, we are in fact constantly drawing inferences
backwards from textual remains that are always later, and often very
much later, than the works they record. This may not have obtruded
as a problem so far, since the stance adopted in this Overview has been
retrospective and broad-brush. When we move on to the finer grain of
historical moments and their interrelation, however, it must be borne
in mind that these are as much the product of interpretation as is
literary interpretation itself.

A final caveat. Just as time passed as inexorably for medieval people
as it does for us, and their world was as inconsistent and varied in its
beliefs as our own, so too they were as busy and productive as we are.
It is wrong to imagine that little survives from the Middle Ages. The
surviving vernacular works prior to about 1150 would fit comfortably
into a slim paperback, but thereafter composition—or what subsists
of it—is voluminous. There is more to be read than there is life in a
medievalist to read it in, and that is to speak only of edited texts. Many
manuscripts are still unedited; there may be many more that remain
unknown. The recent discovery of a fragment from a Tristan poem in
which the lovers drink the philtre is a token of the potentially magical
riches still in store.

The challenges posed by the study of the Middle Ages are both epistemological and ethical. How can we enter into relations with a
period in many ways so other to ourselves? How respond to its fiercely
articulated desires and elaborate decorum, its coarseness and refinement, its ecstasy and its irony? And how give the past its due without
ceasing to live in the present? Our modern sensibility was forged in
the medieval past, which is the source of the greater part of our contemporary culture. At the same time, however, the Middle Ages was
an era radically different from our own. It found expression not
merely in a language different from ours, but in a multitude of differing voices. Such thorough-going polyphony unsettles our most basic
assumptions about language and culture. If we accept that manuscript

technology, with alongside it a vital oral tradition, is defining of medieval 'literature', what implications does that have for reading medieval works? And how, in turn, might it modify our understanding of 'literature', even today? The Middle Ages offer, of course, an abundance of material from which to build a historical understanding. Yet the record is full of gaps. Moreover, there have been such massive fluctuations in its modern scholarly reception that virtually no medieval texts have enjoyed uncontested canonicity except, perhaps, the poetry of the troubadours, the *Chanson de Roland*, and Villon's 'Testament'. We need boldly and imaginatively to venture back, negotiating these gaps and hollows to discover the myriad paths that will support and reward our quest. Perceval's search for the Grail may serve as model here: the crucial point is to keep asking relevant questions, while at the same time acknowledging that we may never find what we are looking for. Indeed, research into the literature of the Middle Ages is more akin to adventure than it is to a specific quest: less directed towards a determinate goal than exhilarated by the variety of encounters on one's path.

The Period in Close-up

THE SAINTS SPEAK FRENCH

What does it mean to 'speak French'? The Roman occupation of the whole of Gaul (55 BC) introduced a spoken form of Latin, one much simpler than the elaborate classical Latin of Roman poets and orators, to its mainly Celtic-speaking inhabitants; the invasions of Gaul by Germanic peoples in the fifth century AD—Vizigoths in the south and Franks in the north—accelerated the drift of this Latin away from the dialects spoken in other parts of the Roman Empire and suffused it with Germanic elements; and the Franks assumed the resulting language as their own, the word 'French' deriving from 'Frankish' just as 'France' comes from 'Frankia', 'land of the Franks'. Throughout these upheavals, scholars, meanwhile, laboured to preserve Latin in something closer to its classical form. The Frankish ruler Charlemagne (742–814), who commanded an empire covering much of what is now France and Germany, promoted their efforts by reforming the teaching of Latin in imperial schools. 'Purifying' Latin meant emphasizing how far the spoken vernacular had become different from it. 'French' as an independent language can be said to owe its birth to the anxiety that 'real' Latin might die.

The oldest document to record this emergent French includes it alongside Latin and German: the Strasburg Oaths of 842 constitute a treaty sworn between two of Charlemagne's grandsons, Louis and his brother Charles the Bald, against the third, a treaty which confirms the division of Charlemagne's empire into three. The framing description of the oath-taking is in Latin. But to guarantee public understanding and witness, each ruler pronounces his oath in the tongue of his brother's supporters: the German Louis swears in French as do the supporters of the French Charles, while Charles swears in German in the same way as the supporters of the German Louis. The French in question is of course very different from the modern language. Louis, for instance, pledges, 'si salvarai eo cist meon fradre Karlo et in ajudha et in cadhuna cosa' (literally, 'and so shall I support this my brother Charles both in aid and in every thing'). The linguistic split within the former Carolingian Empire and the separation of French from Latin are unequivocally recorded in this document.

Some thirty years previously, the Council of Tours of 813 had instructed the clergy to disseminate religious teaching to ordinary people in the vernacular rather than in Latin. This decision, taken in the wake of the Carolingian reforms, confirms how their return to the Latin of the past was, by the same token, an opening to the future of French. Following this remit, virtually all the early (ninth to eleventh century) vernacular texts produced in France—whether in French or Occitan ('Provençal')—are adaptations of Latin devotional works. This may not sound a particularly thrilling start to 'French literature', but recent years have led to interesting re-evaluations of these works.

It is a curious coincidence that the earliest French narrative (it dates from *c*.880) is a liturgical poem recording the death of a female virgin martyr, Saint Eulalia; while probably the earliest surviving narrative work in Occitan (*c*.1070, and maybe earlier) is about another virgin martyr, Saint Faith. The shape of such narratives in the Latin texts adapted by these vernacular writers is traditional. The virgin saint— young, noble, beautiful, nubile—is ordered by a persecutor—a loath-some agent of pagan, Roman tyranny—to abandon her faith in God. He bribes her with offers of worldly pleasures (jewellery, fine clothes, and often marriage, usually to himself, since although he persecutes her he finds her very attractive . . .), and threatens her, should she refuse, with a painful death. She does refuse, of course; and the vanity of the pagan's threats is then exposed by the way his attempts to kill her fail. Typically he has the martyr thrown onto a fire from which God mirac-ulously preserves her. In later texts, mechanisms for killing the saint multiply and become more technologically elaborate, and pagan anger at their frustration appears more comic, but in both the *Eulalia* and the *Faith* when the pyre proves unsuccessful the martyr is beheaded.

This does, indeed, kill her. However, it has the drawback of calling attention to the fact that the saint's resistance to the persecutor lies in her steadfast voicing of her faith. Her neck severed, her physical voice silenced, the saint's testimony ('martyr' is Greek for 'witness') contin-ues to be heard, since the narrative of the saint's martyrdom perpetu-ates her voice beyond the grave, showing its truth to be eternal. The importance of the voice is borne out by the names of both these virgin saints: Eulalia means 'pleasant speech' while Saint Faith, as she defends her beliefs against her tormentor Dacien, speaks both her nature and her name.

Now the coincidence that in both these early texts the voice is a female one is telling. For what language can these young girls be speaking if not the vernacular? The whole structure of these virgin martyr plots relies on the starkness of the opposition between persecutor and saint. On the one hand the physical and political power of the foreign tyrant and his minions, all the resources of an imperial pagan rule, now long since departed; on the other a local girl, powerless and defenceless except for the faith in God which is still shared by the Christian community that reveres her. The concluding lines of the *Sequence of Saint Eulalia* invite all its listeners to entreat the saint, 'Tuit oram que por nos degnet preier' ('Let us all beg that she should deign to pray for us'). It is manifest that saint and audience share the same language. The opening of the Occitan *Life of Saint Faith* celebrates the value of a 'French treatment' of a theme known throughout the Occitan-speaking region of southern France and northern Spain. Saint Faith is represented as speaking in a simple, unaffected style: the language of her people and the poem's audience. For example, she denounces pagan idols as worth less than 'sengle trau de troill | qe l'om agess dolaz enz broil' ('mere planks from a wine press | that someone might have planed in the forest'). Thus when the Council of Tours invited the clergy to transpose religious works into the vernacular, it unwittingly authorized a vernacular literature in which the Church's own language, Latin, is cast in the enemy role. The saints— it appears—speak French.

Speech is also foregrounded in the earliest vernacular saint's life to feature a male protagonist, the late tenth-century French *Life of Saint Leger*. Set in the reign of the Frankish kings Clotaire and Chilperic, the story tells how the wise and eloquent royal counsellor Leger continues to voice his faith even after his tongue has been cut out by the enemies who betrayed him. Interestingly, Christine de Pizan will cite a similar story in her *Cité des dames* of 1405. The author's namesake Saint Christine, another virgin martyr, can also speak after her tormentor has cut out her tongue. When her prosecutor protests, she spits its root into his eye and blinds him. Again a martyr's plot is being used to defend its writer's cause. But this is identified now not as that of vernacular poetry, but of a woman's right to compose it: a cause which French literature has taken over four centuries since the *Sequence of Saint Eulalia* to voice.

It is only in the late eleventh or early twelfth century that we find the vernacular life of a saint whose testimony resides not in speech but in writing. Saint Alexis, who is Roman, barely says a word in the earliest French narrative Life. Instead he commits his story to a written document (*charte*) in order that it can be read after his death. The language in which Saint Alexis composes this document is not indicated, but it must be presumed to be Latin. His story anticipates the theme of *translatio*—the adaptation into French of written models from classical antiquity, and the accompanying transferral and appropriation of classical culture—which rises to prominence in the mid-twelfth century, and to which we return (see p. 42).

INVENTING LOVE POETRY: THE SONGS OF THE TROUBADOURS

The vernacular texts which survive from the ninth to the eleventh centuries do not give the impression of having been written for fun. The contrast with the works of the first known Occitan lyric poet, Guilhem (William) IXth duke of Aquitaine and VIIth count of Poitiers (1071–1126), could not be more emphatic. Reported by a chronicler to have 'distended the jaws of his courtiers with laughter', Guilhem has a surviving corpus of ten or eleven songs, most of them ribald and extravagant confessions of sexual passion. By about 1150, within twenty-five years of his death, the main characteristics of Occitan lyric poetry are becoming established. Addressing topical and moral subjects as well as promoting love and courtship, displaying refinement, desire, and humour in varying proportions, these are performance pieces intended for an audience of courtiers. A single author—their *troubadour* or 'finder'—is responsible for words, music, and usually, in the first instance at least, performance. Songs are strophic, with the same tune being repeated through successive stanzas. Most surviving troubadour melodies deploy a narrow range of notes and little ornamentation except at the ends of lines where flourishes (*melismata*) highlight the rhyme; performance is typically unaccompanied and so also concentrates attention on voice and text. Rhyme schemes are intricate and seldom repeated from one song to another, but content tends to follow more traditional lines. The theme nowadays referred to as 'courtly love', but which the troubadours themselves call *fin' amor*, 'true/refined love', seems to constitute an ongoing debate in which troubadours engage with a recognizable agenda of questions. To what extent is love sensual or spiritual? Rational or irrational? Socially productive or isolating? Pleasurable or agonizing? Morally elevating or degrading? How can one aspire to realize a love that is sustained by aspiration, or seek to overcome the very distance between oneself and the beloved that makes her desirable? Is the lover committed or ironic, delicate or obscene, ecstatic or self-controlled? Is his lady cruel or gracious, monstrous or sublime? In troubadour songs such questioning is not so much answered as amplified, using imagery drawn from the natural world to present the poet as responding to the cycle of the seasons, and a complex vocabulary of value rooted in the moral and social context which he shares with his audience. Initially this common context is the courts of Poitou and Aquitaine in south-west France. As the twelfth century progresses, it extends East into the Toulousain and Provence, then south into northern Italy and Spain. The golden age of the troubadours is between about 1160 and 1230. Later in the thirteenth century the tradition loses momentum, but by this stage its spark has fired imitators in northern France, Germany, the Iberian peninsula, and Italy. Troubadour love poetry is one of the most influential and dynamic poetic forces of the Middle Ages. Many see it as affecting the European erotic imagination to this day.

How did this extraordinarily glamorous and fascinating poetry come into being? There have been various attempts to explain its origins: in Arabic poetry, folk literature, mystical movements, or medieval Latin poetry in the tradition of Ovid. None of these explanations, however, commands widespread assent and in recent years the quest for origins has come to seem increasingly chimerical. Scholars are now more inclined to see the motivation for the rise of troubadour poetry in the poetic tradition itself, and in the courtly milieu in which it arose. The following examples suggest the path this development appears to have taken.

To begin, then, at the beginning, with the songs of the first known troubadour. In one of the more outrageous, Guilhem IX confides in his 'companions' that a lady has complained to him that noisy ruffians keep her under guard. Turning to these guards, he rebukes them (*vos castei*: 'I admonish you') for the vanity of their efforts. Every guard must sleep some time; and any lady, however great her 'faith' (*fei*), if her undertakings (*plait*) or her good grace (*mercei*) are refused, and she is held apart from worth (*proessa*), will have dealings (*plaideiar*) with wickedness (*malvestatz*). The vocabulary of this address invokes religious, moral, legal, and political registers. *Fei*, for example, means 'religious faith' but also 'trustworthiness' and 'fidelity to the sworn word', while *proessa* means 'moral worth' as well as 'physical courage and prowess' and *malvestatz* can mean '(moral) wickedness', '(social) baseness', or even '(physical) cowardice'. Guilhem's mock sermon (*casteis*) may be intended to preserve women's faith from wickedness, or it may mean that a woman refused access to noble warriors will compromise herself with low-born or cowardly men. He deplores keeping women short of what he calls 'good equipment' (*lo bon conrei*; the root *con* in *conrei* is often an invitation to sexual *double entendre* in

Guilhem's songs). A woman will arm herself with what comes to hand, and if she can't obtain a charger (*caval*) she will put up with a riding horse (*palafrei*). Likewise if she can't drink wine, she'll drink water rather than die of thirst: anyone, the singer concludes, would do the same.

The sexual swagger towards the end of this song is unmistakable. The restrictions under which the unfortunate complainant is held are denounced because they prohibit her access to the heady vigour of a potent lover such as himself. The vocabulary associated with her (*fei, plait, mercei*) signals her aristocratic standing. Imposing lack upon her is abhorrent. The song implies that such a lady deserves the abundance of enjoyment which wealth and power can bestow. At the same, these terms provide a cloak for (pseudo)-moralizing: withholding 'prowess' from the lady in its sexual and social manifestations also withdraws 'worth' and condemns her to 'evil'.

This song, one of several 'companion' poems by Guilhem IX, provoked strong reactions in subsequent poets. Marcabru, a Gascon troubadour who flourished c.1130–1149 at, among other places, the court of Guilhem IX's successor Guilhem X, produced a number of reworkings of the 'companion' poems. His 'En abriu' imitates the form while countering the content of Guilhem's. Initially, Marcabru's tone is very different. Evoking Easter as the time when nature grows clear and bright, he embraces the comfort of *fin' amor* as a clear, white, unsullied experience. But love, he goes on, is often treacherous: appearing to serve you nobly, it may prove malevolent. Renewing one of Guilhem's images, he denounces such love as a form of drunkenness: 'qui trop beu que non deu lo vins li tol la vigor' ('for if one drinks more than one should, the wine saps one's vigour'). Rather than wine-drinking representing noble love, it poses a threat of degeneracy and even of impotence.

Marcabru next imagines a nightmarish scenario in which he waits in a queue of lovers outside the lady's room, into which unworthy men are always entering ahead of him. Despite his admonishment (his self-identification as a *castiador* picks up Guilhem IX's *castei*), women's coarse appetites leave them unable to distinguish quality from quantity. He condemns them in shocking terms:

> Aquist con son deziron e raubador;
> tuit cill gartz i clamon partz et ill en lor:
> e qui mieills fa sordeitz a, cum de l'agol' an pastor.

[These cunts are greedy and thievish. All these ruffians claim a share in them, and they in the ruffians; and the man who acts best fares worst, as do shepherds with the lamb.]

Whereas Guilhem IX abhorred restriction and scarcity, here the poet's exclusion from the orgy is taken as an index of his moral worth. Unlike the 'thieving' lovers of plenty, and the lords who presumably own the lamb, the good poet is like a good shepherd: not a rapacious aristocrat but his morally superior subordinate. True he fails to secure sexual favours, but his vision remains undistorted by their inebriating effect. Sex may be a privilege of wealth but true love is a quality of the lowly.

This song may not correspond with modern readers' expectations of 'courtliness' any more than Guilhem's, but songs like this (and Marcabru has some forty surviving pieces) were vital in defining the emergence of 'courtly love' as a stance in which aspiration is more vital than fulfilment. Marcabru recasts Guilhem's parodic 'sermon' along lines more compatible with Christian norms. Although Marcabru positions himself as marginal to the court and as frankly opposed to most troubadours' interpretation of *fin' amor*, his ethical influence on Occitan poetry was decisive and enduring.

The combination of decorousness and passionate desire so typical of 'courtly love' poetry was forged in part by Marcabru's contemporary Jaufre Rudel. Lord of Blaye on the Gironde, and active *c*.1125–1148, Jaufre speaks neither as a great magnate (like the powerful Guilhem) nor yet as a marginal figure within the court (like Marcabru). The themes of his meagre output of only seven surviving songs are crusade, the social and moral complexities of court life, and his love for a distant lady, a love apparently imbued with mystical value as a result of her association with the Holy Land. Rapt in desire for this love, Jaufre's songs move in and out of the world of dreams. His 'Quan lo rius' begins very similarly to Marcabru's 'En abriu' with an evocation of the brightening streams and budding flowers of spring. Just as the little nightingale on the branch shapes his song, so does the troubadour. The love of which he sings is an 'amors de terra londana' ('love of a distant land') for which 'tot lo cors mi dol' ('my whole body aches'). His lady is unique among women. Knowingly, he admits that since satisfaction keeps eluding him, it is not surprising that he burns with desire. The song holds in play religious and sensual registers simultaneously. The lover's appetite is like that of a falcon for the lure, but also one enraptured by the prospect of divine manna; his desire has to be carefully disentangled from the sin of cupidity; his passion, 'sharper than a thorn', but which also 'heals with joy', is reminiscent of Christ's.

In common with Marcabru, Jaufre Rudel can be seen as reacting against the poetry of Guilhem IX. Both see lack (interpreted by Jaufre as unbridgeable distance) as a hallmark of the quality of love. But whereas for Marcabru sexuality is always tinged with abjection, Jaufre represents this state of unfulfilled aspiration as saturated with exquisite, erotic longings. In so doing, he reverses Guilhem's parodic use of religious allusion, restoring it to a thrilling, if precarious, balance with the sensual claims of earthly passion. He makes cerebral awareness of an impossible love combine with celebration of ecstatic aspiration. All this shapes the poet's song which, like that of the nightingale, succeeds in being at once 'natural' and highly crafted. This combination of inspiration and poetic mastery is captured in the portrait of a later troubadour, Folquet de Marselha (Figure 2).

In the great troubadours from later in the twelfth century and into the thirteenth, the legacy of the early troubadours is reworked in a variety of ways and with increasing virtuosity. The careful balance between moral, social, and religious preoccupations, and between refinement, coarseness, and humour, is weighted in different directions by individual poets. Bertran de Born and Raimbaut de Vaqueiras, for example, incline towards the theme of knighthood, Giraut de Bornelh and Raimon de Miraval towards didacticism; Arnaut de Maruelh and Arnaut Daniel explore the contradictions of an unspeakable (or inadmissible) emotion, while Raimbaut d'Aurenga and Peire Vidal revel in confident humour; later troubadours like Peire Cardenal and Guilhem de Montanhagol espouse more overtly religious themes.

The most influential of the great troubadours in defining the parameters of *fin' amor* was Bernart de Ventadorn (active *c.*1147–1170). In 'Pel doutz chan', for example, he depicts himself bursting into song on hearing the nightingale's voice:

> c'aisso es mos melher mesters,
> que tostems ai joi volunters
> et ab joi comensa mos chans.

[for this is my supreme *mester*: that at all times I gladly embrace joy and my song begins with joy.]

The word *mester* means 'craft', but also 'service' and even 'ministry': *faire lo Deu mester*, for example, is to recite the Holy Office. If the spontaneity of Bernart's song echoes the nightingale's, it also encapsulates the supreme value of a joyous, quasi-religious, ecstatic love. In the next stanza he turns to economic imagery, boasting his supreme 'wealth' as a lover. His joy arises from contemplating his lady, so lovely that it would take a year adequately to praise her. In imagination he is with her; and yet in reality he is far away. This decorous

2. The troubadour Folquet de Marselha in the grip
of inspiration at his desk. Pierpont Morgan Library
M 819, fo. 63.

scenario, recalling Rudel, licenses an image more reminiscent of
Guilhem IX: the lover declares himself *garnitz* ('equipped/armed') in
his lady's service. This in turn is quickly translated into the image of
himself as a man pledging his service to another. Less potentially
licentious, this image is nonetheless equivocal since it plays along the
boundaries of gender identity (is his lady his lord?) and social norms
(can a secret love affair really resemble the crucial relation of fidelity
between men?):

> Vostr' om sui juratz e plevitz,
> e vostre m'era des abans.
> Et vos etz lo meus jois primers
> e si seretz vos lo derrers,
> tan com la vida m'er durans.

[I am your man, sworn and pledged, and I was yours from long ago. And you
are my first joy, and you will be the last, as long as my life continues.]

By means of such humble submission, the lover counts on being well
received by his lady when he is next before her. This song is addressed
to Eleanor of Aquitaine, by then queen of England. With its effort-
lessly virtuoso rhyming and its complex web of images, by means of
which *fin' amor* is subtly insinuated into the heart of a whole range of
(not always compatible) experiences, it is characteristic of the broader

European lyric to come, while also echoing the poetry of the very early troubadours.

Even much later songs, and songs by women troubadours (or *trobairitz*), can hark back to these beginnings. The medieval manuscript which contains the 'companion' poem with which this discussion began juxtaposes its selection of poems by Guilhem IX with a group of *trobairitz* songs, and then, after closing that section, repeats the Guilhem songs, as though driving home the women's difficulty in making themselves heard above the male aristocrat's boastful clamour. One of these women's songs, 'Amics, s'ie.us trobes avinen' by Castelloza (first half of the thirteenth century), makes this difficulty explicit. 'Everyone says,' she admits, 'that it is most unseemly for a woman to press her suit with a knight or constantly to detain him with prolonged entreaty':

> . . . dison tuch que mout descove
> que domna prei a cavalier de se,
> ni que·l tenha totz temps tan lonc prezic.

Aware that her lover is unworthy and yet desperate not to lose him, praising him against her better judgement and yet anxious that she herself might be at fault, Castelloza sees no prospect, except in Rudel-like dreams, of the 'joy' which seems to be Bernart de Ventadorn's natural medium. As though in answer to Guilhem IX's assertion that a woman will drink water rather than die of thirst, she realizes 'q'ieu vuoill proar enans qe.m lais morir' ('that I wish to woo rather than allow myself to die'). The first troubadour's crude account of female sexuality has been recast as a complex and tragic avowal of a woman's desire to love and sing, and her sense of being excluded from the poetry of *fin' amor* despite its being seemingly addressed to women like herself.

These examples suggest how the development of the troubadour lyric can be largely explained as a dialogue between individual poets playing in different ways to the fantasies of their courtly audiences. The outrageous offensiveness with which Guilhem IX promotes sexual freedom for upper-caste warriors, his swagger of wealth, power, and potency, and amused conflation of might and right, seem to have provoked a reaction more conducive to the harmonious functioning of court life. This life involved cooperation between widely differing personnel: great lords, lesser lords, knights, religious advisers, diplomats, secretaries, and sundry hangers-on. The debates conducted in troubadour poetry nod to the interests of these different groups and, obedient to the constraints of social decorum, seek to contain them in a balance acceptable to all, while also cultivating a sense of intense inner exaltation and refinement. The figure of the lady, the absent focus and support of this consensus, bears scant relation to historical women. *Fin' amor*, elective and ecstatic, is an imaginary corrective to the marriages dictated by dynastic and territorial interest which were the norm for aristocratic society throughout the Middle Ages and beyond. That it was to prove a winning formula is borne out by the rapid diffusion of courtly love literature to all the courts of Europe. By the late twelfth century, lyric poets known as *trouvères* (the *langue d'oïl* equivalent of 'troubadours') were flourishing in northern French courts. Many—like Gace Brulé or le chastelain de Couci—imitated Bernart de Ventadorn and, indeed, reworked several of his songs. The literary fantasy of courtliness was on its way to becoming a moral and political reality.

THE THREE *MATIÈRES* AND THE MOVE FROM HISTORY TO FICTION

As the twelfth century progresses, literature in the *langue d'oïl*, the French spoken in northern France and Britain, becomes increasingly abundant and innovative. Saints' lives continue to be written, among the most interesting being the *Life of St Catherine* by the Essex nun Clemence of Barking, but most compositions now are secular. And unlike the poetry of the south, they are almost exclusively narrative.

Traditionally, scholars have analysed this surge of narrative composition in terms of genre, under the headings of *chansons de geste*, history-writing, and romances. All three, however, initially posit themselves in some sense as history; their separation into recognizably different narrative genres comes later. An analysis of the various strands of historical subject matter on which they draw was put forward at the end of the twelfth century by the versatile and prolific Arras poet Jehan Bodel. According to the opening lines of Jehan's *Les Saisnes* ('The Saxons'), there are three *matières* or 'matters'. The matter of Britain is empty and pleasing ('vain et plesant'); that of Rome is wise and instructive ('sage et de sens aprendant'); and that of France is constantly revealing its truthfulness ('est voir chascun jour aparent').

The matter of France consists in stories purportedly drawn from French history, usually set in the reign of Charlemagne or one of his successors, and usually (though not always) associated with *chansons de geste*. Probably the most famous of these is the *Chanson de Roland* which describes Charlemagne's wars in Spain and the loss of his nephew, Roland, in the battle of Rencesvals. *Les Saisnes* is a sequel to the *Roland* in which Charlemagne and his surviving nephew subdue Germany, and so in preferring the matter of France to the two others, Bodel is not innocent of self-promotion.

The matter of Rome consists in the translation or adaptation into French of antique texts, a practice theorized in the concept of *translatio*: the claim, central to the twelfth-century Renaissance, that northwest Europe had assumed the imperial and cultural heritage of the ancient world. When the siege of Troy is won by the Greeks the Trojan prince Aeneas escapes and eventually founds Rome; these events are recounted in the *Roman de Troie* of *c.*1160, and the *Roman d'Eneas*, an adaptation of Virgil's *Aeneid* which dates from *c.*1155. Texts which rework antique material into French are collectively known today as the *romans antiques* or *romans d'antiquité*.

The matter of Britain, finally, involves the recasting of the history associated with either Britain or Brittany, much of which seems to derive from Celtic sources. Probably the founding text of this *matière* is the remarkably successful Latin *History of the Kings of Britain* (1136) by the racy writer and folklorist *avant la lettre*, Geoffrey of Monmouth. Geoffrey establishes King Arthur as forebear to the British throne, and introduces the magic and marvels of the Other World.

These three matters all begin, then, as ways of conceiving of the origins and genealogy of twelfth-century culture and institutions. The presence in all of them of legendary and fantastic elements may divorce them from history as we understand it, but the drift into what we would recognize as 'fiction' is nonetheless uneven, while the emergence of what we now see as distinct genres is gradual and uncertain. The generic term *roman*, which it is tempting to translate as 'romance', initially means 'translation (into the vernacular, or Romance, language)'. It is used to refer to the matters of both Rome and Britain, and designates both texts which incline more towards chronicle (like Wace's *Roman de Brut* of *c.*1155, an adaptation into French of the *History of the Kings of Britain*), and texts which are more recognizably fictional stories (like the *Roman d'Alexandre*, a series of long and extravagant *romans antiques* about the legendary emperor Alexander, composed in Britain and in France between *c.*1160 and 1190). The word *roman* also occurs in the manuscript headings ('rubrics') of *chansons de geste* which, in turn, vary greatly as to how far they present themselves as historical, or fictional, narratives.

The attitude of the *romans antiques* to the past combines shock at the crimes of which pagan history was capable with admiration for its astonishing cultural achievements. These two elements fuse in one of their most memorable features: descriptions of the funeral rites, entombment, and fabulous funerary monuments, of dead lovers and heroes. In the *Roman de Troie* especially, the atrocities committed during the relentless siege of Troy—the corpses piled deep on the battlefield, the air oppressive with the stench of rottenness, and the rivers dark with blood—contrast with the exquisite workmanship and jewel-incrusted splendour of its architecture. Embalming skills transform wounded bodies into perennially enduring forms while astonishing automata recast lifelessness as haunting beauty. Analogously, the *romans* can themselves be seen as building on the sublime foundations of antique art, and as gloriously preserving and entombing the morally wounded body of the past.

A very different tone reigns among the mists and marvels of the matter of Britain which seems more readily to drift into fictionality. A noticeable shift in this direction occurs when the material, first elaborated in Britain, is taken up by the mainland French writer Chrétien de Troyes. In Chrétien's hands Arthur becomes even less historical than he was in works composed in England. He is also treated with less respect, becoming increasingly ineffectual and inert as Chrétien's *œuvre* unfolds. The knights of Arthur's Round Table, however, provide an inexhaustible fund of stories. A cast of characters emerges: the slanderous seneschal Kay; Arthur's philandering nephew Gawain; his queen Guenevere; and, starring in Chrétiens's successive Arthurian romances (composed *c.*1165–1190), the young knights Erec (*Erec et Enide*), Yvain (*Le Chevalier au lion*), Lancelot (*Le Chevalier de la charrete*), and Perceval (*Le Conte del graal*; see Figure 3, p. 60).

Chrétien's influential narratives establish the pattern of romances of chivalry for centuries to come. The romance of *Li Biaus Desconnëus* ('The Fair Unknown'), in the late twelfth-century version ascribed to Renaut de Beaujeu, is typical of the model he seems to have inaugurated. An untried and nameless knight arrives at Arthur's court; leaves in quest of adventure; has a range of marvellous encounters in the wild forest with brigands, dwarves, and sundry anti-chivalric figures; triumphs in the supreme adventure to relieve a kingdom and its lady of a spell; learns his true identity, and is consecrated as a hero by the Arthurian court; but, in the course of inner setbacks, loses the lady of his dreams; instead is ceremoniously married to the lady whom he liberated; and leaves with her to found a court of his own. In the masterful hands of Chrétien and his successors, this patterning of forest and court, desire and social obligation, creates a subtle blend of integration and alienation, didacticism and irony.

Another common feature of narratives of the 'matter of Britain' is a mortal hero's encounter with a fairy mistress, as narrated in *Partonopeu de Blois* (probably late twelfth century). This also provides the substance of several of the short narrative *Lais* attributed to Marie de France, the only female author to compose secular narratives in the *langue d'oïl* before Christine de Pizan. For Marie, the Other World alone is judged capable of providing solutions to the injustices and loveless marriages of this one. Women's proximity to supernatural powers may form the mythical background to the *Tristan* legend, in which the young hero Tristan, and Isolt, wife of his uncle King Mark, fall in love under the influence of a love potion. The possibility that the world of our own experience may be lined with an inner world of magic is full of poetic potential, tingeing the everyday with an aura of the marvellous, or else exposing its bleakness when deprived of the golden hue of fantasy. Both the redeeming and the damning effects of invoking magic are explored in what survives of Beroul's version of the *Tristan* legend (second half of the twelfth century). On the one hand, the lovers possess a magical innocence: when King Mark attempts to surprise them together, he in fact finds them sleeping clothed with a sword between them. On the other hand, the text repeatedly denounces the guilt of adultery by associating the lovers with blood, filth, and disease.

Several important texts combine the matters of Rome and Britain. Legend had it that when Aeneas fled Troy to found Rome, he was accompanied by various companions who could be credited with the foundation of other dynasties in northern Europe. Britain was held to have been colonized by, and named after, a certain Brutus (hence the title of Wace's *Roman de Brut*), and Blois by Marcomiris (see *Partonopeu de Blois*, which also includes the 'matter of France' since it features Merovingian kings repelling Saracen invaders). Not to be left out, the French King Philip Augustus also promoted the myth of his Trojan ancestry. Chrétien de Troye's *Cligés* is a hugely enjoyable romp through a travestied *Tristan* plot, using characters who originate in Byzantine Greece, but who seem uncertain whether they belong in Arthurian romance, a *roman antique*, or—most bizarrely of all—the life of a virgin martyr.

If the different matters identified by Jehan Bodel sometimes coincide in the same text, one reason for their compatibility is that all three betray uncertainty about the status of *langue d'oïl* culture. The matter of Rome presents north-west Europe as the latter-day colony of an artistically superior Eastern civilization, but at the same time warns medieval audiences against accepting the moral legacy of the pagan past. The matter of France presents the Franks as barely holding their own against another Eastern civilization, that of the 'Saracens', which is morally inferior (because likewise pagan) but also undeniably wealthier and more technologically advanced than theirs. And the matter of Britain increasingly portrays indigenous origins as absurd or inept (in the figure of Arthur), while his knights of the Round Table are outplayed and undermined by the supernatural powers of the Other World.

The matter of France, whose truth Jehan Bodel extols, may have been the most visible of the three in his own day. But the other two matters were interacting with the love lyric—both that of the troubadours, and that of their northern French imitators the *trouvères*—to produce a literary subject matter that was to prove vastly more influential than either in the long run: that of courtliness. The effect of the rise of courtliness, in turn, was to realign what had previously been *three* historical themes into *two* literary major genres: a courtly one now recognizable as 'romance' and the un- or anti-courtly one of the *chansons de geste*. History-writing, meanwhile, temporarily loses prestige until once more progressing to the literary forefront with the advent of prose. The next two sections deal with courtly romance and the *chansons de geste* respectively; prose history is considered later, in the context of the creation of prose romance.

COURTLINESS AND THE RISE OF ROMANCE

Nothing inherent to the three historical matters would lead one to expect that tales of individual love and adventure would emerge as the major theme of literature in court circles from about 1170 onwards, nor that the meaning of the word *roman* would gradually shift from 'translation' to 'romance'. Neither the ancient epics exploited by the *romans antiques* nor Geoffrey of Monmouth contain much love interest. Medieval *romanciers*, however, built on what little they could find. Whereas Aeneas's marriage to Lavinia earns a brief mention in Virgil's *Aeneid*, in the *Eneas* their love dominates the last fifth of the text; Benoît de Sainte-Maure supplied generations of European poets with his expansive treatment of the love affairs in the *Troie*, notably that between Troilus and Briseïda (later Cressida). Guenevere and the other ladies of the Arthurian world assume increasing importance in the works of Wace and Chrétien. The influence of the poetry of *fin' amors* grows, becoming perceptible on the *Tristan* attributed to Thomas, the *Lais* of Marie de France, and the romances of Chrétien, himself the *trouvère* of at least two lyrics. By the end of the twelfth century, the narrator may pose as a lyric lover who tells his story in the hope of wooing his lady, and keeps breaking off when emotion overcomes him to appeal for her favour (*Partonopeu de Blois*, *Li Biaus Desconnëus*). Early in the thirteenth, the practice develops of including lyric pieces within romances; characters launch into song with all the aplomb of actors in a Hollywood musical. Among the romances that exploit this technique are Jean Renart's *Roman de la rose* (also known as the *Roman de Guillaume de Dole*), and the wonderful late thirteenth-century *Romans dou castelain de Couci*, whose hero, purportedly the historical early thirteenth-century *trouvère*, is represented as composing all his songs for love of the Dame de Fayel. With the first part of the *Roman de la rose*, composed by Guillaume de Lorris, we find a fusion of lyric and narrative as the narrator recounts, in the first person, his dream experience of falling in love (see the section on this text below, pp. 65–8).

The redrawing of literary boundaries in such a way that the love lyric and the narrative works it influences fall together under the heading of 'courtly literature', while other forms remain outside 'courtliness', was to prove decisive in the development of medieval literature. But the process itself was not simple or clear cut. 'Courtly' can, after all, designate anything that has a bearing on courts, their procedures, and their values, and the usage of the Old French word *courtois* reflects this range. Scholars argue, not necessarily productively, about the extent to which specific medieval texts are 'courtly'. The twelfth-century *Tristan* poems are a case in point. Is Beroul's version, which stresses the political implications of the lovers' relationship for Mark's kingdom, thereby 'uncourtly'? Is Thomas's text, with its meticulous intellectual dissection of each protagonist's situation, 'courtly' because of his abstract and restrained treatment of the sexual theme or 'uncourtly' because of his evident disapproval of a life dominated by passion? The story of *Floire et Blancheflor* is another instance where different versions have been labelled 'courtly' and 'uncourtly'. This is an idyllic tale of two children, one a Saracen prince and the other a Frankish slave girl, who grow up together, fall in love, are cruelly separated by the boy's family but then, after many adventures, happily reunited. The story is linked to the matter of France by the fact that their offspring is Charlemagne's mother and is cast in two versions, one more aristocratic ('courtly') than the other.

Such discussions of 'courtliness' point to the possible ramifications of the concept: rhetorically elaborate or at least elegant, avoiding physically crude topics or coarse language, committed to the virtue of restraint, promoting individual sensibility, prizing a chivalric over a warrior ethos, espousing aristocratic interest (for example, in preference to that of the clergy), reflecting aristocratic society . . . The list is a long one before one even mentions 'courtly love', with all the problems which that raises. It is clear that such a complex web of criteria makes it possible for any individual text to be rated as more or as less courtly depending on which of them are applied to it. The thirteenth century sees a prolific production of verse romances that may seem more parodic (*Fergus*, about a Scottish peasant who becomes an Arthurian knight), pious (*La Manneƙine* by Philippe de Remi, about a girl fleeing her incestuous father), folkloric (*Guillaume de Palerme*, featuring a werewolf) or simply idiosyncratic (*Le Roman de Silence* by Heldris de Cornüälle, about a girl brought up as a boy) than straightforwardly 'courtly'.

Rather than lose our way in this critical maze, let us limit this discussion to the major effects of the coalescence just described between lyric poetry and that form of verse narrative which is emerging as 'romance'. The debates initiated by the troubadours regarding the nature of love (see above, 34–5) are absorbed into romance with several shifts of emphasis that result from its more explicit, third-person, narrative character. (1) The question of whether love is a socially positive or negative force is considered in relation to the role of love in inspiring, or distracting from, knighthood. In the lyric, deeds of knighthood are not an issue but this theme (sometimes referred to as the 'chivalry topos') is ubiquitous in Arthurian and other chivalric romances. (2) The value of love is also explored in the context of concrete situations of marriage and adultery. In lyric poetry, adultery is almost never mentioned and ambiguity about the love relationship is encouraged, whereas narrative is inevitably more explicit. Romances which problematize adultery include the *Tristan* poems, Chrétien's *Cligés* and *Lancelot*, and the later thirteenth-century Occitan *Flamenca*, which involves a knight disguising himself as a cleric in order to seduce a married woman. (3) The question of whether love is spiritual or sensual is explored with greater reference to specifically Christian themes, whereas in the lyric, the purportedly spiritual dimension of love is usually treated with a more abstract religiosity. Many of the examples listed under point (2) can be cited here, as also Guillaume de Lorris's part of the *Roman de la rose*. (4) The question of whether the lover is committed or ironic is, as it were, split into two: lovers may well be love-lorn, but the narrator is ironic at their expense, his detachment enabling the humorous suspension of any answer to the earlier questions.

Chrétien's *Lancelot* is an important text in both the development of courtly romance, and its interpretation; the nineteenth-century medievalist Gaston Paris first coined the term 'courtly love' with reference to it. Lancelot's love for Arthur's Queen Guenevere, who has been abducted by the evil Meleagant, inspires him to unrivalled feats of knighthood. He sacrifices his reputation in his lady's service, even climbing on a pillory cart to follow her. When he finds her in Meleagant's kingdom, he worships before her as though she were holy:

> et puis vint au lit la reïne,
> si l'aore et se li ancline,
> car an nul cors saint ne croit tant.
> .   .   .   .   .   .
> Au lever fu il droiz martirs,
> tant li fu gries li departirs
> car il i suefre grant martire.

[and then he came to the queen's bed, and worships and bows down before her, for there is no holy relic in which he has greater faith. . . . When he rose he was just like a martyr, so sorry was he to leave since it makes him suffer such great martyrdom.]

He liberates not only the queen but Meleagant's hundreds of other prisoners. However he also spends the night with her, causing her to be charged with adultery, and then defends in court the knight falsely accused of the crime he himself committed. He is ridiculed by other characters, while his extremes of passion are mocked by the narrator (for example, when he moons over a comb containing Guenevere's hairs, or thinks so obsessively about her that another knight knocks him off his horse into a river). He is also imprisoned and reduced to complete passivity. Maybe the pillory cart (used to punish criminals) represents not supreme self-sacrifice, but a condemnation of the baseness to which love reduces him? This dilemma is encapsulated in the work's medieval title, *Le Chevalier de la charrete*, 'The Knight of the Cart'. Both exalting and undermining of love and chivalry, this romance is typical of the ambiguous and contested character of courtliness, and the entertainment value of its fictions.

THE *CHANSONS DE GESTE*

A counter-blast to the self-conscious cleverness and whimsical refinement of romance is represented by the rough-hewn and often savage narratives of the *chansons de geste*, of which some 100 survive. The earliest of these are the fragmentary *Gormont et Isembart*, the *Chanson de Roland* in its most famous version (known as the Oxford text because the manuscript is preserved in Oxford), and a part of the *Chançun de Willame*. These long narrative songs, which are difficult to date, but which were all in existence by the early twelfth century at the latest, present Frankish, Christian warriors being heroically chopped to pieces by pagan forces treacherously aided by renegade Christians. They are followed towards the middle of the twelfth century by a couple of rather more cheerful poems about the life of the hero William (Guillaume d'Orange) prior to the *Willame*. The Oxford version of the *Chanson de Roland* is one of the Old French poems most commonly studied today, but although the Roland legend was very widely known in the Middle Ages, it was disseminated not by this Oxford text but by the longer versions produced in France later in the twelfth century. Although a handful of early *chansons de geste* pre-date the rise of courtly romances, the heyday of the genre belongs from about 1170 until well into the thirteenth century. It is because the most typical *chansons de geste* seem to dispute the poetic and ideological stance of romances that we have deferred discussion of them until now.

Often misleadingly termed 'epic', these songs are concerned less to glorify war than to grieve over it. Even the Oxford *Roland* admits—in the conflict between Roland and Oliver whether to sound Roland's horn, recall Charlemagne's army, and so avert the disaster of Frankish defeat by the Saracens at Rencesvals—that the closest friendships between men may be fragile and impaired. The large numbers of such poems, generated around Charlemagne and his twelve peers (most famous among them Roland, Oliver, and Archbishop Turpin), collectively constitute what is called the *geste du roi*. Another narrative grouping or 'cycle' (the *geste de Guillaume d'Orange*) takes shape around the figure of William with his innumerable heroic nephews, cousins, uncles, and miscellaneous forebears. Early songs in both of these *gestes* deal with wars against 'pagan' Saracens—the Charlemagne poems typically carrying war abroad to the enemy, the William ones defending Christian homeland from invaders—but increasingly they turn to political criticisms of the French/Frankish regime. In many poems Charlemagne appears ineffectual, deranged, detached from reality, or cruelly vindictive (in *Gui de Bourgogne*, for example, he jealously clings to power although his senility is exposed by the superior fighting skills of young Gui). His son Louis, king throughout the *geste de Guillaume*, is feeble, cowardly, and unjust (in the *Couronnement de Louis* he repeatedly has to be rescued from rebels whom he dares not fight himself, but ultimately refuses to reward his defender William). Both rulers are blind to traitors in their own court and unable to quell disputes among their barons. In the William poems, furthermore, the once cohesive family is torn apart by conflict (in *Les Narbonnais* the aged Aymeri, William's father, drives out all his sons except the youngest from their home in Narbonne, thereby leaving it vulnerable to Saracen attack).

Both *gestes* come to resemble what the author of the late twelfth-century *Girart de Vienne* identifies as a third *geste*, that of the traitors or rebel barons; though if *geste* this is, it is not constituted like the others through recurrent and interrelated characters. These poems dwell on political and social catastrophes internal to the French/Frankish kingdom: bitter warfare between kings and magnates (*Girart de Vienne* itself takes this as its central theme), murderous hatred between close companions (in the Occitan *chanson de geste Daurel et Beton*, a man kills his best friend in order to get his wife and estate), treachery and violence within the family (in *Doon de la Roche*, Doon is persuaded that his wife is unfaithful, repudiates her to marry the daughter of traitors, but is finally brought to book by his son).

Some songs, like the magnificently sombre *Raoul de Cambrai* (late twelfth century), combine several of these themes. The young Raoul is born after his father's death. King Louis decides that his father's lands and widow should be given to another knight. Raoul's mother indignantly refuses the match but cannot prevent Louis handing over the Cambrésis (the region of Cambrai) to his new favourite. When Raoul grows up he demands the restitution of his father's lands, and the reluctant king eventually compromises by promising Raoul the first available estate. Shortly afterwards Herbert de Vermandois dies, leaving vast lands to which Raoul lays claim. Unfortunately Herbert has four adult sons, one of whom is the father of Raoul's boyhood companion, Bernier. The king hesitates to go through with the gift to Raoul, eventually telling him he must win the land himself. Regardless of opposition from his mother and Bernier, Raoul sets out to conquer the Vermandois. His campaign leads to the burning of a convent in which Bernier's mother was abbess; when Bernier protests at her cruel death Raoul strikes him, and he leaves to join the Vermandois army. In the pitched battle which follows, Raoul multiplies acts of savagery and sacrilege before being eventually killed by Bernier. The narrative then progresses through successive wars of revenge until finally all the male characters are killed or exiled.

The horrific account of nuns and townspeople being burned alive in the abbey church imprinted itself on the imagination of the poem's contemporaries, many of whom allude to it:

> . . . li bacon ardent, si chieent li lardie[r].
> Li saïns fait le grant feu esforcier:
> fiert soi es tors et el maistre cloichier—
> les covretures covint jus trebuchier.
> Entre deus murs ot si grant charbonier,
> les nonains ardent, trop i ot grant brasier.
> Totes cent ardent par molt grant encombrier—
> art i Marsens qi fu mere B[ernier],
> et Clamados la fille au duc Renier.
> Parmi l'arcins les covint a flairier;
> de pitié pleurent li hardi chevalier.

[. . . sides of bacon burn and larders collapse. The bacon fat makes the great fire fiercer: it spreads to the towers and the highest steeple—the roofs were brought crashing down. Within the two walls the blaze was so intense that the nuns are burned to death, it was such a furnace. All hundred of them are burning in that great disaster—Marsent, Bernier's mother, is burning to death, and Clamados, Duke Renier's daughter. Amid the conflagration the smell was inescapable and the bold knights shed tears of pity.]

Atrocities such as this make the decorous adventures of individual knights of romance, however earnestly motivated, appear politically irrelevant.

Girart de Roussillon is another powerful story of social disintegration, precipitated in this case by 'love'. The king resolves to marry the younger but prettier daughter of the emperor of Constantinople, even though she was betrothed to his vassal Girart; Girart is obliged to take the older daughter, originally destined for the king. The king's opting for elective love over dynastic marriage leads to a lifetime of warfare; atrocities comparable to Raoul's burning of the abbey at Origny are perpetrated. As though in deliberate contrast with the celebration of desire in courtly romances, here its competitive and destructive dimensions are exposed.

Chansons de geste differ from romances in form as well as in their content. The versions which we have today seem to result from the revision and extension of older songs. Their plots tend to lack both unity (it is easy to imagine their performance as separate episodes) and closure (you could always add another war . . .). Instead of the octosyllabic couplets typical of romance, they are composed in *laisses* of uneven length, in which all the lines share the same rhyme or assonance; for instance, the lines of *Raoul* cited above come from a *laisse* of forty-four lines all ending in *-ier*. *Laisses* are often characterized by ballad-like patterns of repetition, both from line to line (they are said to be 'formulaic') and from *laisse* to *laisse*. In a subsequent episode of

Raoul, where the enraged hero keeps pursuing the wounded warrior Ernaut de Douai, the repetition underlines Ernaut's terror as he flees for his life: 'Fuit s'en Ernaus et Raous l'enchauça . . . Fuit s'en Ernaus broichant a esperon . . . Ernaut c'escrie—poour ot de morir . . . Fuit s'en Ernaus, broichant a esperon . . . Ernaus escrie, poour ot de morir', etc. ('Ernaut flees and Raoul chased after him . . . Ernaut flees, digging in his spurs . . . Ernaut shouts out in fear of his life,' etc.) Such *laisses* give the reader/listener the uncanny impression that the narrator cannot quite fix the precise outline of events in his story, but that he keeps trying to capture them in a welter of tentative, overlapping narrative fragments, and in an oddly restricted and inadequate language. One *chanson de geste* narrator, moreover, is much like any other. They speak in the same formulaic language as their characters and, typically, they are anonymous (Jehan Bodel is an exception). It is as if the songs sing on behalf of a collective identity: perhaps the lost community for which, finding only its mutilated and fragmented remains, they seem to grieve.

We should not underestimate the interest and variety of this community. Shattered by violence are the lives, not only of warriors whose *raison d'être* it is, but of women, children, and townspeople. All suffer the consequences of misrule—which can, it is true, be treated in comic as well as tragic vein. The *chansons de geste* of the late twelfth and thirteenth centuries represent a robust onslaught on the genteel haven of courtly romance, where the main wounds that bleed are those of love and where swordplay is subordinated to play on words.

CLERKS, *JONGLEURS*, AND TOWNSPEOPLE

While it is almost always impossible to determine who is responsible for *composing* the *chansons de geste*, they often imply that those who *recite* them are popular performers who sing or tell stories for a living. In the Middle Ages such performers are called *jongleurs*; often they are men who had begun training as 'clerks' (that is, as members of the order of the clergy, to which their education committed them at least temporarily), but dropped out of schooling to become poets and singers instead. The biographies (*vidas*) of the troubadours composed in the thirteenth century suggest that several of them had taken this route. Many *jongleurs* will have been itinerant, travelling in troupes, able to perform a wide repertoire of texts, and also to act, juggle, and tumble. There are Occitan poems addressed to *joglars* (Occitan for *jongleur*) from the mid-twelfth century onwards which give an admittedly exaggerated and jocular picture of the entertainments people expected from them. *Jongleurs* are usually represented as inferior to 'real' poets, and successful courtly authors who enjoyed long-term aristocratic patronage—Chrétien de Troyes, for example—set themselves apart from them. However, the distinction between poets and *jongleurs* is difficult to maintain since troubadours and *trouvères* typically performed their own compositions, while *jongleurs* composed part of their own repertoires.

The greater or lesser clerical leanings of these *jongleur*-poets are reflected in their compositions. A case in point is the miscellany of stories (known as 'branches') which make up the *Roman de Renart*. Composition of these overgrown animal fables starts in the 1170s, and continues through the thirteenth century. They constitute a *chanson de geste*-like universe of king, magnates, lesser knights, their wives, and court clerics, in which the major figures are Renart the fox, Ysengrin the wolf, Hersent the wolf's wife, and the lion King Noble; the potential for social critique of this material lent it to repeated use in other satirical works. The various individual branches reiterate similar story-lines: the hungry Renart outplays the hungry Ysengrin, not only obtaining food while the wolf fails to, but also having sex with his wife, humiliating and injuring him, and derisively evading punishment. The unregulated violence of these animal-barons is even worse than that of the human world (not surprisingly since it involves foxes stalking and devouring chickens, rats, etc., and being stalked by wolves), yet it never seems to do any harm. The characters can be starved, mutilated, skinned, or flattened, and yet—like today's cartoon strip creations—they spring back into shape at the end of one story ready to face the violence of the next. Their outlines are anyway constantly changing at their narrator's whim, sometimes settling in animal form, then disconcertingly reconfiguring as human.

While some of the branches (like the oldest, usually known as Branch II) remain close to the world of animal fable, others expand this interplay of human and animal world into extravagant parody of courtly romances and *chansons de geste*. In one episode of Branch I, for example, Renart tricks the bear with promises of honey into sticking his head into a cleft tree trunk, and then pulls out the wedge so that the tree springs shut on the bear's muzzle, reducing his head and face to pulp. Renart enquires derisively which religious order he hopes to join, now he is dressed in a red hood? King Noble continues the anodyne, human image: who has removed Brun's 'hat' for him? But animal fury then permeates the king's resolve to pursue legal redress against Renart:

> Qui lors veïst le lïon brere,
> par mautelant ses crins detrere,
> et jure le cuer et la mort . . .

[Whereupon you would have seen the lion roar and tear his mane and swear by (God's) heart and death . . .]

While here, violence shifts back and forth between animal brutality and human institutions, elsewhere it is sexual adventure that veers between animal copulation and a travestied *fin' amor*. Other branches again revive the clerical interests of one of the text's sources, an eleventh-century Latin mock-heroic satire on monastic life called the *Ysengrimus*, in which the fox and wolf are monks. Such branches use the animals to make fun of religious practices such as confession (VII), pilgrimage (VIII), or monasticism (III). They also disconcertingly probe theological issues such as the position of man in nature and the relation of sin to reason. Deceptively simple, disarmingly amusing, these stories also represent a sophisticated engagement with clerical culture.

Another body of texts for which more-or-less clerically qualified poet-*jongleurs* seem to have been responsible is that of the *fabliaux*. Like the branches of the *Renart*, *fabliaux* are short, comic narratives, composed in octosyllabic rhyming couplets, often parodic of the longer genres of *chansons de geste* and romance, which they debase in predictable ways (for example by including graphic sexual and scatological material). They differ from the *Renart*, however, in using human, non-noble characters (innkeepers, pimps, blacksmiths, village priests, beggars) placed in apparently real-world settings (taverns, merchants' houses, craftsmen's shops, busy streets). The earliest stem from the late twelfth century and they continue to be written into the fourteenth. Most *fabliaux* are anonymous, but known authors who experimented with the genre include Jehan Bodel, and the later thirteenth-century poet Rutebeuf (on whom more below, pp. 56–7).

The clerical perspective of these works is, perhaps surprisingly, most visible in the contempt they regularly heap on parish priests. In one *fabliau*, a priest is so incompetent that he gets confused reciting the Good Friday liturgy and, chillingly, finds himself on the wrong side of the story, calling for the liberation of Barabbas. In another, a wood-carver's wife is having an affair with a priest. Suspicious, the wood-carver returns home and the priest tries to hide by removing his clothes and lying outstretched on a cross that the craftsman is preparing for a crucifix. The wood-carver pretends to be taken in by the deception, merely tut-tutting at his poor quality handiwork and 'improving' it by relieving the priest of his genitals. In a third, a clerk is refused hospitality by a woman because she is expecting the priest with whom she too is having an affair. The clerk spies on her activities, returns to the house when her husband is home, and ingeniously informs the husband of his wife's misdeeds: he compares his travels that day to the various preparations for her transgression which the wife has concealed around the house, the climax coming when he claims to have been attacked by a wolf which looked at him just like the priest hiding in the larder. As these examples suggest, the *fabliaux* despise stupidity and prize intellectual resourcefulness, typically expressed as the ability to concoct convincing representations. Priests are simply unequal to their task of representing Christ; the *fableor*, by contrast, can transform them into a Jew, a statue or a wolf, and castrate or animalize them at will. The myriad trickster figures who dominate their stories succeed because they have a clerk's keen wits and powers of invention. The way they manipulate other people's perceptions leads to their gaining access to valued commodities: money, sex, lodging, food. Through these figures, the *fableors* enact the linguistic and intellectual bases of the *jongleurs*'s success with the townspeople.

The urban settings of most *fabliaux* may reflect the fact that in the thirteenth century, performance conditions for *jongleurs* grew more stable precisely in the towns. A genre that reflects this change is drama. Very early plays (if 'plays' they can be called) consist in vernacular insertions into Latin liturgical texts and were performed as part of the office. The twelfth-century *Ordo representacionis Adae* (or *Adam Play*) is the most developed representative of this tradition. In the thirteenth century, however, theatre moves from church to town; by the end of the century, a vernacular word for 'play', *jeu*, has been created. Two of the best-known plays of this period were produced in Arras, and clearly intended for an audience of local townspeople: the *Jeu de saint Nicolas*, another work by Jehan Bodel, a poet-*jongleur* who clearly dominates Arras at the turn of the twelfth and thirteenth centuries, and the *Jeu de la feuillée* by the later, equally prominent Arras writer Adam de la Halle (active in the last third of the thirteenth century). In the *Jeu de saint Nicolas*, the traditional miracle of Saint Nicholas's restoring a treasure stolen by thieves is entirely recast. The thieves are colourful gamblers who hang out in an Arras tavern; the treasure belongs to an exotic Saracen king who is winning the war against crusaders but who promptly converts when his stolen treasure is returned. The play stages a nice balance between promoting religious truth and indulging material appetite. Contemporary street life in Arras is also vividly portrayed in the *Jeu de la feuillée*. Adam him-self is the central figure and observer. Initially resolved to leave his family and friends in order to resume his studies as a clerk in Paris, he is overwhelmed by the throng of people (including a madman, an imbecile, a quack doctor, and a begging monk), bewitched by fairies, and induced to remain in Arras. At the play's conclusion he with-draws to the inevitable tavern.

Such plays imply their authors' confidence in a local audience. Adam de la Halle, like other Arras poets, enjoyed the support of the 'Confrérie des jongleurs et bourgeois d'Arras', a poetry society of a kind that sprang up in several cities during the thirteenth century. Known as *puys* (perhaps from the podium whence contributions were judged), these societies were funded and attended by local mer-chants eager to retain and reward the services of successful *jongleur*-poets. It is thought that the *Jeu de la feuillée* was first performed at the Confrérie. As well as the patronage of the burghers of Arras, Adam de la Halle enjoyed that of Count Robert of Artois, for whom he wrote another witty play staging the rustic goings-on of a shep-herd girl and her boyfriend as seen through the lens of aristocratic condescension (the *Jeu de Robin et Marion*). Adam also composed a *chanson de geste* and a prolific corpus of lyric poetry since, in addition to being an able versifier, he was an accomplished and innovative musician.

Another major thirteenth-century *jongleur*-poet whose success was grounded in an urban context was Rutebeuf (active in Paris *c*.1250–1280). He likewise wrote in a range of genres (*fabliau*, drama, lyric, saint's life, and social satire exploiting material from the *Roman de Renart*) but he is chiefly remembered for his *dits*: informal self-mocking first-person narrative poems usually on a humdrum topic. Rather like Adam in the *Jeu de la feuillée*, he cuts a deliberately poor figure, always down on his luck. So far as poetic skills are concerned, however, he revels in his clerk's mastery of language, his command of different metres, and his flair for word-play. The following passage, from 'La Griesche d'hiver', a first-person poem representing Rutebeuf as a down-at-heel gambler, displays a Mallarméan fascination with the dice-like roll of words. The repeated word-play on *voie* ('path'), *fet* (Modern French *fait*), and their com-pounds, make it virtually untranslatable. *Voie* further puns with forms of the verbs *avoir* and *savoir*, while *enviail*, a dicing term meaning 'stake', or 'bet', also resonates with *envoier* (Modern French *envoyer*, 'to set on its path, send'). There is a final, disturbing pun on *dé*, 'dice' and 'gods'.

Il ne me remaint rien souz ciel, tout va sa voie.
Le enviail que je savoie
m'ont avoié quanque j'avoie et forvoié
et fors de voie desvoié.
Fols enviaus ai envoié, or m'en souvient.
Or voi je bien, tout va, tout vient,
tout venir, tout aler convient fors que bienfet.
Li dé que li decier ont fet
m'ont de ma robe tout desfet; li dé m'ocient,
li dé m'aguetent et espient,
li dé m'assaillent et desfient.

[Nothing at all is left to me, everything has gone on its way. My knowing bets have brought me everything I had and sent it astray again, far away from the path. I've set up stupid bets, I remember now. Now I can see that everything comes and goes, everything must come and go, except good things. The dice which the makers made have stripped me of my clothes; the dice/gods are killing me, lying in wait for me and spying on me, attacking me and declaring war on me.]

Rutebeuf seems not to have invented the *dit* but his self-presentation as a luckless but matchless poet influenced its development in the following century in the hands of Guillaume de Machaut and others (see below, pp. 75–80).

PROSE: HISTORY, ROMANCE, AND THE GRAIL

Before 1200 there is virtually no vernacular prose. By the middle of the thirteenth century literary prose is well established. By the end of that century it is the standard medium in which factual texts such as histories are written. By the late fourteenth century it is the standard medium for narrative. These are radical changes which, as we try to account for them here, we admit we cannot fully explain.

The oldest works in prose in both French and Occitan are either legal (like the earliest written French, the Strasburg Oaths, and charters) or religious (sermons, biblical translations). Was this association of prose with authority and truthfulness the reason why, at the turn of the twelfth and thirteenth centuries, patrons and audiences grew suspicious of verse texts? Did the success of *jongleuresque* entertainment—the works referred to in the previous section are all in verse—lead to verse being devalued as too frivolous for serious composition? Did the increasing refinement of courtly lyric and romance make verse appear, on the contrary, too artificial and abstruse? Or did the spread of education create more literate expectations, so that audiences expected works to be read rather than recited, and liked them to reflect Medieval Latin narrative where prose is more common than verse?

Prose histories begin to be composed in the early thirteenth century. Their protestations that verse texts are untruthful rapidly become a cliché. Probably the earliest was a translation of the Latin *Chronicle of Pseudo-Turpin*, a text purporting to narrate the history of Charlemagne and his peers, including the events of the *Chanson de Roland*, from the eyewitness testimony of Archbishop Turpin. A French translation was commissioned by the countess of Saint Pol in 1202; other commissions by patrons in Flanders and Hainault for French adaptations of Latin histories followed. These northern lords were anxious about their future, threatened, as they saw it, on two sides. Below them, the merchants in thriving cities such as Arras were fast outshining them in wealth and splendour. Above them, King Philip Augustus was working to centralize power and administer it bureaucratically. His rapacity and modernizing initiatives were depriving the old aristocracy of land and influence. The patrons of these early prose histories traced their descent back to Charlemagne, and regarded the Capetian King Philip as a newcomer. Prose, the medium of charters and of Latin historiography, would avoid the artificiality or frivolity of verse narrative and confirm the legitimacy of their claim to be the 'peers' of the king, just as the Carolingian barons had been.

The supposedly eyewitness authority of the *Pseudo-Turpin* finds a parallel in another genre in which vernacular prose was pioneered: that of the historical memoir. There were twelfth-century verse histories narrated by authors who had personally participated in the events they describe, such as the Third Crusade. But the Fourth Crusade of 1202–4 saw a switch to prose. This shameful fiasco, in which the crusaders were induced to turn aside from the Holy Land and attack instead the Christian city of Constantinople, inspired two contrasting accounts. Robert de Clari—ignorant of higher-level strategy, but all agog at the splendours of Constantinople—gives a worm's eye view. Geoffroi de Villehardouin, by contrast, has a top diplomat's suave authority and a leader's eye for the aesthetic of war—the splendid sight of a fleet, or the noble heroism of a ruler. For both authors the medium of prose seems to convey the purported authenticity and transparency of lived experience. Later in this same tradition belongs the notable *Vie de Saint Louis* by Jean de Joinville (early fourteenth century), which testifies both to its author's admiration for Louis IX, and to pride at his intimacy with the king.

There is another early flowering of prose which historians of literature in the *langue d'oïl* tend to overlook. From very early in the thirteenth century, Catalonia and Italy (the regions abutting Occitania) produced Occitan prose texts teaching people how to understand and compose troubadour songs. Raimon Vidal's *Razos de trobar* is a linguistic manual intended to teach Occitan to Catalans. In northern Italy, Uc de Saint Circ (active 1217–53) inaugurated the genres of *razo* and *vida*. We have already referred to the *vidas*, or biographies, of the troubadours. Generally quite short, they outline the troubadour's social and regional background, principal patrons, and romantic entanglements (these last seemingly on no better authority than a literal reading of the songs themselves). They sometimes also sketch a summary critical judgement ('good tunes but poor words', 'master of the troubadours', 'difficult rhymes', 'worthless'). *Razos* provide the alleged historical context of an individual song. The earliest were composed to help listeners navigate the sea of political allusions in the songs of the troubadour Bertran de Born. Unlike prose histories, these Occitan prose texts do not protest their truthfulness. Offering themselves as a means of access to foreign poetry, they imply that prose is simpler and more straightforward than verse.

It may have been the same impulse to reach a wider public that led to the first examples of *dérimage* (the recasting of a verse narrative in prose) in northern French. But the association of prose with historical, religious, and especially biblical narrative may also have been a factor, since the earliest examples of *dérimage* are Robert de Boron's romances about the Holy Grail. Grail literature flourished in the aftermath of Chrétien de Troyes's *Conte del graal* of the 1180s, an unfinished romance in which the fruitless wanderings of a painfully naïve hero, Perceval, are worked in counterpoint with the equally unsuccessful adventures of the much more knowing Gawain. Because none of Chrétien's characters finds the grail, his audience remains ignorant of what he thought it was. The grail (or, as the text has it, *un graal*, 'a flat dish') makes a single appearance, carried in a mysterious procession together with a lance that bleeds, at the castle of the Fisher King who, we later learn, is sustained by eating the sacrament from it (see Figure 3, p. 60). If the right questions can be asked at the Grail Castle, the king will be healed of his thigh wound, and his lands, which lie waste, restored to fertility. Various poets supplied continuations with the aim of bringing Chrétien's tantalizing narrative to a satisfying conclusion.

Rather than compete in this market, however, Robert de Boron began the story again from scratch. Around 1200 he composed two,

3. Perceval arrives at the Grail Castle and witnesses the Grail procession with the Fisher King. Chrétien de Troyes, *Le Conte del graal,* Bibliothèque Nationale fr. 12577, fo. 18ᵛ.

possibly three verse romances (only one and a fragment of the second survive) that identify the grail as the Holy Grail, the vessel from which Christ drank at the Last Supper, and in which his blood was collected by Joseph of Aramethea. Drawing on material from apocryphal gospels, Robert then created a chain of transmission whereby the Grail passed from the crucifixion to Arthurian Britain. Around 1220 these verse texts were recast as a prose trilogy which concludes with Perceval's quest for the Grail and the fall of Arthur's kingdom (adapted from Geoffrey of Monmouth's *History of the Kings of Britain*). Just as early verse romances are intricately connected with historical themes, so is this pioneering experiment in prose. The *Petit Saint-Graal*, as this cycle based on Robert de Boron is known, deploys the matter of Britain but downplays that of Rome, substituting for the myth of Trojan ancestry a genealogy reaching back to the Holy Land. The various associations of prose—with historical truth, legitimacy, sacred authority, seriousness, transparency, accessibility—coincide in this trilogy. The foundations of future prose romance are laid.

Shortly after *Petit Saint-Graal*, between about 1225 and 1230, there came into being the monumental prose cycle which unites the stories of Arthur, Lancelot, and the Grail, and which is known rather unprepossessingly as the 'Vulgate Cycle'. Parts of the enormous central book, known as the *Lancelot* proper, are based on Chrétien's *Lancelot*. The order of composition of the other books is uncertain and nor is it known to what extent they were conceived as part of a vast cycle. The concluding two, the *Queste del saint graal* and the *Mort Artu*, narrate the zenith and nadir of the Arthurian world: the supreme achievement of the Grail quest and the destruction of the kingdom by guilt and strife. The two prefatory books, the *Estoire* and *Merlin*, on the other hand, were probably added later, the *Merlin* in part borrowed from the prose *Merlin* of Robert de Boron.

Despite the Vulgate Cycle's debts to previous texts, its world has been altogether reconceived. Galahad, Lancelot's son, replaces Perceval as the knight who reaches the Grail. His story is threaded against that of his father (also originally called Galahad) whose illicit love for Guenevere is the source of both his greatness and his downfall. The romance simply juxtaposes the terms of this contradiction, leaving the reader to puzzle over the thunderous silence between them:

Lancelos ainme la reïne Guenievre des le premerain jor que il reçut l'ordre de chavalerie, et pour l'amour de la reïne, quant il fu nouviaus chevaliers, fist il toutes les proesces qu'il fesoit.

[Lancelot has loved Queen Guenevere since the very first day he received the order of knighthood, and when he was newly knighted he performed all his great deeds of prowess for love of the queen.]

'Maleoite soit l'eure que onques ceste amor fu commenciee; car ge ai doutance que il ne nos en soit encore moult de pis.' 'Cestres,' fet Hestors, '. . . vos verroiz encore entre nostre parenté e le roi Artu la greignur guerre que vos onques veïssiez et tout por ceste chose.'

['A curse on the hour that love was ever begun; for I am afraid it might yet be much the worse for us.' 'Indeed,' said Hector, '. . . you will yet see between our kin and King Arthur the greatest war that ever was, and all because of this.']

Lancelot is not so much guilty or innocent as magnificent in his noble, tragic love; while the Arthurian world, corroded by animosity and corrupted by incest, hastens anyway to its doom.

The success of the Vulgate Cycle led to other important examples of *mise en prose*, notably those of the *Tristan* and the *Troie*. These fascinating, if seemingly endless, prose narratives rivalled and gradually eclipsed verse romance within less than a century of its rise. Wilder and more exuberant than their verse forebears, they madly dilate themselves by cannibalizing other texts. Just as the Vulgate Cycle absorbs its predecessors, so the *Prose Tristan* conflates the Lancelot and Grail elements of the Vulgate Cycle with the Tristan story. Other genres were also absorbed into prose: saints' lives (which until the thirteenth century had been written in a variety of verse metres) and eventually, with Jean d'Outremeuse's *Myreur des Histors* (early four-teenth century), *chansons de geste*.

A major effect of the success of prose was that it retrospectively designated verse narrative as somehow defective. The word *vers* ('verse, verses'), which the troubadours often punningly align with *vers* (Occitan for 'true, true things'), becomes associated with twisting (*vers* from *vertir*, 'to turn'): verse is indirect and contorted, whereas prose (fancifully derived from *prorsum*, 'in a straight line') is straight-forward and truthful. However prose, having set itself up to speak the whole truth and convey all meaning to everyone, finds that ultimate authenticity keeps eluding it. Instead of proceeding 'in a straight line', prose romance develops the intricate structure known as 'interlace' whereby various story-lines twist in and out of view. Endlessly seek-ing to supplement the shortfall in truthfulness of the texts with which they compete, prose narratives find that they endlessly produce more of themselves (thereby reflecting the thirteenth-century tendency towards compilation, see next section). By the same token they draw attention to the great cultural achievement of the twelfth century: the creation of fictions. But try as they might to rid themselves of the fictionality of such fictions by 'de-rhyming' them, prose romances merely develop larger-scale and more ramifying fictions in their place. Translated into all the neighbouring vernaculars, these fictions play a leading role in subsequent European literatures.

TREATISES, ENCYCLOPEDIAS, AND COMPILATION IN THE THIRTEENTH CENTURY

We have mentioned the existence of poems instructing *jongleurs*. Similar verse *ensenhamens* (Occitan for 'teaching'), composed between the late twelfth and early fourteenth centuries, impart courtly instruc-tion to other social groups such as young noblewomen or knights, and to courtly society in general. In the *langue d'oïl*, poems entitled *enseignement* or *chastoiement* ('admonishment') are also vehicles of social and moral engineering. Such works amplify the didacticism latent in much courtly literature; conversely, however, *chastoiements* may be inserted into narratives, with the not infrequent result that their directives are undermined by the plot. The *œuvre* of the early thirteenth-century Robert de Blois combines courtly romance and lyric with *enseignements* on a number of courtly and religious topics. It tends to be transmitted as a unity, and in one manuscript all of his didactic works are transcribed in the middle of his Arthurian romance, *Beaudous*, in such a way as both to emphasize his central project of edification, and to betray the complexity of such an undertaking.

Courtly instruction tends to cling to verse; in Occitan, even vernacular encyclopedias—notably Matfre Ermengart's late thirteenth-century *Breviari d'Amor*—are in octosyllables. Nevertheless didactic or informative literature turns increasingly to prose. The early thirteenth-century Occitan prose treatises on language and versification mentioned in the previous section lead on to the massive *Leys d'amors* ('Laws of love') in the fourteenth. This was compiled in a succession of redactions (the last in 1356) for the Toulouse Consistori del Gay Saber, a poetry society founded to foster what remained of troubadour poetry after the success of the Albigensian crusade against the south of France and its subordination to northern rule. The terminology used by the *Leys* to describe the genres and verse-forms of troubadour poetry is still in standard use among modern scholars.

There are no thirteenth-century French poetry manuals, but Brunetto Latini continued a tradition of French and Latin encyclopedic writing with his *Livre dou tresor* of *c*.1270. This vast copendium is a fascinating source for anyone who wants to read a potted account of contemporary views on the elements, the humours, the properties of different animals, the structure of universal history or, indeed, any subject whatsoever (including rhetoric), since it exhibits to a high degree the impulse towards exhaustiveness so characteristic of thirteenth-century prose. Brunetto's choice of French over his native Italian indicates the cultural pre-eminence of French as a language of learning in this period. Indeed, French produces an abundance of prose texts by which we can be edified or informed. Some are translations from Latin, but increasingly French is the original language, as for instance in Philippe de Remi, lord of Beaumanoir's legal compendium, *Les Coutumes du Beauvaisis*. (This Philippe de Remi is probably the father of the author of *La Manneƙine* mentioned on p. 47.)

To the historian of literature, the most interesting manifestation of thirteenth-century interest in encyclopedias and compendia is the way literary texts themselves are transmitted. While there are very few pre-1200 vernacular manuscripts, those of the thirteenth and fourteenth centuries are almost without exception compilations. Their principles of organization vary, but one which emphatically does not operate is that of the integrity of the single work. Just as prose seeks to make good the deficiencies of verse narrative, so manuscripts supplement the individual text by including others with it. Indeed, the boundaries of particular works are often erased in this process. For example, there are compilations of *chansons de geste* from a particular cycle which run together what scholars identify as originally distinct poems. Such manuscripts are called 'cyclic manuscripts'. Scribes sometimes modify beginnings and ends to facilitate the seamless progression of the cycle. Arthurian romances may be treated similarly, as in one manuscript where Chrétien's romances are inserted into the middle of Wace's *Roman de Brut*, and their prologues and epilogues excised, dissolving their fictions into a series of episodes within the history of Britain. Our knowledge of the *Roman de Renart* is likewise owed to cyclic manuscripts; the traditional numbering of the branches reflects their order in a particular manuscript group. When the compilers of the *Petit Saint-Graal* or the architects of the Vulgate Cycle set out to compose a cycle of works, they were reproducing as authors the practices of the compilers of cyclical manuscripts.

The identity of a particular author is only very rarely the organizing principle of a compilation. Of the thirty-one manuscripts containing romances by Chrétien de Troyes, none includes his lyrics or is devoted exclusively to him, while his works form an uninterrupted sequence in two at most. Organization of manuscripts by genre is quite common, especially for lyric poetry which is transmitted in anthologies known as *chansonniers*. The troubadour *chansonniers* date from the mid-thirteenth century onwards. Internally, they are usually arranged by author although subdivision by genre is also found. Each author section may be prefaced by a portrait and the author's *vida*, and individual songs introduced by an explanatory *razo*. *Trouvère* manuscripts are similar except that they lack the prose introductions, and are more likely to contain musical notation. Whereas troubadour *chansonniers* usually order the poets according to whose poetry is most highly esteemed (often starting with Giraut de Bornelh), *trouvère* ones order them by rank, beginning with the thirteenth-century Thibaut de Champagne because he was king of Navarre. There are also manuscripts exclusively given over to romance, but it is more common for narrative works to be gathered in large, wide-ranging compilations containing several different genres.

Medieval books are therefore quite unlike modern ones, which are habitually defined by the identity of the author and the boundaries of the individual work. The literary interpretation of compilation is a growing area of medieval studies. The challenge to ideas of authorship and authority associated with recent post-structuralism has an interesting precursor in the material practices of the thirteenth century and beyond.

THE *ROMAN DE LA ROSE* AND THE ALLEGORICAL TRADITION

Jean de Meun, famous above all for his continuation of Guillaume de Lorris's dream-vision poem the *Roman de la rose* (*c*.1276), is the epitome of a late thirteenth-century author. A clerk living in Paris, his wide learning is reflected in his translations into French prose of the classical military theorist Vegetius's *Art of War*, the fifth-century philosopher Boethius's *Consolation of Philosophy*, and the correspondence between the twelfth-century philosopher Abelard and his lover Héloise. His nearly 18,000-line addition to Guillaume's *Rose* displays an encyclopedic knowledge of mythology, history, natural science, philosophy, and theology, as well as of contemporary university politics. Its sprawling length bespeaks an urge—exhaustive and sometimes exhausting—to anthologize, compile, and endlessly supplement what went before.

What went before is itself a landmark text. The first part of the *Rose* (composed between 1225 and 1240) is a mysterious first-person dream narrative, whose 'characters' are a large cast of personified abstractions arranged round three successive settings. First the dreamer is admitted by the elegant young woman Oiseuse ('Leisure') to the garden of Deduit ('Pleasure') and finds, dancing there, a whole series of courtly qualities: Jeunesse, Courtoisie, Largesse, Beauté, and so on. Then he wanders off to the spring (or fountain) of Amor, where he sees a rose garden reflected in the water, lights on a single choice bud, and is struck by Amor's darts (Beau Samblant, etc.), i.e. he begins to 'fall in love'. Amor delivers a *chastoiement* on the nature of love, enjoins him to obey his Ten Commandments, and recommends to him the support of Ami and others. Thirdly, the dreamer tries to enter the rose garden but finds his access to the rose blocked by Jalousie (which can mean both 'zealousness' or 'jealousy' in Old French: is it his own excessive enthusiasm, or the begrudging attitude of others, that causes the lover's frustration?). Jalousie has built a castle around the rose and installed further personifications—Honte ('Disgrace'), Malebouche ('Bad-mouth') and so on—to guard it. The lover's attempts to get closer mainly take the form of interplay between Bel Acuel ('Fair Welcome') and Dangier ('Rebuff'), who in turn meet with support or opposition from other personifications. Raison harangues the lover for preferring Amor to her; he consults briefly with Ami. Although the lover persists faithfully in his suit, Bel Acuel is locked up and the text breaks off with the lover lamenting his unfulfilled desire:

Ha! Bel Acuel, biaus dous amis,
se vous estes en prison mis,
gardés moi au mains vostre cuer
e ne soffrés a nes un fuer
que Jalousie la sauvage
mete vostre cuer en servage
aussi cum el a fait le cors.
   .   .   .   .
Se li cors en prison remaint,
gardés au mains que li cuers m'aint.

[Oh Bel Acuel, my fair friend, even though you are in prison, keep your heart for me and never for a moment allow wild Jalousie to enslave your heart as she has your body. . . . If your body remains confined, make sure at least that your heart loves me.]

   Guillaume's 4,000-line narrative, enigmatic in both its content and its lack of an ending, has been divergently interpreted. It displays consummate brinkmanship over sensitive issues on what we have been calling the 'courtly agenda', like the relationship between spiritual and physical love, or the rival claims of reason and passion. At times suffused with dreamlike unreality, it offers a wonderfully lyrical exploration of a first initiation to love. At the same time its self-conscious deployment of the vocabulary and motifs of the troubadour love lyric suggests a desire to scrutinize and systematize the language in which love is formulated. The dream-vision framework presents Amor as a real, supernatural entity governing all our lives. And yet the text also conveys a sense of intense interiority, and is dedicated to an individual 'who deserves to be called Rose', so perhaps its concern with names (such as those of the personifications) reflects the poet's effort to abstract a generalizing vocabulary from individual, concrete events. Certainly the text drips with sensuality just as powerfully as it evokes spiritual analogies for the love experience. That it should break off with a plangent address by one young man to another (see the quotation above) provides yet a further impetus to reflect on the complexity and equivocations of the conventions and rhetoric of love.

   The use of personified abstractions is often equated with 'allegory', but this is misleading. For a text to be allegorical, it must invite its readers to interpret it as meaning something other than what it first appears to mean. While personification may point to the possibility of an allegorical reading, it does not of itself institute one. If Guillaume's *Rose* is 'allegorical', this is due less to the personifications themselves than to the thoughts we have seen them provoke on the nature of love, and on wider issues such as the relation of experience to language. In its day, Guillaume's poem was by far the most subtle and elaborate French example of a literary tradition, previously almost exclusively in Latin, in which a dreamer receives visions that reveal to him the nature of the abstract essences by which his life is determined. Its two most important antecedents are Boethius's *Consolation of Philosophy* and the twelfth-century Alan of Lille's *Complaint of Nature* in which, as their titles imply, the revelations concern the power of, respectively, Philosophy and Nature. Putting Amor instead in the starring role makes it ambiguous whether what is being upheld is a lofty ideal or a physical experience, an enquiry into the nature of man or an exposure of his limitations. The use of personified abstractions, meanwhile, calls into question whether such abstractions are real entities, or else intellectual responses of our own to individual instances of the lovable, beautiful, or pleasurable—especially when physical enjoyment may be the key to understanding them. This equivocation reflects and mocks the debate in the medieval philosophy of language between realists (who held that universal abstractions *were* real entities) and nominalists (who thought they were names for our reactions to individuals).

Guillaume's exquisite balance between the courtly exaltation and philosophical dissection of love seems to have fascinated Jean de Meun. The narrative of his continuation essentially repeats the main lines of Guillaume's. Its major episodes are the lover's meetings with Raison (who tries to put him off love), one with Ami (full of hot tips for seduction), the lover's reassertion of his obedience to Amor (an episode expanded by the long monologue of Fausemblant, a dissembling friar), and his further attempts to contact Bel Acuel. These last foreground a character mentioned but not developed by Guillaume: the Vielle, an old tart turned chaperone, who delivers a long *chastoiement* to Bel Acuel on the art of exploiting men. Following this episode, Jean's narrative innovates. Nature makes a long speech and her priest Genius delivers a 'sermon'. Then, in another rerun of Guillaume, Venus arrives with her torch. This time her intervention is definitive and the lover gets the rose.

Jean de Meun seems to have been attracted to Guillaume's unfinished text because it both runs parallel to the dream poems of Boethius and Alan of Lille, and undermines them. Jean's own text is to a very considerable extent made up of tongue-in-cheek adaptations of these Latin philosophical works. First, Boethius supplies the greater part of Raison's long opening address to the lover; but the lover, bored, doesn't listen except for one interesting moment when Raison says *couille* ('bollocks'). (This is *not* in Boethius and nor is

Raison's lengthy explanation that words like *couille* and *relique* ('relics') are determined only by convention and are thus in principle interchangeable.) Alan of Lille is the source of the new characters of Nature and Genius. Nature's role is pivotal since her job is to ensure that all species reproduce themselves; man's failure adequately to do so was the core of Alan's diatribe against homosexuality. Nature accordingly deplores Jalousie's hostility and summons reinforcements. She also, meanwhile, delivers a long Boethian tirade on the structure of the cosmos, free will, and the Trinity: this text is full of surprises. Nature's speech is followed by that of Genius, a figure also taken from Alan of Lille for whom he represents the universal spirit of generation, but who in Jean de Meun's hands is a parodic bishop, a penis in a mitre (mitre in turn being a slang term for 'glans'), preaching to Amor's followers that having sex will gain them access to heaven. Jean's recasting of both Boethius and Alan is supremely disrespectful since he appears to argue, a good deal more explicitly (not to say graphically) than Guillaume, that our access to knowledge is ultimately through not supra-sensory realities but individual bodily experience.

The text ends with a real phantasmagoria in which Raison's observations on bollocks and relics, and Genius's claims for the religious rewards of sex, are combined. The lover, now in the guise of a pilgrim equipped with a phallic staff, approaches an arrow-slit in Jalousie's burning castle beyond which stands a beautiful statue, like a saint in a reliquary; he kneels down to worship it and thrusts his staff into the arrow-slit (see Figure 4); the next minute, he is wrestling with the rose bush and spilling the bud's seed.

> Ainsint oi la rose vermeille.
> Atant fu jorz, et je m'esveille

[Thus I had the scarlet rose. Then it was day and I woke up]

the text laconically concludes.

On the way to this foregone, but seemingly indefinitely deferred conclusion, Jean packs in a great deal of humour, satire, and instruction. But the whole project of education through compilation, so dear to thirteenth-century writers, is imperilled by his text which leaves us uncertain whether the lover, or we ourselves, have learned anything from it, and if so, what. The authors of the *dits amoureux* of the next century will have to grapple with these uncertainties. Before we turn to them, however, we need to take in significant changes in lyric poetry in the later Middle Ages.

4. The final moments of the lover's 'pilgrimage'. Jean de Meun, *Roman de la rose*, Biblioteca de la Universidad, Valencia, MS 387 (formerly 1327), fo. 147ᵛ.

FROM THE *GRAND CHANT COURTOIS* TO THE *FORMES FIXES*: THE FRENCH LYRIC AT ITS HEIGHT

Although the spread of prose sounded the knell of medieval verse narrative, it did nothing to diminish the prestige of lyric poetry. On the contrary, lyric composition became the expression par excellence of literary artistry and personal refinement. There is scarcely a significant author of the fourteenth or fifteenth centuries who did not excel in this genre: a situation without parallel in the literature of the *langue d'oïl* either before or since. Most practitioners of the lyric in this period were engaged by powerful rulers as diplomats or administrators. And almost all of them were also engaged to write history, usually in prose. This exceptional relationship between lyric and history is one of the most significant features of late medieval literature. We shall see, in the next two sections, how historical frames are placed around lyric poetry in the *dit amoureux*; and how history-writing, like lyric poetry, lends itself to moral reflection. But first we review the major transformations in form and content that accompany this canonization of the lyric.

The *trouvères* who adapted troubadour songs for northern courts from the later twelfth century onwards had continued the Occitan lyric forms, chief among which was the *canso* (Occitan for 'song'), or *grand chant courtois*. This consists in a variable number of stanzas, sharing the same metre (so that the same musical setting can be repeated for each stanza) and linked by a rhyme scheme often of breath-taking intricacy. The same metrical form is seldom repeated from one song to another except where a poet is deliberately evoking an earlier composition. Exact formal imitation (*contrafactum*) is a powerful vehicle of dialogue or polemic, as when Marcabru mimics Guilhem IX, or when late twelfth-century love songs by Gace Brulé are rewritten as songs to the Virgin by Gautier de Coinci early in the thirteenth.

By the end of the thirteenth century, however, the value attached to formal variety wanes and the *grand chant courtois* cedes to a number of so-called *formes fixes* ('fixed forms') which closely prescribe a poem's length and rhyme scheme. Most of these seem to hark back to dance songs, thereby signalling their collective accessibility in contrast to the solo virtuosity of the *canso*. The *ballade*, *rondeau*, and *virelai* (and later the *chant royal*) are also characterized by refrains, which could be sung collectively, and which lead a semi-independent existence as a minor genre in their own right, migrating from song to song.

The simplest and most repetitive of the *formes fixes* is the *rondeau*, possibly so-called from its association with a round dance. The amount of repeated material in a *rondeau* varies, but this example by the great fourteenth-century poet Guillaume de Machaut is typical of his age and conjures remarkable emotional complexity from apparent verbal simplicity. (The capital letters designate refrain lines, and the small letters the lines that rhyme with them.)

1	Se par amours n'amiez autrui ne moy,	A
2	ma grief doulour en seroit assez mendre	B
3	car m'esperance aroye en bonne foy,	a
4	se par amours n'amiez autrui ne moy.	A
5	Mais quant amer autre, et moy laissier voy,	a
6	c'est pis que mort. Pour ce vous fais entendre	b
7	se par amours n'amiez autrui ne moy,	A
8	ma grief doulour en seroit assez mendre.	B

[If you loved no one else, nor me, my dreadful hurt would be greatly lessened, for I could have hope in good faith if you loved no one else, nor me. But when I see you love someone else, and turn away from me, it's worse than death. And so this is why I want you to understand that if you loved no one else, nor me, my dreadful hurt would be greatly lessened.]

Vast melancholy overflows this seemingly slight work, as a result of its reiterated return to suppositions known to be untrue. The bleak reality 'seen' (*voy*) in line 5 is that the singer's lady loves someone other than the poet, and that his pain is deathlike (line 6). But this admission is surrounded, and as though muffled, by the refrain lines which reverse the terms of lines 5–6, replacing them (albeit hopelessly) with a hypothetical situation in which the poet's lady might not love someone else, and his hurt might be less than it is. The poet wishes his audience to *entendre* this (line 6) as though by repeatedly making us 'hear' he could erase what he himself 'sees'; yet, since the imagined state of affairs is avowedly unrealizable, the refrain reinforces the desperation of his love as much as it seeks to disguise it.

The *ballade*, the most successful of the *formes fixes*, likewise turns around repeated material. Initially a three-stanza song with a one-line refrain concluding each stanza, this form was extended to include an additional half-stanza often containing an address (*envoi*) to the *ballade*'s recipient. The prolific fourteenth-century poet Eustache Deschamps, author of no fewer than 1,175 *ballades*, paid tribute to Machaut at his death in a *double ballade* of six stanzas exhorting all to lament, in the words of its refrain, 'La mort Machaut, le noble rhetorique' ('The death of Machaut, that noble poet'). At the turn of the fourteenth and fifteenth centuries, Christine de Pizan composed *ballades* which reverse the traditional stance of a male lover longing for an unattainable lady by instead mourning for her dead husband, and by casting doubt on the value, for women, of the so-called love addressed to them by men. By far the most memorable lyricist to compose *ballades* was Charles d'Orléans. A casualty of the Hundred Years War, Charles was taken prisoner by the English at Agincourt in 1415 and detained in England until eventually being ransomed in 1441. His output during this period is overwhelmingly of *ballades* (after his return to Blois he instead preferred the denser form of the *rondeau*). These create a wistful, melancholic universe, where the self, distantly haunted by death and suffering, wisps away into semi-allegorical transfigurations, or disperses itself in strange settings and objects, as if permanently alienated from its own sensibility.

Sundered from the heart and its obsessive passion, the 'I' in this *ballade* is agitated and rootless:

> Quant je suis couchié en mon lit
> je ne puis en paix reposer;

> car toute nuit mon cuer lit
> ou Rommant de Plaisant Penser,
> et me prie de l'escouter;
> si ne l'ose desobeïr
> pour doubte de le courroucer:
> ainsi je laisse le dormir.

[When I have gone to bed I cannot rest peacefully because all night long my heart keeps reading aloud from the Romance of Pleasant Thoughts, and begging me to listen to him; and I dare not disobey for fear of angering him, and so I leave off sleeping.]

The second stanza tells how the heart 'takes sovereign pleasure' in the romance's contents, made up of the lady's deeds, which even 'I' cannot weary of, 'and so I leave off sleeping'. Even when the eyes cannot bear to read any longer, in stanza three, still the heart remains gripped by thoughts of love. No longer enraptured by its Romance, it is lonely and fretful, the 'I' anxious and appeasing: and so sleep seems more distant than ever. Throughout the *ballade*, then, the 'I' is a point of consciousness that cannot submerge itself in slumber but instead records, in the form of the *ballade* itself, its anxious alternation between colluding in the heart's enjoyment and fearing its displeasure. In the *envoi*, 'I' finally confesses its inability to control the heart's emotions: the heart obeys not 'I' but Love, and this unstinting service is what imposes ceaseless vigil on them both:

> Amour je ne puis gouverner
> mon cueur; car tant vous veult servir
> qu'il ne scet jour ne nuit cesser,
> ainsi je laisse le dormir.

[Love, I cannot control my heart; for it desires to serve you so much that it cannot leave off night or day, and so I leave off sleeping.]

Charles d'Orléans's *ballades* may perhaps encode, in the acceptable discourse of love's sorrows, his unhappiness as a prisoner and exile.

Other *formes fixes* include the *virelai*, usually used for love songs, and the *chant royal*, increasingly associated with songs to the Virgin. But the most demanding and consequently most prestigious of these forms is the *lai*. Not to be confused with early medieval narrative *lais* such as those ascribed to Marie de France, the lyric *lai* is a stellar feat of versifying. Its twelve stanzas must each have a different metrical form and different rhymes from all of the others, except that the final one repeats the form and rhymes of the first. Each stanza, furthermore, is in two halves, the second formally mirroring the first; often each half can be divided in half again; lines vary in length, with a preference for including some as short as three or four syllables, so that a very high proportion of syllables is affected by rhyme. The form thus combines disarray with resolution, jarring dissonance with obsessive harmony. Whereas the shorter *formes fixes* are more apt to freeze and eternalize the poignant moment, *lais* lend themselves to extended meditation on the complexities of love or religion. In his *Prison amoureuse*, Froissart wryly reveals the poetic stakes of these various *formes fixes*. *Ballades* may be turned out in batches of three, and *virelais* can be tossed off by amateurs, but a *lai* is a six-month assignment even for so skilled a poet as Froissart. With nine months before him, Froissart composes the first three stanzas before being sidetracked by other commissions. Eventually, to his relief, he manages to complete the remaining nine. Staggered between two separate parts of the *Prison*, the resulting *lai* is over 200 lines long and reflects elaborately on its central themes of love and friendship. Miniatures of poets wrestling with the complexities of the *lai* are found in various manuscripts; an example can be seen in Figure 5 (see p. 74).

Other longer lyric forms are similarly composed to a mathematical formula of some kind. Both Machaut and Froissart wrote *complaintes* ('laments') containing 100 different rhymes. *Ballades* were likewise assembled in numerically determined collections, such as Christine de Pizan's *Cent Ballades d'amant et de dame*, in which male and female voices exchange *ballades* that pinpoint moments in their evolving relationship and expose the woman's vulnerability to the social consequences of illicit passion. This systematic and quasi-mathematical approach to poetry assumes that texts will be transmitted in written form. So does the flourishing of other poetic devices, such as the use of anagrams and acrostics (where the initial letters of each line spell out a message, such as the name of the poet or the dedicatee), or what are called 'rebus' poems where, instead of the rhyme words being copied on the page, they are represented—often punningly—by a picture.

The codification of literary composition in the *formes fixes* also goes hand in hand with the first poetic treatises in French (they had existed in Occitan since the early thirteenth century). In the Prologue composed shortly before his death in 1377 to preface manuscript compendia of his works, Machaut represents himself as created by Nature in order to explicate the value of love. Nature assigns three of her 'children' to assist him: Sens (meaning), Retorique, and Musique. Rhetoric and Music both serve to promote love; but Music, being more remote from Meaning, evades the inevitable slide into melancholy of a lover's language. Indeed, like Orpheus whose playing almost enabled him to

5. A lover in the throes of composing a *lai*. Below the image is the musical notation of the *lai* which, like the other *forme fixe* lyrics in the *Remede*, is set to music. Guillaume de Machaut, *Remede de Fortune*, Bibliothèque Nationale fr. 1586, fo. 26.

bring back to life his wife Eurydice, Music can resist grief and death. It seems, then, that for Machaut, the sublime, timeless quality of lyricism lies in its musical setting. The relation of poetry to music is treated quite differently by Eustache Deschamps in his *Art de dictier* ('Art of composing poetry') of 1392. Poetry is no longer seen as a branch of rhetoric, but instead placed among the sciences: geometry, mathematics, astronomy and music. Specifically, says Deschamps, poetry is 'natural' as opposed to 'artificial' music: not language accorded to music, but an *alternative* form of music. In this, the first French treatise on versification, Deschamps highlights the mathematical qualities of the *formes fixes*, exemplifying them from among his own compositions. The divorce between poetry and music was, in reality, far from complete; many lyrics were composed to be sung well into the early modern period. Nevertheless, all the major lyricists of the fourteenth and fifteenth centuries have left songs for which we have neither music nor evidence that a musical setting was ever intended.

Unlike the troubadours, whose compositions energetically debate moral, political, and satirical as well as amorous themes, the *trouvères* overwhelmingly rehearse the commonplaces of *fin' amor*. The relatively conventional content of the *grand chant courtois* is as though offset by its formal variety. The *formes fixes*, by contrast, while determining the formal outline of compositions, seem to have left poets more freedom as to their content. Deschamps's *œuvre* contains *ballades* on surprising topics: medicine, diet, baldness, old age, misogyny.

It became common to compose in a borrowed voice. Assuming that of an old woman, or a young girl, constitutes a kind of poetic drag act; in more macabre vein, one can speak hanging from the gallows or from beyond the grave. Examples of such fantastic ventriloquism are common in Villon who, in his 'Testament', provides a framework for the voices of, among others, his mother, an aged prostitute, a drunkard, and a pimp.

Because many lyric poets were also political advisers and historians, their poetry was often political, reflecting on the situation of their patron. References to specific events tend to be heavily cloaked in allegorical and other rhetorical embellishments, thus imputing to them a level of generality. The poet assumes the public voice of one who articulates and preserves moral values; the formal control exhibited by his compositions parallels the sense of order and hierarchy which their content promotes. Attached to royal or ducal courts, such poets extolled their activities in ever more elaborate verses as the fifteenth century wore on. Works of this kind are not easy to like nowadays. They form part of the broad current of didacticism that affects much later medieval literature. Such admiration as they excite in modern critics tends to be grounded in their formal inventiveness and virtuosity. It is worth bearing in mind, however, that the official moralizing of this poetry often goes hand in hand with obscenity and quite sadistic misogyny. The voice of public morality, that is, is also one which indulges in public fantasies of exposure and punishment. Such prurience is implicit in much didactic writing and explicit in the fracas surrounding Alain Chartier's 'La Belle Dame sans mercy', which we discuss shortly. Chartier was the most important 'official' poet of this kind in the first half of the fifteenth century; he worked first for Yolande of Anjou, and then for Charles of France, later Charles VII. In the second half of the century there develops a poetic school known as 'les grands rhétoriqueurs' of poets and historians, of whom the most important are Jean Molinet and Jean Lemaire de Belges (see Part II, pp. 111–16).

THE *DIT AMOUREUX*: BETWEEN LYRIC AND HISTORY

Already in the fourteenth century, in the newly constituted genre of the *dit amoureux*, history was being invoked as a framework that both circumscribes, and is dissolved by, the erotic and moral reflections of the lyric. These complex compositions frequently celebrate the relationship between the real-world patron and his poet, and hence between aristocracy and clergy, experience and language, politics and writing. The way they are compiled, with their multiple framing devices and insertions, blurs the boundaries between these categories, allowing the texts to tug now one way, now another.

Initially the *dit*, a reflective, sometimes moralizing, sometimes comic first-person verse genre, had been pioneered in the thirteenth century by authors such as Rutebeuf. Although its content often had a narrative cast, the centring of the *dit* on the reactions of a first-person speaker made it also an offshoot of lyric; the terms 'lyrical narrative', or even 'lyrico-narrative', are used to describe its hybrid character. In the fourteenth century, when the unparalleled prestige of lyric and history inflect the *dit* towards courtly love and the courtly patron, its hybrid nature becomes more pronounced.

Dits amoureux are often studded, jewel-like, with shorter lyrics in the *formes fixes* which pick out their structure and serve as prisms for refracting or focusing emotion. In this respect, they hark back to thirteenth-century romances with inset lyrics such as the *Romans dou castelain de Couci*. They may also incorporate exchanges of letters, resulting in an alternation of verse and prose that is reminiscent of Boethius's *Consolation of Philosophy*. Indeed, Boethian consolation, or *confort*, is often called upon to assuage the melancholy afflicting the *dits'* protagonists, and to help them withstand the blows of Fortune. Guillaume de Machaut's *Remede de Fortune* adapts this Boethian theme, providing examples of each of the *formes fixes* to create a literary showpiece that will, at the same time, serve as a bulwark against life's vicissitudes (see Figure 5). But the *dits amoureux* owe an especial debt to the *Roman de la rose*. They incorporate the paraphernalia of allegory: personifications, dreams, the settings of garden and fountain. They also renarrate Ovidian myths such as also feature prominently in the *Rose*. These *dits amoureux* are not merely hybrid works, then: they are anthologies or compilations. Although they speak and sing in the first person, they are also *books*: performing books, and books that record and comment on their own performance. Throughout the *dits amoureux* their poet-narrators reflect on their compositions and the reception they elicit—as Froissart comments, in *La Prison Amoureuse*, on the difficulty of writing a *lai*. In addition to being author and commentator, the first-person narrator is often also a secretary and administrator who assembles and files the various letters and *formes fixes* contributed, according to the fiction, by the *dit*'s protagonists before releasing them for publication. This fictional role accords, indeed, with the reality of their historical authors: Machaut, Froissart, and Christine de Pizan all supervised the preparation of manuscripts of their own collected works, sometimes in sumptuously illustrated presentation copies intended for their real-world patrons (cf. Figure 1).

The longest and most complex of the *dits amoureux*, and one which illustrates the way the genre performs its own genesis as a book, is Guillaume de Machaut's *Voir dit*, composed 1364–5. It is orchestrated around the relationship between an elderly poet and a young girl, in which the poet successfully imposes his authority as a writer from whom the girl is trying to learn, and yet pathetically fails to win her love. The title means 'True telling', but the vast array of letters and poems contained in the *dit* defies arrangement into a coherent narrative, so that whatever the 'truth' of the purported relationship may be, its 'telling' spirals uncontrollably into competing fictions. In this case, then, the anthologizing tendency of the genre extends to its plot, since this can be told in a collection of different ways. The 'truth' of the text is more about the *dit* as a process of 'telling' than about what is 'told', more about art than love, writing than life.

Especially intriguing are those *dits amoureux* in which the first person of the poet is distinct from the lover, since in these cases the play between love and art, and between history and writing, is enacted within the fiction. One person feels love but, enigmatically, his feelings find their voice in another; the lover has a magnate's political commitments yet these can only be comprehended and moralized by his clerk. This situation gets more paradoxical the more figures are introduced: ladies and their attendants, personified abstractions, mythological figures, the shades of earlier poets whose influence shapes the *dit* . . . Unsurprisingly, concepts of identity and experience are much diffused as they are captured by this array of figures; and they are as much refracted as reflected in the *dits'* anthology-like structure. The presence in the text of recognizable historical personages situates all this disparity within a determinate historical frame, yet simultaneously absorbs that frame into the lyric and reflective world of the poet.

In the opening scene of Guillaume de Machaut's *La Fontaine amoureuse* (1360), the narrator, a comic, self-deprecating figure, is kept awake by a knight in the next-door bedroom bewailing his unreciprocated love; the poet spends the night transcribing this lament which, in his masterful hands, becomes an elaborate lyric effusion 1,000 lines long, containing 100 different rhymes, and elaborating the myth of Ceyx and Alcyone (Figure 6). Although in some sense the grieving knight is the 'author' of this lament, he also is unaware of its existence until he commissions the narrator, at the fountain, to compose 'some *lai* or *complainte*' for him, and finds the poet all ready with

6. A love-lorn nobleman and a poet-scribe collaborate to produce a *dit amoureux*. Guillaume de Machaut, *La Fontaine
amoureuse*, Bibliothèque Nationale fr. 1584, fo. 155ᵛ.

a presentation copy of it! Lover and poet then fall asleep by a fountain
richly sculpted with the history of how the Trojan prince Paris won
Helen. Venus appears to the two men in a dream and retells the story
at greater length.

These reminders of the fall of Troy invoke the sombre menace
which love poses to society, while at the same time celebrating the
value of art. Representations of the past offer the means to master and
interpret the tragedy of historical experience. When the men awake
the narrator discourses learnedly on the phenomenon of the shared
dream, but in the final lines, as the lover puts to sea, he wonders
whether he did not dream the whole experience alone:

> Armez s'en va de toutes armes
> contre desir, souspirs, et larmes.
> Ensi parti; je pris congié.
> Dites moy, fu ce bien songié?

[He leaves, fully armed against desire, sighs and tears. Thus he departed; I
took my leave. Tell me, was that well dreamt?]

The metaphorical 'armour' provided by the poet against love's sorrows reminds us that the knight's real task is war. Venus is at best a

distraction, at worst a disaster, as the Trojan myth made plain. The aristocrat should not let love stand in the way of military accomplishment, nor participate in its dreams. The text, ironically representing its author as a dreaming clerk, may thus be an oblique warning to its real-world patron Jean, duke of Berry, portrayed in the text as suffering military setbacks. The fabulous, mysterious world of art is the poet's glory and the aristocrat's *confort*, but they should join in it only to sublimate love, not to pursue it.

Froissart's *La Prison amoureuse* (1372–3) further elaborates the interplay of lord and poet, disconcertingly placing historical reality and literary artifice if anything closer together than Machaut had done. This intricate and self-reflexive *dit* was composed for Wenceslas, duke of Brabant, during his imprisonment after a military defeat. Its title comes from the 'amorous prison' in which the unsuccessful lover-protagonist dreams that he is confined after having been defeated in a battle waged between personified virtues. The dream narrative, then, is both parallel and counterpoint to Wenceslas's real-world reversal. But the title also, of course, alludes to *La Fontaine amoureuse*, thereby acknowledging Froissart's relationship with Machaut. Wenceslas and Froissart signal their intimacy, and their debt to the *Rose*, by calling one another Rose and Flos ('flower') respectively; since the rose is a sub-species of flower, the names also imply that the clerk belongs on a higher plane of abstraction than the aristocrat. Froissart-Flos advises Rose on his courtship and, at his commission, composes an Ovidian myth. Unlike those narrated by Machaut, however, Froissart's mythographic essay is entirely his own invention. The retreat into fictionality of the purportedly classical example is another means of implying that 'real' history takes second place to art; unless, that is, we assume Froissart to be ironically drawing attention to his own limitations. The pseudo-Ovidian tale is then subjected to elaborate scrutiny, and to comparison with a dream dreamt by Rose; letters and *formes fixes* wing their way back and forth between the various characters. An emotional bond connects the two men more than either of them to their ladies and heterosexual love is not so much sublimated as dispelled through this network of interlinked texts. Indeed, the plot seems designed for nothing so much as to accumulate the vast portfolio of documents which finally, grumbling, Flos assembles to form the *dit* itself. A presentation copy of it is sent, in the concluding lines, to Rose.

Where Froissart allies the figures of poet and patron in a tangle of text, whimsy, and inter-male intimacy, Christine de Pizan uses the position of poet to criticize men's treatment of women in *Le Duc des vrais amants* (1403–5). The first person of the text is the duke of the title, but he is assisted by a woman poet. Aided by his cunning cousin, the duke gains access to the lady; eventually, after a prolonged courtship, a love affair begins; but it soon runs into difficulties. His lady, who is a more prominent figure in this *dit* than in any of the male-authored *dits*, writes to consult her friend, Sebile de Mont Hault, Dame de la Tour. Like the Sybils (prophetesses of antiquity) or Reason in the *Rose* (who similarly lives in a lofty tower), Sebile is a figure of authority. She warns the lady that, while the affair may exalt her lover's honour, it is damaging her own, a theme also found in Christine's *Cent Ballades d'amant et de dame*. Eventually the lovers stop meeting, but too late: gossip is rife and the lady's reputation is ruined. Although the narrative is still told in the duke's voice, we no longer believe his protestations of undying devotion. The voices of Sebile, the lady herself, and the female author whose words preface the *dit*, have created a bond of solidarity in which the sufferings women experience in love now appear more important and authentic than the cliché-dominated, self-serving desires of its male first person. Christine's words in the prologue, which seemed then to announce no more than her willingness to help the duke record his experiences:

> Je diray en sa personne
> le fait si qu'il le raisonne

[I shall recount, using his character, the action as he conceives it]

seem, with hindsight, to open up an ironic gap between her voice and his perceptions. None of the *dits amoureux* exalts love. But Christine's *Duc des vrais amants*, although sympathetic to the lure of passion, is the only one to decry its harmful effect on women. Contrary to its title, it exposes the refined and uplifting emotions which Machaut and Froissart ascribe to their courtly protagonists as false and self-deceiving. The fictional world of the *dit* admonishes real, historical people to renounce it.

WRITING HISTORY

If *dits amoureux* seek to sublimate, dispel, or condemn desire, this may be because the pursuit of individual happiness seemed less and less an acceptable goal in these troubled times. Machaut alludes, at the beginning of his *Jugement dou roi de Navarre*, to the ravages of the Black Death of 1349 in which France lost a third of its population. Froissart's lyrics and *dits amoureux* may be 'consoling' but they have much to be consoling about: they are, after all, composed at roughly the same time as his great *Chroniques* which starkly juxtapose to the elegant abstractions of courtly poetry the material realities of war-torn France. When Charles V came to the throne in 1364, the Hundred Years War had been raging for nearly thirty years and France had recently lost half of her territory in the treaty of Brétigny (1360, about the date the *Chroniques* were begun). In the *Chroniques* we see that women, far from being objects of adoration, are mainly used as pawns in the marriage market to forge alliances between magnates' families. They may intervene powerfully in political crises, but more often than not the alliances founder, as do the marriages themselves. The decorous clashes between personifications in the *dits* similarly contrast with the real-world violence of the *Chroniques*, the paradise settings of gardens and fountains with the horror of sieges and battlefields. No wonder, then, that historical references in the *dits* seem designed to reduce courtly love to a merely literary pastime, and summon magnates to resume their political responsibilities.

The *Chroniques* start by reworking those of an earlier author, Jean le Bel. More interesting, however, are the later volumes, from Book III onwards, when Froissart himself becomes the central figure. Instead of the chronicle issuing from an authoritative, impersonal source it appears to be the transcript of Froissart's conversations as he travels round interviewing informants. They provide most of the text; he listens, prompts with occasional questions, follows up loose ends, and probes mysteries. He thereby poses as intermediary between the true sources of history—those who enacted or witnessed it at first hand—and its future readers. His relationship as secretary and scribe to those who have borne arms resembles that of writer and clerk which he assumes towards the knightly lover in *La Prison Amoureuse*. History writing has, as we have seen, been the site of literary innovation from the very early Middle Ages. It was here that the three *matières* of Rome, France, and Britain were first explored, and the use of prose pioneered. When Froissart transforms the writing of a chronicle into a staging of the chronicler's activity he likewise uses history-writing as a laboratory for literary experiment, recasting prose narrative as a performative genre like the *dit*.

Christine de Pizan also composed historical works that share common ground with her *dits*. In her long verse *Mutacion de Fortune* (1400–3), an account of world history takes the form of a dream narrative in which she describes the paintings in the house of Fortune. This device of presentation echoes both the *Rose* (which similarly describes the house of Fortune) and the fountain sequence in

Machaut's *La Fontaine amoureuse*. This dream is, furthermore, inserted into an allegorized autobiography in which, with a nod to the myth of Ceyx and Alcyone (also found in *La Fontaine amoureuse*), she describes her husband's death at sea and her own metaphorical transformation into a male writer. Another of Christine's historical works with marked affinity to the *dit* is her *Ladvision Cristine* (1405), a prose dream vision which interweaves a universal history with reflections on the moral decay of France.

As was the case for many of his predecessors, romance ideals of chivalry shape Froissart's conception of history. Like the courtly refinements of the lyric and *dit*, these ideals confer moral beauty and abstraction on events, however violent. A native of Hainault, at that time not under the French crown but allied with England, Froissart was well placed to witness the war from both sides and he traces its reversals from a position not of partisanship but of poised distance and aesthetic admiration. He is much less interested in politics or strategy than in individuals' feats of arms and their repercussions on noble families. He writes glowingly, for example, of Jean de Luxembourg's courage at the battle of Crécy in 1346: although blind, Jean headed the charge against the English and was killed. The *Chroniques* are torn between adherence to the values of chivalry—the splendid martial display of the noble elite—and the growing perception that such values cannot compensate for, far less avert, military disaster. Sometimes we are allowed to sense that nobility of rank does not necessarily guarantee nobility of character—an admission which, although it hovers in the background of many a twelfth- or thirteenth-century romance, will not become explicit until the sardonic and embittered *Memoires* of Commynes (composed 1489 onwards).

Thus in both Froissart and Christine we see how the *dit amoureux* forms a bridge between the two prestigious genres of lyric poetry and history-writing, borrowing from the first to influence the second. The lyric first person is posited as a subject in history, while history is confirmed as a medium of first-person reflection which, like the lyric, can elevate itself above the momentary to the timeless world of order and truth.

HUMANISM, DIDACTICISM, LICENCE, AND DEATH

Another reason why history enjoyed high status in the later Middle Ages is that the literary culture of this period was more clerical and less courtly than that of earlier centuries, and thus more obviously oriented around the value of instruction. Didacticism found an especial ally in history-writing. Not only is history a body of knowledge which it is one's duty to pass on, it is also a repository of exemplary lives or events (known as *exempla*, Latin for 'examples') from which one may learn. The advanced study of ancient texts for their own sake created circles of humanist scholarship similar to those of the Renaissance. A leading figure in one such circle was the Italian poet Petrarch, who spent part of his career in Avignon, and whose writings were known in France from the late fourteenth century onwards, although 'Petrarchism' as a mannered poetic style was not adopted until the sixteenth. This focus on classical antiquity, a historical activity in itself, encouraged the reading of Latin historians, whom the more learned vernacular writers then adopted as models. Livy's history was translated into French by Pierre Bersuire between 1356 and 1358. The first work in French to be printed in Paris, in 1477, was the official chronicle of Saint Denis, the *Grandes Chroniques de France*.

Education in the late Middle Ages was more than ever dominated by Aristotle, although he was still known in Latin rather than the original Greek. The first vernacular translations of any of his works—the *Ethics*, *Politics*, and *Economics*—were undertaken by Nicole Oresme, again under the patronage of Charles V, between 1370 and 1377. The choice of works is revealing: learning is valued for the moral and practical lessons that can be drawn from it. The Stoic moral philosophy of Cicero and Seneca was also influential, with French translations being produced in the fifteenth century. Even in less learned milieux, writing and moral reflection were closely associated. Meaning became identified with analysis, and analysis with teaching; for writers with a Christian agenda, teaching tended to edge into preaching. Frequently, given the exclusively masculine make-up of clerical culture, such teaching was profoundly misogynistic. In Latin, anti-feminist writing was widespread. The Latin *Lamentations* of Matheolus, a virulent diatribe against women's alleged iniquities, were translated into French by Jean Lefèvre in the late fourteenth century. There is some pro-feminist writing, but the accusation which one modern critic has levelled against Christine de Pizan—of inventing misogyny in a desperate attempt to make her own stance against it seem important—is baseless given the almost routine way vernacular poets accuse women of polluting men's bodies and imperilling their souls. Marriage is often seen as the source of untold woes, as for example in the sarcastically entitled *Quinze Joies de mariage*.

The impulse to didacticism is everywhere apparent in late medieval literature. Relatively discreet in courtly verse genres such as lyric and *dit amoureux*, it is more insistent in prose works. The more learned the writer, the greater his obligation to instruct. In his *Quadrilogue invectif* of 1422 Alain Chartier seeks to rally each social group within French society by having them harangue each other in learned, Latinate prose. Didacticism infiltrates even relatively unlearned material like the legend of Mélusine, fairy progenitor of the house of Lusignan from which Gui de Lusignan, leader of the First Crusade, would stem. In the version attributed to Jean d'Arras (around 1395), Mélusine herself, although in a sense less than human since she is transformed into a serpent from the waist down on Saturdays, also has access to superhuman wisdom which she does not hesitate to impart. The mother of ten sons, she determines their careers, even ordering one of them to be killed. She delivers long *chastoiements* expounding the crusading and chivalric values that her eldest sons should follow. Thanks to her, they fight nobly in Christian causes and establish successful dynasties across Europe and the Near East.

The convergence of historical, scholarly, and didactic currents finds its apogee in the writings of Christine de Pizan, and notably in her *Livre de la cité des dames* of 1405. Long despised as a tiresome bluestocking, Christine is now avidly appreciated, as indeed she was in her own day. The *Cité des dames* is a compilation of exemplary lives of historical women, adapted mainly from two Latin texts: Boccaccio's *Of Famous Women* and the section on female martyrs in Vincent of Beauvais's *Mirror of History*. Christine's compilation is structured by two allegorical schemes. First, the author figure dialogues with three personifications, Raison, Droiture, and Justice (Reason, Equity, and Judgement). Each in turn dominates one of the *Cité*'s three books, and each is represented as relating the women's lives in answer to Christine's questions about women's character, and as consoling her for the ubiquity of anti-feminist writings like those of Matheolus, which she has just been reading. Second, the stories are combined with the image, adapted from Augustine's *City of God*, of constructing a moral, spiritual, and eternal city in the midst of the cities of this world. The lives in Book I and the first part of Book II of the *Cité* make up the foundations, walls, and principal dwellings of the city of ladies. The remainder of Book II populates it with exemplary historical women and Book III fills its highest towers and chambers with female saints, led into the City by the Virgin Mary who becomes its queen. Christine's project, then, involves taking on some of the most authoritative male writers in the Western tradition and synthesizing their writings, while at the same time reversing their teaching.

Women's experience, instead of being disregarded or condemned, should be valued, says Christine, their contribution to civilization applauded, and their virtues imitated. Misogynists, in short, are to be taught a lesson, as she says to the ladies assembled in the completed City: 'Faites les tous menteurs par monstrer vostre vertu et prouvez mençongeurs ceulx qui vous blasment par bien faire' ('Make liars of them all by showing forth your virtue and prove, by acting well, that those who reproach you are lying').

Such learned and didactic strains inevitably provoked scepticism and even derision. The recasting of Boccaccio's *Decameron* for the court of Burgundy in the *Cent Nouvelles nouvelles* of *c*.1456–61 results in a fascinating mix of tragic, moral, and scurrilous tales, purporting to relate events that recently took place in the duke's domains. Many parody the very idea of learning from example. In story xxix, for instance, a naïve newly-wed has sex with his wife for the first time, whereupon she immediately delivers a baby: shocked to 'learn' that reproduction is so rapid and efficient, he decides to abstain from then on. The tale gains in piquancy from being told in a pseudo-allegorical manner (mocking the tradition of the *Rose*) about a knight fighting for control of a fortress, from which a prisoner (the baby) is then yielded up. Other stories revel in the punishment of unfaithful wives or mistresses—unfaithful husbands or lovers are rarer. The audacity or ingenuity of the infidelity often exerts more fascination than its sanctioning. The didacticism of the misogynist tradition reveals its obsession with precisely those impulses which it appears to condemn.

It has been suggested that the *Cent Nouvelles nouvelles* were written by Antoine de la Sale (*c*.1385–1460), and certainly the writings of this author bring a new twist to the various strands of prose-writing—historical, learned, didactic, and lubricious—which we have so far identified. La Sale was squire and tutor in a number of noble families, and the author of various pedagogical and didactic works deploying historical *exempla*. His most accomplished, but also most puzzling, work is *Jehan de Saintré* (1456), the story of how a young squire is trained by a beautiful widow, the Lady of Belles-Cousines, to be a perfect knight in public and her lover in secret. All goes well until the young man tries to assert his independence by devising chivalric undertakings of his own. Furious, Belles-Cousines withdraws to her estates where she indulges in a wild love affair with a well-built abbot of peasant stock. Together they mock Saintré when he tries to talk to her; in revenge he humiliates her in front of the whole court by telling them in anonymous form the story of her misdemeanours and inviting them to condemn her.

This text has obvious links to history-writing because the hero and others of its characters are recognizable historical figures; to didacticism, because it opens with a protracted *chastoiement* by Belles-Cousines to Saintré; and to humanism, because some of this *chastoiement* is taken (via a French translation) from the Latin of Valerius Maximus. Yet the spectacular degeneration of Belles-Cousines from chaste widow to sacrilegious debauchee undermines the value both of her teaching, and of its product, Saintré himself. La Sale's revelation of her perverse nature may be an attack on women who try to usurp the role of educator, perhaps especially on Christine de Pizan who identifies herself repeatedly as a widow qualified to deliver moral instruction. But if, in Belles-Cousines, didacticism slides into licence, the end of the story, where Saintré denounces Belles-Cousines to the court, shows courtesy slipping into cruelty. We are left suspecting that the displays of faultless elegance on which courtly performances depend—including those of chivalry and storytelling—betray, at the same time, an underlying viciousness of intent.

Didacticism often relies on eliciting and then organizing a sexual impulse. The other unspeakable entity that furnishes it with a dynamic is death. The ability of *exempla* to induce compliance often lies in their representing the death of their protagonist as a threat or a promise to the reader. The didactic impact of eros and death combined explains the canonicity of such exempla as Narcissus, Lucretia (who committed suicide after being raped), or Dido (who likewise killed herself after being abandoned by Aeneas). The combination is treated mockingly in story lv of the *Cent Nouvelles nouvelles*, in which a young girl sick with the plague decides that she would feel more reconciled to dying if she could first know the pleasures of sex. Various gallants whom she has previously resisted are delighted to oblige; but one after another they are exhausted by her appetite, contract the plague, and die. Insatiable, the 'ouvriere de tuer gens' ('killer-worker') survives, 'Qui est notable et veritable exemple a plusurs jeunes filles de point refuser ung bien quand il leur vient' ('Which serves as a true and noteworthy *exemplum*/example to many young women not to turn down a good thing when it comes their way'). This concluding 'lesson' parodies the traditional didactic menace of death as a warning *against* sexual indulgence; it is self-undermining in so far as her behaviour proves lethal to others. Uncannily, however, her desire *does* save her and so the 'lesson' is also true: women's lust rages even more powerfully than the plague. Villon's 'Testament' likewise, and with explosive effect, runs moral, punitive, and humorous treatments of death and sex together.

Late medieval literature exudes a sense of the ubiquity of death. It is often suggested that this is because death was a more palpable reality in the Middle Ages than it is today, insulated as we are from it by medical and other institutional shields. However, this ubiquity may not be the *cause* of its being so much referred to by medieval writers, as the *effect*: the effect, that is, of didactic traditions in which, far from being a cosy familiar, death is the ultimate horror that can frighten readers into obedience. All the medieval resources of scurrility—boundless as they are—cannot detract from its nightmarish powers.

THE 'QUERELLE DU *ROMAN DE LA ROSE*' AND 'LA BELLE DAME SANS MERCY'

The dividing line between edification and disgust is a fine one, and mobile, too, since different readers may respond differently to the same text. Such divergences are responsible for two early fifteenth-century literary debates: one over the *Roman de la rose* and the other over Alain Chartier's poem 'La Belle Dame sans mercy' of 1424.

We have already seen the decisive influence of the *Rose* on authors of *dits amoureux* throughout the fourteenth century. The text of Jean de Meun's continuation, however, is littered with attacks on women and marriage, mostly pronounced by the personifications Ami, the Vilain Jaloux (Jealous Husband), and Genius. Fourteenth-century readers seem to have especially relished these passages; manuscript copies are covered with marginal exhortations to *Nota Bene* ('note well') and little drawings of hands with the finger pointing to the good bits. The *Rose* as a whole, then, fuelled both *fin' amor* and anti-feminist satire. These contradictions are already legible within Jean de Meun's continuation, which stages a vigorous debate between the various personifications over the value of love. Its conclusions, if any, are ambiguous, given the narrator's own ironic stance.

Predictably, Christine de Pizan did not share her contemporaries' enthusiasm for the *Rose*. In 1399 she wrote a verse *dit*, the *Epistre au dieu d'amours*, condemning its plot as the callous seduction of a young girl, and criticizing men who hold women responsible for men's desire for them. But the *querelle* proper flared in 1401 with the production of a treatise, now lost, by the humanist Jean de Montreuil. Jean seems to have identified his namesake Jean de Meun as fellow scholar, and defended the display of learning in the *Rose*. He sent the treatise to Christine, provoking an exchange of open letters. A friend of Jean de Montreuil, Gontier Col, joined the pro-*Rose* faction; Jean Gerson, a conservative theologian, Chancellor of the Sorbonne and precursor of those *Sorbonniqueurs* denounced by Rabelais, preached against it. There were various further sympathizers on either side. Early in 1402, Christine assembled all the papers in the case, provided them with a dedication and a narrative framework promoting her own point of view, and submitted them—for all the world like a character in a *dit amoureux*—to Queen Isabelle of Bavaria. A second round of the *querelle* took off in 1402, this time sparked by Gerson, who wrote his own treatise on the *Rose*. This provoked further exchanges of letters into which Gontier's brother Pierre was drawn. Christine contributed more letters and—as if again to cement the resemblance to a *dit amoureux*—some *rondeaux*. Once again, she was responsible for gathering up the paperwork and ensuring its survival.

Detractors of the *Rose* claim that it is obscene, prejudiced against women and marriage, and that, in its finale where the lover plucks the rose, it endorses rape. Its defenders maintain that Jean de Meun is the model of the learned clerk. Criticisms of him are unfounded, either because Jean's views are sound, or because his critics don't read him properly, confusing the literal and the allegorical, or the characters and the author. The argument, however, is not ultimately about the meaning of a poem which, by this date, was well over 100 years old.

In part it is about the status of women. The humanists are scandalized that Christine should dare to criticize what they see as men's prerogative to hold a monopoly of writing. They refer to her only in the third person, and dismiss her as no better than an animal or a prostitute, thus replicating against her—as Christine sees it—the violence which Jean de Meun authorizes against women in the *Rose*. Indeed, the pro-*Rose* writers endorse misogynistic views of women. If Christine doesn't like such views that only proves their truth. For Christine, however, generalizations are to be mistrusted, and the blanket condemnation of women is harmful to everyone. It is no coincidence, in her view, if the *Rose* supports both courtly love and misogyny, since both collude in ignoring the rights and interests of women, blind men to their own faults, and prevent everyone from enjoying what should properly be valued: the support and safeguard of a happy marriage.

The debate is also about the status of literature. The view of it as entertainment, which was predominant if not universal in the twelfth and thirteenth centuries, has given way to the assumption that it is a source of moral and intellectual understanding. And the responsibility for subject matter has shifted away from tradition. Henceforth authors are to be held liable—to what extent is precisely what is at issue—for the content of their work; their identity, whether as cleric or woman, is a major factor in determining how their work is received; emergently, at least, writers are now conceived as the source of 'authority' for their work. By entering into controversy with established authors Christine secures a foothold among them, while by correcting their views she asserts her authority over theirs. Despite the humanists' best efforts, female authorship—temporarily at least—is the beneficiary of this dispute. Indeed, as the author of lyrics, *dits*, histories, didactic and reflective works, where the first person is vigorously promoted as an authoritative, moral perspective, Christine de Pizan emerges as the towering literary figure of late medieval literature.

Similar issues of the status of women in love, and the responsibility of the author for his work, are rehearsed in the debate over Chartier's poem. 'La Belle Dame sans mercy' consists in a dialogue between an anonymous lover and lady in which the lover presses his suit and the lady rejects him. They speak in alternating stanzas, the woman's words often echoing, dismantling, and mocking the lover's pleas, which are couched in the highly conventional rhetoric of *fin' amor*. The dialogue is overheard by a frame narrator whose own lady has died. At the end, he tells us that the knight died of grief, while the callous lady 'aux dances se deporta' ('amused herself at dances'). The final lines warn women not to be cruel and to eschew the example of the 'belle dame sans mercy'. The poem sparked a series of verse sequels in which the lady is variously defended or punished, and Chartier attacked or vindicated. The undercurrent of sexual violence is even more marked in this debate than in the *querelle de la Rose*. It is not clear whether actual women participated in the *querelle*, although the opening sally censuring Chartier for representing the *belle dame* in such a cruel light is said to emanate from the ladies of the court. A social as much as a literary document, the debate lays bare the interconnections between courtliness, misogyny, the didactic exploitation of love and death, and the self-promotion of writing as a privilege of the male *clerc*.

Together these *querelles* imply that the social and moral importance of French literature is inseparable from controversy about the status of women, issues that would be revived in the sixteenth-century *querelle des femmes* (see Part II, pp. 120–1).

THEATRE IN THE LATE MIDDLE AGES

The increasing prestige of the book in the later Middle Ages, far from allowing literary works to circulate more freely than hitherto, tended on the contrary to confine them to wealthy or educated circles. Thus, while the elite was reared on a diet of lyric and narrative, popular audiences came to rely on a different staple: theatre. Performances ranged in scale from short dramatic monologues to immense mystery plays that took large casts and several days to perform.

We have seen the beginnings of drama in thirteenth-century cities. In the fourteenth, miracle plays—dramatized episodes from lives of the saints—become popular. Rutebeuf, as well as being an important pioneer of the *dit*, seems also to anticipate this transition from narrative saint's life to miracle play, since he wrote examples of both. His *Miracle de Theophile* recasts for the stage a well-known miracle of the Virgin Mary in which she rescues a cleric who has sold his soul to the devil. In the fourteenth century there develops a cycle of forty such Miracles of the Virgin, based on earlier, narrative miracles, which were performed annually between 1339 and 1382 under the auspices of the Goldsmiths' Guild. Since the reason for the Virgin's interventions is the terrible mess which ordinary people get themselves into, these plays are more entertaining than one might expect. In the Miracle of Theodora, for example, piety is spiced with adultery, transvestism, and same-sex seduction, and enlivened by the well-worn theatrical devices of mistaken identity and eventual recognition. Other Miracles show the seamier side of life's rich pageant: illegitimate births, absconding nuns, and unchaste clerics, sensual misadventures the consequences of which are miraculously undone by the Virgin. The religious endings of the plays are accompanied by the altogether human satisfaction of everything returning to its rightful designation and everyone seeing where they went wrong.

In the fifteenth century, miracle plays were overtaken in popularity by morality plays (in which events are acted out by allegorical personifications) and mystery plays (which dramatize historical events, usually taken from the Bible or saints' lives). Morality plays were small-scale but the mysteries could require the cooperation of a whole town to stage. There were also straightforwardly comic genres, *soties* (where all the characters are *sots*, or fools, delivering a mixture of nonsense and satire), and farces (whose plots are very similar to the earlier *fabliaux*). The most elaborate and watchable of the farces is that of *Maître Pierre Pathelin*, a drama centring on a down-at-heel lawyer who fools a cloth merchant into giving him some cloth in the hope of getting paid later. Pathelin persuades his wife to help him dupe the merchant by pretending that Pathelin is on his deathbed and so can't have agreed to buy the cloth. Pathelin makes a show of mistaking the merchant for a doctor and tells him grisly details of his symptoms; he also rambles more or less intelligibly in a series of different dialects. The merchant departs, unable to make sense of the two accounts in his mind—that Pathelin is his debtor, and that Pathelin is dying. The merchant, who is not very good at accounts, decides to make good his lost cloth by claiming back from his shepherd the value of some sheep that the shepherd has stolen from the merchant's flock. The shepherd engages Pathelin as his lawyer and, just as Pathelin had instructed his wife how to speak and act in front of the merchant, now he tells the shepherd to say nothing but 'Baa' in front of the judge. Pathelin thus scripts, acts, and stage-manages events, a *farceur* within his own farce. In the courtroom the merchant recognizes Pathelin, and this increases his mental confusion. He keeps muddling up the story of his unpaid cloth with that of the stolen sheep, until eventually the judge loses patience. The shepherd, meanwhile, is taken for an idiot. The case against him is dismissed. But when Pathelin asks the shepherd to pay him, he gets nothing but 'Baa'. One injustice counteracts another or, as Pathelin puts is, the one who thought he was the best deceiver has been duped by a mere rustic.

Much of the pleasure of this plot comes from reversing hierarchies: the richer you are, the more likely you are to be made a fool of. Pathelin who is a poor man gets the better of the rich merchant but is worsted by the even poorer shepherd. The merchant, for his part, loses cloth to the lawyer and mutton to the shepherd; his sheep are stolen from him, their wool going to the one, their flesh to the other. Since the legal profession is known as 'the order of the robe', Pathelin's need for cloth defines his status. He gets his 'robe' for nothing but then, when the shepherd manages to avoid paying him, he exercises its functions for nothing too. As in the *fabliaux*, control over representation is the key to success: fictions and misrepresentations are piled up one on another, and the play revolves joyously around different kinds of linguistic excess, from Pathelin's delirious volubility to the shepherd's single 'Baa'.

It is significant that, unlike in the *fabliaux* where the successful trickster figure is usually a clerk, in farces it is more likely to be a lawyer. Indeed, comic play on the similarity between play-acting and the practice of the law runs through the *Pathelin*. In some of the *soties*, too, the fools present their complaints before a judge in a mock court. Of the large numbers of people involved in these popular entertainments in fifteenth-century Paris, many were law clerks. Others were clerks, graduates of the University, who had been unable to secure patronage from the aristocracy or a living from the Church. Villon, who has even been thought by some to be the author of *Pathelin*, may well have spent some time as a member of a theatre troupe. His 'Testament' resembles these late medieval plays in its satirical attacks on society and its constant conjuring of the law and its enforcers. One of its inset *ballades*, the *Ballade de bonne doctrine*, captures the simultaneous liveliness and degeneracy of the player's life where acting, deceiving, and gambling are all intertwined and everything ends up (in the words of the refrain) 'at the tavern and with the tarts':

> Rime, raille, cymbale, fluctes,
> comme fol feintif, éhontés;
> farce, brouille, joue des flûtes;
> fais, ès villes et ès cités,
> farces, jeux et moralités,
> gagne au berlan, au glic, aux quilles,
> aussi bien va, or écoutez!
> tout aux tavernes et aux filles.

[Rhyme, rail, play the cymbals or the flutes, shameless ones, like some feigning fool; play-act, blague, pull a fast one; put on farces, shows, and morality plays in cities and their outskirts; win at card games or skittles: it makes no difference, for it all ends up—mark my words!—at the tavern and with the tarts.]

All of these fifteenth-century theatrical genres continue to be hugely popular well into the sixteenth century. The 1545 printed edition of *La Farce du Cuvier* (in which a hen-pecked husband gets the better of his wife) announces the 100-year-old play as a *farce nouvelle tres bonne et fort joyeuse*. Performances come to an end not because they are abandoned by their audiences, but because they are condemned by the civic and religious authorities.

THE FUTURE OF A POET WITH A PAST: FRANÇOIS VILLON

Villon's poetry has featured in several contexts in the course of this history. His 'Testament', which we have just likened to contemporary drama, has also been identified as a *dit*: a poetic *montage* in which a semi-comic first-person narrative frames a number of inset *forme fixe* lyrics that ventriloquize a range of different voices. Its themes of antifeminist and anti-clerical satire, and of the pervasiveness of death, anchor it firmly in the poetic traditions of the later Middle Ages. Even the form of the mock will, in which Villon's 'Testament' and his earlier 'Lais' are both couched, is a medieval genre that goes back at least to the *Roman de Renart* and was cultivated by other late medieval poets. Yet Villon's bravado in bequeathing his work to the future has conspicuously succeeded where the endeavours of lesser poets failed. Indeed, the form in which the 'Testament' is most commonly read today, with each of the inset lyrics prefaced by a descriptive title, is due to its having found an enthusiastic reader and editor in the sixteenth-century poet Clément Marot. Since then Villon has been taken up and imitated by many subsequent French poets, including Apollinaire. His poetry may serve to end this discussion of the medieval period with the reminder that, regardless of what the format of this book might imply, periods do not have neat ends. Like late medieval drama, Villon's poetry reaches forward into the century that follows. It forms a continuum with the compositions of the *grands rhé-toriqueurs* with which Part II: *The Period in Close-up* begins, and its influence stretches on into the modern period.

It is worth comparing the 'Testament', composed in 1461, with Guillaume de Machaut's *Voir dit* of almost exactly a century earlier to see why Villon's poem should have succeeded in speaking to later generations in a way that Machaut's did not. Both poems are pseudo-autobiographical and centre on an elderly poet-protagonist who is unlucky in love but skilled at his craft. Choice specimens of different *formes fixes* are interspersed throughout both texts, many of them drawn from a pre-existing stock (in addition to those included in the 'Testament' some twenty-two other short lyric poems by Villon sur-vive). Both works assume a quasi-legal form: *voirdit* is medieval French for 'verdict' while the 'Testament' follows the protocols of contemporary wills. Each is its author's longest, most ambitious work, a summa of his achievement on which it passes a 'verdict' or which it leaves as a 'legacy' to the future. Both lodge a claim to truthfulness, Machaut's through use of the adjective *voir*, 'true', Villon's through play with the biblical sense of 'Testament'. But both equally draw attention to their artifice, Machaut allegedly compiling his correspon-dence with Peronne and Villon picturing himself dictating his last words to his scribe—in fact the poem presents him as dying shortly before it is completed! Why, then, has Villon become the best-known poet of the Middle Ages whereas Machaut, though widely revered in his own day, is now read mainly by specialists?

Villon's success is due in part to the way he breaks out of the courtly mode and raises the stakes of composition. The first person of the 'Testament' is a strident, angry figure who uses the poem to reward his few friends (the companions of his misspent youth) and curse his many enemies (mostly associated with the forces of law and order). His 'will' is mainly composed of legacies of things that don't exist, or that he does not own; their wording is intended to lampoon or insult their recipients, not enrich them. Villon thereby implies that those who oppress him are undeserving fat cats who have abused their position at his expense, while he has been cheated of the material success to which his poetic skill should have entitled him. The 'Testament' is a socially disruptive work aiming radically to refashion the poet's world; and it exudes a rawness that is far removed from the cautious intelligence of much medieval poetry. Written from under the threat of death, it demands that it be heard.

Poetic conventions as well as the social status quo are the targets of Villon's vindictiveness. Individual passages within the 'Testament', and especially its inset lyrics, often open on a noble or melancholy note, but this is soon undermined by the systematic lowering of register and tone known as 'burlesque'. Even the famous 'ballade des dames du temps jadis' falls prey to this systematic degradation. Lament for the fair women of antiquity (stanza one) gives way to reviewing dangerous or castrating loves of the medieval past (stanza two), and a miscellany of more recently departed women who were prominent politically (stanza three). With these shifts, the famous refrain 'Mais ou sont les neiges d'antan?' changes connotation. From evoking whiteness and purity, 'last year's snow' comes instead to suggest coldness and transience. The *envoi* stigmatizes the quest for these irrecoverable and possibly undesirable women as anyway futile:

> Prince, n'enquerrez de semaine
> ou elles sont, ne de cet an,
> qu'a ce refrain ne vous remaine:
> mais ou sont les neiges d'antan?

[Prince, you'll not ask this week where these women are, nor yet this year, without my bringing you back to this refrain: but where are last year's snows?]

As a later *ballade* in the same group will derisively remark, everything passes, and a good thing too: it is simply blown away like dust in the wind. The use of mock Old French in this later *ballade* underlines the folly of attempting to cling to the past.

But if the past is mere dust, and all of us are doomed to be swept away by the wind, how is the poet's plea for recognition to reach the future—especially if his language, like earlier forms of French before it, is bound for obsolescence? The strength of Villon's 'Testament' is that it achieves survival precisely by renouncing it. It consigns everything to oblivion; there is no nostalgic hankering for immortality. Instead there is an intense jubilation in the present. The sensual delights of red wine or soft pillows, the satisfaction of venting wrath, the tight-rope walker's thrill in managing a difficult verse form, these are things of value precisely because they are of the moment. The form of this will is a shell curiously at odds with its contents, as it para-doxically perpetuates in the form of a written document the trace of an irrecoverable, urgent voice.

Villon's 'Testament' berates his contemporaries for using him ill, and so he may always have intended that he himself should be its chief beneficiary. In material terms his success seems to have been limited. Condemned to death in 1462 for his part in a riot, his sentence was commuted on appeal in 1463 to ten years of exile, and that is the last we know of Villon the man. The legend and the poetry, however, have remained undimmed. Thief, murderer, rioter, this brilliant but ill-starred poet shows how a sustained future is still possible for the medieval past.

Part II

The Early Modern Period 1470–1789

Overview of the Period

During the three hundred years from 1470, when the first printing press was established in Paris, to the Revolution of 1789, French culture changed almost beyond recognition. To juxtapose Christine de Pizan with Madame de Graffigny, Alain Chartier with Voltaire, the *Farce de Pierre Pathelin* with Beaumarchais's comedies, Charles d'Orléans's 'I' with Rousseau's, or again the image of François I as a patron of early sixteenth-century humanism with that of Madame de Pompadour as an incarnation of Enlightenment culture (see Figures 7 and 11, and pp. 116 and 169), is to move between different languages, different mental worlds, and radically different conceptions of form and style. Fifteenth-century literature arises from a locally organized manu-script culture, concentrated for the most part in the hands of a relatively few members of the privileged classes. In the eighteenth century, print culture is expanding beyond the control of censorship and reaching a large literate public in the form of inexpensive books, journals, and newspapers. A centralized court culture has come and gone. Above all, a national literary canon is well on its way to being recognized, a set of texts already perceived to encapsulate the genius of the French nation.

During these three centuries, there is still a large and predominantly illiterate peasant population whose way of life changes slowly if at all, but in the larger towns and cities cultural change is rapid. People with the means to do so move around a good deal: despite intermittent wars in various parts of Europe, travel is increasingly easy and well organized. Columbus's voyage was still barely conceivable when Villon was writing; by the late eighteenth century, the Americas are a major feature on the economic, political, and cultural map. Journeys in late medieval literature are liable to lead to fabulous encounters with strange and monstrous beings; in eighteenth-century texts, Persians, Peruvians, and Hurons—all of them eminently civilized in their own way—visit Paris, and fictional travellers from France insatiably explore other cultures. Travel-writing has become a popular genre in its own right. Visitors from outer space are beginning to arrive, too. For fifteenth-century astronomers, the planets and the 'fixed stars', endowed with souls, marked the concentric spheres of a geocentric universe, generating a celestial harmony; Voltaire's Micromégas travels from a planet of the star Sirius to Saturn, and thence, with a Saturnian philosopher, to a small planet in the solar system, just past Mars, where they are astonished to find that the minute inhabitants have made considerable scientific discoveries. In 1500, anyone who had suggested that the body and mind consisted solely of matter, with no immortal soul, would have been thought mad or (more probably) possessed by the devil. In the late eighteenth century, such ideas are being explored, more and more openly and imaginatively, by a number of thinkers.

These are the changes that have led historians to describe this whole period as 'early modern', a long phase of transition towards a world that appears familiar to us. Yet such terms are always problematic. Is it justifiable to speak of the period as inaugurating 'modernity'? Writers of that time often register a perception of change, and the word 'modern' is one they themselves use. Yet they were self-evidently unable to think of themselves as 'early modern', since they can have had no conception of what we call modern; the features we recognize as anticipating our mental world were perceived differently by them. All period terms are of course themselves relative, being similarly the result of attempts by historians of a later age to make sense of *their* past. Labels like 'Renaissance', 'Baroque', 'Classicism', 'Enlightenment', which are routinely used to characterize medium-scale cultural shifts within the early modern, are at best convenient markers. They should never be allowed to impose an artificial coherence on the complex and conflicting evidence of cultural history. They draw attention to some phenomena at the expense of others and will thus be used sparingly and cautiously here. We shall often find, in fact, that they are at least partly mythical, being the later outgrowth of stories and aspirations conceived in the period itself in order to construct a cultural identity.

In Rabelais's *Gargantua*, published in the 1530s, the wise old king Grandgousier tells a henchman of the fanatical imperialist Picrochole that 'Le temps n'est plus d'ainsi conquester les royaulmes avecques dommaige de son prochain frere christian' ('The time is past for conquering kingdoms in this way at the expense of our Christian neighbour and brother'). By the sixteenth century, the idea of a European empire was in decline, to be revived much later in the legendary career of Napoleon and in our own times by the Nazi attempt to found a Third Empire. Rabelais's episode may be interpreted as propaganda in favour of French national sovereignty. The king, François I, had himself aspired to the title of Holy Roman Emperor; when he failed, he helped instead to lay the foundations of what in the next two hundred years was to become the most powerful nation state and a model for European culture. France was close to achieving geopolitical unity, even though its eastern and south-eastern borders would remain in dispute for a long time, and a sustained policy of centralization of the administrative and legal systems had begun to gather momentum, laying the foundations for the absolutism of Louis XIV, the Republicanism that followed the French Revolution, and a modern state in which most of the key powers are exercised from the capital (the liberal monarchy and relative regional autonomy which evolved in the British Isles provide a striking contrast to this history). The process will be a long one. In the sixteenth century, there are still many regional centres with their own cultural identity: the phenomenon of Lyons, a cosmopolitan city with a flourishing economy, a prolific printing industry, and a literary output to match, is only the most prominent of these; likewise, the peculiar intensity of the wars of religion (1562–93) would not have been possible if the warring factions had not had access to formidable independent power-bases. Yet the wars of religion also helped to erode the power of the nobility, making it vulnerable to the centralizing policy of the seventeenth-century monarchs and their ministers.

The evolution of the French language, and its eventual emergence as the international medium of diplomacy and polite society, follows a similar path towards centralization and standardization. By 1500, *francien*, the idiom of the Île-de-France, was already established as a national language; a series of royal edicts, culminating in the Edict of Villers-Cotterets (1539), made it the required vehicle for legal proceedings and depositions throughout France, marginalizing regional forms and dealing a crucial blow to the survival of Latin as the language of professional culture. Calvin first wrote the *Institution de la religion chrestienne*, his massive work of reformist theology, in Latin, but translated it into French five years later (1541). Ambroise Paré, a leading medical authority, also wrote in French. Although Latin remained for hundreds of years the cornerstone of education and an international vehicle for the transmission of knowledge, the vernacular was by the mid-seventeenth century established as its natural successor over the whole range of literacy and as the focus of an increasingly triumphalist sense of national and cultural superiority.

The formation of a centralized culture focused on the royal court, rather than the regional courts of earlier times, is a major aspect of the same process. Cultural display has always been used as a way of advertising political and economic power, and François I embarked on an impressive programme of building and interior decoration at

Fontainebleau and in the Loire valley, using artists imported from Italy. He brought humanists to court (see Figure 7) and, together with his sister Marguerite de Navarre, herself a major writer, presided over an extraordinary flowering of literary activity. By the later seventeenth century, the spoken language of the court was to become a model for elegant writing of all kinds. The Académie Française, founded in the mid-1630s, legislated for proper linguistic usage and the observance of standard literary conventions, especially in the newly emergent the-atre. This formidable institution has demonstrated what a powerful cultural function it fulfils by remaining an influential feature of French public life up to the present day.

This story of the building of a national identity is not unproblematic, however. Early modern literary culture was never wholly separable from the religious and political domains, where authority took on a more directly coercive form: for example, the function of the Académie Française, which exercised cultural control, was not so different from that of the Sorbonne (the Faculty of Theology of the University of Paris), which made critical decisions throughout the early modern period on what was or was not to be regarded as orthodox belief. Such authorities never went unchallenged, although the nature and extent of dissident opinion, and the way it was expressed, varied very widely. One important strand, which we shall return to at several points along the way, is an increasingly relativistic view of France in its relation to other cultures. More broadly, the scientific and philosophical question-ing of established principles which becomes insistent in the course of the seventeenth century and overwhelming in the eighteenth generates tensions of all kinds, often ones which run *through* individual works.

There are thus many kinds of crossings-over. The construction of narratives of national origin in Jean Lemaire de Belges's *Illustrations de Gaule et singularitez de Troye*, Ronsard's unfinished *La Franciade*, or Chapelain's epic version of the Jeanne d'Arc legend, *La Pucelle*, pro-vides clear evidence of a desire for collective identity, a tangible sense of Frenchness. Yet none of these—or any other similar works—estab-lished themselves as canonic works comparable with Homer's *Iliad* or Virgil's *Aeneid*. And there are counter-stories: Voltaire deflated the religiosity of the Jeanne d'Arc story in his mock epic *La Pucelle*, and his *Siècle de Louis XIV* takes a sharply analytic look at the king who had become a myth in his own lifetime.

A different group of examples, one much closer to the mainstream of French literary history as it is generally perceived, would begin with the two key *arts poétiques*, Du Bellay's *Deffence et illustration de la langue françoyse* (1549) and Boileau's *Art poétique* (1674). Du Bellay dismisses

7. François I, surrounded by his sons, a French cardinal, the court dwarf and assorted pets, listens to the humanist Antoine Macault reading from his translation of a Greek historical work (*c.* 1532).

virtually the whole of French medieval literature in order to promote a radical renewal based on the most illustrious ancient (Latin and Greek) and Italian models; the French language, thus glorified, will become the medium of works fit to join that timeless canon. Yet his argument is based on a notion of the *passing* of cultural superiority from one people to another; it is full of metaphors of change, decay, and death, and Du Bellay's own poetry often emphasizes the fragility of individual experience in the face of the great monuments and institutions of human history. Boileau's perspective is very different in that he places tragedy and comedy rather than lyric and epic poetry at the centre of the ideal canon, but he too rejects the French poetry of preceding ages (including notably that of Du Bellay's contemporary Ronsard) and insists on the superiority of ancient models. Both works participate in the sustained current of literary energy which produced, in the sixteenth century, some of the finest French lyric poetry, and, in the later seventeenth century, an unparalleled burst of creativity. But it is important not to take their claims too literally. The ironies of literary history will make both look from some perspectives like a mere publicity stunt, an exercise in special pleading to justify the literary taste of the moment. Boileau is scathing about the poetic movement that Du Bellay inaugurated; his own contemporary adversaries, the 'Moderns', whom he also treats with crushing scorn, will in turn soon take their revenge.

The invention of printing (more strictly, of movable type) is arguably the single event that most decisively transformed the cultural landscape of Europe. Once the first press was established in Paris, others soon followed, both in the capital and in regional centres such as Lyons. The commercial success of the new technology depended on an expanding and increasingly prosperous urban population, and the demand for literacy grew as reading matter became more and more readily available. Some of the early printed books were luxury objects, but plainer, cheaper books soon began to be produced in larger numbers, reaching new markets. Reading habits changed: material which had in earlier times been delivered orally and consumed in public— sermons, pedagogical writings, stories, poetry—began to be read privately and silently.

These changes are essential to the redefinition of literary culture in the early modern period. Printing from its earliest beginnings was exploited by the *humanistae* ('humanists'), scholars who inaugurated a programme of studies based on a scrupulous respect for classical Latin as opposed to the modernized Latin used by the scholastics, on a revival of classical Latin style ('rhetoric'), and on the literary legacy of antiquity. One of the first books printed in Paris was a handbook of Latin rhetoric by the French humanist Guillaume Fichet. Yet it was inevitable that the market would also demand printed versions of books which were already popular and of new ones in the same vein: the standard pedagogical handbooks of late medieval learning, including treatises on logic (regarded by the scholastic establishment as the key to all intellectual enquiry) and philosophical and theological commentaries; popular works of devotion in both Latin and French; and vernacular narrative fictions, from the short, racy *nouvelle* to the vast structures of romance.

The map of French print culture in the sixteenth century may thus be roughly divided into three areas: learned or scholarly culture, written almost exclusively in Latin at first, but increasingly in French; court culture, self-consciously elitist but by no means always learned; and a wider realm of popular culture, requiring literacy but not claiming social or intellectual supremacy. Popular culture as defined here should not be confused with the mass culture of modern times, based on almost universal literacy and a global media network, nor should one assume that there is a clear-cut social and ideological opposition between high culture and popular culture.

What we now call literature is distributed across all three areas, since many humanists wrote Latin poetry and drama, while vernacular poetry and fiction were avidly consumed by all literate readers. One of the most widely read books of the sixteenth century was the Protestant translation of the Psalms into French verse, begun by the court poet Clément Marot. It certainly belongs to the history of literature, but it also shows how the availability of the printed book could promote far-reaching ideological change: such a widespread dissemination of biblical texts among the laity—one of the central aims of sixteenth-century religious reformers—would not have been conceivable a hundred years earlier. It was for this reason that the Sorbonne attempted to suppress printing in the 1520s, attacked unorthodox printers (Estienne Dolet was burned at the stake in 1546) and published lists of prohibited books.

The turbulence of the early years of printing was superseded, after the wars of religion of the late sixteenth century, by a long period in which an increasingly powerful religious and political establishment imposed a kind of stability. Scientific or philosophical writings that ran counter to orthodox belief were routinely subjected to censorship: Descartes's works, for example, were mostly published outside France. However, dissident voices could also find forms of public expression. An avalanche of satirical and propaganda pamphlets appeared in the mid-seventeenth century in the context of the Fronde; in this period, too, the forerunners of the modern newspaper began to appear in the form of broadsheets and gazettes. These developments were crucial for the dissemination of heterodox and dissident ideas in the eighteenth century. Censorship continued to be widely imposed, but the *philosophes* and their allies—often operating from outside France— became adept at using the spread of print culture for their own ends, whether in barely disguised satirical form in Voltaire's *contes* or in the *Encyclopédie*, whose articles conceal explosive ideas beneath apparently bland titles. How far these intellectual uses of print prepared the ground for the Revolution is still a matter for debate; recent work suggests that another and perhaps more pervasive factor in this historically critical shift was the popular press. However one looks at it, the powers and constraints of print are central to the story of early modern culture.

We may now focus on the broad outlines of literary production in France from the invention of printing to the French Revolution. Early modern literature inherited a complex mapping of literary genres from medieval writing and progressively superimposed on it generic models derived—or rederived—from classical antiquity and Italy. The elaborate forms of religious drama and the farces that were popular in the later Middle Ages were not replaced overnight by humanist reconstructions of tragedy and comedy on ancient models, but such experiments were the forerunners of a crucial shift in the nature and status of theatre in France. Similarly, in the 1540s, a newly imported love poetry in the mode of the Italian lyric poet Petrarch (1304–74) was grafted on to the courtly love poetry that had existed in France long before Petrarch's day, creating fresh opportunities for French poets. The sixteenth century was indeed remarkably rich in poetry, with wave upon wave of poets who made a distinctive and lasting contribution to the history of French verse: this was the period in which the sonnet, made famous by Petrarch, was naturalized in France, while the native alexandrine, thus called because it had been used in the medieval *Roman d'Alexandre*, began to come into its own as a metre peculiarly suited to the rhythms of the evolving French language.

All the established genres, including epic and drama, were perceived as varieties of poetry throughout the early modern period. Rhetorical theory recognized a hierarchy of prose styles and forms from letter-writing to formal declamation, but the kinds of prose fiction we now regard as central to literature had no recognized status before they began to be theorized in the later seventeenth century. Even then, the novel and its forerunners were regarded as less serious genres, serving primarily as entertainment. However, despite the suspicion that hung over prose fiction in some high-culture circles, readers consumed it in ever-increasing quantities: the *nouvelle* and the *conte* (varieties of short story) were popular throughout the early modern period, and extended prose narratives steadily gained ground from the beginning of the seventeenth century.

The literature of the 'long sixteenth century' (say 1470–1630) is marked by the variety and vigour of its experimentation. Not only do writers try out every existing form and discover new ones (the invention of the 'essay' by Montaigne is the most striking of these), they also have few inhibitions about mixing generic and stylistic levels in a single work. Rabelais's comic fictions combine elements from epic (medieval and classical), romance, popular story, classical satire, farce, and many other literary modes, so that they are impossible to assign to any single generic category. Marguerite de Navarre's *Heptaméron* embeds the *nouvelle*, both Italian and French, within the newly fashionable dialogue form derived mainly from recent Italian handbooks of courtly conduct, thus producing a new variant of the long-standing *querelle des femmes*. And Montaigne's *Essais* are a model of what is often in this period called a *mélange*, a kind of writing that embraces many different themes and is open-ended in construction. The unresolved character of much sixteenth-century writing is a consequence not only of restless experimentation but also of a predominant taste for richness and abundance: leading humanists—particularly Erasmus—exploited the notion of the 'copious style' (*copia*) from Latin rhetorical theory, and this preference seems to have caught on among vernacular writers also. Ronsard, the most prolific French poet before the nineteenth century, experimented across the whole stylistic and generic range, explicitly advertising the richness and variety of his output, and not a few others—including the epic Protestant poets d'Aubigné and Du Bartas—emulated him.

During and after the widespread disruption caused by the wars of religion, tastes and cultural patterns show signs of significant mutation. This is a period which is difficult to characterize owing to the sheer diversity of its literary production. One may nevertheless trace the emergence of a new literary economy which corresponds broadly to the increasing power and confidence of the court as a cultural as well as a political centre. The prestige of humanist studies as a prerequisite of literary production begins gradually to wane; whether in prose or in verse, writers become less eager to advertise their classical learning in the form of *recherché* vocabulary, esoteric mythological figures, quotation, and allusion. The linguistic and stylistic norm moves from richness of texture and prolixity towards lucidity, accessibility, and control. Descartes's transparent and economical prose, reflecting his preoccupation with clarity of thought, has sometimes been regarded as a turning point, the founding gesture of a new rationalizing aesthetic, but it is rather a symptom of changes which had been prepared long since and which are crystallized at precisely the same moment in the founding of the Académie Française. By about 1640, Ronsard's poetry is perceived as ridiculously pretentious and pedantic; by 1674, Boileau in his *Art poétique*, speaking as it were from the summit of Parnassus, is able to trace a concise history of the progress of French poetry from barbaric disorder to the new age of reason and taste, conveniently heralded at the beginning of the seventeenth century by Malherbe (Boileau's phrase 'Enfin Malherbe vint' has become a notorious commonplace of French literary history).

A firm hierarchy of genres is established, each respecting its own level and register on a model analogous to the structures of socio-political organization and control. The prominence of theatre as a publicly sponsored art form, endorsed by the emphasis on tragedy in Aristotle's *Poetics*, gives tragedy undisputed status as the noblest genre, rigorously separating it from its junior counterpart, high comedy. Poets with any ambition invest their creative energies in dramatic verse: no one reads epic, and lyric poetry is now regarded as a minor social art. La Fontaine's *Adonis*, a short mythological narrative poem of unparalleled elegance, is a special case; so, equally, are his better-known *Fables*, which forge a distinctive poetic idiom from the politest register of everyday speech traversed by all kinds of parodic idiolect. Yet the *Fables* are also an exemplary instance of a literary form that derives its purpose from a social *milieu* deeply preoccupied with the uses of language. Seen from this angle, they belong generically with the works of the so-called *moralistes* (a term invented in later times), writers who reflect on human behaviour, ethics, and psychology without falling into the rhetoric of didacticism. The later seventeenth-century moralists prefer short, epigrammatic forms: La Rochefoucauld's *Maximes* and La Bruyère's *Caractères*, like La Fontaine's *Fables*, are presented as collections of easily consumable fragments, ready to be absorbed once more into the witty conversations from which they emerged.

The preference for concise, coherent forms also produces an important mutation in prose fiction. The romances which were popular in the earlier seventeenth century, and which lent themselves to endless possibilities of further *salon* conversation, are superseded by the *nouvelle historique*, set in recent history and focusing on the love affairs of the court. The question whether this mutation, of which Madame de Lafayette's *La Princesse de Clèves* is the most celebrated example, anticipates the emergence of the novel as we know it, will be considered later; meanwhile, the fact that such *nouvelles* attracted enormous quantities of critical discussion turning most often on questions of *vraisemblance* shows that the generic features of tragedy could be extended to prose narrative, giving it a new and more elevated status in the hierarchy of literary forms.

The normative aesthetic which was championed by Boileau and which as its keynote flaunted a reverence for Greek and Latin antiquity, flourished from the 1660s to the 1680s. Its heyday coincided with the moment when the abolutism of Louis XIV was at its zenith to produce the 'Golden Age' that nationalistic literary historians of later generations celebrated as the most perfect realization of the French native spirit and of the French language. But it has often been pointed out that in many ways the coherence and supremacy of this aesthetic is only a mirage. Corneille's plays fit uneasily into the prescriptive Aristotelian poetics which became progressively institutionalized during his lifetime, yet they continued to be popular in the period of Boileau and Racine. *Timocrate*, a so-called *tragédie à fin heureuse* composed by Corneille's younger brother Thomas, has always been regarded as marginal even though it was one of the most popular plays of the later seventeenth century. Similarly, the blockbuster 'heroic novels' of Mademoiselle de Scudéry, published around 1650, were scorned by many critics of the next generation, but they did not become extinct overnight, and Madame de Lafayette's *Zaïde* is a romance with a complex and exotic plot rather than one of the newly fashionable *nouvelles historiques*.

Taste for extravagant spectacles was insatiable in the circles that could afford them, and was at its height at the very moment when Boileau produced his *Art poétique*. Louis XIV laid on complex theatrical and mythological displays in the palace of Versailles and its gardens, with instrumental music, singing and dancing; one of them, a *tragédie-ballet* called *Psyché*, was composed jointly by Molière, Corneille, Quinault, and the Italian court composer Lully. This was also the period in which opera, invented in Florence towards 1600, came to France. In the light of such cultural phenomena, the apparently austere aesthetic of, say, Racine's *Bérénice* looks like a special case rather than the keystone of the monument.

These manifestations of a taste which had little to do with Greek and Latin paradigms, with fine generic distinctions, or with authoritarian rule-making, emerged in the later seventeenth century as a revisionist aesthetic constructed around the concept of the 'modern' and admitting the need for change and innovation. Promoted vigorously by women patrons and writers in the *salon* culture which forms a persistent thread in the seventeenth-century weave, drawing also on the Cartesian call for a *tabula rasa* (clean sweep) of existing habits of thought, and on the interest in science which was beginning to spread in polite society, this cluster of literary conceptions gains confidence as the personal power of Louis XIV and the prestige of the inner court circle begin to decline, and may be seen as the forerunner of many eighteenth-century developments.

In the period between the death of Louis XIV and the Revolution of 1789, the normative aesthetic which is generally referred to by literary historians as 'Classicism' continued to flourish (the term 'neo-Classicism' is sometimes used to describe its eighteenth-century variants). The preference for tragedy continues in full spate: this was the genre in which Voltaire wished above all to excel, a fact which has never ceased to disconcert future generations. Lyric poetry remains a minor genre (although dozens of *salon* poets subscribe to it), while long verse narratives and didactic poems are still cultivated by writers of Voltaire's stature (*La Henriade, Poème sur le désastre de Lisbonne*).

Yet a retrospective view of French literary history marks these phenomena, however vigorous, however self-evident they may have appeared at the time, as regressive; they are features which, within a few decades, will move to the edge of the literary map. To us, the eighteenth century is a period of innovation, of intense debate, of controversy and dissension: the so-called 'Enlightenment' is the very embodiment of an early modern world about to come of age. Many of the works that are now regarded as representative of the period were in their day published clandestinely or anonymously and attracted censorship or at least official disapproval: Montesquieu's *Lettres persanes* and Voltaire's *Lettres philosophiques* and *contes*, Rousseau's *Discours sur l'Inégalité* and *Du contrat social*, the *Encyclopédie*, many of Diderot's works, Beaumarchais's *Le Mariage de Figaro*, Laclos's *Liaisons dangereuses*. The aesthetic of such works, in so far as it is possible to speak of a single aesthetic across such a wide range, represents a fine balance between communicability and indirection. Sensitive ideological targets are discreetly veiled (while always guessable); disturbing new ideas are advanced by means of humorous displacement, embodiment in narrative form, or complex analogies. But the point is always to *advertise* new ways of thinking, and this determines over and over again the mode of presentation: the letter-form in particular, used earlier for polemical purposes by Pascal, comes into its own as a disarmingly accessible, quasi-oral medium that carries a potent explosive charge. Dialogue has a similar function, whether in philosophical dialogues such as Diderot's or in narratives like Voltaire's *contes*, where the characters enact a questioning of conventional ideas and practices, institutionalized doctrines, and every kind of authority. The key *persona* of eighteenth-century satirical letters, dialogues and fictions, from the *Lettres persanes* via *Candide* and *L'Ingénu* to *La Religieuse*, is a naïve observer who sees the world without its veil of cultural and intellectual prejudice; the matrix of eighteenth-century communicative enquiry is the *Encyclopédie*, a gigantic collaborative undertaking which, in order to achieve commercial success and maximal ideological diffusion, required a large literate public and a printing industry serving that public's needs.

Similar conditions surround the gradual transmutation of longer narrative fiction. Subject matter is seldom drawn now from the charmed circle of romance or of the court world. Whether in updated versions of the picaresque, in shorter first-person narratives like *Manon Lescaut*, or in the ubiquitous letter-novel, the settings are more often those of everyday life; characters are drawn from the bourgeoisie or the minor aristocracy; plots give rise to moral and psychological crises not too far removed from the possible experience of the ever-increasing reading public. In Madame de Graffigny's best-selling *Lettres d'une péruvienne*, the apparently exotic situation of the Peruvian letter-writer promotes relativizing comment on the French scene in a manner wholly consistent with the epistolary works of the *philosophes*.

Prose narrative also allows the taste of this period for exacerbated sensibility, visible also in the dramatic genres, ample room to expand: it seems that weeping became an especially intense pleasure in the age of Rousseau. Alongside *sensibilité*, often inextricably linked with it, eroticism penetrates the fabric of eighteenth-century narrative, whether disguised by a thin veil of moral reprobation (as in *Manon Lescaut*) or openly asserting itself in the novels of Crébillon fils and of Restif de La Bretonne. Voltaire, the champion of reason and enlightenment, was capable of writing semi-pornographic verse. The marquis de Sade—whose work was written during and after the Revolution—is in a category of his own, but the note of excess had already been sounded in the permissive society of pre-Revolutionary days, despite the institutionalized disapproval exercised by the censors. Besides, Sade also illustrates the strange mixture of philosophical reflection and dark desire which recurs in less violent forms in so many works of the period.

Finally, major developments are taking place in theatre. Alongside neo-Classical tragedy and comedy, a new genre comes into being: the *drame*, written in prose and focusing on social and psychological problems in bourgeois families. Although a number of leading writers—Graffigny, Diderot, Sedaine, Beaumarchais—experimented with this genre, their plays have never been successful on the stage. Yet the *drame* is a barometer of aesthetic and social change in the second half of the eighteenth century, and it also anticipates important nineteenth-century European developments, including *verismo* and the theatre of Ibsen and Chekhov.

These, then, are the major questions posed by the early modern period of French literature: does the phrase 'early modern' have a sense other than that of a convenient label to be applied more or less neutrally to a large and diverse segment of literary culture? What major changes take place during the period? Are they only apparent retrospectively to a modern gaze that knows what is going to happen next and reads the story accordingly? Are literary texts in any sense the vehicles—rather than merely the reflectors—of large-scale shifts in the forms of knowledge and understanding that are in place at particular moments during the period? What is the value of early modern literature as a means of access to history? Such questions can never be fully answered, least of all within the compass of a short history. They can, however, provide a frame of reference within which particular moments and texts may be more closely examined without premature foreclosure of the broader contexts and issues.

The Period in Close-Up

FROM BURGUNDY TO THE FRENCH COURT:
JEAN LEMAIRE DE BELGES

Between Villon, who was writing in the mid-fifteenth century, and Rabelais, whose *Pantagruel* first appeared in 1532, there are no French writers whose names are widely remembered. During this period, the rich and powerful culture of Burgundy is in decline, while the political and economic shift which, by the third decade of the sixteenth century, brings about a concentration of affluence and cultural resources at the French royal court and in the trading city of Lyons, is still in process.

The career of the versatile poet and chronicler Jean Lemaire de Belges, who might well have achieved lasting fame in different circumstances, belongs to and illustrates this phase. His wittiest poem, *L'Épître de l'Amant Vert*, was immediately successful and was read appreciatively in many European courts. Composed in 1505, when Lemaire was working under the patronage of Marguerite d'Autriche, daughter of the Holy Roman Emperor Maximilian, it takes the form of a kind of suicide note in verse written by a pet parrot of Marguerite who was eaten by a dog while she was away from home. The 'Green Lover', parroting the laments of innumerable pseudonymous courtly lovers, relates how he fell in love with Marguerite, was admitted to her most intimate company—even to her bedchamber where he watched her undress—and suffered such pangs of unrequited love that he decided to throw himself into the jaws of the dog. One of the interesting things about this poem is that it combines native French conventions (courtly love, parody, verse-form, and style) with a newly revived classical model, the verse epistles attributed to ancient heroines in Ovid's *Heroïdes*. Another is that it shows a certain multicultural awareness: the parrot, who comes from Ethiopia, learns the languages of the imperial court in order to integrate himself into the elite culture of Europe.

Jean Lemaire was not a foreigner in that milieu, but he was certainly mobile. His career took him from the Burgundian territory of Flanders, where he was born, via Savoy (at the time of the parrot episode, Marguerite was the newly widowed spouse of the duke of

Savoy), to the entourage of Anne de Bretagne, who was married to the French king Louis XII. Brittany was one of the last independent duchies to be integrated into the kingdom of France, and Anne had wanted to preserve this independence by marrying her daughter Claude into the imperial family. In the end, however, she was obliged to marry her to the young prince François de Valois, who became king of France in 1515. By the time Lemaire worked for her, this outcome was in practice inevitable, so that the later part of his career is situated on the very threshold of François I's construction of a cultural milieu corresponding to the newly centralized political identity of the French nation.

A snapshot of the literary modes with which Lemaire would have been familiar will be helpful here. He was the godson of the major poet Jean Molinet, who enjoyed the patronage of Charles the Bold, duke of Burgundy. Molinet was a chronicler, as were many other poets employed by noble patrons wishing to bolster their claims to permanence and power; similarly, his long allegorical poem *Le Trône d'Honneur*, lamenting the death of Charles the Bold, shares with other funerary poems the function of mediating a crisis in a noble house. Lemaire too will write substantial allegorical poems on the death of patrons, or husbands of patrons. At the other end of the scale, Molinet used the so-called *formes fixes* which had become fashionable in the later Middle Ages, such as the *rondeau*, the *virelai*, the *chant royal* and the *ballade*. Poets were currently developing these structures in increasingly complex ways, displaying considerable virtuosity in metre and—especially—rhyme: a taste for intricate form seems to have been fostered by the culture particular to the courts of Burgundy, with their love of elaborate and finely wrought artefacts. It is in this period and this milieu also that the 'art' (we would nowadays say 'theory') of vernacular rhetoric was most intensively explored: Molinet himself, for example, produced an *Art de rhétorique*.

Towards the end of the fifteenth century, however, the word 'rhetoric' was beginning to acquire other—not necessarily incompatible—associations. Jean Lemaire had studied in Paris at a time when the *humanistae* (also known as *poetae*, 'poets') were promoting a pedagogy based on a correct and elegant use of Latin and a scrupulously philological study of classical Latin literature. This programme was initially introduced unofficially alongside the logic-based pedagogy of the scholastic philosophers and theologians who had long dominated the scene at the University of Paris. But it was inevitable that the two approaches would come into conflict, especially as the *humanistae* were contemptuous of the heavily adapted, modernized Latin used by the scholastics as a medium for their programme of studies. This story will continue for a very long time: it is dramatized in comic mode by Rabelais, it recurs in a wholly different form in Montaigne's *Essais*, and traces of it can still be detected in Pascal's satire of Sorbonne pedantry in the *Lettres provinciales*.

For the young Lemaire, however, the handbooks of Latin grammar and rhetoric produced by the newly established Paris printing presses must have provided a refreshing new angle on the vernacular rhetoric practised in his day and led him to experiment with a variety of styles in French poetry and prose. The allegorical landscape and building of his *Temple d'honneur et de vertu*, commemorating the death of Pierre de Bourbon, is like that of many other contemporary poets, except that it is written in a style that shows clear signs of an attempt to emulate the textures of classical Latin. The *Illustrations de Gaule et Singularitez de Troye*, an ambitious legendary history tracing the origins of Gaul to a time before the Trojan War, likewise has much in common with medieval narratives blending the matter of Rome with the matter of France, yet its language and iconography are also more directly indebted to classical models.

This celebration of the antiquity of French power and culture belongs to the later phase of Lemaire's career, when he was working for the French monarchy; at about the same time he also acted as a mouthpiece for an early form of Gallicanism, that is to say the relative independence of the French Church from Rome (not to be confused with the schismatic Anglicanism adopted by Henry VIII of England some thirty years later). His *Concorde des deux langaiges* of 1511 defends yet another nationalistic cause, the value of French culture in relation to Italian. The fifteenth century is the period of the great flowering of Italian art and literature which set in motion the European Renaissance. Italian *humanistae* had come to lecture in Paris in the later part of the century, and the writings of Petrarch and Boccaccio had been known in France since the late fourteenth century; other factors which served to bring the two cultures into contact with one another were trade, especially via Lyons, and the intermittent military campaigns of Charles VIII and Louis XII in Italy. The opening part of the *Concorde* celebrates Italian love poetry: Petrarch features prominently, and this part of the work is written in *terza rima*, the verse-form adopted by Dante in the *Divine Comedy*. The second part, by contrast, leads the reader out of the 'Temple de Vénus' to the 'Temple de Minerve', the more sober domain of French literary culture, where historiography and moralizing writing have pride of place; here, in an oddly prophetic gesture, Lemaire opts for the alexandrine metre. No one could have foreseen at that time that this metre would later achieve canonic status, yet Lemaire seems already to want to promote it as a characteristically French form. In these ways, on the threshold of the sixteenth century, French culture and the French language begin to assert themselves on the international stage as vehicles of nationhood, rather than as local manifestations of a European-wide cultural network.

RABELAIS: *PANTAGRUEL* AND *GARGANTUA*

By the early 1530s, when Rabelais's first comic fictions were published, the scene is shifting again. A new wave of religious reform is gaining adherents in France, including the king's sister Marguerite de Navarre; François I himself, although distracted by continuing conflict with the Emperor Charles V, is encouraging the intellectual and pedagogical priorities of the humanists by acting as patron to leading scholars such as Guillaume Budé and by establishing royal 'readerships' in Latin, Greek, and Hebrew, an initiative which was to develop into the Collège de France (see Figure 7, p. 103). Rabelais was well placed to appreciate these developments. He had spent the earlier part of his life in monastic orders, where he had displeased his superiors by acquiring the fundamental skills of humanism (in particular, a knowledge of Greek), and subsequently gained dispensation from holy orders so that he could study medicine at Montpellier. He then moved to Lyons, where he practised medicine and gave lectures on ancient medical texts. In a famous letter to Erasmus, dated 1532, he speaks of his admiration for the great Dutch scholar, who was both setting the agenda for the development of humanism in northern Europe and advocating a thorough-going but non-schismatic reform of the Church.

Rabelais's comic fiction, written over a period of twenty years, draws on almost every literary and cultural source available to a writer in the second quarter of the sixteenth century and is difficult to classify. In the broadest possible terms, it may be regarded as a heavily mutated descendant of Jean de Meun's *Roman de la rose*, being a narrativized compendium of the intellectual preoccupations and anxieties of its day. Like the *Rose*, which was still being read at the time, it is also a text which connects the mind (sixteenth-century writers would have said 'the soul') with the everyday needs and desires of the body. At the same time, it belongs to a later phase of European fiction which includes Ariosto and Cervantes, and which gives a new impetus to the still-popular genres of medieval epic and romance narrative by treating them in an exaggerated or burlesque mode (see below, pp. 164–5).

This is especially true of the first two books, *Pantagruel* (1532) and *Gargantua* (1534/5), each of which takes the reader through the birth, early feats, education, and heroic military exploits of its giant hero. *Pantagruel* follows openly in the footsteps of *Les Chroniques gargantuines*, a popular account of the astonishing deeds of the giant Gargantua: Pantagruel, an invention of Rabelais's, is Gargantua's son. *Gargantua*—the second book in order of composition but the first according to the narrative sequence—retells the story of the father. Rabelais enriches the entertainment with elements drawn from the *fabliaux,* anti-feminist literature, late medieval sermons, the oral skills of the mountebank, and perhaps above all farce: he himself acted in farces while a student at Montpellier, and dialogue is central to his comic scenarios. Each of the giants is paired with a wayward and resourceful sidekick: the trickster Panurge becomes Pantagruel's perpetual companion, while Gargantua gives the energetic lapsed monk Frère Jean his protection and favour.

However, while the *Chroniques gargantuines* had no intellectual pretensions, *Pantagruel* and *Gargantua* bristle with sophisticated textual allusions and complex representations of controversial issues. Materials that any French reader of the 1530s would easily recognize are fused with fashionably erudite elements drawn from the satirical fantasies of the ancient Greek writer Lucian, the writings of Erasmus, and the *Utopia* of the English humanist Thomas More. Education becomes a major issue: the giants are exposed to suitably hyperbolic versions of the new humanist pedagogy, and in *Gargantua* this programme is used to rescue the young giant-prince from an interminable and stultifying education by caricatural Sorbonne theologians. The obscurities of the legal process are sent up at length in a major episode of *Pantagruel*. Battles between the giants and grotesque opponents feature as a site of reflection on the ethics and conduct of war. Above all, perhaps, religious controversies are engaged with at every turn: monasticism is subjected to a corrosive critique in *Gargantua*, and becomes the pretext for the construction of the utopian Abbey of Thélème, one of the most famous episodes of these earlier books.

Gargantua is regarded by some as a more intellectually satisfying rewriting of *Pantagruel*, since its political and religious references are more acutely contemporary and developed at greater length. Yet this interpretation amputates the work of its prime source of energy, the presence of the expanding giant bodies which are virtually metaphors of Rabelais's own new-found mastery of comic fiction. In fact, he delivered some of his most brilliant scenes on the very threshold of his writing career: Pantagruel's first encounter with Panurge centres on the new arrival's astounding polyglot display and hence on issues such as the rise of national languages in Europe and the nature of language itself; towards the end of the book, another encounter is staged when the narrator ventures into Pantagruel's mouth and meets a native of the country he finds there, who thinks that his world is the 'old' one, and that those who come from outside belong to some strange 'new world'.

Taken together, these two episodes suggest a penetrating insight into the changing spatial and political horizons of the earlier sixteenth century: Rabelais is constantly aware of time-frames and time-shifts. Gargantua's letter to Pantagruel (*Pantagruel* 8) refers to the dramatic cultural transformation which has taken place within his lifetime: like many humanist propagandists, he caricatures the late Middle Ages as a time of 'Gothic darkness' dispelled by the light of the new learning. The educational episodes of *Gargantua* re-enact this shift, while Thélème belongs to a kind of time-warp of its own. Thus the cultural mixture of which Rabelais's work is made up, the old and the new, the popular and the erudite, becomes the very emblem of a mutation in process. It is a work that refuses to be classified by monolithic period terms such as 'Renaissance' and 'Reformation', but which yet provides crucial evidence of what those terms could mean when broken down and dissolved in the substance of everyday culture.

RELIGIOUS CONTROVERSY AND LITERATURE: THE CIRCLE OF MARGUERITE DE NAVARRE

We turn now to the role of the French court as a mediator of literary culture in the reign of François I. The story begins and ends with questions of religion, although many other factors are also in play. Already in the early works of Rabelais one can see clear signs of support for the rapidly expanding group of moderate French reformers known as 'evangelicals' (*évangéliques*). Their main contention was that the Bible (especially the New Testament), not the abstruse formulations of the medieval theologians, constituted the true source of Christian faith and that it should be made widely available through translations, paraphrases, sermons, and other kinds of religious literature. They also called in question the practice of observances, rules laid down by the Church for the conduct of the faithful, which had in many cases become purely mechanical: of these, the prohibition of meat during Lent aroused the most controversy.

The success of the evangelicals was such that the theological establishment, represented primarily by the Sorbonne, had already begun to take severe repressive measures. A religious poem by Marguerite de

Navarre, printed in 1531, was condemned for its potentially Lutheran theology; those responsible for the condemnation were in turn accused of *lèse-majesté*. The scene is set for two decades in which Marguerite gathers round her at court a circle of writers and eminent figures sympathetic to her cause while the Sorbonne marshals its opposition.

One indicator of the rapidly changing situation in these decades is the emergence of a young scholar called Jean Calvin who began his career as a *humanista* but was drawn towards the more radical end of the evangelical spectrum. In 1536, he dedicated to François I a Latin treatise which he later translated into French under the title *Institution de la religion chrestienne*. This is the first extensive work of theology written in French, and is a powerful literary work in its own right: it is written in tough, lucid prose with a strong biblical flavour. Within a few years, Calvin had left France with some of his supporters for Geneva, where he set up a new political order based on an austere reformed Church. This clearly schismatic move constituted a direct challenge both to Rome and to the Sorbonne, and made it difficult for the more moderate French evangelicals to pursue their programme of non-schismatic reform. The Sorbonne began to draw up lists of prohibited books (Rabelais's were among them). In 1545, the Council of Trent was called in an attempt to resolve the European-wide religious crisis, but the hawks rapidly gained the upper hand and the Council ended, some twenty years later, by reformulating traditional Roman theology in such a way that it was definitively incompatible with the theology of the various reformist sects. François I died in 1547 and was succeeded by the orthodox hardliner Henri II; Marguerite de Navarre herself died two years later, bringing the era of moderate evangelical reform in France to an end.

Meanwhile, however, Marguerite had presided over a richly productive literary scene which bears traces at every point of her influence. We shall return to secular poetry later, but it is essential to mention in this context the most widely disseminated poetic work of the sixteenth century, Marot's paraphrases of some fifty psalms. The psalter was completed later by the Calvinist poet Théodore de Bèze, set to music and sung by French Protestants everywhere. Marot's style, deliberately plain and unpolished, reflects the predominant aesthetic of Marguerite's circle. This is perhaps surprising at first sight: was the reign of François I not the embodiment of the French Renaissance, with its dazzling architecture (the châteaux of Fontainebleau and of the Loire valley were begun at this time), its court humanists, and its enthusiasm for Italian painting, poetry and manners? But it is important to emphasize that these two very different strands coincided in the

1530s and 1540s and were often fused, defining a distinctive and many-sided cultural milieu.

The most striking example of this phenomenon is the *Heptaméron*, a collection of stories commonly attributed to Marguerite herself, although it was not published until after her death and no direct evidence of her authorship has survived. Its prologue describes the way the project was conceived by leading members of the royal family as a French rival to Boccaccio's *Decameron* (of which Marguerite had also commissioned a new translation). As in its Italian predecessor, ten noble men and women courtiers were each to tell a story a day for ten days. At the death of Marguerite, however, the project remained incomplete. The *Heptaméron* consists of just over seventy stories linked by the conversations of the story-tellers (*devisants*). This feature, too, was borrowed from Boccaccio, but Marguerite transformed it by increasing enormously the amount of space devoted to the conversations and raising through them a wide range of serious topics revolving round the central theme of love and marital relations. Many of the stories read like their late medieval forerunners, and some of them are in fact refurbished versions of existing stories (from the *Cent Nouvelles nouvelles*, for example; see above, p. 85): they abound in intriguing, amusing, and often highly improbable situations which the characters—lecherous or brutish husbands, adulterous wives, unscrupulous monks—either manage to get out of by clever ruses or succumb to catastrophically. Many others, however, concern pairs of lovers who show varying degrees of constancy in love; these are often tragic in outcome. There is a good deal of violence: frustrated lovers resort to desperate behaviour (rape is a recurrent motif), as do cuckolded husbands and wronged wives.

The *devisants* agree at the outset that their stories, unlike Boccaccio's, will be true. We do not have to take this claim in its most literal sense, but its metaphorical sense is crucial to the nature of the collection. In Marguerite's circle of evangelicals, the plain truth was valued above beauty of form and style, and the touchstone of that truth was Scripture. Thus in the *Heptaméron*, each day of storytelling begins with a reading from the New Testament by the oldest of the *devisants*, a woman called Oisille. The Bible is also often quoted in the course of the conversations and even in the stories themselves. The effect is that religious questions, both ethical and theological, are brought into direct contact with everyday human experience rather than being restricted to a special domain monopolized by priests and the monastic orders. Conversely, the psychology, morality, and metaphysics of love, which had formed the substance of the courtly love lyric, of medieval romance, and of the *querelle des femmes* (see above, pp. 87–9), are revived here in a new form.

One of the ingredients in this new mixture is the use of neo-Platonist themes and images. Platonist thought, already a persistent strand of medieval philosophy, had been revived in late fifteenth-century Florence as a direct challenge to the Aristotelian logic-based philosophy of the scholastics: it forms an important source of inspiration for Renaissance fine art as well as literature. In the first half of the sixteenth century, it was transmitted to France primarily through Italian handbooks of courtly behaviour in dialogue form, which treat the etiquette and ethics of love as a central preoccupation of the refined courtier. The expansion of the storytellers' dialogue in the *Heptaméron* owes a good deal to these 'courtesy books', some of which were translated into French by members of Marguerite's circle.

This new strain of neo-Platonist thought, which stresses the perfectibility of human nature and which valorizes love and art as stepping-stones to contemplation of the highest forms of spiritual experience, is one of the distinctive markers of the 'Renaissance'. Marguerite's spokeswoman Parlamente draws on it—most famously in the discussion after story 19—to counter the arguments usually put forward by the male *devisants* in favour of a purely sexual view of love; Jean de Meun's *Rose* is standing in the wings here, and is indeed quoted in the discussion following story 9. But Parlamente's references are always cautious, subjecting neo-Platonist arguments to a pessimistic evangelical theology of human fallibility, and the characters in the stories who rely on their own powers to achieve high moral aims invariably come to grief.

These convergences and divergences may finally be illustrated by a comparison between two utopian texts, the opening scene of the *Heptaméron* and Rabelais's Thélème. At the end of *Gargantua*, the giant rewards Frère Jean by endowing for him an abbey conceived as the antithesis of everything that the monastic system stood for: rules, rigorous observances, chastity, poverty, and obedience. In place of the ignorant and ill-bred who, according to this account, were the usual candidates for monastic life, Thélème welcomes the well-off, the well-born, and the well-educated and offers them a luxury residence built on the lines of a Loire château. Men and women live together in harmony; they have books, music, art, games and sports, good food and drink, and above all *freedom*: they can leave whenever they want, particularly in order to get married. The motto of the Abbey is 'Fay ce que vouldras' ('Do as you will'). This moral freedom is possible because the Thelemites—being well born, well educated, etc.—have a natural instinct prompting them to good and discouraging them from vice. Each thinks first of the good of the others; self-love is banished in favour of the evangelical principle 'love your neighbour'. This extraordinarily optimistic vision is of course utopian: it is a vision, not a model of the world as it is. But it *is* optimistic, drawing on an Erasmian evangelism which places faith in human capacity and allows a full harmonization of ethical values with aesthetic ones; this is a beautiful place full of beautiful people. Marguerite's elite group of storytellers are of course also, socially speaking, beautiful people, and they too gather in an abbey, marginalizing the rather unsavoury abbot and his monks: they attend mass, but their Scripture readings are more relevant to their discussions of human behaviour. Yet this utopia is temporary and fragile, a haven in a threatening world. Some of the *devisants*, despite their noble birth, are far from being paragons of moral virtue. And the prologue makes it clear that 'gens de lettres' (scholars and humanists) have been excluded from the group, lest their learning and love of beautiful style should get in the way of the truth. Both of these texts belong to the French Renaissance; both are deeply marked by evangelical ideas; but they combine and represent these elements in entirely different ways, and one should be careful to avoid using period labels in such a way that they erase that difference.

RABELAIS'S LATER WORKS

The difference between *Gargantua* and the *Heptaméron* owes something, no doubt, to the increasingly threatening situation in which moderate reformers found themselves in the 1540s. Rabelais too had his problems. His exemplary patron Guillaume Du Bellay died in 1543 (an event referred to twice in the later books), his writings were subjected to censorship, he was often constrained to take cover abroad, and there were depressing examples of what could happen to scholars who fell foul of the Sorbonne: the truculent humanist and printer Estienne Dolet was burnt at the stake in 1546. It was in that same year that Rabelais published his *Tiers Livre*, which he dedicated to Marguerite de Navarre. His own name now appears on the title-page, replacing the earlier comic pseudonym Alcofrybas Nasier, and the prologue refers to an unspecified disaster in which the author lost everything but his book. The giant stories have disappeared; Panurge is now in the foreground, and most of the book consists of a series of episodes in which he consults experts for advice on whether or not he should marry. This is the most intellectual of Rabelais's books. Essentially, it explores the sources of human knowledge, from divination and dream-interpretation via the traditional branches of learning (theology, law, medicine) to the divine insight of fools: in some ways, the *Tiers Livre* may be regarded as a profoundly transformed rewriting of Erasmus's widely read *Praise of Folly*. We are now in the fallen world outside Thélème, whose motto is reformulated in the question Pantagruel puts to the dithering Panurge: 'N'estez vous asceuré de vostre vouloir?' ('Have you no confidence in your own will?'). Unlike the Thelemites, Panurge is riddled with self-love: he is unable to interpret correctly the messages he receives from the experts because he is obsessed with his own desires. This is still very much a comedy, enacted almost entirely in dialogue form, but the comic tone is darker and less exuberant.

Two years later, a fragmentary *Quart Livre* appeared, but it was not until 1552, the year before Rabelais's death, that the complete version was published. Pantagruel and his friends have now departed on a voyage to seek the 'Holy Bottle' which may provide the definitive answer to Panurge's question. They take the north-westerly route, stopping at many exotic ports and islands, are nearly shipwrecked in a storm, hear the frozen sounds of a battle as they thaw out, are becalmed, but always sail on. When the book ends, they appear to be no closer to their goal, although a *Cinquiesme Livre* of dubious authenticity, printed some ten years later, takes them to the Holy Bottle and Panurge gets his answer. The *Quart Livre* is Rabelais's strangest and most imaginative book, full of grotesque and beautiful inventions. It is partly allegorical, staging islands of old age, malevolent figures of both Lenten fasting and gross over-eating, an erstwhile utopia now ruled over by the stomach, fanatical Papists and impoverished anti-Papists. Yet the central issue, the one that preoccupied Rabelais from beginning to end of his works, remains constant and indeed acquires new intensity in this fantastic decor: language, its sounds and textures, its capacity for carrying meaning, for deceiving, for signifying nothing, for cursing, and for bringing joy and friendship, is always present whether as theme or as medium. The comedy of language was never explored more exhaustively and inventively than in Rabelais's four books.

POETRY: (I) FROM MAROT TO LABÉ

It is customary to speak of a significant break in French literary culture in the mid-sixteenth century, and there are good reasons for this. The arrival on the scene in 1547 of Henri II and his queen Catherine, from the great Florentine family of the Medici, together with the death of Marguerite de Navarre two years later, brings to an abrupt end the court culture established by Marguerite, with its evangelical leanings and its austere aesthetic; simultaneously, Joachim Du Bellay's *Deffence et illustration de la langue françoyse* claims to make a dramatic break with the past and inaugurate a new era in French poetry. On the other hand, Henri II continued his father's ambitious architectural programme, while Catherine ensured that Italian influence remained strong. Since, moreover, the generic and formal constraints of poetry ensure continuity even at times of maximum change, it is better to consider the story of sixteenth-century French poetry as a chronological whole.

In 1532, the year that *Pantagruel* appeared, Clément Marot produced his first printed collection of verse, the *Adolescence Clémentine*; some of the poems it contains may date back to the beginning of the reign of François I. His father Jean Marot, a well-known *rhétoriqueur* poet, had been *valet de chambre* to the king; on his death in 1526, Clément had succeeded him. He also enjoyed the patronage of Marguerite de Navarre, to whom he remained closely attached until his death in 1544. The *Adolescence* includes a large number of poems in *formes fixes* (*ballades* and *rondeaux*) as well as a longer allegorical poem called *Le Temple de Cupidon*. Unlike many of the poets of the preceding generation, the younger Marot meets the demands of the *forme fixe* while sustaining a transparent poetic style close to the rhythms and vocabulary of spoken language, as in the following *rondeau*, which plays on the courtly theme of the exchange of hearts between the lover and his married mistress, and where the repeated phrase 'Toutes les nuictz' shifts in meaning at each appearance:

> Toutes les nuictz je ne pense qu'en celle,
> Qui a le Corps plus gent qu'une pucelle
> De quatorze ans, sur le poinct d'enrager,
> Et au dedans ung cueur (pour abreger)
> Autant joyeulx qu'eut oncque Damoyselle.
> Elle a beau tainct, ung parler de bon zelle,
> Et le Tetin rond comme une Grozelle.
> N'ay je donc pas bien cause de songer
>   Toutes les nuictz?
> Touchant son cueur, je l'ay en ma cordelle,
> Et son Mary n'a sinon le Corps d'elle:
> Mais toutesfois, quand il vouldra changer,
> Prenne le Cueur: et pour le soulager
> J'auray pour moy le gent Corps de la belle
>   Toutes les nuictz.

[Every night I think of nothing but her: she has a body lovelier than a 14-year-old virgin about to go wild, and inside it a heart (to cut things short) as lively as any young woman's. She has a beautiful complexion, she's an enthusiastic talker, and her breasts are as round as redcurrants. So haven't I got good reason to dream every night? As for her heart, I have it in my keeping, and her husband only has her body; all the same, if he wants to swap, he can take her heart, and to relieve him I'll have her lovely body to myself every night.]

This sexy, streetwise poem belongs to a strand of French poetry that reaches back to Villon and forward to Prévert and Brassens; but it also belongs to an age where a new-found confidence in the French language as an oral as well as a written instrument is changing the very conception of poetic form. At the court of Marguerite de Navarre, the complexity and intricacy prized in the Burgundian courts gives way to a new kind of virtuosity, characterized rather by directness and fluency.

Another major genre prominently featured in the *Adolescence* is the *chanson*: Marot had written a number of lyrics for the highly popular series of song collections printed in this period by Pierre Attaignant. Lyric poetry is still very close to music throughout the sixteenth century, even if the links are progressively loosening. The setting of poetry to pre-established musical forms had important consequences for the symmetrical patterning of the verse-form, and one should remember also that Marot's later psalm-paraphrases were designed for musical setting. The *chansons* are printed separately in the *Adolescence* as poems rather than songs; like his *rondeaux*, they show the lightness of touch which was to become his hallmark, and which is illustrated above all by his *épîtres*, quasi-fictional letters in verse-form written over a considerable span of Marot's career. These last follow the fashion set at the beginning of the century by Lemaire's *Amant Vert* poems, extending it in a virtuoso display of different voices and styles; they are also reminiscent of the letter-poems in the late medieval *dits amoureux* (see above, pp. 75–80). They enable the poet's persona to develop through the use of the first-person singular which is constitutive of the letter as a literary form; they thus belong to a rapidly expanding body of writing which will eventually include both quasi-autobiographical prose such as Montaigne's *Essais* and the letter-novel.

The *formes fixes* and the *rhétoriqueur* style are by this time beginning to look dated: in his *Art poëtique françoys* of 1548, the theorist and poet Thomas Sebillet describes the *rondeau* but says that it is no longer fashionable. One reason for the change of taste was the evangelical preference for a plain style fostered in the circle of Marguerite de Navarre. Another was the growing interest in classical models: a good deal of Latin poetry was translated into French during this period, and poets were experimenting with classical forms. Marot wrote a series of eclogues in which echoes of Virgilian pastoral are easily traceable, and some free translations of verse epigrams by the Latin poet Martial together with others of his own. These two strands are not incompatible: in keeping with the evangelical aesthetic, the poets who imitate classical models tend to avoid or play down the richer, more sensuous textures of Latin poetry. Classical forms are blended with elements from existing French traditions rather than replacing them.

This convergence of native and imported models is plainly visible in Sebillet's description of the genres and forms available to the French poet in the 1540s. His account of the epigram, for example, confirms what one would have deduced from a reading of Marot's compositions in the genre, namely that this micro-form, usually comprising eight or ten lines, was used by French poets as a vehicle for love poetry as well as for satire in the Latin mode. The *dizain*, he says, being the perfect form of the French epigram, is the equivalent of the Italian sonnet: although it only has ten lines as opposed to the fourteen prescribed for the sonnet, it has a tightly organized structure and a rigorous rhyme scheme. A number of Petrarchan sonnets had been rendered into French—by Marot among others—during the preceding decade, but the sonnet was still seen as a foreign form. Thus when Maurice Scève came to compose the first French cycle of love poetry on the model of Petrarch's *Rime*, it was the *dizain* rather than the sonnet that he chose as his medium, and in an introductory stanza, he called his poems 'épigrammes'.

Scève's *Délie* was printed in 1544, the year of Marot's death. It is a strange and dazzling collection in which the love-experience is communicated with an unparalleled intensity. This 'love-experience' is an amalgam of the courtly love tradition of unrequited or unconsummated love, the Petrarchan variant of that tradition, which attaches a single exemplary passion to the quasi-mythological figure of the beloved ('Délie' is identified with the moon-goddess Diana, born on Delos), and some elements borrowed from the neo-Platonism fashionable in France in this period. The intensity derives in part at least from the compression of the form: the language is terse, the syntax elliptical, the word-order unorthodox. Contrast, for example, this evocation of the jealous lover's plight with the racy diction of Marot's *rondeau* (above, p. 124):

> Seul avec moy, elle avec sa partie:
> Moy en ma peine, elle en sa molle couche.
> Couvert d'ennuy je me voultre en l'Ortie,
> Et elle nue entre ses bras se couche.

[Alone with myself, she with her consort; I in my torment, she in her soft bed. Covered in misery, I wallow in a bed of nettles, and she lies naked in his arms.]

Conventional figures of speech (love as a fusion of light and dark, ice and fire, life and death) are delivered with an uncompromising density, conventional similes are so impacted that they become disconcerting metaphors, as in these lines encapsulating the effects on the lover of his mistress's mood-swings:

> Tant que sur moy le tien ingrat froid dure,
> Mon espoir est denué de son herbe:
> Puis retournant le doulx Ver sans froidure
> Mon An se frise en son Avril superbe.

[While your ungrateful coldness endures, my hope is stripped bare of its grass; then, when the sweet spring returns without cold, my year curls ('puts out leaves') in its proud April.]

Scève has been compared with the English metaphysical poets; although his work is precisely defined by its own historical moment, he resembles them in his demand that poetry carry an unusually high intellectual charge. Poem after poem uses verbal means to construct a relationship between abstract and concrete, soul and body, as where Délie's return after an absence is figured in an embrace which is both sensual and spiritual, local and cosmic:

> Car en mon corps: Mon Ame, tu revins,
> Sentant ses mains, mains celestement blanches,
> Avec leurs bras mortellement divins
> L'un couronner mon col, l'aultre mes hanches.

[For into my body, my Soul, you returned, feeling her hands, hands of celestial whiteness, with their mortally divine arms, one crowning my neck, the other my waist.]

Scève belonged not to the court circle but to the erudite milieu of Lyons, where both Rabelais and Estienne Dolet had been central figures and where a good deal of prose and verse was written in humanist Latin (Scève's unusual vocabulary and word-order are often Latin-based). Highly educated women were also active in this society, as is shown by the poetry of Pernette Du Guillet, often said to be Scève's 'Délie', who died in 1545 at the age of only 25. Du Guillet's love poems are in fact similar in character to Scève's, and should be read in conjunction with the *Délie*; here, for example, is a variation on the theme of light and dark which is so obsessive in the *Délie*:

> Ja n'est besoing que plus je me soucie
> Si le jour fault, ou que vienne la nuict,
> Nuict hyvernale, et sans Lune obscurcie:
> Car tout celà certes riens ne me nuit,

> Puis que mon Jour par clarté adoulcie
> M'esclaire toute, et tant, qu'à la mynuict
> En mon esprit me faict appercevoir
> Ce que mes yeulx ne sceurent oncques veoir.

[I no longer need to care if the daylight fades or the night comes, a dark winter night with no moon; none of that, I know, can harm me, since my Daylight with its gentle radiance shines full upon me, such that at midnight it makes me perceive within my mind what my eyes could never see.]

The intricate syntax, the elisions, the compressed metaphors, the etymological word-play ('clarté/m'esclaire'), and the 'metaphysical' character of the poetic argument are all in the Scève manner. This should not, however, be taken to mean that Du Guillet is a derivative poet. The relationship between Scève and Pernette is one of equality and exchange, despite the conventionally submissive stance adopted by both poets, and constitutes a remarkable testimony to the collective making of love poetry in this period.

Louise Labé, also from Lyons, is often mentioned in the same breath as Du Guillet, but her love poetry was written a crucial few years later when Du Bellay and Ronsard had published their first cycles of Petrarchan sonnets. Her complete works, printed in 1555, carry a now celebrated preface in which she defends the right of women to acquire a serious education and to rival men in the cultural domain, the time having come 'que les severes loix des hommes n'empeschent plus les femmes de s'apliquer aus sciences et disciplines' ('when the severe laws made by men no longer prevent women from applying themselves to the various branches of knowledge'). She became something of a legend in her own time as an emancipated woman, and was condemned by Calvin and others for her sexual adventures; it seems likely, however, that the legend arose primarily from her passionate love poems, in which she adapts Petrarchan conventions to a woman's perspective and animates the sonnet form with a strikingly free and resonant voice, as in this concluding sonnet, asking other women not to judge but to understand her plight:

> Ne reprenez, Dames, si j'ay aymé:
> Si j'ay senti mile torches ardentes,
> Mile travaus, mile douleurs mordentes:
> Si en pleurant, j'ay mon tems consumé,
> Las que mon nom n'en soit par vous blamé.
> Si j'ay failli, les peines sont presentes,
> N'aigrissez point leurs pointes violentes...

[Do not reproach me, Ladies, if I have loved, if I have felt a thousand burning torches, a thousand labours, a thousand gnawing pains, if I have consumed my days in weeping: alas, let my name not be blamed by you. If I have done wrong, I suffer present torments for it: do not make their violent points still sharper.]

POETRY: (II) THE *PLÉIADE*

In 1556, Pierre de Ronsard published a poem in which the name 'la Pléiade' is used for the first time to designate the new generation of poets. The founder members of the group were Ronsard, Du Bellay, and Jean-Antoine de Baïf, who had studied together under Jean Dorat at the Collège de Coqueret in the later 1540s; membership of the group fluctuates somewhat over the years, but the term has survived and is a convenient way of referring collectively to this prolific and formative phase in the history of French poetry.

Ever since Du Bellay's *Deffence et illustration* first appeared, its claim to represent a radical new departure has been vigorously disputed. The rapidly changing scene of the 1530s and 1540s undoubtedly helped to prepare the ground for the further innovations of the Pléiade; Du Bellay differs from his predecessors not so much in advertising the value of classical and Italian models as in his wholesale rejection of native French forms. Perhaps above all it is the tone that counts here: like Rabelais's hyperbolic opposition between scholastic and humanist educational methods, Du Bellay's advertisement of ancient genres at the expense of his French predecessors creates a *perception* of change which may be overstated but does in fact help to make changes happen.

At all events, over a period of some ten years the Pléiade poets produced a fertile series of experiments in different poetic genres, from the shortest and lightest of lyrics to weighty mythological and cosmic 'hymns' and epic fragments, from odes and sonnets to tragedies. The principal motor for this enthusiasm seems to have been close encounters with Greek and Latin poetry. New editions were appearing thanks to French humanists such as Henri Estienne, and the whole antique corpus was by now becoming available for study in the University of Paris through the teaching of men like Dorat. Pléiade poetry is a direct consequence of humanist reform, uninhibited now by evangelical suspicions of erotic content or stylistic elegance, although attacks will soon come from Calvinists in Geneva and elsewhere for precisely these features. Ronsard and his fellow poets also draw on the theory of multiple imitation which had been popularized in northern Europe chiefly by Erasmus: while some humanists had advocated a purism of language and style based on a single ideal model, Erasmus insisted on the need to draw on the widest range of potential models. By assimilating these borrowed elements and 'digesting' them (this metaphor is commonly used in sixteenth-century poetics), modern writers would be able to speak with an individual voice grounded in an experience of the world and culture they lived in. Many of Ronsard's earlier poems, in particular, are extraordinary amalgams of materials culled from quite different Greek, Latin, and Italian models, creating a sense of extreme profusion and richness.

Ronsard and Du Bellay were not merely learned poets, however. They were socially and professionally ambitious, seeking a place of favour at court. Themes of patronage, and complaints about lack of it, are frequent in their poetry: it seems that Henri II was more interested in his architects than in his poets, and in jousting and hunting than in either. A whole galaxy of court figures appear in Ronsard's writing from his first major publication (four books of odes) in 1550 onwards. Often inserted into mythological scenarios that raise them to an ideal world of power, prosperity, and fame, these figures are seen reciprocally to bestow on the poet the highest dignity as creator of the nation's culture and instrument of its prestige. The ancient theory of the poet's divine inspiration, revived and Christianized by the neo-Platonists of fifteenth-century Florence and imported by French translators in the 1540s under the patronage of Marguerite de Navarre, was also appropriated by the Pléiade and advertised triumphally by Ronsard, for whom it became a central poetic theme. He clearly loved the sumptuous mythological images of transcendental energy which served as its vehicle for Renaissance painters as well as poets—the Muses in the *Ode à Michel de L'Hospital*, Bacchus in the *Hymne de Bacchus*, the four seasons in the *Hymnes des saisons*.

The elevated subject matter and allusive style favoured by the Pléiade in its earlier years were not always appreciated at court. Partly for this reason, Ronsard experimented with a 'style bas' in his love poetry of the mid-1550s, favouring pastoral themes and a more accessible diction. At exactly the same time, Du Bellay, who was at the papal court in Rome with his diplomat uncle, was writing a collection of sonnets which he called *Les Regrets*. These are poems bewailing the poet's 'exile', expressing nostalgia for France, and satirizing the decadent morals of his Roman milieu. The sense of exclusion from a familiar world, and also from the ideal poetic landscape Du Bellay had evoked in his early love-cycle *Olive*, sometimes emerges with peculiar intensity, as in this quatrain which echoes a theme made famous by Villon's 'mais où sont les neiges d'antan?' ('but where are last year's snows?'; see above, p. 94):

Où sont ces doulx plaisirs, qu'au soir soubs la nuict brune
Les Muses me donnoient, alors qu'en liberté
Dessus le verd tapy d'un rivage esquarté
Je les menois danser aux rayons de la Lune?

[Where are those sweet pleasures that the Muses used to give me in the evening, under a dusky sky, when in freedom, on the green carpet of some secluded river-bank, I led them away to dance in the moonlight?]

Yet what Du Bellay chooses to advertise in his opening sonnets is rather the 'everyday' style of this collection, his lack of pretension to the inspiration and poetic grandeur affected by Ronsard:

Je me plains à mes vers, si j'ay quelque regret,
Je me ris avec eulx, je leur dy mon secret,
Comme estans de mon cœur les plus seurs secretaires.
Aussi ne veulx-je tant les pigner & friser,
Et de plus braves noms ne les veulx desguiser,
Que de papiers journaulx, ou bien de commentaires.

[I complain to my verses, if I have some cause for sorrow; I share my mockery with them; I tell them my secrets, since they are the most trustworthy secretaries of my heart. And so I don't especially want to comb and curl them, or disguise them with more ambitious names than diary entries, or perhaps commentaries.]

At this stage in their career, both Ronsard and Du Bellay also use the letter-poem, written in the poet's name and addressed to a fellow poet or a court figure, as a vehicle for this more familiar register: one notes again here the association of the letter-form with an intimate, quasi-autobiographical use of the first person. These are all, of course, highly sophisticated literary devices, often with classical and medieval antecedents; we are not speaking here of a direct transposition into poetry of personal experience. Yet important changes occur over a long period of time in the perception of what it means to write as a unique individual, and such poetic experiments certainly provide clues to that development.

By this time, the sonnet has been thoroughly naturalized and will remain a canonic form in France. The earlier French sonnet cycles—Du Bellay's *Olive*, Ronsard's *Amours*, Louise Labé's sonnets—are written exclusively in decasyllabic metre, but by 1554 Ronsard is experimenting with the more capacious alexandrine: the *Continuation des amours* of 1555 is divided into groups of decasyllabic and alexandrine sonnets, Du Bellay's *Regrets* are exclusively in alexandrines, while both metres are used in Ronsard's *Hymnes* of 1555–6. It was believed at first that the alexandrine was suited to less elevated themes and style:

Ronsard wrote his unfinished epic *La Franciade* in decasyllables but later decided that this had been a mistake. The two large-scale poems which dominate the late sixteenth century, Agrippa d'Aubigné's *Les Tragiques* and Du Bartas's *La Sepmaine*, use the alexandrine. If the most often-quoted lines of sixteenth-century poetry—lines such as 'Heureux qui, comme Ulysse, a fait un beau voyage' ('Happy the man who, like Ulysses, has made a fine journey') from the *Regrets* and 'Cueillez dés aujourd'huy les roses de la vie' ('Don't wait till tomorrow to pick life's roses') from Ronsard's late *Sonnets pour Hélène*—are alexandrines, it is perhaps mainly because the alexandrine has since become the standard French metre.

It is impossible to illustrate in a short space the richness and diversity of styles generated by the great outburst of poetic energies in this period. Many of the best poems achieve their effect cumulatively, and many are also highly allusive and thus require detailed explanation. One sonnet in particular stands out, however, as a paradigm of what the Pléiade poets at their best were capable of. This is the celebrated elegy on the death of Marie, which Ronsard apparently wrote to mourn the mistress of Henri d'Anjou (later Henri III), but which he eventually included in the cycle of poems dedicated to the Marie of his 'second book' of love poems:

> Comme on voit sur la branche au mois de May la rose
> En sa belle jeunesse, en sa premiere fleur,
> Rendre le ciel jaloux de sa vive couleur,
> Quand l'Aube de ses pleurs au poinct du jour l'arrose:
> La grace dans sa fueille, et l'amour se repose,
> Embasmant les jardins et les arbres d'odeur:
> Mais batue ou de pluye, ou d'excessive ardeur,
> Languissante elle meurt fueille à fueille déclose.
> Ainsi en ta premiere et jeune nouveauté,
> Quand la terre et le ciel honoroient ta beauté,
> La Parque t'a tuee, et cendre tu reposes.
> Pour obseques reçoy mes larmes et mes pleurs,
> Ce vase plein de laict, ce panier plein de fleurs,
> Afin que vif et mort ton corps ne soit que roses.

[Just as one sees on the branch in the month of May the rose in her youthful beauty, her first flowering, make the sky jealous with her vivid colour, when Dawn sprinkles her with tears at sunrise: grace dwells in her petals, and love, steeping the gardens and trees in scent; but beaten down by rain or excessive heat, she languishes and dies, petal after petal unfolding: thus in your first youth, your life still new, when earth and sky honoured your beauty, the Fates have killed you, and, mere ashes, you lie at rest. As funeral offerings, receive my tears and lamentations, this vase full of milk, this basket full of flowers, so that in life and death your body will be nothing but roses.]

With its leisurely yet elegant symmetries, its internal rhymes and echoes, and the complete circle of its form, culminating in the return to 'fleurs' and 'roses' as the final rhyme-words, this is a sonnet which has few rivals. It borrows motifs from classical Latin and Greek poetry, the comparison between woman and rose is one of the most well-worn of all the tropes of love poetry, and the use of a simile to articulate the son-net's structure is a standard device of the Petrarchan tradition. Yet it creates a freshness and a sense of suspended time that allows it to inhabit any age, any reader's imagination, as if it had just been written.

Finally, the close of one of Ronsard's *Hélène* sonnets, remarkable for its combination of technical poise with a dry, self-mocking manner. As in most Petrarchan love-cycles, the name of the mistress provides a repertory of classical allusions and tropes, but here the epic world of the Trojan war is evoked ironically:

> Maintenant en Automne encores malheureux
> Je vy comme au Printemps de nature amoureux,
> A fin que tout mon age aille au gré de la peine:
> Et ores que je deusse estre exempt du harnois,
> Mon Colonnel m'envoye à grands coups de carquois
> R'assieger Ilion pour conquerir Heleine.

[Now, in autumn, still wretched, I live as in the spring, amorous by nature, and so my whole life goes by in the thrall of misery; and just when I ought to be exempt from military service, my Colonel (i.e. Love) sends me off with great blows of his quiver to besiege Troy once more and conquer Helen.]

This is a witty poem, but it is also many other things: a graphic and painful representation of old age, an expression of the poet's weary search for perfection as his career declines, and perhaps too an echo of the war-torn world Ronsard found himself in, against all the Pléiade's brave promises of a new Golden Age.

THE LATE SIXTEENTH CENTURY: MONTAIGNE'S *ESSAIS*

The cultural and political optimism of the early Pléiade years was indeed ill-founded. Henri II died in a jousting accident in 1559; the house of Valois was never to recover, and the absence of a strong leader opened the door to the savage if intermittent civil conflicts known as the wars of religion. Ronsard's poetry had immediately reflected this changed world: in a series of major polemical poems of the early 1560s he adopted an anti-Protestant position which drew some fierce answering fire. The early love poetry of the Huguenot poet Agrippa d'Aubigné, who belongs to a younger generation, mingles Petrarchan commonplaces strangely but powerfully with images of war, blood, and death; d'Aubigné will soon begin to write *Les Tragiques*, which is at once an evocation of contemporary atrocities, a virulent satire against the corruption and effeminate manners of the French court, and a visionary panorama of the sufferings and ultimate salvation of the elect. His consciousness of the changed circumstances of the poet in his day is explicit: 'Ce siecle, autre en ses mœurs, demande un autre style. | Cueillons des fruicts amers, desquels il est fertile' ('This age, different in its manners, demands a different style. Let us pick the bitter fruits in which it is so fertile'); the exacerbated tone and style of his writing has often been regarded as the epitome of the 'Baroque' in France.

At about the same time, the more moderate Huguenot Du Bartas published an imposing creation epic in hyperbolic Pléiade style entitled *La Sepmaine*; it became famous throughout Europe, was translated into several languages, and influenced Milton's *Paradise Lost*. Meanwhile, perhaps because of the fragmentation brought about by the wars, dozens of poets and would-be poets sprang up in provincial centres. Religious poetry in particular flourished in every conceivable style, primarily as an outgrowth of the devotional practices encouraged among the laity by both Catholic and Protestant authorities. Women played a major role in this diffusion of poetic energy, partly no doubt because devotion was by definition respectable: unlike Louise Labé, Georgette de Montenay and Gabrielle de Coignard didn't run the risk of censure.

This is a time above all of dramatic changes and contrasts. D'Aubigné's abrasive manner was formulated in explicit contempt of the 'style doux-coulant' ('sweetly flowing style'), the elegant and smooth-textured style cultivated by Henri III's favourite poet Philippe Desportes, who was fashionable enough to rival even the ageing Ronsard's reputation. Atrocities such as the Massacre of Saint Bartholomew's Day (1572) alternated with court entertainments designed by the regent Catherine de Médicis, widow of Henri II, to mediate between the warring factions: Ronsard and other major poets of the day contributed the text for these events, which included mythological tableaux and embryonic anticipations of ballet and opera.

Himself at times a mediator, shuttling between the different parties, Montaigne was thoroughly familiar with this turbulent, often violent world and with all its cultural manifestations. He is bound to be a central figure in any history of early modern French literature and thought, if only because his *Essais* are an enormous reservoir of evidence of the different things that could be thought and the different ways in which they could be thought in the late sixteenth century. But he is also a problematic figure, partly because his writing appears to a modern reader to lie awkwardly across the divide between imaginative literature and intellectual reflection, partly because when one reads him one seems to hear pre-echoes of so many things that seem familiar, necessary, and valuable to us. His place in history is, as it were, already booked. He is the originator of a new genre, the essay; his *Essais* is the first extended work of introspective self-reflection in European literature, acknowledged as an antecedent for Rousseau's *Confessions* and thus for autobiographical fictions from Constant to Proust and beyond; his use of relativistic and sceptical strategies opens up a whole range of questions, including the status of religious belief and of European political and cultural norms; he is an inquisitive and open-minded traveller; he adopts a liberal attitude towards witches in a period when the persecution of witches was rife; he hates cruelty, violence, and prejudice; he is a well-read humanist who wears his learning lightly, forging an accessible vernacular style in which to speak of the most important issues.

These characteristics look rather different, however, when one replaces them in the context of late sixteenth-century culture. Montaigne's grandfather had bought his title to nobility; Montaigne thus belonged to the new *noblesse de robe*, a class of lawyers and regional administrators, rather than the old landed *noblesse d'épée*. He is deeply preoccupied with the values appropriate to the nobility, and there is a streak of conservatism which is immediately visible in the *Essais*, above all perhaps in his insistence that the traditional teaching of the Church must be respected and his consequent dislike of Protestantism, which he believed threatened the very fabric of orderly society. At the same time, he shared the views of the *politiques*, the moderate faction in the wars of religion, who supported the monarchy as the key to a unified France in which religious toleration was preferable to civil strife.

The question of his private religious beliefs has been hotly debated and remains open. Were his professions of Catholic orthodoxy sincere, or a façade adopted to protect him against condemnation in dangerous times, or a consequence of his social and political conservatism? The question arises principally because the longest chapter of the *Essais*, the 'Apologie de Raimond Sebond', while purporting to defend a late medieval devotional work against accusations of unorthodoxy, devotes most of its considerable space to an exposition of Pyrrhonist arguments. Pyrrhonism is a radical form of scepticism, elaborated in antiquity and preserved mainly in the works of the late Greek writer Sextus

Empiricus. It was known to sixteenth-century humanists (including Rabelais) through other sources, but it was not until 1562, when the French humanist Henri Estienne translated Sextus' *Hypotyposes* into Latin, that the full range of Pyrrhonist arguments began to be widely available. By paraphrasing some of the most crucial of these in French, in a work which was to become virtually a coffee-table book and was translated almost immediately into several other European languages, Montaigne released a powerful current of scepticism for assimilation by writers and thinkers of all kinds in the following centuries. This philosophy of hyperbolic doubt is represented by Montaigne's formula 'Que sais-je?': the form of the question allows him to avoid asserting that he knows anything, or even that he knows nothing. Pyrrhonism clearly fascinated Montaigne, and was compatible with his own sense of the mobility and mutability of human forms of knowledge and belief. Throughout the *Essais*, sceptical formulations serve as an anti-dote against prejudice and dogmatism. Yet the cautious conservative streak is always there too, creating a delicate balance which can at times look like contradiction (although Pyrrhonism too recommends adher-ence to the customs and laws of one's country, since one cannot be sure of offering a better alternative). The coexistence of both strands should be accepted as evidence of a late sixteenth-century mindset. Later thinkers will use sceptical arguments to undermine the very founda-tions of religious belief and political orthodoxy, but it is wrong to assume that Montaigne shares their radical view while prudently deny-ing it. His contemporaries used scepticism to *defend* religion by attack-ing would-be rational assaults on it; Montaigne goes considerably further, nearer to the brink, but he still belongs to that world.

Much the same can be said of Montaigne's 'self-portrait'. There are signs in the very earliest chapters of an interest in recording the stream of unstable and elusive reflections which passed through the writer's mind (see for example I.8); a more substantial chapter, probably writ-ten two years later, tells the story of how Montaigne was accidentally thrown off his horse one day and of his state of consciousness while hovering between life and death (II.6). His brief preface to the first edition (1580), comprising Books I and II only, presents the *Essais* as a self-portrait for friends and family. In a new edition of 1588 containing a third book, a good deal of additional self-commentary has been added to the first two books, and Book III carries the self-portraiture into previously uncharted territory, including intimate details of Montaigne's sexuality (III.5) and of the gall-stones from which he suf-fered (III.13). The scale of this enterprise is unprecedented. There had been plenty of memoirs and 'external' autobiographies; there had been collections of published letters—Erasmus's being the most monumental example—in which the first-person mode is naturally linked to details of everyday life and reflection: as we have seen, the letter-poem was another important vehicle of such writing; there had also been confessional narratives with a moral and theological aim; but there had been nothing comparable to Montaigne's secular introspection. At times, indeed, Montaigne seems to be trying to invent a new metaphorical language in which to make tangible the outlandish journey into the intestines of the self that he had embarked on. Listen for example to this passage from 'De la præsumption', where the reflexive movement is conveyed through a constantly shifting pattern of repetition:

Le monde regarde tousjours vis à vis; moy, je replie ma veue au dedans, je la plante, je l'amuse là. Chacun regarde devant soy; moy, je regarde dedans moy: je n'ay affaire qu'à moy. Je me considere sans cesse, je me contrerolle, je me gouste. Les autres vont tousjours avant,

nemo in sese tentat descendere,

moy je me roulle en moy mesme.

[People are always looking at other people; as for me, I turn my gaze inward, I fix it there, I detain it there. Others look at things outside themselves; as for me, I look inside myself: my only concern is with myself. I observe myself continuously, I monitor myself, I sample myself. Others always go forwards, *no one attempts to descend into himself* [a quotation from the Latin poet Persius]; as for me, I wrap myself up in myself.]

Yet the *Essais* are only a distant forerunner of full-scale autobiographical works such as Rousseau's *Confessions*, and despite the intensive use of a first-person grammar, they contain no instance of the noun-form 'le moi' ('the self'), which only became common in the seventeenth century. Montaigne's writing is also many things besides a record of self-observations and self-analyses. It is first and foremost a repertory of anecdotes, examples, philosophical commonplaces and quotations (many in verse) drawn from ancient texts, a genre much favoured by humanists. Montaigne's increasingly bold uses of the first person singular may indeed emerge in part at least from humanist theories of imitation, which emphasize the need for writers to appropriate such borrowed materials and reissue them in their own voice. The *Essais* are also a collection of 'Morall, Politike and Millitarie Discourses', as the title of the first English translation has it: they contain serious reflections on the wars of religion, the ethics of statecraft, education, personal conduct, relations between the sexes, the intricate interweavings of nature and culture, and many other topics. The importance of the intensive use of the first person is not that it assigns authority to these observations as part of a didactic discourse, but that, on the contrary, it marks them as being items of an individual's momentary thought, which may change the next year, the next month, the next moment: as Montaigne puts it, 'Je n'enseigne poinct, je raconte' ('I don't teach, I tell'). The title is not (yet) a genre term, but a word that retains the meaning 'trials', 'experiments', 'soundings'. In this sense, it marks the fullest and most explicit realization of the exploratory, open-ended types of discourse that had characterized sixteenth-century French writing from Rabelaisian comedy and the dialogues of the *Heptaméron* onwards.

NEW DIRECTIONS IN THE EARLY SEVENTEENTH CENTURY

Montaigne's death coincided almost exactly with the end of the wars of religion, which is also marked by the publication of a remarkable work of post-Rabelaisian satire called the *Satyre menippée*: composed by several hands, it reflects the perspective of the *politiques*, lampooning the ultra-Catholic *Ligue* and its allies. Satirically and politically motivated texts of the kind one finds throughout the sixteenth century will now be in abeyance for some time. With the accession of the Protestant Henri IV, who in 1593 underwent a strategic conversion to Catholicism, a period of tolerance and reconciliation ensues: the Edict of Nantes of 1598 gives the French Protestants relative freedom of worship.

One marker of the early seventeenth-century mood is provided by the micro-culture of Annecy, just over the border from Calvin's Geneva. It was here that François de Sales, bishop of Geneva in exile, wrote his *Introduction à la vie dévote*, which was to become one of the most popular devotional handbooks ever written in French; François himself was canonized in 1665. Designed to make devotion attractive to members of the laity, particularly women (it is written in the second person and addressed to a fictional woman), it is bathed in pious emotion and consistently indulgent to human feelings, especially amorous ones; its rhetoric is gently passionate, its metaphors frequent and flowery.

François was a member of the local 'Académie florimontane' of Annecy, to which Honoré d'Urfé also belonged. The first volume of d'Urfé's gigantic pastoral novel *Astrée* appeared in 1607, and two others came out before the author's death in 1625; a conclusion was added posthumously by his secretary. This too became a best-seller in its day, and remained popular throughout Europe until the eighteenth century. Just as the *Introduction à la vie dévote* mixes worldly feelings into its devotional effusions, so too *Astrée*, set in an imaginary pastoral landscape where the aristocratic characters, disguised as shepherds, practise a Druidic religion presided over by the priest Adamas, weaves a hedonistic devotional strand into its story of amorous severance and misfortunes. The moral optimism of the novel is best illustrated by an episode where Adamas advises the despairing lover Céladon to disguise himself as a girl and infiltrate the dormitory where Astrée is living with her girl-friends so that—always keeping his mind of course on spiritual things—he can contemplate her higher attributes without offending her by his presence. This complex and many-sided novel is also full of dialogues about how lovers should behave and other moral and social questions; its success was largely due to the fact that it provided ample materials for polite literary discussion in well-to-do circles. It was in fact at exactly this time that the marquise de Rambouillet designed a new town house in Paris containing a suite of *salons* (an architectural novelty), where, until her death in 1665, she gathered around her a social and cultural elite whose views on literature and manners were regarded as a touchstone for good taste. D'Urfé's *Astrée* was doubtless a frequent topic of conversation there.

POETRY: (III) MALHERBE AND HIS CONTEMPORARIES

For another perspective on the early seventeenth century, we return now to poetry, since this is the domain of François de Malherbe, long regarded as the herald of 'le Grand Siècle'. The turn of the century is marked by the publication of an important series of anthologies which offered to readers both a conspectus of the poetry of the previous fifty years and a generous sample of the prolific verse-writing, sacred and profane, which still continued unabated. The evident commercial success of these anthologies suggests a markedly pluralistic taste: it would be hard to elicit from them any clear direction that poetry was likely to take in the new century. Malherbe's own early poetry is absorbed into this flood. But by the first decade of the seventeenth century, he emerges as a ruthless critic of his predecessors. His personal copy of Ronsard's poetry, in which page after page has simply been crossed out as if in scorn or in anger, has been preserved, and he was only marginally less severe towards Desportes. He published no treatise on poetics, but his doctrine can be derived from his marginalia and from his own later poetry. He insists on rigorous discipline in the use of both poetic language and verse-form: there are to be no obscure allusions or signs of erudition, metaphor is to be kept on a tight leash, the structure of the line and stanza must be firm and clear, with *enjambement* reduced to a minimum. In other words, the preference for profusion, stylistic enrichment and poetic energy which characterized the Pléiade and its successors is now replaced by an aesthetic of control, order, and rational plausibility.

Of course there had been anticipations of this change. Ronsard himself progressively revised his poems, removing untidiness and improving clarity; the language of his late *Sonnets pour Hélène* is much more transparent than that of his early *Amours*, and their movement is more elegantly measured. Other poets such as Desportes, Du Perron, and Bertaut have also been claimed as forerunners of the new aesthetic. Yet it is not clear that there was a 'movement' in the direction Malherbe was to take, rather than a proliferation of different styles among which one is bound to find some examples of relative austerity.

Caution is needed, too, in assigning a cultural significance to the would-be Malherbian reform. Was it an early sign of the centralized control of culture which was to be one of the features of the period from the 1630s onward? Did it anticipate a 'rationalism' which crystallized in the thought of Descartes? It is hard to see why these possibilities should be other than a projection back from later phenomena that we regard as important. Sixteenth-century writing continued to be admired in the first third of the seventeenth century. Marie de Gournay, Montaigne's *fille d'alliance* who helped his wife prepare the posthumous edition of his *Essais* in 1595, actively defended the poetry of Ronsard in this changing climate while also speaking out for women's rights to education and equal cultural status, and the lively satirist Mathurin Régnier (the nephew of Desportes) also challenged the new Malherbian purism. This is a resolutely pluralistic period which should neither be hijacked for the mythical 'Grand Siècle' nor regarded as a kind of appendix to the sixteenth.

The prefatory poem to the 1621 edition of the *Œuvres poétiques* of Théophile de Viau recognizes Malherbe's status while asserting the freedom to adopt an entirely different style: 'Imite qui voudra les merveilles d'autruy, | Malherbe a tres-bien fait, mais il a fait pour luy' ('If anyone wants to imitate other people's marvels, let them; | what Malherbe did was fine, but he did it for himself'). Entrusting his poetry to the judgement of the woman to whom the collection is addressed, Théophile sketches a poetics of discontinuity and improvisation, heedless of all rules: 'Je ne veux point unir le fil de mon subjet, | Diversement je laisse et reprens mon object . . . La reigle me desplaist, j'escris confusément' ('I have no desire to make my subject matter follow a single thread, | Randomly I abandon my theme, then pick it up again . . . I dislike rules, I write confusedly'). This claim is of course to be taken, not literally, but as a counter-move to the Malherbian fashion. It is realized primarily in the associative movement of Théophile's poems, which can shift their focus disconcertingly: in his best-known sequence, *La Maison de Silvie*, the second *Ode* dazzles with its mythological transformations, the play of light on water, and a delicately evoked snowy landscape.

The theme of mutability, together with the use of imaginative association as a formal device, links a number of early seventeenth-century poets. The *Stances à l'inconstance* by the short-lived court poet Estienne Durand, executed for intriguing against the king, is a famous example. A wayward, sometimes introspective imagination also characterizes the work of two other poets, Saint-Amant and Tristan l'Hermite, who outlived Durand and Théophile by many years and participated in the great literary upsurge of the mid-seventeenth century. Tristan's *Le Promenoir des deux amants*, which has affinities with *La Maison de Silvie*, was to appeal to the impressionistic taste of Debussy, who set a selection of stanzas from the poem.

Théophile, Saint-Amant, and Tristan have traditionally been grouped together as *libertin* (that is to say freethinking) poets. The use of the word in this context is approximate: only Théophile got into seriously deep water for impiety. But this is more than a straw in the wind. *Libertinage* is an increasingly important aspect of early seventeenth-century culture. It is often associated with the influence of Montaigne: the associative thought and quasi-improvised style of the *Essais* are arguably recognizable in the form if not the subject matter of the *libertin* poets. A suspicion of deviant 'freedom' hangs over some of the most attractive writing of this period, and—retrospectively— begins to contaminate the *Essais* themselves.

QUESTIONS OF LANGUAGE AND STYLE

A year before his death in 1628, Malherbe published a *Recueil des plus beaux vers des poètes de ce temps*, an anthology of his own and his disciples' poetry. This served, if not as a landmark, at least as a benchmark for the progressive consolidation of a normative, 'regular' poetic style. At about the same time, the young prose stylist Guez de Balzac, who belonged to the same generation as the *libertin* poets, was beginning to publish works designed to establish norms for prose-writing. At the centre of this project was the letter-form. We have seen how important this epistolary genre was in the sixteenth century, in both prose and verse, as a vehicle of informal, first-person discourse. Balzac now uses it as the model for a vernacular style which is at once colloquial and polite, refined and unpedantic. Balzac admired the writers of classical antiquity, but he reacted against the ostentatious 'quotation rhetoric' which had become prevalent among humanist writers from the late sixteenth century onwards and which had spread to sacred prose: the richly allusive sermon style of Jean-Pierre Camus is a prominent example. Elegance in prose style was to be achieved by wearing one's learning as lightly as possible. Montaigne's prose already anticipates this shift of taste in some respects: it eschews pedantry and high rhetoric, and the 1,200-odd quotations in the *Essais* are always subordinate to— often absorbed into—the flow of the surrounding text. But Montaigne's style, like that of his favourite Latin author Seneca, combines long, rambling periods with tersely epigrammatic formulations, and the reader encounters lines of Latin verse at every turn. Guez de Balzac chose as his model the letters of the Roman orator Cicero, which combine elegance with informality; at the same time, he looked to the polite language of the court as a criterion for what was accessible and acceptable. His *Entretiens*, not published until after his death, consciously seek to remake the manner of the *Essais* according to these criteria: the replacement of a title signifying the exercise of personal judgement by a title invoking conversation is a clear indicator of this shift of emphasis. It is also a sign of the times that Marie de Gournay, who had vigorously defended Montaigne against his detractors, produced in 1625 an edition of the *Essais* in which the language is updated and the quotations translated.

Montaigne himself had remarked that the French language was changing so fast that, within fifty years, no one would be able to read the *Essais*. The changes were perhaps not quite as rapid as that, but pressures on the vernacular to become the standard vehicle for virtually all forms of speech and writing had continued unabated since the late thirteenth century. After the period of geopolitical fragmentation brought about by the wars of religion, the imposition of a highly centralized monarchic regime gathered new momentum, and a standardized national language was one of the consequences—indeed one of the principal instruments—of this policy. A unique combination of political, ideological, social, and aesthetic factors thus gave rise to a more or less coordinated effort to construct enduring norms for the use of French in speech and in writing, in prose and in verse.

At the centre of this effort was the foundation of the Académie Française. This remarkably powerful institution evolved from an informal circle of writers who had been meeting since the late 1620s. In 1634, under the auspices of the king's first minister the Cardinal de Richelieu, the Académie acquired an official status which was finally ratified by Parlement in 1637. Its role was to monitor and police linguistic usage, and by extension literary standards, especially in the theatre, that most public of all forms of literary practice. It began to compile a dictionary, and included among its projects both a normative French grammar and a rhetoric. In the event, these works were either completed much later or never completed, but the important thing was that the Académie was seen to embody an absolute standard of correctness and linguistic purity, a function which it retains to this day. In its wake, individuals such as Vaugelas produced their own minute observations on lexical and grammatical usage: Vaugelas's celebrated *Remarques sur la langue française* appeared in 1647, providing a kind of manual of how to speak and (above all) how not to speak in polite circles.

THEATRE: A RETROSPECT

The stage is now set for a remarkably intense, and intensely focused, phase of literary production. And 'stage' is the right word. Not only will the theatre itself be at the centre of cultural activity for the next fifty years at least, but other genres—pulpit oratory is one, 'moralist' writing another—will often assume a quasi-theatrical character. This phenomenon is connected with the progressive emergence of a highly self-conscious court society which itself is a kind of theatre, both in its internal codes of language and costume and in its self-presentation for wider consumption; that process, in turn, will facilitate the construction of an absolutist monarchy whose every public and even private move is carefully choreographed.

Such metaphorical generalizations are of course always liable to qualification, and it is important to recall that a deep and abiding distrust of theatre is also written into the history of the early modern period. In the 1630s, those developments are in any case only just beginning. It is therefore necessary at this point to make a retrospective detour in order to put in place, if not to explain, the extraordinary rise to prominence of theatre in the second third of the seventeenth century.

Medieval dramatic genres and practices—mystery plays, morality plays, and farces—continued to be popular in France until the late sixteenth century, even though an edict of 1548 banned the performance of mystery plays in Paris on the grounds that the theatre was associated with public disorder and immorality. It may indeed have been the popularity of the plays that gave rise to alarm. The nearest thing to a permanent theatre at that time was a building constructed for the performance of religious plays by the Confrérie de la Passion, a kind of devotional society or guild. Temporary structures were erected by travelling troupes of players, and in some cases plays were performed by students in their colleges or in other suitable buildings.

An entirely different conception of drama emerged in the course of the sixteenth century as humanist scholars edited and translated the corpus of ancient tragedy and comedy and investigated the conditions of performance in antiquity. In 1552–3, the poet Estienne Jodelle wrote a tragedy called *Cléopâtre captive* which was immediately celebrated by the budding Pléiade as marking the rebirth of authentic tragedy in France; other poets followed suit with both comedies and tragedies modelled in some sense on ancient examples. Drama, it should be remembered, was normally regarded as one of the genres of 'poetry' and—with significant exceptions such as Molière's *Dom Juan*—verse was its primary medium until the rise of the eighteenth-century *drame*.

French drama of the late sixteenth century is rich in serious subjects—political and religious issues were often alluded to, especially in plays written during the wars of religion—conveyed in a flamboyant rhetorical style. The tragedies of Robert Garnier in particular have stood the test of time. His *Marc-Antoine* is a powerful version of the Antony and Cleopatra story, and *Les Juifves*, an elegiac Old Testament play, illustrates the way in which writers of this period used the colours and textures of biblical language in close juxtaposition with a humanist eloquence derived from classical Latin. His principal model is in fact the Latin playwright Seneca, who himself reworked subjects from the Greek dramatists: Garnier's *Hippolyte*, for example, has its place in a genealogy which runs from Euripides via Seneca to Racine's *Phèdre*. We know that his plays were performed, but unfortunately little evidence of stage practices in this period have been preserved. What does seem clear is that such dramatists were not in a position to work with experienced troupes of actors in an established theatre, so that their plays, despite their many merits, do not lend themselves to modern revival on the stage as do those of their celebrated English contemporaries.

Things begin to change in the earlier seventeenth century with the rise of the actor-playwright Alexandre Hardy, who wrote and performed a large number of plays, most of which have been lost. Adopting the classical, historical, and romance subjects of his sixteenth-century predecessors, Hardy treats them freely and with an unruly energy: violence on stage is frequent, and his considerable contemporary reputation suggests that he managed to draw in big audiences. He worked for a while with a company of actors who had taken over the playhouse of the Confrérie de la Passion, the Hôtel de

Bourgogne, which remained the leading Paris theatre for most of the century. The fact that, by the end of his life, Hardy's plays already appeared impossibly unrefined is a measure of the rapid evolution of taste in a medium which was now becoming well established as a focus for public entertainment and, potentially, a vehicle for high culture. What seems to have happened is that, as audiences increased in size and social range, the presence of wealthier and more powerful customers created a demand for a better-policed institution (public theatre was notoriously linked to rowdyism and petty criminal behaviour) and for a more upmarket programme. Going to the theatre became fashionable, and writing for it began to attract the best talents.

These developments coincide with an intensive revival of Aristotelian poetics, no doubt invoked largely in order to *authorize* the new enthusiasm for the theatre: if drama were subject to a set of rules guaranteeing its seriousness and rationality, the Church's deep suspicion of its capacity to seduce and subvert could in some measure be countered. The foundation of the Académie Française provided the ultimate seal of authority. Among its first official pronouncements was a somewhat severe judgement on the sensationally successful play *Le Cid* by the young dramatist Pierre Corneille. This episode makes visible the balance that had to be achieved in order to operate within the constraints of contemporary sensibility. On the one hand, the audience needed visceral entertainment: Corneille himself records that a *frisson* of excitement was caused by the scene where Rodrigue comes to visit his beloved Chimène carrying a sword still covered with her father's blood. On the other, the *bienséances* of polite society had to be observed, women should not be shocked, and reasonably strict conditions of plausibility should be observed. If Corneille's plays were often controversial yet nearly always successful, it was because he was constantly, and brilliantly, walking that tightrope.

THEATRE: CORNEILLE AND HIS TIMES

The new-found confidence of the theatre in the mid-1630s is explicitly advertised in *L'Illusion comique*, where Corneille manipulates a complex plot in such a way as to foreground the successful creation of theatrical illusion. In the denouement, it turns out that the protagonists, who have just enacted a tragic scene, are not dead: they are actors. The scene was an illusion, the actors are earning a good income, and the profession they have taken up has become socially acceptable. The magician Alcandre's speech in defence of the new theatre (a sort of upbeat counterpart to Prospero's famous resignation speech in *The*

Tempest) is worth reading in itself as an indicator of the rapid changes taking place at this time.

L'Illusion comique is also a showcase for the different genres in which Corneille was experimenting at this early stage in his career—comedy, romance, tragicomedy and tragedy. Generic uncertainty hangs over a good deal of his writing for the theatre: for example, *Le Cid* was first described as a tragicomedy, later as a tragedy. The development of Aristotelian poetics in this period leads to a sharpening of the distinction between genres as norms are set more and more firmly; Corneille yields in part to this pressure, but he also refuses to accept that Aristotle's so-called rules necessarily apply in modern times. Again, he responds to contemporary demands for a simplified and more coherent plot by progressively removing physical action from the stage and focusing on emotional and moral dilemmas. This is the period when the 'three unities' of time, place, and action were firmly established as a pre-condition of plausibility (*vraisemblance)* in the theatre, and the older stage practice of using a *décor simultané* (a set representing several scenes simultaneously to allow for changes of place without moving scenery around) was giving way to a single theatrical place in which all the action had to be set. Yet in Corneille's theatre there are still many episodes of physical panache, as in *Le Cid*, while several plays—*Cinna* and *Polyeucte* in particular—have surprise denouements in which the characters are transported by a quasi-divine moral enlightenment. In his prefaces and other critical writings, Corneille seeks to justify such spectacular plots and the superhuman actions of his heroes by adding *admiration* ('wonder' as well as 'admiration') to pity and fear as emotions to be aroused by a tragedy, and by claiming, against contemporary orthodoxy, that *invraisemblance* is not only acceptable but desirable in a tragic plot, as long as it is founded in historical truth.

Corneille's plays, together with those of important contemporaries like Jean Rotrou, reflect a widespread taste for heroic action accompanied by equally heroic moral dilemmas such as the choice between personal happiness and family honour or national glory. Similar themes are found in the *romans héroïques* of the same period, especially Madeleine de Scudéry's *Le Grand Cyrus* and *Clélie*. This cult of the hero was nourished by the exemplary exploits of the warriors of ancient Rome, where many of Corneille's plays were set; it runs parallel, too, with a predominantly optimistic view of human nature in philosophical and theological thought. The humane, almost indulgent, values of François de Sales and of the pastoral tradition are echoed by the teaching of the Jesuits, currently at the height of their power (Corneille was educated at a Jesuit school): the relative freedom of humans to make moral choices is emphasized in Jesuit theology and, from a different perspective, in the moral thought of Descartes, another pupil of the Jesuits. Of course these issues were not problem-free, and one cannot assume that Corneille's plays were designed simply to glorify the moral status of the hero. The Roman warrior Horace, in the play named after him, not only defeats his enemies, he also kills his own sister in a fit of rage when she calls the morality of his deeds into question, and his exclamation at this point, 'C'est trop, ma patience à la raison fait place' ('It's too much, my patience yields to reason') reveals a sinister equation between loss of control and supposed rationality. Likewise, the obstinate defence of family honour by Chimène in *Le Cid* and Émilie in *Cinna* is eventually perceived to be wrong-headed, and there are also negative heroes and heroines such as Cléopâtre in *Rodogune*, who—according to Corneille—evoked *admiration* in the audience through the sheer enormity of her actions.

This analogy between the implications of Corneille's drama and the sensibility of his day is meant only as a broad-brush sketch: such connections are always oblique and usually much more complex than they appear at first sight. On the other hand, dramatists as successful as Corneille are likely to be more sensitive to the prevailing moods, tastes and preoccupations of their day than any other kind of writer, at least in periods before the age of the mass media. They have to make an immediate appeal to their audience across a relatively broad social and intellectual spectrum; in the right circumstances, their fine adjustment to the plural mindset of that audience will lead to dramatic re-enactments of issues which are elsewhere treated with less freedom and in a more one-dimensional manner.

One further point may be made about Corneille's period via his theatrical representations. His plays are often intensely political, in the sense that they enact tensions between rulers and their henchmen or military commanders: heroes like Rodrigue, Cinna, Horace, and Nicomède are needed by the state, but they often diverge from its purposes, for good or ill, for the sake of their own glory. Some plays end with the reimposition of order by a monarch whose power coincides with moral justice; more often, tyrants are worsted by heroic underlings, whose task is to ensure that a Machiavellian *raison d'état* does not prevail. It is likely that this constantly redrawn equation reflects a critical tension between the increasingly centralized monarchy of Louis XIII and the old landed aristocracy (the *noblesse d'épée*), who had hitherto enjoyed some freedom of jurisdiction on their own terrain. This struggle came to a head in the 'Fronde' of 1648–53, a series of civil skirmishes which ended with the defeat of the old aristocracy and the assertion of the absolute power of the monarch. By this time, Louis XIII was dead and the minister Mazarin was wielding power on behalf of the young Louis XIV, but when in 1661 Mazarin died and Louis XIV came of age, the young king took all power into his own hands. A reign of unparalleled autocracy ensued.

DESCARTES AND PASCAL: THE MID-CENTURY TURN

The publication of Descartes's *Discours de la méthode* coincided with the emergence of the new Aristotelian poetics, the rise of Corneille and the founding of the Académie Française. The coincidence is interesting but should not be overinterpreted. Descartes is a key figure in the history of philosophy; his role in the construction of a seventeenth-century French 'Classicism' is more problematic. The founding gesture of Cartesian thought is the initial *tabula rasa*, the clean sweep made of all previous philosophies, authorities, preconceptions, whereas 'Classicism', if it has a sense, must entail the privileging of ancient models and authorities (Aristotelian poetics being itself a prime example). As for the clarity and rigorous method which Descartes insists on as the only route to truth, they are quite distinct from anything in the literary world. Cartesian philosophy makes a decisive break with the whole humanist tradition, not only through the *tabula rasa*, but also through its rejection of rhetoric as a valid instrument of knowledge; in its most fundamental conception, it is a *logic*.

To this may be added a warning about the first building block that Descartes establishes on his cleared surface, the proposition 'je pense, donc je suis' ('I think, therefore I am': the so-called '*cogito*'). The radical nature of the move, together with its first-person syntax, have led some historians of ideas and literature to regard Descartes as the founder of a modern subjective consciousness; epistemological histories of the period tend to organize themselves around this moment as around some quantum shift in human intellectual evolution. This is again a question for historians of philosophy to investigate, but there is no evidence that first-person genres of writing began to proliferate from this particular date, and it is obvious that Montaigne's *Essais* (or indeed Augustine's *Confessions*, translated into French in 1649 and immediately influential among secular as well as religious writers) provided a much more wide-ranging and central model of the possibilities of first-person discourse than anything in Descartes's philosophy.

This is not to say that Cartesian thought exists in some entirely separate cultural domain. In the first place, Descartes chose to write his *Discours* in French, rather than the Latin of his more extensive philsophical writings, and in a French which was lucid, non-technical and transparent for the reader: his initial dictum 'Le bon sens est la chose du monde la mieux partagée' ('Good sense is the most widely shared thing in the world') may be read ironically, but the message of accessibility that it carries is unmistakable. Secondly, he regarded the elaboration of a practical psychology and ethics as the 'topmost branch' of his philosophical endeavour: his last work, *Des passions de l'âme*, again written in French, contains a detailed classification, definition, and analysis of the passions (what we would call the emotions) and of the means of controlling them. Although it is distinctively Cartesian, and therefore cannot be directly 'applied' to any contemporary literary work, one can gain from it considerable insight into the meanings that could be attributed to words for the emotions in the earlier seventeenth century. The role of terms like *étonnement* (the initial shock that precedes any particular passion), *gloire*, and *générosité* in Descartes's ethical psychology is germane to issues not only in Corneille's drama, but, *mutatis mutandis*, in many other seventeenth-century works where the passions are centrally featured.

As a mathematician and scientist, Descartes also played a significant role in a long-term movement of scientific change, which included both the gradual (if often unwilling) acceptance of the heliocentric model of the universe and the evolution of the science of optics which made that fundamental reconfiguration possible. Descartes agreed with Galileo, and ran into difficulties with the authorities for doing so, but his preference for the deductive method of scientific reasoning over the inductive, experimental method led him, for example, to reaffirm the ancient dictum that 'Nature abhors a vacuum' in the face of increasing experimental evidence to the contrary. By contrast, his younger contemporary Pascal, an equally brilliant mathematician, repeated and extended the experiments of the Italian scientist Torricelli, demonstrating the difference of air pressure at different altitudes and ultimately calculating the weight of the entire atmospheric envelope of the earth. In an important preface to a treatise on the vacuum which he never completed, Pascal argued that in mathematics and the physical sciences no 'authorities' were valid and that knowledge in these domains could be infinitely extended by a proper combination of the deductive and the experimental methods; in all domains dependent on documentary evidence, however—history, geography, literature and, above all, theology—the reverse was true. Here, human reason was useless since everything depended on a testimony given once and for all. In Pascal's non-scientific writings, this opposition has a fully theological force, since it depends on a deeply pessimistic view of the fallibility of human reason as an instrument for knowing the things that really matter.

The predominantly optimistic theological and moral sensibility of earlier seventeenth-century writers such as François de Sales, d'Urfé, Corneille and indeed Descartes had already been countered by religious movements where the emphasis was placed on theological and moral severity. One of these evolved in the late 1630s under the leadership of the Abbé de Saint-Cyran at the reformed convent of Port-Royal. The theology he fostered there was nourished by the treatise *Augustinus* of the Dutch theologian Jansenius, published posthumously in 1640, an exposition of Augustine's doctrine of the entire dependence of man in his fallen state on divine grace as a means to salvation. Port-Royal also provided schooling for well-to-do lay pupils—Racine was educated there—and became an interface between a group of powerful theological minds and their lay sympathizers from *le beau monde*. The rise of Jansenism might have been simply another episode in the internal theological disputes of the Church, but such contacts ensured that it had a decisive influence on the sensibility of the later seventeenth century.

In this osmosis from the theological to the secular domain, Pascal turned out to be the prime mover. In the 1650s, he became the Jansenists' most potent ally in their running battle with the Sorbonne theologians and with the Jesuits (a battle which they none the less lost), composing a series of fictional letters in support of their cause, supposedly written to a friend in the country (a 'provincial': hence the title, *Lettres provinciales*). His lucid, if polemically slanted, interpretation of the quarrel made it accessible to lay readers; his ironies and, in the later letters, his indignant satire of what he saw as the lax theology and ethics of the Jesuits and their friends, were so brilliantly conceived that the Jesuit order has never quite recovered from the caricature; and the deployment of a supposedly naïve persona to unmask an establishment which hides its corruption beneath obscurantism is a device which will be borrowed and used to devastating effect by very un-Pascalian authors in the eighteenth century.

When the quarrel of the *Provinciales* was over, Pascal began to work on a more ambitious project, nothing less than an apology for the Christian religion itself, conceived as a set of arguments designed to persuade *libertins* (the rising tide of freethinkers) of the truth of the Christian religion and of the desirability of embracing it. He never completed this work, leaving only, on his premature death in 1662, a baffling collection of fragments and notes, together with some ambiguous traces of his reflections on how to order them. An edited selection, entitled the *Pensées,* was published by Port-Royal in 1670; thereafter, editors regularly adopted a heavily interventionist policy until the mid-twentieth century, when it was shown that these editions had obliterated the signs of incipient order in the original collection. Most modern editions follow one of the two manuscript copies made soon after Pascal's death.

Pascal admired Descartes but rejected his purely philosophical search for the truth through reason. He was also a close reader of Montaigne, while disparaging him for his moral laxness and for 'le sot projet qu'il a de se peindre' ('his foolish project of self-portraiture'). Whereas Descartes had used the pyrrhonist arguments first popularized by Montaigne as a strategic device to clear the table on which his edifice of rational thought was to be built, Pascal used them to disable reason as an instrument of moral and transcendental knowledge. Humans, he argues, know God not through the reason but through the *cœur,* and then only when the heart is informed by grace, since the fallen heart is also the seat of concupiscence. Imprisoned in a fallen world and a fallen body, their reason vitiated, their only claim to *grandeur* is that they have enough lucidity to perceive their *misère,* although not enough to escape from it. Such an argument lands Pascal with a virtually insoluble problem of presentation. If he sets out a series of neat, rational arguments to convince his *libertin* antagonist, he will contradict his own fundamental view of man's predicament; besides, rational arguments are for Pascal cold and will never be able to deliver the fire of faith. It is clear that he was experimenting with a presentation in letter-form, or dialogue-form, or perhaps a combination of the two, as in the *Provinciales.* But perhaps it is less damaging for this work than for any other imaginable that it should have been left as a set of fragments. The teasing, enigmatic nature of the text, its provocations and paradoxes, its maxim-like formulations left hanging in the air (although often elaborated in other fragments), its constant shifts of tone and subject matter, arguably give a more deeply engaging and *appropriate* image of the problem Pascal wished to tackle than any elegantly completed work could have done. He himself seemed to see this: 'J'écrirai ici mes pensées sans ordre et non pas peut-être dans une confusion sans dessein. C'est le véritable ordre et qui marquera toujours mon objet par le désordre même' ('I shall write my thoughts down here without any order and perhaps not in an unplanned confusion. That is the true order and it will always indicate my objective through disorder itself').

There is another point which is essential for the reader who may not share Pascal's commitment to the Jansenist theology of grace and its consequences. Seen simply as a writing endeavour, the *Pensées* is a work of almost heroic proportions. Pascal was ready to impose on himself the most excruciating constraints in order to achieve his high aim—an aim so high, indeed, that he knew it was unreachable. The writing cracks and buckles under the strain; seismic caverns open up, dark spaces which suddenly fill with the promise of constellations. The text of the *Pensées* is like an unfinished musical score, or an extremely modern one which accepts fragmentation and silence as part of its condition of being. It is also like a gigantic prose poem, striving to say something beyond poetry, beyond language. Not until Mallarmé will another French writer conceive such a project, and then the religion will be explicitly a secular one, a kind of transcendental poetics.

LITERATURE AND POWER IN THE AGE OF LOUIS XIV

Not long before Pascal died in 1662, Corneille had published an edition of his complete dramatic works, together with three short essays on the poetics of drama and a collection of retrospective *examens* of his plays. This was a monument; yet his career was to continue for another fourteen years. Meanwhile, a new dramatic talent had appeared in Paris: Molière's *Les Précieuses ridicules* (1659), followed by the more ambitious *L'École des femmes* (1662), were provoking a storm of applause and disapproval, the latter equally good for box-office returns. Another young would-be dramatist called Jean Racine was writing his first tragedy about the sons of Oedipus, to be called *La Thébaïde* (1663). The ageing and disillusioned duc de La Rochefoucauld, defeated in the Fronde and in close touch with Port-Royal, had compiled a collection of polished if rather bleak epigrams which were already circulating and would in 1665 be published as the *Maximes*. And Louis XIV had newly asserted his authority at a court which would rapidly become a cultural hothouse, demanding constant entertainment and recreation at the very highest levels, in conscious imitation of the great Augustan age of Rome.

It is hardly surprising that, in the culture of this period, representation of the monarch and of his power becomes a collective, myth-making enterprise. The ideal figure of the King is consecrated in portraiture and statuary, in public celebrations and dedications, in theatre (see Figure 9), music, dance (see Figure 8), culinary confections, in an intensely formalized court etiquette, and above all, no doubt, in court architecture: the history of the enlargement of what had originally been a hunting-lodge into a palace of unparalleled splendour at Versailles, purpose-built for the king and his court and projecting their

8 and 9. Two theatrical representations of the monarch: 8. The young Louis XIV acting the part of the Sun in the *Ballet de la Nuit* (1653). 9. Louis XIV depicted as Alexander the Great against the backdrop of the scenery for Racine's play *Alexandre* (1665).

cultural supremacy to an astonished and admiring Europe, encapsulates the extravagant self-advertisement of Louis's reign.

Among the most notorious celebrations of the monarch and his power staged by a contemporary text is the final scene of Molière's *Tartuffe*: just as the villain seems about to triumph, a messenger arrives to say that the all-seeing king has saved the victims and decreed the punishment of the wicked. This is the role usually reserved for the *deus ex machina* of ancient drama, the god who comes down in a stage machine in order to unravel the plot. Modern readers find it difficult not to read this as a caricature: the device is so threadbare, the flattery so egregious. It *is* a comic twist, but one in which the device is renewed by placing ultimate power in the hands where it really resides. Some twenty years later, in the preface to *Athalie*, Racine will defend the plausibility of Joas's precociously astute handling of his interrogation by Athalie by claiming that Louis XIV's 8-year-old grandson was capable of an even more astonishing brilliance: all the members of the royal family seem to be endowed with a quasi-supernatural aura.

If the absolutist theme has a less celebratory underside, it is to be found rather in the recurrence in literary texts of scenes of power enacted between individuals. There are certainly absolutist tyrants like Amurat in Racine's *Bajazet*, whose word is law, but in general what one witnesses in the fictions of this period is the grim combat of antagonists whose interests are opposed: power is disseminated throughout the system. One sees this in the world of La Fontaine's *Fables*, where animals (and humans) endlessly exploit, subjugate, and destroy one another; in Molière's comedies, where Arnolphe imposes a tyrannical regime on Agnès (*L'École des femmes*) and Dom Juan conceives all his relationships in terms of power; and in the diplomatic yet savage encounters of Racine's characters. In Madame de La Fayette's *La Princesse de Clèves*, royal power and its loss appear as the paradigm of hidden struggles within the fabric of a court society where self-interest rules and no quarter is ever given. The protagonists of Racine's plays, endowed though they often are with considerable political and personal authority, are always disabled at some critical point which makes them the victim of another's power: Titus the emperor cannot choose whom he would marry (*Bérénice*); Agamemnon must sacrifice his daughter if he is to lead the Greeks to glory against the Trojans (*Iphigénie*); Thésée the king and monster-slayer cannot control the outbreak of monstrous passions in his own family (*Phèdre*); Athalie the tyrant hesitates momentarily and is lost. The power of only a few shadowy offstage figures—Amurat again, the gods in *Iphigénie* and *Phèdre*, God in *Athalie*—remains undiminished.

QUESTIONS OF PSYCHOLOGY AND ETHICS

The motive of virtually all the dramatis personae of later seventeenth-century French literature is self-interest; their fatal vulnerability is a failure of self-knowledge. Self-interest may be mitigated by more or less heroic attempts to impose a moral imperative: Alceste in Molière's *Le Misanthrope* seeks sincerity against all the odds in a society addicted to hypocrisy and secrecy; the Princesse de Clèves desperately struggles to maintain her marital fidelity in a world no less addicted to seduction and passionate affairs; Phèdre would rather die than speak—let alone enact—her shame. Yet these three great test-cases show the more clearly that moral intention is always undermined in advance by the character's own hidden desires. Alceste wants to be *seen* to be distinguished from the common crowd ('Je veux qu'on me distingue'), and he is also fatally in love with Célimène, the most dissembling and gossip-prone woman at court; the Princesse makes endless small concessions to her incipient passion for Nemours and in the end encourages him as much as she keeps him at bay; Phèdre lets herself be persuaded to confess her love for Hippolyte to her nurse Œnone, and after that it won't be long before she is confessing it to Hippolyte himself. In each case, self-deception is central: when Phèdre approaches Hippolyte in the great confession scene (II.5), she has resolved to speak to him of the political situation in the wake of his father's reported death, but in his presence cannot help her language deviating towards the subject she most wants to talk about; in fact, the scenario is repeated with different characters and different emphases no fewer than five times in the first two acts of *Phèdre*.

Another very different example which movingly reveals the delicacy of Racine's psychological and linguistic instruments occurs in *Bérénice*, the most formal, decorous, and *inhibited* of Racine's tragedies. Whereas Phèdre, at the moment where her passion finally breaks through the diplomatic façade she has struggled to maintain, switches famously and dramatically from the 'vous' form of address to 'tu' (*Phèdre*, line 670), the noble characters of *Bérénice*, however hard-pressed they may be in the endgame of their amorous triangle, never deviate from the polite form in addressing one another. But when Titus at last manages to tell her that they must part, she breaks into a bitter tirade ostensibly blaming him for not telling her this long ago, before she had fallen so irreversibly in love with him; and this tirade contains two and a half lines in which she imagines him, in that happier past, addressing her with the intimacy of the 'tu' form:

> Que ne me disiez-vous: «Princesse infortunée,
> Où vas-tu t'engager, et quel est ton espoir?
> Ne donne point un cœur, qu'on ne peut recevoir.»

[Why did you not say to me: 'Unhappy Princess, what commitment are you making, what hopes have you? Do not give a heart that cannot be accepted.']

On the surface, the speech she invents for him is correct, even frosty, but the pronouns tell a different story: the story of a love admitted and exchanged, which had been theirs and to which they can never now return.

This focus of interest depends first on a psychology in which conscious *intention* is always undermined by hidden or unconscious *motive*; on this premiss is built a pessimistic ethics in which the possibilities of moral achievement or transcendence offered by surface values such as honesty or generosity cannot be fulfilled, because the values themselves are already flawed by self-deception. This is a world in which the heroes of Corneille's theatre could not survive, and Racine chose in the earlier part of his career to write two successive tragedies on Roman themes in which he expressly inverted the values of his predecessor. In *Britannicus*, the young emperor Néron, apparently poised on the brink of a reign of virtue, slides unstoppably into vice and thus provides a counter-example to the conversion of Auguste portrayed in *Cinna*; in *Bérénice*, Titus, forced by Roman custom to renounce his beloved Bérénice, embraces his *gloire* with reluctance, something which none of Corneille's heroes would have dreamt of doing: his key line 'Et, puisqu'il faut céder, cédons à notre gloire' ('And, since we must yield, let us yield to our glory'), would have unleashed a tide of contemptuous rhetoric from the likes of Rodrigue (*Le Cid*) or Horace.

The blueprint for this pessimistic vision of human powers is already present in Pascal's *Pensées*, although one should remember that only a partial text was available in this period, and then not until 1670. In Pascal, the vision is set in its full theological context, yet already translated into a French which would be accessible to a wide range of lay readers. The other essential mediating text here is La Rochefoucauld's *Maximes*, still traceably in contact with Port-Royal, but one decisive step closer to full secularization. Virtually all theological reference is excluded from this text, leaving only the unsparing analysis of moral values and perceptions which are intrinsically fallible: 'Nos vertus ne sont, le plus souvent, que des vices déguisés' ('Our virtues are most often only disguised vices'). Even qualifications such as 'le plus souvent', which appear to leave space for authentic values, actually increase the uncertainty of moral knowledge: in these crystalline formulations, there is always a blur at the centre, a flaw in the diamond of lucidity.

One can trace the force of the *Maximes* as a vehicle for such conceptions in many works of the period. When Dom Juan in Molière's play decides in the final stages of his abandonment to amorality to adopt the mask of hypocrisy, he defends himself with a 'maxim' which sounds just like La Rochefoucauld's: 'l'hypocrisie est un vice à la mode, et tous les vices à la mode passent pour vertus' ('hypocrisy is a fashionable vice, and all fashionable vices are regarded as virtues'). La Fontaine dedicates one of his fables (I.11, 'L'Homme et son image') to the author of the *Maximes*, portraying the book as a mirror in which everyone sees their true face and which no one can evade. And in his *Caractères*, first published in 1688, La Bruyère absorbs many of La Rochefoucauld's themes into a mixed work which contains 'maxims' alongside caricatural portraits and longer reflective fragments.

At the centre of these issues is the question of the *honnête homme*, a focal instance of the preoccupation with politeness and the rules for proper behaviour which spread through Europe in the sixteenth and seventeenth centuries. Ideally, it is a concept in which social and moral values are fused. In the eighteenth century, the moral connotation will become dominant, but in the age of Louis XIV, the *honnête homme de cour* is a social being whose behaviour never offends, never obtrudes, whose politeness is so flawless that it is almost invisible. He is instantly distinguishable from the pedant, the prude, the boaster; his dress is never flamboyant, his gestures always restrained. Yet the word *honnête* connotes moral value, as if the highest ethic were a form of social poise. This is a key example of the way in which the competitive, claustrophobic society of the court (and by extension the upper bourgeoisie, who strove to imitate the court) sought an accommodation between different and often conflicting value-systems: the behaviour admired at court wasn't intrinsically moral, but it had a moral name. The so-called *raisonneurs* of Molière's comedies (the sensible characters who try to restrain and pacify the manic central characters) are *honnêtes gens*: they are always discreet, moderate, flexible, sympathetic, but their discretion usually takes the form of recommending the form of behaviour which risks least public embarrassment—it's better to be a cuckold than to make a fuss about fidelity, it's better to be only mildly devout than to advertise one's devotion. The scandal of Dom Juan is that he is an *honnête homme* who is seen to break all the moral rules acknowledged by society, and who, to make matters worse, is a freethinker. The scandal of *Le Misanthrope* is that it is not Alceste, the moral standard-bearer, who is the *honnête homme*, but Philinte, who makes endless accommodations with society. In these ways, Molière's theatre relentlessly exposes the value-clashes which were endemic in contemporary society, and it is perhaps Molière who provides the most compelling behind-the-scenes view of what makes the *honnête homme*. In his short play *L'Impromptu de Versailles*, written in defence of *L'École des femmes*, he appears in his own name as actor-director-playwright, casting his latest piece (*L'Impromptu* itself). He tells each actor how to play his role—the pedant, the *petit marquis* and so on; to the actor who will appear as his spokesman, he says: 'Pour vous, vous faites un honnête homme de cour ... c'est-à-dire que vous devez prendre un air posé, un ton de voix naturel, et gesticuler le moins qu'il vous sera possible' ('As for you, you're playing a court gentleman ... that is to say that you must adopt a relaxed manner, a natural tone of voice, and gesticulate as little as you possibly can'). Such moments remind one how self-aware Molière's audience was, how intimate the relationship between stage and social scene.

LUCIDITY AND UNCERTAINTY

In the works of this period, despite differences of genre, there are formal similarities which operate at the level of language. As we have seen, language and linguistic usage had become a particularly intense focus of cultural reflection in the seventeenth century: it had been linked to notions of common sense, rationality, or the natural in an attempt to give everyday polite usage a stable and permanent grounding. The form of the maxim, the form of the fable, the comic and the tragic forms all strain towards economy and lucidity. They place little emphasis on concrete denotation, reference to the physical world, whether literal or metaphorical; instead, they strive to handle abstraction with a precision that comes not from extensive definition but from the precise placing of terms in context, and in relation to one another. This means that it would be a mistake to think that the abstract vocabulary of late seventeenth-century France is endowed with fixed meanings. Users of the language behave as if their words (*honnêteté*, for example) had a strong and reliable sense, but there is an unease that comes when that sense shows signs of cracking under pressure. This is the blur that I mentioned earlier as characteristic of La Rochefoucauld's maxims; it appears again in La Fontaine's *Fables*, where there is notoriously often some discrepancy between the fable itself and its purported moral message ('Les Compagnons d'Ulysse' is a good example). In Racine, the failure of language to deliver full meanings—its deviations, its evasive silences—becomes the instrument of tragedy itself. Thus, to return to an earlier scene from *Bérénice*, Titus' moral and psychological inability to tell Bérénice that they must part is translated into the figure of aposiopesis, into sentences stammered and left unfinished (she has asked him whether he is tired of her):

> Non, Madame. Jamais, puisqu'il faut vous parler,
> Mon cœur de plus de feux ne se sentit brûler ...
> Mais ...
> BÉRÉNICE
>   Achevez.
> TITUS
>   Hélas!
> BÉRÉNICE
>   Parlez.
> TITUS
>   Rome ... l'Empire ...
> BÉRÉNICE
> Hé bien?

TITUS
Sortons, Paulin: je ne lui puis rien dire.

[TITUS: No, Madam; never ... since I must speak to you—did my heart burn with more passionate fires ... But ... BÉRÉNICE: Say everything. TIT: Alas! BÉR: Speak. TIT: Rome ... the Empire ... BÉR: Well? TIT: Let us go, Paulin: I can say nothing to her.]

The force of this exchange lies in the collapse of the elegant if impassioned rhetoric which the characters seek to maintain at all times. In a world where politeness is itself a tragic constraint, the breakdown of language is a sign that the characters' world is itself about to fall apart.

Images of a surface brilliance precariously suspended above darkness are hard to avoid in the culture of Louis XIV's reign. The collective effort to achieve a civilization of unparalleled glory and power seems to have promoted in equal measure a brooding on the murky depths of human moral blindness, on deceit and self-interest, and on the transience of all these trappings of magnificence. Both are present in some of Bossuet's *Oraisons funèbres*, where the—at times quite unsavoury—lives of the great are paraded as examples of human vanity, and where the supremacy of the monarch and his court is adulated at the very moment when the curtain is about to fall. Contemporary engravings show that these too were theatrical events (see Figure 10, p. 160). The whole court gathered to hear Bossuet's eloquent performance, to celebrate their unique status, and to contemplate their own imminent demise: 'Jetez les yeux de toutes parts', he declaims:

voilà tout ce qu'a pu faire la magnificence et la piété pour honorer un héros: des titres, des inscriptions, vaines marques de ce qui n'est plus; des figures qui semblent pleurer autour d'un tombeau, et des fragiles images d'une douleur que le temps emporte avec tout le reste; des colonnes qui semblent vouloir porter jusqu'au ciel le magnifique témoignage de notre néant; et rien enfin ne manque dans tous ces honneurs, que celui à qui on les rend.

[Cast your eyes around you, and you will see everything that pomp and piety have been able to do to honour a hero: titles, inscriptions, vain marks of something that no longer exists; statues that seem to weep around a tomb, and fragile images of a grief that time carries away with all the rest; columns that seem to strive to carry up to heaven an extravagant testimony to our nothingness; in all these honours, in short, nothing is lacking except the one for whom they are intended.]

Finally, in Racine's *Athalie*, written during the decline of the reign in a stifling atmosphere of devotional rigour, the worldly power-game is played out by characters who are, on both sides, tyrannical, fanatical, and violent. When Joad, the high priest of Jehovah, finds his enemy

*Funebris pompa, ac cenotaphium quod Henricæ Annæ ab Anglia, A Rege
christianissimo Ludouico xiuᵒ pio felia semper augusto in Basilica Diui Dionisÿ
in Francia die vigesima prima augusti. M.D.C.LXX. exitatum est.*

10. The highly theatrical decor for the funeral of Henriette d'Angleterre (Henrietta
Maria, the widow of Charles I of England, who had fled to France after her husband's
execution) at the royal cathedral of Saint-Denis.

Mathan, priest of Baal, within the temple precincts, he bursts into
crude invective: 'de quel front cet ennemi de Dieu | Vient-il infecter
l'air qu'il respire en ce lieu?' ('how does this enemy of God dare come
into this place and infect the air he breathes?'); Mathan replies coolly
enough: 'On reconnaît Joad à cette violence' ('Such violence is characteristic of Joad'), but Joad launches into a stream of Old Testament
curses, predicting that the dogs that ate Jezabel are waiting for him too,
and Mathan departs, fatally shaken. At the denouement, the ultimate
triumph of God's protected orphan is belied by the prophecy that he too

will in turn become a tyrant and an idolater. Other prophecies and allusions anticipate the Redemption: *Athalie* was after all written for a Christian audience. Yet, for the characters, that hope is as distant and as uncertain as the 'Dieu caché' of the Jansenists, and they are condemned to the endless clashing of wills on a crumbling human stage.

The representations of the court I have sketched out here through the texts of the period are of course not concrete images of the 'real' court, but a historical model constructed selectively from the perceptions and imaginations of contemporaries. It might be compared, for example, with the social and ethical constructions one can derive from medieval courtly poetry, or with representations of the city in the nineteenth-century novel and elsewhere. What emerges is the sense of a *place*, of a crowded and anxiety-ridden environment where there was little privacy and everyone was constantly subjected to the hostile gaze of everyone else.

'ANCIENTS' AND 'MODERNS'

This dense cluster of like-minded texts was of course not confined to the court: it spilled out via theatrical performance and the printed text to the whole of literate society. And it was to be enormously influential: La Rochefoucauld and Pascal were read and internalized by writers as diverse as Baudelaire, Nietzsche, Gide, and Proust; Racine provided a benchmark for French tragedy, all the more powerful because controversial. The claim of these texts to canonic status is not specious. The problem begins when they are allowed to assert themselves collectively as the paradigm of a French 'Classical age', indeed of French literature, of French literate expression as a whole. For whatever one may think of that, the consequence is that many other types of writing, often vigorous and forward-looking ones, are jostled to the sidelines.

This effect is partly a long-term consequence of the propaganda campaign that was waged against those who refused to conform to the new orthodoxy. But if one reads against the grain, one can easily see that such attacks demonstrate the presence—and indeed the popularity—of the writers and styles they attempt to occlude. One of these writers is Corneille himself, who has usually been regarded as one of the twin stars of a French classical tragedy. In his *Impromptu de Versailles*, Molière parodies the supposedly inflated acting style of the Hôtel de Bourgogne, where Corneille's plays were often performed, and claims to replace it with a 'natural' style. Yet Molière's troupe themselves staged some of Corneille's plays, and audiences continued to enjoy *Le Cid* and *Cinna* throughout the period when Racine was in vogue (Racine's own attacks on Corneille, in his prefaces to *Britannicus* and *Bérénice*, also prove this). Similarly, when in *Les Précieuses ridicules* and *Les Femmes savantes* Molière satirizes women's desire to play an active role in high culture and the advancement of learning, that is because women were indeed culturally active and would continue to be throughout this period; Boileau's more direct and scathing attacks in his late *Satires* are a sign that the old guard is *not* winning this battle.

In many ways, in fact, the aesthetic that Boileau, Racine, and certain of their contemporaries subscribed to is a conservative reaction against more positive and optimistic ways of writing and thinking. Viewed in the long term, this is merely another phase in the controversy over the choice of cultural models which flared in the imitation debates of the humanist period (see above, pp. 129–30, 137) and in which writers as different as Du Bellay, Montaigne, Corneille, Descartes, and Pascal played distinctive roles. In the late seventeenth century, it re-emerges as the 'quarrel of the Ancients and the Moderns'. The *anciens*, as their name implies, insist on the supremacy of ancient models, ancient genres, ancient poetics, and many of their masterpieces place themselves openly and self-consciously in relation to such models. La Fontaine rewrites Babrius, Phaedrus, and Aesop. Racine seeks an ever-closer relationship to the great tragedies of ancient Greece. Like the *Ars poetica* of the Latin poet Horace, Boileau's *Art poétique* encodes the 'rules' of poetics for a cultivated lay audience in the form of a poem. La Bruyère publishes a translation of Theophrastus' *Characters* as a prelude to his own *Caractères*, which opens with the famous dictum 'Tout est dit, et l'on vient trop tard depuis plus de sept mille ans qu'il y a des hommes et qui pensent' ('Everything has already been said, and we come too late: mankind has existed, and has been thinking, for more than seven thousand years'). Explicitly or implicitly, these writers attack the *modernes* who prefer to start afresh, like Descartes with his *tabula rasa*, or at least to adapt to a new age the principles adopted by ancient writers and thinkers.

Meanwhile, as we have seen, the *modernes* remain active and well organized. There are groups which discuss Cartesian ideas (attacked by La Fontaine in his *Discours à Madame de Sablière*) and the new developments in science and scientific technology—optics, the telescope, astronomy, dissection; others deplore the social and marital disadvantages women were subjected to, even questioning the institution of marriage itself; others again put forward a programme for a renewal of literature, defending modern genres such as the novel and the opera, modern subjects, and modern styles.

Among the latter were Desmarets de Saint-Sorlin, who had been active in the Académie from the period of Richelieu's supremacy, and

Charles Perrault, who was to play a major role in the later stages of the quarrel: between them, they illustrate the staying-power of these issues. Perrault's *Contes*, his brilliant rewritings of folk stories as what we now call 'fairy tales', launched a whole new vogue in which women writers (Henriette-Julie de Murat, Marie-Catherine d'Aulnoy, Marie-Jeanne L'Héritier) were to feature prominently; here, too, he was a quintessential 'Modern', eschewing ancient models in favour of a domestic culture. Meanwhile, Corneille's late plays, contemporary with Racine's, continue to stage articulate and principled women who are formidably capable of using language as a weapon against tyrants and seducers. Saint-Évremond, exiled in London, writes essays defending Corneille as a model of what a modern playwright should be, and in the process touches on the theme of human potential, the possibility of intellectual and cultural progress, which is at the core of the debate between *anciens* and *modernes*.

The quarrel broke out actively and violently in 1687, when Charles Perrault read his poem *Le Siècle de Louis le Grand* at the Académie Française, for it celebrated the achievements of the reign without referring to leading *anciens* such as Racine. The Académie Française was indeed at this stage dominated by the *modernes*, with Boileau leading the counter-attack. An uneasy reconciliation was reached in the 1690s, but the polemic between individuals and coteries is less important than the long-term issues which are at stake: the role of classical antiquity in education and in culture at large, the innate capacity of humanity for improvement and progress, and the value of scientific and technological discovery.

Equally important are the crossovers which show that changes in the deep structure belie the drawing of ephemeral battlelines. Pascal's view of mathematics and science is unequivocally 'modern', but his pessimistic view of human nature affiliates him to the *anciens*. The achievements of Racine and other *anciens* provide ammunition for the claim of the *modernes* that the present age can outdo classical antiquity in cultural brilliance. La Bruyère, firmly entrenched in the camp of the *anciens*, is capable of an astonishingly relativistic perspective: in one of his prefaces, he imagines readers of future ages encountering the strangeness of seventeenth-century French society; in the *Caractères* ('De la cour' 74), the French court is seen as from the supposed point of view of North American native peoples ('Hurons' and 'Iroquois'). These techniques of defamiliarization will become potent vehicles of innovating thought in the eighteenth century. On the other hand, in a *Digression sur les anciens et les modernes* (1688), the arch-*moderne* Fontenelle predicts an exponential expansion of human knowledge together with constant improvements of 'method' (a Cartesian word) in order to handle this flood of data, while writing in a witty, lucid, refined prose that places him in the stylistic mainstream alongside the best of the *anciens*. Fontenelle is a forerunner of the innovative polymaths who will come to be known as *philosophes*; indeed, he will himself survive until the mid-eighteenth century, a living symbol of continuity.

OUTLINES OF THE NOVEL

Seventeenth-century prose fiction is a genre cultivated above all by the *modernes* and their forerunners. In a retrospective history, it may well look like the crossover point between older traditions of narrative fiction and the rise of the modern novel in the other sense of 'modern', that is to say the realist novel that reaches its peak in the nineteenth century. It is all the more important not to judge early modern prose fiction by the criteria of later forms: it responded to different sensibilities, different functions, different ways of reading. A brief sketch of its principal varieties will also show the mutations it began to engender as the age of Louis XIV came to an end.

The most popular and prolific mode of fiction throughout this period is what may loosely be called romance. These long, rambling narratives, featuring love and adventure in equal measure, together with abductions, foundlings, hidden identities, separations, trials of prowess and fidelity, and sometimes incursions into the world of the supernatural (magic islands, enchanters and enchantresses, fabulous creatures and the like), are the direct descendants of the medieval chivalric romance, although the influence of late Greek novels like Heliodorus' *Aethiopica* is added to the mix from the mid-sixteenth century. Other variants include the pastoral novel of which *Astrée* is the canonic example, and the heroic novel in the manner of Madeleine de Scudéry: the intense interest in the modalities of love which characterizes d'Urfé's work reappears, for example, in the famous 'Carte de Tendre' ('Map of the Land of Tender Love') which was inserted in the first volume of *Clélie*.

The extravagances of romance begin from an early stage to spawn hyperbolic versions and parodies. The Italian Ludovico Ariosto's *Orlando furioso* (1532), based on the story of the epic French hero Roland, was translated into French and remained popular until well into the seventeenth century. Rabelais's comic fictions provide another kind of example, where the deeds of chivalric heroes are grossly inflated, the heroes become giants, and the quest turns into a wild goose chase. The classic European example of the parodic romance, however, is *Don Quixote*, where the romance plot is explicitly presented as a product of the imagination: Quixote has not only read too many romances, he also fails to understand that they are only fiction (Emma Bovary will later suffer from a similar error). This shows that romance, like the practices of chivalry itself (crusades, jousts) and the socio-political structures it was dependent on, is already perceived as out-moded. *Don Quixote* was translated into French in 1614 and was widely read and imitated.

The picaresque novel is essentially a variant of this same class of fic-tions. Here, however, the hero is usually of humble origins, and his adventures, equally unglorious, take place in everyday settings such as provincial towns, country roads, and inns. This transposition of the chivalric romance plot into familiar, down-to-earth surroundings is intrinsically parodic, and may be accompanied by burlesque uses of high style: Scarron's *Roman comique*, for example, which provides an entertaining glimpse of the lifestyle of a group of travelling actors in the early seventeenth century, opens with a highly ornate sentence, full of mythological references, describing the coming of dawn. In this case, the hero and heroine appear to be characters of noble birth who have fallen on hard times—the novel is incomplete, so it is impossible to be certain. This kind of interplay between social levels will remain an important feature of novels in the picaresque mode in the eighteenth century: it recurs, for example, in Marivaux's *La Vie de Marianne* (1731–41) and *Le Paysan parvenu* (1735–6), and seems to be a symptom of the transference of the subject matter of prose narrative from a socially privileged setting to the lives of ordinary people. The very title of Furetière's *Roman bourgeois* (1666) is another indicator of this change. In the nineteenth century, when virtually all novels have a bourgeois setting, such a title would be virtually meaningless.

All these types of fiction are characteristically long and episodic. They engage the reader's interest by constantly interrupting the vari-ous strands of the story at moments of high interest, adding further sec-ondary narratives which may be more or less remote from the main line of the plot, and systematically deferring narrative outcomes. Indeed, many of these works—Rabelais's fictions, *Astrée*, Scarron's *Roman comique*, and Marivaux's *La Vie de Marianne*—remain unfinished because the author either dies or loses interest, although it is usually possible to guess what the ending will be (marriage of hero and heroine, recovery of noble identity, entry into the power and privilege which that entails). What the readers seem to enjoy is rather the continuous polyphony of the plot, the suspense and the surprises, and—in many seventeenth- and eighteenth-century variants from *Astrée* to *La Vie de Marianne* and beyond—various kinds of reflection on the amorous ethics and psychology to which the story gives rise. In other words, romance was closer to soap opera than to what we think of as the novel. It implies semi-public consumption of narrative: daily episodes read aloud and discussed in small groups over an indefinite period of time (the longer the better) in a social world where people have plenty of leisure and not many other forms of entertainment. Of course, such novels were also read silently, in private, and many of those readers were literate members of less privileged classes, but the *model* of read-ing—the model projected or implied by the fictions themselves—remains the same. Here again the picaresque shows a social muta-tion: secondary stories are told by innkeepers, chance acquaintances encountered en route, and other members of the motley cast of characters.

Romance was consumed in a social world dominated by women, the world of the *salons*, and women were usually represented as its princi-pal readers. It is not surprising, therefore, that many women writers chose the novel as their preferred medium: this is a phenomenon which will continue until modern times. A further type of narrative fiction in which women writers made a major impact and which proves to be important for the history of prose fiction (not least because it gave rise to the English word 'novel') is the *nouvelle*, or short prose fiction. Collections of *nouvelles* such as Marguerite de Navarre's *Heptaméron* (see above, pp. 120–2) were popular in the sixteenth century; during the wars of religion the subject matter of such collections was often grim, and the *histoire tragique* becomes a sub-genre. In the later seventeenth century, this genre reappears in new guise in the *nouvelle historique*, where the subject matter is drawn from recent history. Segrais's *Nouvelles françaises* (1656–7) set in train a crucial series of experiments which include Madame de Lafayette's early story *La Princesse de Montpensier*, *Les Désordres de l'amour* by the prolific Madame de Villedieu, and Lafayette's *La Princesse de Clèves*, where an allusion to the *Heptaméron* suggests that readers would have been expected to recognize Marguerite de Navarre's stories as an important precur-sor. Segrais and other contemporary critics even devised a poetics for this genre on the analogy of tragedy, demanding *vraisemblance* and a stretched form of the tragic 'unities' in explicit opposition to the loose, open-ended form of romance (now widely ridiculed). In some ways, this was a local experiment, rather than the 'birth of the novel'. But it certainly provided models for a more concise novelistic form whose plot-structure was tighter and more urgently directed towards a denouement. There are secondary narrative episodes in *La Princesse de Clèves*, but they are all firmly linked to the main narrative, whether thematically or causally, and it is difficult to imagine Madame de Lafayette's novel as a soap opera.

The desperate, and unsuccessful, attempts of the Princesse de Clèves to find peace and privacy provide a graphic illustration of the fact that the late seventeenth century was an intensely public age, at least for those at court. This is no doubt one reason why private and personal forms of writing began to proliferate at this time. In the *nouvelle historique* itself, the great events and dramas of history only provide the backdrop for the inner life of its characters. Similarly, memoirs of the period document the *secret* world of the court, the intrigues and gossip and amorous entanglements that official historiographers leave out. The vast and rambling memoirs of the duc de Saint-Simon, one of the least read masterpieces of the age, provide us not only with a picture of the squalor and pettiness which often lay behind the glittering façade of the court, but also with the precise angle of perception of a senior courtier. This is prose narrative on a monumental scale; how much of it is fiction is hard to tell, but in this area the distinction is not paramount, since what matters is the imaginative reconstruction of a lost world (Proust owes not a little to Saint-Simon).

Women too wrote memoirs, as well as fictions that read like memoirs. But perhaps above all they wrote letters: Madame de Sévigné's colourful, spirited, and often moving letters to her daughter Madame de Grignan and others are a microscopic record of the everyday comings and goings, moods and opinions of a well-born family and its intimates as refracted by an unusually acute sensibility. That they were not meant for publication removes them from the formal epistolary genre as it had been practised for some two hundred years, yet the letter remains here the vehicle of a first-person narrative. It is not an accident that the most successful new mutation that emerged from the teeming gene-pool of seventeenth-century narrative was the letter-novel. In 1669, a sensation was caused by a slim anonymous volume containing five letters purportedly written from the convent by a young Portuguese woman who had been abandonded by her French lover. Although it is now generally believed that they were composed by the sieur de Guilleragues, contemporary readers assumed that these *Lettres portugaises* were, as the preface claimed, a French translation of an authentic Portuguese original; the pathos of the woman's situation thus acquired a peculiar intensity. A trend had been set. The vogue for letter-novels in the eighteenth century will culminate in the brilliant *Lettres d'une Péruvienne* of Françoise de Graffigny (who herself wrote an enormous number of letters, full of graphic and moving personal details), Rousseau's *La Nouvelle Héloïse* and Laclos's *Les Liaisons dangereuses*, all of which go to some length to persuade the reader that the correspondence is authentic. Authenticity is here deeply linked to the use of an intimate, personal form and to a first-person discourse. There is no omniscient narrator; the letter-writers are all imprisoned within their own subjective perspectives, and often make disastrous errors as a result. As it moves away from the world of romance towards the private lives of contemporary characters, prose fiction is here becoming an instrument for exploring individual consciousness and its limitations.

THE END OF A REIGN: LITERATURE AT THE TURN OF THE CENTURY

The story of the court as a primary focus for French culture, which had begun in the early sixteenth century, comes to a close with the fading of Louis XIV's reign in the early eighteenth. Economic problems, unsuccessful military adventures and the king's failing health had progressively stifled the energies of the court as a cultural organism.

The career of Fénelon, archbishop of Cambrai, illustrates the constraints of court culture in this terminal period as well as its devout leanings. Highly favoured by Bossuet, Fénelon was the author of *Télémaque*, a novel in the style of the 'Moderns' about the son of Odysseus, and intended as an educational aid for the king's grandson. However, an episode in *Télémaque* depicting an ideal city state was held to be critical of the regime, and the archbishop was permanently exiled from the court. Yet his novel continued to be popular throughout the eighteenth century and was read retrospectively as an anticipation of Enlightenment ideas. Such are the crossings-over that characterize the last phase of Louis XIV's reign, where innovative ideas are often present in conjectural form in works that otherwise appear to be conformist.

In the early eighteenth century, the comic energies released by Molière also underwent significant transformations. Molière had used controversial issues such as religious hypocrisy, libertinage, and the education of women as materials for 'problem comedies' (*Tartuffe*, *Dom Juan*, *Les Femmes savantes*) which have remained intractable to interpretation ever since. Was he primarily a brilliant entertainer who enjoyed provoking his audience, or is his critique of the society he lived in grounded in intellectual and moral commitment? Perhaps—as with Rabelais—one should avoid this false antithesis between the 'comic' and the 'serious', and understand Molière's theatre as the product of a fertile imagination capable of seizing on the most sensitive questions of his day and embodying them in a dramatic form which preserves their problematic character. There is, in any case, little sign that Molière had some carefully thought-out intellectual agenda.

The comedies of Lesage—notably *Crispin, rival de son maître* and *Turcaret*—already shift the balance. The satire is sharper, and the theme of the *valet* who rises to a position of supremacy over his master by the end of *Turcaret* (a remake of *Le Bourgeois Gentilhomme*) has a markedly subversive edge. Marivaux's comedies, mostly composed in the 1720s and 1730s, take place in a kind of fantasy realm liable to the strangest inversions—not only in the world of Parisian society, where manipulation of language can make almost anything happen (*Les Fausses Confidences*), but also on imaginary islands: the scenario of *La Nouvelle Colonie* experimentally inverts the power-relations of the sexes, while *L'Île des esclaves* gives the comic convention of role-reversal between masters and servants a much sharper edge.

After the death of Louis XIV in 1715, Parisian society had in fact entered a phase of at least superficial freedom in reaction to years of repression. Censorship will continue to be rife, especially in matters of religion and politics, but it is more frequently challenged, freethinking attitudes are fashionable, and the moral atmosphere becomes visibly laxer, more effervescent. Henceforth, inventive literary activity will no longer be organized primarily as an instrument of the monarch's power. Shifting initially to the *salons* of the 'Moderns', it will still seek patronage in high places, but often in less orthodox forms. Louis XV's mistress Madame de Pompadour, for example, will preside over the activities of some the most avant-garde writers and thinkers: a famous painting by La Tour pictures her with a musical score in her hands and with leading works by *philosophes*, including a volume of the *Encyclopédie*, on the table beside her (see Figure 11, p. 170).

THE LETTER-FORM: MONTESQUIEU, VOLTAIRE, GRAFFIGNY

The utopias of Fénelon and Marivaux, like Lesage's satires, are still confined within what is virtually a self-censoring form: their unreality is marked by a fictional mode outside which it is assumed that established values continue relatively undisturbed. This is true neither of Montesquieu's *Lettres persanes* nor of Voltaire's *Lettres sur les Anglais*, later renamed *Lettres philosophiques*. Both use the technique exploited so brilliantly by Pascal in the *Lettres provinciales* of staging an innocent, uninformed first-person voice in search of knowledge. Both use it to

11. This portrait of Madame de Pompadour by Maurice Quentin de La Tour (1755) represents her as a patroness of the *philosophes* and an incarnation of eighteenth-century *salon* culture. She holds a musical score, key works of the *philosophes* are placed on the table at her side, and other elements evoke her interest in painting and engraving.

turn a critical searchlight on an unprecedentedly wide range of questions: religion, government, social organization, gender relations, science, literature and the arts. Both also extend the cultural relativism of Montaigne, in particular of his chapter 'Des cannibales': Montesquieu's protagonists are a small party of Persian travellers who come to Paris to admire its renowned civilization; Voltaire writes in his own name as a traveller to England who is given a grand tour of its institutions and achievements. The effect in each case is to defamiliarize French institutions and culture, much as La Bruyère had defamiliarized Versailles in 'De la cour' 74, but again on an immeasurably larger scale. The naïve observer is a kind of *tabula rasa* sweeping away all forms of cultural conditioning and allowing the most hallowed beliefs and traditions to be seen from a detached viewpoint. The Persian Rica says that the French king has amazing powers, but that he is subservient to an even greater magician: 'Ce magicien s'appelle *le Pape*: tantôt il lui fait croire que trois ne sont qu'un, que le pain qu'on mange n'est pas du pain ou que le vin qu'on boit n'est pas du vin, et mille autres choses de cette espèce' ('This magician is called *the Pope*: sometimes he makes him [the king] believe that three is only one, that the bread one eats isn't bread or that the wine one drinks isn't wine, and innumerable other things of that kind'). This deflating reference to the doctrines of the Trinity and of transubstantiation is a typical example of a device systematically exploited by the *philosophes*.

Montesquieu's work, however, has a feature not shared by Voltaire's: it is also a rather loosely composed letter-*novel*. The Persians have left their wives behind in the harem under the strict surveillance of eunuchs. As the husbands increasingly familiarize themselves with European culture, staying much longer than originally intended, the wives become restive and finally stage a revolution. One implication of this story is that each culture has its own internal logic and equilibrium; cross-cultural influence can cause profound change. Another theme is the violence locked up in tyrannical regimes, always waiting to be released, and Montesquieu crucially embodies tyranny here in gender relations rather than in systems of government. The women's revenge blows apart the fabric of the text: all those intelligent, civilized letters sent by the Persians, their whole experiment in cultural tourism, are shown to rest on a blindness, a taking for granted of absolute male supremacy. The final letters come exclusively *from* the harem; a kind of sexual turbulence breaks out, with consequences that remain unpredictable.

The reflections on society, law, and government sketched out in the harem story and in episodes like the 'myth of the Troglodytes' (letters 11–14) were later to be systematically elaborated in the vast *De l'esprit des lois*, which analyses the way in which different types of government, topography, climate, commerce, religion, and culture generate sharply contrasted legal systems. This thorough-going relativistic appraisal of the foundations of law is a landmark in the history of European political and social thought and was to be influential also in the drafting of the American constitution; it is highly visible among the works selected to embody the Enlightenment in the portrait of Madame de Pompadour (see Figure 11).

Montesquieu's later forays into philosophical *fiction*, however, were undistinguished; Voltaire, by contrast, discovered its potential in mid-career and thereafter used it again and again to give graphic form to his intellectual, political, and moral reflections. *Zadig*, a story about the inscrutability of Providence, was the first to be published (1748), but it is likely that *Micromégas* was begun as early as 1739: it is a short tale, influenced by Swift's *Gulliver's Travels*, in which a giant from Sirius visits earth, admires the scientific achievements of humankind, but is shocked by its folly and cruelty. Both of these stories exploit the point of view of an uninformed or perplexed character, whether he is simply an observer and outsider or, as in *Zadig*, experiences the problem of evil and injustice in the world through the ups and downs of his own life. In 1759 this paradigm bore fruit in *Candide*, where the hero, as his name indicates, is the personification of naïveté. *L'Ingénu* followed in 1767: this time the allegorical name is conferred on a young Frenchman raised among the Hurons (an echo of La Bruyère?) who comes to France and experiences its corruption. Voltaire's philosophical *contes* are narrated in the third person rather than in the first-person form of the *Lettres persanes* and the *Lettres philosophiques*. They swing with a kind of frantic energy between the farcical, the grotesque, and the tragic, setting traps for the reader at every twist and turn of the narrative.

Philosophical fictions take many forms in the eighteenth century. Some, like Rousseau's controversial pedagogical novel *Émile*, sacrifice narrative interest to ideas, but other variants are as inventive as Voltaire's. One instance is Madame de Graffigny's *Lettres d'une Péruvienne*, which looks at first like a straight letter-novel but turns out to be much more. The sole letter-writer is an Inca princess who has been abducted by Europeans on the eve of her wedding and taken to Europe. The Frenchman in whose ship she travels falls in love with her and treats her well, but his family objects to this bizarre passion. Meanwhile, she hopes her Inca fiancé, who later turns out to have been taken separately to Spain, will join her. The story is told through the letters she sends him, supposedly translated from the *quipos* (the Inca equivalent of writing, consisting of coloured knots tied on cords) she uses in order to communicate with him. The reader is thus aware of the complex acts of cultural translation which are required to make the princess's perspective comprehensible. It takes a long time for her to understand what is happening to her: she has never been on a ship before, she has no idea what the Frenchman's demonstrations of affection signify, and when she gets to France, she becomes a naïve heroine, a female counterpart of the Ingénu. Eventually she learns French and begins to be able to sort things out for herself, by which time we have been given an abrasive satire on French customs, morals, and social prejudice. *Lettres d'une Péruvienne* is thus, in one sense, a more extreme example of cross-cultural fiction than *Les Lettres persanes* (to which the preface refers). Although it contains no lengthy disquisitions on political and religious questions, it also ends with a remarkable declaration of autonomy and self-possession on the part of the heroine: far from falling victim to the alien culture of France, or being subjected to the will of a Peruvian or French lover, she will henceforth make her own way. Just as one thought that everything was ending in disaster, Zilia walks out of the novel with her life firmly in her hands:

Le plaisir d'être; ce plaisir oublié, ignoré même de tant d'aveugles humains; cette pensée si douce, ce bonheur si pur, *je suis, je vis, j'existe*, pourrait seul rendre heureux, si l'on s'en souvenait, si l'on en jouissait, si l'on en connaissait le prix.

[The pleasure of being, that forgotten pleasure that so many blind human beings are even unaware of, the sweet thought, the pure joy of knowing *I am, I am alive, I exist*, would alone be capable of making us happy if we remembered it, if we savoured it, if we knew its value.]

Lettres d'une Péruvienne lies at a tangent to the fictions written by the *philosophes*, but by reading it in their company, one begins to unsettle the French Enlightenment canon in a way the Inca princess might have approved of.

THE *PHILOSOPHES* IN ACTION: THE *ENCYCLOPÉDIE*

The philosophical fictions of Montesquieu and Voltaire will give us a first definition of the *philosophe*. The term belongs to the period itself—there is, for example, an article 'Philosophe' in the *Encyclopédie*—as does the phenomenon it refers to. The *philosophes* are not systematic philosophers like Aristotle or Descartes. They share an attitude rather than a precise set of doctrines. Their chief aim is the exposure of every kind of prejudice, whether conditioned in the individual by society and education or entrenched in institutions which retain their power by inertia. Their method, as we have seen, is comparative and relativizing: travel (whether literal or fictional), cultural difference and cultural interchange exert the leverage which shifts the unthinking assumption that the culture one happens to inhabit is natural and superior. A belief in tolerance, humane behaviour, liberal values, flows from this radical reappraisal: English Protestants, Persians, Peruvians, Hurons all have their distinctive worlds that should be respected. Repressive regimes, laws, and religions must be untiringly attacked, and the self-interest and love of power which keeps them in place must be unmasked.

The common mission of the *philosophes* is indicated by their choice of broadly literary means of expression. Fiction and other literary modes provided them with a way of disseminating their ideas among a wide public and allowed them to present problems in practical rather than theoretical terms. Narrative fiction is their primary vehicle, but the letter-form and the dialogue are also standard *philosophe* forms. Voltaire used tragedy as a platform for his polemic against religious bigotry, and wrote a poem on the catastrophic Lisbon earthquake of 1755. His *contes* are thought-experiments, often leaving the issues raised by the story unresolved: when the angel explains to Zadig that all the evil in the world is there for a good purpose, he replies 'Mais...', and there the story ends; *Candide* concludes famously with the ironic non-conclusion that it's best to cultivate one's own back yard ('Il faut cultiver notre jardin'). The quest, the process of enquiry and reappraisal, matters more than the precise outcome.

The trajectory of Voltaire's life illustrates the active commitment of the *philosophes* to changing the world. Already imprisoned more than once in his earlier years for speaking out against individuals and abuses, Voltaire constantly defied censorship, public vilification, and threats to his personal safety, while at the same time seeking protection from well-placed sympathizers. In 1758, he retired to a comfortable semi-exile at Ferney, close to the Swiss border, where he was visited by a constant stream of leading intellectuals, crowned heads, nobility, and would-be hangers-on. But he also used his later years to wage campaigns for the rehabilitation of victims of injustice, notably Jean Calas and the Chevalier de La Barre, both executed for supposed religious crimes. He was deeply conscious of the problem of evil in the world and was by no means a naïve optimist: the subtitle of *Candide*, 'ou l'Optimisme', is of course ironic (although Voltaire is here referring to a hyperbolical form of philosophical optimism, promoted by Leibniz and others, and not to the everyday variety). Yet in the *Lettres philosophiques* he delivered a scathing attack on Pascal's pessimism, and everything he did and wrote indicates that he believed in the possibility of moral progress.

The collective contribution of the *philosophes* to the European value-shift generally referred to as the 'Enlightenment' is most clearly embodied in the *Encyclopédie* (see Figure 11, where the recently published fourth volume of the *Encyclopédie* is prominently placed on Madame de Pompadour's table). This awesome publishing enterprise was first launched in the mid-1740s, but encountered a series of managerial difficulties as well as hostility and suspicion from the political and religious establishment. The first two volumes were published in

1751, and the complete seventeen-volume work was in print by 1765. The word 'encyclopedia', as the article 'Encyclopédie' in the *Encyclopédie* reminds us, is derived from Greek roots meaning 'the circle of knowledge'. In the Renaissance, it was used to refer to the total horizon of human knowledge, not to a single work containing that knowledge; the modern sense—the encyclopedia as a reference book—emerges in the eighteenth century.

In comparison to modern encyclopedias, however, the *Encyclopédie* is a strange and hybrid beast. It represents the last moment in European culture when what we call science was still regarded as a branch of philosophy and the whole range of human knowledge was potentially accessible to a single person. At the same time, it marks the moment when experimental science was poised to make a great leap forward and when new and powerful ways of classifying the phenomena of the natural world were being devised. It is at once a grand compendium of knowledge and a random collection of articles on different topics, some of which look bizarre or trivial to the modern reader. Many read more like essays than encapsulations of knowledge. Most important of all, the claim of the *Encyclopédie* to present a precise and dispassionate corpus of data disguises another quite different aim: to undermine beliefs and institutions which the *philosophes* regarded as an obstacle to enlightenment. Sometimes this propaganda aim is openly flaunted: there are whole articles on political representation ('Représentants'), the freedom of the press ('Presse'), slavery ('Traite des Nègres'), equality ('Égalité naturelle'), superstition ('Superstition') and many similar topics. Elsewhere, articles on apparently innocuous or obscure subjects hide blistering attacks on credulity ('Agnus scythicus' is a famous example), on religious institutions and observances, or on tyrannical or corrupt forms of government. The hybrid character of the *Encyclopédie* is a direct product of its times: this is a period where, as we have seen, daringly new forms of thought are regularly embodied in fiction, where the very idea of an encyclopedia in this sense provokes official suspicion and censorship, and where the strategy of indirection—the strategy on which literature itself flourishes—is not a local device but an intellectual necessity.

Two *philosophes* were appointed as the principal editors of the *Encyclopédie*: the mathematician and scientist Jean d'Alembert, who wrote the 'Discours préliminaire', and Denis Diderot, still virtually unknown at that time. Diderot also seems to have researched and composed an astonishingly large number of articles, including some of the most intellectually and ideologically challenging. Voltaire, by contrast, made only a few minor contributions, apparently believing that this mammoth work would become a white elephant, too costly for ordinary people to buy and thus unsuited to the work of enlightenment. He even composed his own *Dictionnaire philosophique*, ambitious enough in its own right but marketable as a single portable volume, unlike the seventeen vast tomes—some 20 million words—of the *Encyclopédie*. In fact, the *Encyclopédie* sold surprisingly well and became a benchmark for future encyclopedias. It's true that ordinary people didn't read high-culture works like the *Encyclopédie*, but it seems certain that the attitudes it embodied, together with the vast range of knowledge it offered, cascaded down via cheap editions and other modes of popularization and were in that way quite widely disseminated. If not a cause, it was at least a visible symptom of change in both the prevailing conception of knowledge and the ideological agenda of the age.

ROUSSEAU: AUTOBIOGRAPHY AND FICTION

Despite their common purpose and relativistic habit of mind, the individual *philosophes* also formulated their own religious, political, social, or scientific beliefs. In these areas they diverge from one another; indeed they often quarrelled violently among themselves. Rousseau—who, it should be remembered, was Swiss, not French, although he spent many of his most productive years in France—is the most dissenting, the most idiosyncratic of the *philosophes*. He was a friend at various times of Voltaire and Diderot, he contributed some articles on politics and on music to the *Encyclopédie*, and he was as scathing as any *philosophe* about the political and religious institutions of his day. What he did not share was their belief in cultural and scientific progress. In the *Discours sur l'origine et les fondements de l'inégalité*, he presented a quasi-mythical explanation of what he regarded as the central paradox of human existence: man is naturally good, but human behaviour as witnessed in modern civilizations is corrupt and degenerate. Humans were born to live in society, argues Rousseau, but they have chosen the wrong social and political forms. In certain instances, he believes, political reform might still be possible, and *Du contrat social* proposes such a reform, albeit in general and abstract terms. Rousseau's utopian scheme gives sovereignty to the people, who freely, as individuals, make a pact with each other to give power not to a monarch or to any other individual, but to the state as a whole. *Du contrat social* became the most celebrated political tract of the eighteenth century, and is widely regarded as a pre-Revolutionary work founding the modern concept of democracy. Rousseau himself, however, claimed that it was a purely philosophical treatise and that he was utterly opposed to revolution in any form.

There is a case for reading *Du contrat social* and similar works not as purely intellectual and rational constructs but as the product of the dilemmas and torments of Rousseau's own life, which at times—as he himself observes—reads like a wayward fiction, somewhere between the romance and the picaresque. He had written almost nothing before he was 39, when his prize-winning essay entitled *Discours sur les sciences et les arts* made him famous overnight (1751). In an astonishing burst of creative energy in 1761–2, he produced three major works, *La Nouvelle Héloïse*, *Du contrat social* and *Émile*, together with his first experiment in autobiographical self-defence, the four *Lettres à Malesherbes*. *La Nouvelle Héloïse* was an immediate success, and became one of the most widely read novels of the eighteenth century. The other two works, however, generated violent reactions. *Du contrat social*, published in Amsterdam, was immediately banned in France; the Paris Parlement condemned *Émile*, and a warrant was put out for Rousseau's arrest. He fled to Switzerland, where he began the *Confessions* in 1764. By this time, as well as upsetting the authorities in both Switzerland and France, he had quarrelled with Diderot, d'Alembert, and Voltaire. Much of his life thereafter was spent in escaping or confronting his enemies and in writing works of self-justification.

Of these, the *Confessions*, completed in 1770 and published posthumously, is by far the most important. Historically, it appears in retrospect as the moment of crystallization of a characteristically French autobiographical mode which will recur in fictions from Chateaubriand and Constant to Proust and beyond. Its major predecessors, of which Rousseau was fully conscious, were the *Confessions* of Saint Augustine, popularized in a mid-seventeenth-century French translation, and the *Essais* of Montaigne. Rousseau rewrites the Christian narrative of fall, conversion or illumination, penitential self-examination and redemption which is also visible in palimpsest in his political writings: on the opening page of Book I, he announces that he will confidently appear at the Last Judgement armed with his *Confessions*. The loss of an original paradise is, however, fully internalized here and its structure is radically different. The 'fall', explicitly marked by a reference to the eviction from Eden, takes the form of an episode in which he is falsely accused and punished for an action which he did not commit; his youthful misdemeanours, by contrast, are either glossed over or attributed to a false social consciousness, externally imposed. Similar arguments are extended to questionable actions of his later years—most notoriously, his decision to give his five children to a foundlings' home. The whole point of the work, in fact, is to demonstrate, against the claims of his enemies, that he is fundamentally innocent, even one of the best men who ever lived. 'Conversion' is also reinterpreted: Rousseau claims that, on the way to visit Diderot in prison at Vincennes in 1749, he had a moment of illumination in which he suddenly understood why humanity was in its present condition, the insight that is successively unpacked in the two *Discours*. This insight launches his career as a famous writer, but it also inserts him into the very culture which, in his view, was the source of humanity's moral decline. Thus the 'conversion' is another kind of fall, marking the passage from an almost timeless phase of tranquil obscurity to a world of controversy and public vilification from which he can no longer extricate himself. The nearest he comes to redemption, in his own account, are his moments of meditative solitude, above all on the Île Saint-Pierre during the period of his Swiss exile, in which time seems again to expand infinitely and his inner world becomes anxiety-free, transparent like the waters of the lake. These moments are recorded in Book XII of the *Confessions* and in the fifth of the *Rêveries du promeneur solitaire*, his final work. The pages he devotes to them are celebrated: they influenced a whole generation of nineteenth-century writers, and not only French ones (Thoreau's *Walden* is a striking example).

Rousseau only grudgingly acknowledged Montaigne as a precursor, claiming that his self-portrait was partial and insincere (sincerity was the all-important virtue for Rousseau). Yet the *Essais* provided the paradigm of an identity forged through the accumulation of idiosyncratic detail and apparently inconsequential thoughts and actions, an identity constantly in change to the point at times of discontinuity, while always returning to a central core. Montaigne also opened up a vein of sexual frankness which will be carried much further in Rousseau, who describes, for example, the pleasure he derived from childhood spankings. The connection between childhood and sexuality is in fact one of the ways in which Rousseau's work seems to foreshadow future theories of the psyche, or at least to signal a major shift in the terms of reference of autobiographical writing. In Rousseau, childhood becomes a critical element in the structure of a life. It is a time of innocence and transparency which, for the adult, becomes in retrospect the memory of a lost paradise, an inaccessible place of special intensity. Yet it is a place already traversed by the sinister and corrupting pressures of society, the place where things began to go irremediably wrong.

La Nouvelle Héloïse stages yet again the crossing of a threshold from innocent youth into the problematic world of adult society, and the social and political theme is also developed at length in the central sections of the novel. These are devoted to reflections on the economy and ecology of a household, its estates and its inhabitants, which form a semi-autonomous micro-society. This utopian episode is often referred to as the 'Clarens idyll', Clarens being the country estate where Julie lives for a while in fragile harmony with both her *philosophe* husband Wolmar and her former tutor and lover Saint-Preux. Clarens may seem a long way from the world of the *Discours* and *Du contrat social*, but in fact it embodies the same problems and a comparably ideal solution. The patriarchal family, isolated from the corrupting influence of larger and more complex social systems, reconciles the human need for society with the exercise of an intrinsic sense of virtue; it also reconciles religion in the person of Julie with the sceptical philosophy represented by Wolmar.

The social theme is in fact important from the beginning of the novel because Julie's aristocratic father is implacably opposed to the idea of her marrying the low-born Saint-Preux; he has already promised her to his old friend Wolmar. Julie is deeply attached to her father and in the end decides to obey him, but not before he has lost his temper with her and, in a scene of extraordinary violence, knocked her to the ground. As a result, she loses the baby which she had conceived and which would have made a marriage to Saint-Preux compulsory. The staging of this disturbing scene is one of Rousseau's most extreme representations of the clash between natural goodness and social deformation. Similarly, the young lovers' intense sense of guilt as they progressively yield to their desires is shown to be induced entirely by social pressures. Yet their agonizing separation allows a transmutation of their love into something higher, the ideal world of Clarens. There are no easy solutions: tensions remain, Julie dies before any final outcome is clear, but Saint-Preux will become the tutor of the children of Wolmar and Julie and thus perhaps assure the happiness of the next generation.

These themes are important as symptoms of the changing world of the eighteenth century: one only needs to glance back at *Astrée* or *La Princesse de Clèves* to see the difference. But perhaps what remains longest with the reader of *La Nouvelle Héloïse* is the double charge of emotion and erotic feeling which runs like an electric current through the first sequence of letters and returns intermittently thereafter. The young lovers' desperate assertions of virtuous intention are invaded, then saturated, by desire: this is not a sexually explicit narrative, yet the letters describing the first kiss and a night of love-making make an unexpected impact. Unexpected, because in the surrounding letters there is a good deal of emotional rhetoric which can easily look like gross over-writing. In fact, it is Saint-Preux whose style is inflated: his sexual energy emerges as an excess of rhetoric. Later in the novel, the tone is gradually modified; Saint-Preux's pain eventually knocks most of the high-flown verbiage out of him, and other more moderate voices intervene. Yet *La Nouvelle Héloïse* is above all a novel of *sensibilité*—a key word in the eighteenth century, and one which, as we shall see, has a wide range of reference.

THE SENTIMENTAL AND THE EROTIC

By the time *La Nouvelle Héloïse* appeared, the letter-novel was already well established in France as a vehicle for inward dramas of peculiar intensity. In 1751, the Abbé Prévost had published a translation of Richardson's letter-novel *Clarissa*, to which he gave the title *Lettres anglaises*, and it is no accident that Rousseau's novel features an English lord of moderate yet sterling temper who is favourably contrasted with the likes of Julie's father. Prévost himself wrote a number of fictional works, including some with English characters and settings, but he is known almost exclusively for *Manon Lescaut* (1731). Originally published as an episode in the *Mémoires et aventures d'un homme de qualité*, a so-called memoir-novel, it is a first-person retrospective account of a *coup de foudre* and its fatal consequences. The older and wiser chevalier Des Grieux recounts his unfortunate love affair with the irresistibly seductive and wayward Manon to his yet older mentor, the narrator of the memoir-novel. The story is erotic and occasionally violent, penetrating the seamier sides of Paris life in the early eighteenth century. Des Grieux's role is far from edifying, and his act of narration is primarily a self-defence: he famously claims that, if he did wrong, it was because his sensitive nature, his capacity for intense feeling, made it impossible for him to do otherwise. Thus, while the framework narrative places the love affair in perspective as a youthful folly, the rhetoric of the narration points in the opposite direction, turning it into an advertisement for *sensibilité*.

In such fictions, *sensibilité* is not easily separated from the erotic. We have seen how they are interwoven in Rousseau, who traces his own erotic and emotional bent to his early canings by Mademoiselle de Lambercier; Saint-Preux has more orthodox desires, but that doesn't make it any easier to unravel the double intensity of his rhetoric. In fact, the two strands can be disentangled, and not only for the purposes of analysis. A taste for intensity of emotion is already apparent in the later seventeenth century: both Boileau and Racine use the verb 'toucher' to render the tragic pity of Aristotelian poetics. Audiences seem to have wept openly at the theatre throughout this period, which favoured the *tragédie à fin heureuse*. The *comédies larmoyantes* of the mid-eighteenth century, a genre to which both Marivaux and Madame de Graffigny contributed, and later the prose *drame*, with its deliberately emotive scenarios, are further symptoms of this sensibility; another more tempered variety is the savouring of the pure pleasure of existence advocated by Zilia on the final page of *Lettres d'une Péruvienne* (see above, p. 173). As institutionally enforced morality was increasingly called in question by the *philosophes*, an inward, 'natural' criterion was sought to take its place. Openness to the finer feelings, and thence to powerful emotions, becomes a sign of natural nobility, even of natural goodness. Under these circumstances, the *amour-passion* which eroded the will and undid the lives of characters in late seventeenth-century fictions is revalued; sexuality is relieved of its association with original sin. The point is neatly made by Dominique-Vivant Denon's witty and sexy story *Point de lendemain* (later to be quoted by Balzac in his *Physiologie du mariage*), where adultery is presented in a scrupulously amoral perspective.

Of course this kind of argument only explains a part of the process by which values change. Another important factor is the growth, after the death of Louis XIV, of a society more publicly addicted to pleasure: erotic adventures become the stuff of a good deal of eighteenth-century fiction, from Crébillon *fils*, exiled for several months for his novel *Le Sopha* (1742), in which a sofa recounts the amorous scenes it has witnessed, via Diderot's early *Les Bijoux indiscrets* (1748) which exploits a similar motif, to Restif de la Bretonne, whose sexual narratives at the end of the century cross the borderline into pornography. Fine art shows the same inclinations: the paintings of Boucher, for example, graphically illustrate the erotic preoccupations of the period.

The overlapping of the emotional or sentimental and the erotic gives rise to all kinds of ambiguity. It is often hard to know whether the reader is supposed to make careful moral distinctions between what is acceptable and what is dissolute in the behaviour of fictional characters, or to enjoy the intensity and ask no questions. This ambiguity is of course intrinsic to the predominant forms of the day. The first-person mode of both confessional narrative and letter-novel precludes any authorial commentary that might resolve the issue, except in prefaces and other paratextual materials which may easily be dismissed as a strategy for deflecting criticism. It can in fact be plausibly argued that all of these phenomena are intimately linked, and that they are symptomatic of the uncertainty caused by a series of rapid and far-reaching value-shifts. In that view, the letter-novel, for example, is not only the vehicle of a new and heightened inwardness, or of a relativism spreading into fresh cultural domains, although it is certainly both of those, but a mutating gene which helps determine the transformation of the whole social organism.

This view is reinforced by the way in which social themes interact with the sentimental and the erotic. *La Nouvelle Héloïse* is once again a key example, but so are Marivaux's novels, which show how characters can move across social frontiers in ways that still seem transgressive but are also liberating. The female narrator of *La Vie de Marianne* is ignorant of her social origins, but she feels like a well-born girl, she looks a million dollars, and she's going to make sure that she gets what she deserves, despite the obstacles that a prejudiced society puts in her way (see Figure 12). The trick here, as elsewhere, is to appeal to the moral sensitivity of the right people, to be both heart-breakingly beautiful and heart-breakingly 'good'. If some theatrical bravura is required, *tant mieux*: people love good theatre, too. Similarly, Manon may be a low-born slut, but let no one call her that; she has a fineness of feelings which in the end makes good her sexual deviousness. The novel is opening itself to new materials, new settings, new modes of feeling; the excitement is palpable.

That such changes continue productively right up to the outbreak of revolution is shown by a group of contrasted examples from the 1780s, Isabelle de Charrière's *Caliste*, Laclos's *Les Liaisons dangereuses*, and Bernardin de Saint-Pierre's *Paul et Virginie*. Isabelle de Charrière is the married name of Belle de Zuylen, a Dutch woman who spent most of the later part of her life in Switzerland. Her remarkable and extensive correspondence has been preserved, together with loosely woven sequences of fictional letters such as the *Lettres écrites de Lausanne*, letter-novels and *contes*, which, like Prévost's, owe much to English models (some are actually written in English). *Caliste* is a novella of some fifty pages appended to the *Lettres écrites de Lausanne*. Although not strictly a letter-novel, it is narrated as a kind of confession in letters sent by the English male protagonist William to the central woman figure in the *Lettres* themselves. As in *Manon Lescaut*, the well-born narrator forms an attachment to a 'fallen woman'; all prospects of marriage are blocked by his father. Caliste is, however, no Manon. A woman of taste, intelligence, and sensibility, she is determined to prove that she is now entirely respectable. The indecisive narrator is unable to rise to her implied challenge and loses her, with disastrous effects on both. This is a theme which will be treated in similar first-person mode

12. An illustration from Marivaux's *La Vie de Marianne*. Marianne has pretended to injure her ankle, and is allowing it to be inspected by a doctor; Valville, a young man whose attention she wishes to attract, shows his appreciation of the display. Such images were clearly designed to help sell the book in a rapidly expanding market for the novel.

in Constant's *Adolphe* (in which Charrière herself figures as the 'vieille dame') and in Mme de Staël's *Corinne*; the intensity of Charrière's tale rivals them both, and it is astonishing that her work has only recently begun to receive the recognition it deserves. Through the metamorphoses of the twin theme of the déclassée woman and her vacillating lover, one may also trace the progressive questioning of values fundamental to the society of the *ancien régime*.

Les Liaisons dangereuses is the supreme example of the letter-novel—
La Nouvelle Héloïse looks technically clumsy by comparison. Laclos
designs a distinctive style and mindset for each of his several letter-
writers, creating what is often called a polyphonic effect. The complex
chronology of their letters, full of gaps and collisions, informs the
reader while leaving the writers themselves in the dark about each
other's strategies. The word 'strategy' is especially apposite here, as
Madame de Merteuil and Valmont, the central figures, conduct a campaign of seduction against others and what turns out to be a duel to the
death with each other. Merteuil's account in letter 81 of her sexual self-
education and of her flawlessly amoral performance in what she calls
'le grand théâtre' of amorous relations makes Marivaux's Marianne
sound like an *ingénue* and Des Grieux like an apologetic adolescent.
She is a proto-feminist, not because she cares about other women, but
because she perceives the disadvantages women are born with in the
world of sexual competition and finds ways of reversing them. She
learns to control herself, even her facial expressions; she learns how to
control her lovers; but what she learns to control above all is secrecy, the
confidential world of the erotic. The novel exploits that secrecy for all it
is worth: the reader is after all looking through the keyhole, reading
stolen letters. Yet its existence as a novel also presupposes the breaking
of confidentiality, the inevitable leak, and thus the downfall of the protagonists. It comes because Valmont succumbs, despite his own
amorality, to his *sensibilité*: in seducing the virtuous Présidente, he also
feels pity for her and finally realizes that he has fallen in love with her.
Whether we are meant to cling to this as a way out of the theatre
of exploitation Merteuil and Valmont have constructed, or whether
sensibilité is itself merely another theatrical effect, remains an open
question.

Such questions hardly arise in *Paul et Virginie*, first published as the
fourth volume of Bernardin's popular *Études de la nature*. For
Bernardin, an admirer of Defoe's *Robinson Crusoe* and of Rousseau, the
connection between authentic feeling and an intrinsically good nature
is unambiguous. 'Nature' in this case is symbolized by the island of
Martinique, an early example of the exotic landscape as a utopian paradise remote from the decadent values of Europe: one of the attractions
of the book is its lush descriptions, which anticipate Chateaubriand's.
To the paradise island is added the soon-to-be-lost paradise of childhood. Paul and Virginie grow up innocently as brother and sister, but
also as potential lovers. The idyll is interrupted when Virginie, who
unlike Paul comes from a well-to-do family (shades of *La Nouvelle
Héloïse* again), is sent to be educated in France. Social difference,

hitherto innocuous, now causes fracture and ultimately catastrophe. Virginie remains true to Paul and sails back to be reunited with him, but the ship is wrecked within sight of shore. She will be saved if she takes off her clothes and allows a sailor to carry her ashore; she refuses and is drowned; Paul dies of grief.

This sentimental and for many readers slightly comic conclusion reiterates in symbolic terms Rousseau's analysis of social consciousness and its malignant effects. Virginie can never return to paradise. She has been irreversibly dressed up in the polite French culture of the *ancien régime*. Like the whole of that social world—the one ruthlessly stripped naked in *Les Liaisons dangereuses*—she is doomed. Of course it would be absurd to read this slight but immensely successful novel as an allegory of imminent revolution. Yet the fable is a more potent one than it appears at first sight, meriting its place in the competitive world of eighteenth-century narrative fiction.

DIDEROT: THE *PHILOSOPHE* AND HIS DOUBLE

Diderot, writing at the very end of the early modern period, anticipates many of the intellectual and aesthetic experiments of more recent times. As his work on the *Encyclopédie* shows, he was a polymath of extraordinary range; some of his later works display such a wide and detailed knowledge of contemporary debates in science and the arts that they are difficult to interpret. Perhaps for this reason, his reputation as one of the three leading writers of the eighteenth century has only recently become fully established.

The early part of his career was devoted primarily to the *Encyclopédie* and to philosophical writings such as the *Lettre sur les aveugles* of 1749. In the 1750s, however, he produced an important series of writings on dramatic theory, together with two plays, *Le Fils naturel* and *Le Père de famille*, designed to illustrate those theories. The plays themselves have had a bad press on the grounds that they are sententious and sentimental, although it is perhaps time that this prejudice was reconsidered: Diderot's imagination is never trivial, and if they are read with sympathy, they can be peculiarly moving. However, it is the concept of the *drame*, or *drame bourgeois*, which makes this body of writing especially important. Diderot here announces a definitive break with the predominantly Aristotelian poetics of the previous hundred years. The hierarchical separation of tragedy and comedy is abolished, and bourgeois life, rather than the doings of monarchs, nobles and famous heroes, becomes the material of serious drama. Other major French dramatists subscribed to the new genre within the following decade: Sedaine's *Le Philosophe sans le savoir*, first performed in 1765, has a particularly well-judged combination of agonizing emotional dilemmas and moral uprightness, and two years later Beaumarchais, to whom we shall return later, wrote an *Essai sur le genre dramatique sérieux*. However, French audiences were not especially impressed by the *drame*. It was in Germany, in the age of Lessing, that Diderot's theories flourished, establishing a major point of reference for the domestic drama of the next century. And of course, this development in the theatre runs parallel with shifts in the tone and subject matter of the novel.

Diderot's own novels, however, fit into no single literary historical schema: they experiment with ideas, with moral and psychological problems and with fictional form in unpredictable and often unsettling ways. The idea for *La Religieuse* arose in 1760 from a hoax: in order to lure a potential patron back to Paris, Diderot and his friends composed some letters purporting to be written by an unhappy and mistreated nun. The novel itself was not published until 1780. It is another example of a fiction presented from the point of view of a naïve protagonist, literally a *novice*: when she is forced to take the veil, Suzanne knows nothing of the self-interest, power-struggles, sadism, and sexual intrigues which are rife in the cloister. The world of the convent is thus defamiliarized and unmasked in a way which is both comic and brutal, rephrasing the caustic narrative mode of works like *L'Ingénu* in terms of a female voice and a single satirical target. Yet the novel is not simply an attack on the monastic system and the society that makes use of it for its own ends. The erotic strand is insistent, sometimes in a covert form (the sadistic treatment of a young and pretty girl), and openly in an episode where Suzanne is lured into sexual encounters with her current Mother Superior. Once again, the effect of this sequence derives from the innocence of the observer: Suzanne herself has no idea what is going on when the Mother Superior clings to her, masturbating, while the novice plays the harpsichord. What Diderot is interested in here is not only the technique of calling on a sexual knowledge the narrator herself does not have (Henry James will use a similar technique in *What Maisie Knew*), but also what one might call the physiology of sensibility. The strings of the instrument vibrate in harmony with the Mother Superior's erotic sensations and with Suzanne's unwittingly aroused nervous system; 'feeling' or 'passion' is transmitted here via a physiological path which explicitly bypasses any less material organ (the heart, the soul).

Diderot explores this physiological domain with immense wit and daring in the three dialogues, composed in 1769 but not published until the nineteenth century, which are now known under the title *Le Rêve de d'Alembert*. Already in a letter of 1765 he had asserted that *sensibilité* is a universal property of matter, and he now investigates the ways in which it might be possible to understand the relationship between mind and body, thought and sensation, from a purely materialist standpoint, that is to say without reference to any notion of an immaterial soul. Thought must arise, on this model, from matter alone; sensibility—the sympathetic vibrations transmitted throughout the physiological system—becomes the crucial mediating factor. The doctor Bordeu explains these hypotheses to Julie de Lespinasse, one of the most progressive and intelligent young women in Paris, while d'Alembert sleeps, although he also talks in his sleep. Sleep is of course itself a state where consciousness is suspended yet apparently continues, the paradigm of a thought-mode utterly inseparable from the material body. An echo of *La Religieuse* occurs when Mademoiselle de Lespinasse tells Bordeu that d'Alembert has masturbated in his sleep while holding her hand, thus making her heart beat faster, but now the context is scientific: the discussion concerns the evidence for spontaneous generation and the examination through the microscope of creatures resembling sperm. The sexual scenario, hilarious in itself, is here a way of connecting scientific hypothesis with physiological reality; Diderot is especially fond of this technique of cutting between different angles of perception. Another key technique is the use of heuristic analogies—the spider in its web, the *réseau*, the cluster of bees—in order to probe the way in which an organism can coordinate many different functions across the spectrum from the mental to the physiological; these are comparable to the image of sympathetic vibrations in the harpsichord scene. *Sensibilité*, in the materialist sense, is throughout the dominant note.

Le Neveu de Rameau, which was again not published until the nineteenth century, seems to belong to this same phase of Diderot's career and dramatizes in an entirely different way the relation between mind and body. Two voices, 'Moi' and 'Lui', converse in a Paris café. 'Lui' is the nephew of the composer Rameau, 'Moi' the archetypal *philosophe*, and not Diderot himself, as some have too easily supposed. 'Moi' thinks, 'Lui' performs: he is among other things a brilliant mime artist. 'Moi' is an orderly member of society, 'Lui' is anarchic, amoral, and parasitic on a society which he regards with contempt. They are polar opposites yet mirror-images of one another, the two modes of being which must in a materialist model be manifestations of a single physiological system. The subcutaneous energies of the dialogue are far-reaching: it was translated into German by Goethe, admired by Hegel, and read by some as a forerunner of the Freudian opposition of ego and id. Yet it clearly belongs to a precise moment in the later eighteenth century when *philosophe* thought is moving beyond its earlier assumption of the universal validity of reason. An opaque and unruly force now complicates the issue, a profound creative irrationality which disrupts both ethical and aesthetic criteria and makes reason look like a surface mirage.

Diderot's experimental novel *Jacques le fataliste* is nowadays perhaps his best-known work. Written in the 1770s and published posthumously, it belongs to the genre of picaresque and parodic fictions. The valet Jacques and his master wander from place to place, telling and listening to stories, including Jacques's own endlessly interrupted love-story, and discussing various philosophical issues. The burlesque master–servant relation is reminiscent of comedy, especially as much of the novel is in dialogue form, but it is also a variant of the 'moi–lui' dialectic of *Le Neveu de Rameau*, and this enormously enriches the perspective within which its ethical, aesthetic, and metaphysical themes are presented. In addition, there is an implied dialogue between the author/narrator and the reader, focusing on the status of the fiction and its relation to reality. The reader is teased, infuriated, and always outwitted; in the process, the mechanisms by which such fictions operate are exposed to view. *Jacques le fataliste* is thus in the direct line of *Don Quixote* and other mock-romances. Diderot goes much further, however, by disrupting the very means by which the reader can make sense of the novel: as the author/narrator says, 'ceci n'est point un roman' ('this is not a novel/romance'). His model is rather Laurence Sterne's *Tristram Shandy* (1759–67), which carries out a similar demolition process, at one point leaving several pages blank for readers to fill in the story for themselves. It is not surprising that these two 'anti-novels' attracted enormous attention in the later twentieth century as exemplars of the reflexive mode which also characterized the *nouveau roman* (see below, pp. 279–82).

One crucial aspect of this reflexive turn is the way it affects the issue of fatality alluded to in the title. Questions of causality are constantly raised in the dialogues between Jacques and his master, often emerging from apparently accidental incidents in the narrative; Jacques exhibits a naïve fatalism, claiming that everything they do is written 'up above' on a 'scroll'. The reader perceives, of course, that it is the novel which is the scroll, and the characters' 'fate' consists only in the arbitrary decision of the novelist to tell a story in a particular way. The thematization of causality in certain of Voltaire's *contes* recurs here in the form of a secularized (even materialist) poetics of narrative. The supernatural guarantee which enabled earlier fictions to end with predestined recognitions, marriages, victories, or deaths, has now been wholly eliminated. Fictional narrative is a labyrinthine pathway designed by the author and miming the strictly deterministic sequences of the human world. It is on this premiss that the 'realist' novel of the nineteenth century will be based.

CROSSING THE DIVIDE

Another kind of fatality hangs over the story of late eighteenth-century French culture. An event as monumental as the French Revolution inevitably casts a shadow backwards in time as well as forwards, at least for us who look back on those events as an end-directed narrative. We scrutinize everything that came before for signs of impending change, and—as we saw with *Les Liaisons dangereuses*— signs are not hard to find. Similarly, although none of the three leading *philosophes* lived to see the Revolution (and none of them would have welcomed it), their radical re-examination of the political, social, and cultural world they lived in is now readable as the early warning of a seismic shift. The form that shift would take was not pre-ordained, but once it had happened, it uncovered in works written earlier meanings which subsequently appear self-evident. This is true, for example, of the final sentence of Rousseau's *Discours sur l'origine et les fondements de l'inégalité*:

il est manifestement contre la Loi de Nature, de quelque manière qu'on la définisse, qu'un enfant commande à un vieillard, qu'un imbécille conduise un homme sage, et qu'une poignée de gens regorge de superfluités, tandis que la multitude affamée manque du nécessaire.

[it is manifestly contrary to the Law of Nature, however that law be defined, that a child should give orders to an old man, that an imbecile should guide a wise man, and that a handful of people should wallow in superfluous luxuries while the hungry multitude lacks the necessities of life.]

These same ideas are to be found—in a more indirect form, it is true— on the last page of Montaigne's 'Des cannibales' (which Rousseau undoubtedly knew), and one would certainly not want to say that Montaigne was a prophet of the Revolution. One needs, therefore, to remember in each case that the meanings added by subsequent history are just that: *added* meanings.

The works of writers whose lives crossed that dramatic borderline are of course even more liable to be reinterpreted in this way, and we shall now look finally at three such writers. The eldest is

Beaumarchais, who started his theatrical career as an exponent of the *drame*: *Eugénie* is a *drame larmoyant* or tear-jerker. Beaumarchais's two dazzlingly successful comedies belong to a single brief period of his eventful life. *Le Barbier de Séville* (1775) and *Le Mariage de Figaro* (1781) are among the most frequently performed plays in the French theatrical canon, and their fame has been spread still more widely by their transformation into operas by Rossini and Mozart respectively (the play that completed the trilogy in 1792, *La Mère coupable*, was a flop from the start). This is indeed an operatic age, and one in which opera itself was crossing the divide between an elite entertainment and a popular one—Mozart's *Magic Flute* is the most famous example. Beaumarchais was no revolutionary: he preferred backers who had money and power, and only narrowly escaped the September Massacres of 1792. But he incorporated into *Le Mariage de Figaro* a violent tirade by the servant Figaro against the privileges of the nobility, as a result of which Louis XVI blocked the performance of the play until it was finally put on in a modified form in 1784. These, then, are comedies of the *ancien régime* which incorporate elements of the *drame* and at the same time display a socially disruptive truculence, using the conventional formula of the servant who outwits his master in ways that are visibly more threatening than anything one finds in earlier comedy. Molière's *Dom Juan* had been a potentially dangerous and disquieting figure, as is shown by the banning of the play soon after it was first performed, but his servant was the farcical and always servile Sganarelle, whereas Figaro has become the star of the show.

The contextual shift brought about by the events of 1789 casts a vivid and indeed poignant light on the work of a thinker who, having subscribed to the ideals of the *philosophes*, espoused the Revolution but did not survive it. The marquis de Condorcet was a mathematician and scientist and a protégé of d'Alembert. He took an early interest in politics, supporting the American Revolution; after 1789, he became caught up in the factional disputes of the revolutionary parties and in 1793 was forced to go into hiding for eight months. The day after his arrest, he was found dead. In those final months he wrote the work for which he is best known, the *Esquisse d'un tableau historique des progrès de l'esprit humain*. It is an eloquent apology for human perfectibility in both science and morality. It reasserts all the essential values of the *philosophes* in a triumphalist history of enlightenment, culminating in the Revolution itself and looking forward to a utopian future in which the new science will enable humankind to progress indefinitely. Yet in retrospect, the story reads like an ironic comment on the whole 'Enlightenment' movement and the hopes it engendered.

We end this close-up view of the early modern period, as we began, not with a thinker but with a poet, although he too was preoccupied with human progress, leaving an unfinished *Essai sur les causes et les effets de la perfection et de la décadence des lettres et des arts*. André Chénier is the only lyric poet of the eighteenth century whose name is remembered. Like others before him, he experimented unsuccessfully with epic form, and his *Iambes*, written not long before his execution, belong strictly speaking to the public satirical mode. Yet these poems are memorable above all as the vehicle of an eloquent personal voice, denouncing the Terror and declaring his own moral certainties. His lyric and pastoral poems reflect his unqualified admiration for antiquity, especially for Greek poetry; they are elegant and harmonious, while displaying a marked metrical freedom. These various qualities recall the heyday of the Pléiade in the sixteenth century, but they also anticipate several strands of nineteenth-century verse, and it is hardly surprising that the Romantics turned the story of his death into a heroic legend and regarded him as a precursor. Indeed, for any reader of French literature in its history, the sounding of this clear but fragile note amid the cataclysmic ending of an age has an undoubted imaginative reach: Chénier's voice is both the last echo of a mythical golden age and a premonition of things to come.

Part III

The Modern Period
1789–2000

Overview of the Period

The Revolution of 1789 represents an exemplary moment of discontinuity in the social and political history of France, and certain of its consequences are still unfolding over two hundred years later. If we look closely at the events and personalities of the Revolutionary decade we can see all manner of institutional, artistic, and intellectual survivals from the *ancien régime*, but for most practical purposes it makes more sense to think of 1789, in the manner of the Revolutionaries themselves, as the beginning of a new epoch. Social changes that had previously been the stuff of fantasy suddenly became possible. And, together with the American revolution of the previous decade, the upheaval of 1789 became the inspiration and the model for later revolutions in France and around the globe. In the ferment of these extraordinary times, a variety of new social roles became available to writers, and French literature became a scene of paradox, contradiction, and restless formal innovation.

The Republic declared on 22 September 1792 gave voting rights to adult French males who met certain financial and residential conditions, and if we look simply at the range of literary works and genres that flourished between 1789 and the July Revolution of 1830, writers, including female writers, seem to have enjoyed enfranchisement of their own. Whether in support of the Revolution or in opposition to it, they had work to do, as essayists, historians, and pamphleteers, and the period of Napoleon's ascendancy during the early years of the new century again saw them taking sides and pressing their verbal skills into political service. But if the expanded sense of opportunity writers enjoyed at this time allowed them to look outwards into the life of French society at large, it also opened up paths to the interior world of individual subjectivity. The careers of Benjamin Constant, Madame de Staël, Chateaubriand, and Lamartine are all remarkable for double journeys of this kind—into and away from the public sphere. For writers of this generation, introspective prose fiction or intimately confiding verse were not alternatives to political awareness so much as its complements and extensions. The writer was a figure of authority and prestige even if his political choices placed him for a while on the losing side. He was a licensed explorer of new worlds.

It would, however, be unwise to attribute the enhanced status enjoyed by writers in the long aftermath of the Revolution solely to political causes. The material conditions in which literary works were published and disseminated, together with the social conditions in which they acquired their readers, were changing rapidly. And many of these changes, particularly in matters of printing technology and educational reform, were gradual and cumulative, and affected surprisingly little by the switches and reversals that are to be seen in the political sphere. Between 1780 and 1850 we witness in France, as elsewhere in Europe and North America, the progressive industrialization of the printing process and the emergence of mass-market publishing on a pattern that is still familiar today.

Modern books require paper, and multitudes of them require it in very large quantities. Until the late eighteenth century, paper had been made by means of slow and laborious hand-operated devices, but a machine introduced in 1798 soon brought a tenfold increase in the rates of production. By 1824 paper prices had fallen in France by 25–30 per cent, and by 1843 by a further 20 per cent. At the same time major improvements were being made to the printing press itself. In 1804 Charles, the third Earl Stanhope, replaced the familiar wooden press with an iron structure that could print a large-format sheet in a single pull of the operator's hand. The new machine is the subject of an argument between two generations of the Séchard family in the opening chapter of Balzac's *Illusions perdues*. 'La vie des Stanhope est la mort du caractère' ('The life of the Stanhopes is death for the character'), the father complains to his commercially ambitious son: the pursuit of speed will damage the type, compromise the typographer's art, and generally weaken his 'character'.

Increasing speed of production was, however, to be the ruling passion of the printing trade in the nineteenth century. The introduction of steam-power and stereotype plates, of cylinder printing and multiple-feeder machines, brought an order-of-magnitude increase in output levels. Whereas a Stanhope press was limited to about 250 impressions per hour, the four-feeder cylinder machine manufactured by Pierre Alauzet in the late 1840s could produce 4,200 (see Figure 13). Technological advances prompted by the requirements of mass-circulation newspapers were quickly adapted to the book trade. Simplifying somewhat the story of authorship in its relations with the new industrial processes, we could say that this huge increase in productive capacity created a correspondingly eager demand for new books, and new editions of old ones. In the 1780s upwards of 1,000 officially recognized—non-pirated—new titles per annum appeared in

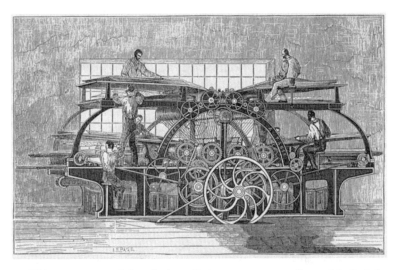

13. This steam-powered, four-feeder cylinder press was manufactured in Paris by Pierre Alauzet, and introduced for newspaper printing in the late 1840s.

France; for 1850 the *Bibliographie de la France* records 7,608 titles, and by 1875 this figure had almost doubled. *Illusions perdues* itself is a complete handbook on the splendours and miseries of the professional writer in this newly mechanized print culture.

This upsurge in the availability of printed matter is a social and political fact of overwhelming importance, and the fortunes of 'literature' occupy only a small place in the overall historical picture. The Republican ideal set great store by public education and the advancement of literacy. The ability to read was thought of by successive regimes as a right of the citizen and as an agent of democracy and social progress. When François Guizot as education minister in 1833 required each commune to provide an elementary school, and when Jules Ferry, two generations later, made primary education free, universal, and compulsory, they were upholding and implementing the Enlightenment ideas codified in the 'Déclaration des droits de l'homme et du citoyen'. Print brought textbooks and reference works to future citizens during their school years, instruction manuals to craftsmen and industrial workers, and standardized documentation to the increasingly complex local and state bureaucracies. Parisian newspapers, public information leaflets, decrees and government regulations, together with tracts, advertising flyers, and electoral materials travelled back and forth across France, and, because these were almost always written in French, they became powerful instruments in the campaign for a single national language.

In 1794 the abbé Grégoire had calculated that 6 million inhabitants of France, from a total population of 28 million, were ignorant of the French language, and that as many again had only a rudimentary knowledge of it. The continuing strength of Breton, Occitan, Basque, and a variety of local *patois* was thought by successive governments to be inimical to the very idea of a national democracy, and the presence of German and Flemish speakers in the border territories of the hexagon, and of Italian speakers offshore, gave the project of linguistic unification outlined by Grégoire still greater urgency. French was to be the language in which French citizenship was claimed and affirmed, and the bulk dissemination of printed matter written in that language was itself a warning against dissidence. *Francien*, which had until now been the language of the court, of centralized government, and of the professional bourgeoisie, was being aggressively repromoted as the language of national identity.

A special role was played in this newly militant print culture by material designed to serve the needs of the observant Christian population. Bibles, prayer books, catechisms, and popular devotional works were produced in impressive quantities, and across the entire price-range from pedlar's brochures to finely printed and luxuriously illustrated volumes. Against this background, two works enjoyed huge popular approval during the middle years of the century. Félicité de Lamennais's *Paroles d'un croyant* was the single most successful new publication of the July Monarchy, and in the early 1860s Ernest Renan's *Vie de Jésus* became a pan-European publishing phenomenon. Both books owed much of their popularity to their boldly amphibious character. Lamennais married elements of biblical diction to an exuberant pamphleteering style, and in the process seemed to free an essential Christian message—of concern for the poor and of human solidarity in the face of suffering—from the elaborately codified dogmas of the Church. The more Renan's 'historical' Jesus was shorn of his supernatural, miracle-working powers and released from ecclesiastical tradition, the more fully he became an inspired moral visionary. The dynamic, modernized Christianity that each work proposed had appeal for two audiences at once: it offered the devout a slightly scandalous retelling of the biblical narratives, and sceptical secularists a compelling view of morality in action in the social sphere.

The presence of these works on the best-seller lists gives us a further reason for being cautious when it comes to the claims of imaginative literature. If we were to measure these claims solely in terms of the new titles listed in the national bibliography they would indeed be rather unimpressive. In the years 1840–75 the categories 'fiction', 'poetry', and 'drama' together account for fewer than 6 per cent of the new works listed. By 1900–5 this figure has risen to 11 per cent, and by 1922–5 to 19 per cent. The increase is striking, but by 1925 four-fifths of new books still have other than artistic primary purposes. If we measure the 'market penetration' of literature by different criteria, however, an altogether more favourable picture begins to emerge. Print runs for literary works were much larger than for most other categories; many works stayed in print over long periods; cheap popular editions brought new readerships into play; and 'literature' for many publishers did not have to be new to be profitable: acclaimed works from the past offered a steady source of income and involved little commercial risk.

The *cabinets de lecture* that had been introduced in Paris and other major cities in the eighteenth century spread rapidly in the early decades of the nineteenth. These were the predecessors of the modern public library, and by 1835 there were 500 of them in the capital alone. Such records as we possess suggest that prose fiction, together with newspapers, was the pre-eminent attraction offered by these print-filled rooms. Whether hired out for reading on the premises, or borrowed and taken home, novels were consumed voraciously. Newspapers themselves, by way of the serialized novels they often carried, fed this appetite, and were in turn its beneficiaries: *Le Constitutionnel*, for example, increased its daily sale from 3,000 to around 24,000 by recruiting Eugène Sue as the reliable supplier, episode by episode, of *Le Juif errant* (1844–5). Other novelists who flourished during the heyday of the *roman-feuilleton* in the 1840s included Alexandre Dumas senior, the author of *Les Trois Mousquetaires* and *Le Comte de Monte-Cristo*, and Paul Féval, whose *Les Mystères de Londres* reused a number of winning devices first exploited in Sue's *Les Mystères de Paris*. All three produced written material by the yard. Dumas was not only a high-output text-producing machine in his own person, but at the zenith of his career supervised a number of ghost-writers, charged with producing 'Dumas' in industrial quantities. The new printing and paper-making equipment, the newly energized newspaper trade, and the storytelling talents of these prolific authors combined to give prose fiction the status of a commodity. It could be written, printed, and distributed in bulk, and bulk—the sheer corpulence these serial novels displayed when finally issued in volume form—became a reliable selling point. From the commercial point of view, big was beautiful.

What other reasons were there for the popularity of these works? To some extent the *feuilleton* novelist, in spinning his yarns, was providing a mixture of excitement and reassurance on a time-honoured pattern. He could concoct a dizzying array of plots and sub-plots, contrive all manner of cliff-hanging endings for his successive episodes, consort with demons, condense into the pages of his fiction all the man-made horrors of the urban environment, yet still manage to suggest that the world was hospitable, rule-governed, and intelligible. Plots had denouements, mysteries had solutions, and, after many delays and detours within the narration, a sense of order could be restored. The novel opened itself up to the dangerous and insanitary labyrinth of the modern city, yet created a closed, self-sustaining world into which the inhabitants of city and countryside alike could escape. The reader, as he or she turned the pages of newspaper or book, was a solitary, lost in a private world of adventure and reverie, operating alone the complicated rules of narrative grammar, yet at the same time the conscious participant in a craze, a pattern of collective behaviour by means of which a precarious sense of community could be forged. In the *roman-feuilleton* the extraordinary prestige that was later conferred upon the 'art-novel' can already be glimpsed. The novel, purveying mere stories, was to become an instrument of cognition and consensus, a device by which an entire society could begin to achieve a critical understanding of itself.

The great novel cycles of Balzac and Zola, together with the astonishing prose epic that is Hugo's *Les Misérables*, enlarged the horizons of an audience that still belonged principally to the middle class. The primary aim of many readers choosing the novel over other literary genres may well have been that of 'reading for the plot', but fiction also had a role that is nowadays more likely to be played by the documentary film or the feature article: it took its readers to unusual destinations. The middle class was transported into factories, urban tenements, and criminal dens, and invited to eavesdrop on racy languages they would otherwise be unlikely to hear; provincials could explore the city and city-dwellers the inscrutable wasteland that lay beyond the metropolis. Sitting in their chairs at home or in the *cabinet de lecture*, consumers of the novel could enjoy unaccustomed social mobility. Down into the Paris sewers with Hugo's Jean Valjean, up into aristocratic salons with Balzac's Rastignac, or across to the rolling fields and open skies of the Beauce with Zola's Jean Macquart, the reader's fictional journeys gradually gave him or her an ecstatic sense of ubiquity within the territory of France. The *Voyages extraordinaires* of Jules Verne extended this freedom of travel to include the sea-bed, the centre of the Earth, and the trackless reaches of outer space. The novel told stories still, but it also satisfied a passion for knowledge. The novelist made things up and sometimes pursued his flights of fancy to preposterous lengths, but he also drew convincing maps of the real world. He told his readers how things were.

As literacy increased and bookseller-publishers competed with each other for lucrative popular markets, serial publication became much less common. With the exception of the 'Fantômas' adventures, which ran in instalments from 1911 to 1962, complete works launched in volume form became the order of the day. Aficionados of fiction continued to borrow books, but increasingly they bought their own supplies as well. Flammarion printed 600,000 copies of Victor Margueritte's mildly pornographic *La Garçonne* in 1922; 1.13 million copies of Zola's *Germinal* had been sold by 1972, most of them as modern paperbacks. The industry began to think of individual authors and their works as distinctive 'brands', and, with the willing compliance of the authors themselves, resorted to new marketing strategies.

Among the latter none now seems more bizarre than the vogue for the *roman-fleuve* in the aftermath of the First World War. Such multivolume productions as Romain Rolland's *L'Ame enchantée*, Roger Martin du Gard's *Les Thibault*, Georges Duhamel's *Chronique des Pasquier*, and Jules Romains's *Les Hommes de bonne volonté* were all works of healing and reconciliation: to a nation traumatized by war and a sense of irreparable loss these vast fictions offered the consoling spectacle of continuity within the family and the nation state. Romains's twenty-seven-volume novel, the longest by far of these very long works, has an entire apparatus of résumés, indexes, and apostrophes to the reader, all designed to suggest that the whole experience of modern France has been turned into a single verbal fresco. The formula was a compelling one, and was to have its after-echo in the uncompleted novel cycles launched by Louis Aragon and Jean-Paul Sartre in the 1940s. Yet the commercial motive behind these projects is clear: first capture your audience, and then keep it supplied, year upon year, with further slabs of text. Within the single-volume format the profitable idea of serial publication had been artfully reinvented.

Even when novels were of relatively modest size, their titles often spoke with unashamed grandeur. Who could resist the exalted perspectives promised by *Voyage au bout de la nuit* and *La Condition humaine*, by *Le Désert de l'amour*, *La Chute* or *L'Espoir*? Novelists had been appointed as the conscience of their age, and the writing of novels had come to be thought of as the literary activity par excellence. The Dreyfus affair, the battles of the First World War, and the experience of occupation, collaboration, and resistance after 1940 were novelized even as the events themselves were unfolding. Literary prizes and domestic squabbles within the house of fiction were front-page news. When the new novelists of the 1950s and 1960s attacked Balzac as the embodiment of an obsolete 'realist' approach, they did so the more resonantly to proclaim the glorious rebirth of novel form for which they themselves were responsible. When a major new social movement emerges—feminism, say, or decolonization, or gay rights—the novel still offers it a straightforward expressive outlet and an already primed audience. For many readers of today the automatic answer to Sartre's celebrated question 'what is literature?' would be 'novels'.

The fiction industry in twentieth-century France has, however, a dispiriting lesson for aspiring novelists: the chances of any new novel still being available in print a generation, or even a decade, after its first appearance are low. The industry calls new works into being, but rapidly loses interest in them. Novels are produced, consumed and forgotten on a massive scale. This merchandising of the writer's craft was characteristic not just of literature in French but of many other Western traditions. As courtly and ecclesiastical patronage gradually disappeared across Europe the market provided writers with an alternative, and equally precarious, means of support.

We come closer to a specifically French cultural landscape when we consider genres other than prose fiction, and other roles for the writer than that of supplying raw materials for the newly mechanized print industry. Particularly striking, in the literature of the twentieth century, are the fluid interchanges that are to be observed between 'high' and 'popular' literary forms, and between the printed word and other media. Many writers had parallel careers as journalists, and in times of national emergency—during the two World Wars, for example, or the Algerian crisis of 1954–62—addressed a broad public on the contentious issues of the day. French writers were expected to have views and espouse causes. On such matters as the right to oppose the Algerian war, the repeal of the law on abortion, or the freedom to publish without state censorship, writers in loose ad hoc groups made their voice heard. That a given writer had a given view was itself often headline news.

Even in the absence of crises and *causes célèbres*, major literary figures were prepared to immerse themselves in popular culture and the daily life of the capital: the Surrealists read Hegel but also rummaged gleefully in the flea-market; Sartre was a philosopher and political theorist who joined demonstrations and edited the Maoist newspaper *La Cause du peuple*; Raymond Queneau was a polymath and encyclopedist who found poetry in the lives of fairground workers and the urban poor.

In two areas of French cultural life, such crossovers between different kinds of language and different forms of expression have a long-established and still secure place. In popular song, first of all. When Georges Brassens sang lyrics by Villon, Hugo, or Aragon he was doing at one remove what they themselves had done: absorbing and reinflecting an ancient oral idiom. And when, as was more often the case, Brassens wrote lyrics for himself to set and then perform he was continuing an almost unbroken tradition that dates back to the troubadours and *trouvères* of the Middle Ages. The world of Brassens and fellow singer-songwriters such as Léo Ferré, Serge Reggiani, and, from Belgium, Jacques Brel is one in which the daily concerns of ordinary people, transformed into song, suddenly became rich and memorable; a new sense of community is created between artists and the *petites gens*. The large corpus of texts and recordings left by these singers, together with the work of Mistinguett, Josephine Baker, Edith Piaf, and Juliette Greco among the *chanteuses*, are a musicalized social history of the age, and a unique archive of linguistic exhibits. The modern singer-songwriter was to become an international and pre-dominantly anglophone phenomenon in the later decades of the twentieth century. But although he, and increasingly she, were part of what Jean-Jacques Servan-Schreiber in a best-seller of 1967 was to call 'le défi américain' ('the American challenge'), the origins and the finest achievements of this complex creative personality were unmistakably French.

The second of these areas of interchange is the cinema, to which French directors, actors, writers, and musicians made decisive contributions throughout the century. Again the distinction between high and popular art is distinctly unhelpful here. Even if one thinks of the two terms as marking the outer limits of a spectrum, where on it can one place Jean-Paul Belmondo's performance in *Borsalino* or Yves Montand's in *Jean de Florette* and *Manon des sources*? And where exactly does the category 'literature' fit inside the extraordinary web of skills and signifying practices that a film in production brings together? Even in the work of Jean-Luc Godard, who seems so envious of literature and so anxious to claim for himself the designation *auteur*, cinema is a defiantly hybrid, plural, and collaborative medium.

No single figure occupies the shifting borderlands between literature and film with more assured versatility than Jacques Prévert (see Figure 14). He wrote the screenplay for Jean Renoir's *Le Crime de Monsieur Lange* during the Popular Front, and for Marcel Carné's *Quai*

14. Jacques Prévert
(1900–1977) as drawn
by Maurice Henry
(1907–1984) for an
encyclopedia article.

des Brumes and *Le jour se lève* shortly after. Under the German occupation, he was the principal writer for Carné's semi-clandestine *Les Enfants du paradis*, and began producing the poems that were to be collected as *Paroles* immediately after the war. Prévert's poems enjoyed huge popular success, both in their printed form and as song lyrics. 'Les Feuilles mortes', set by Joseph Kosma and sung by Juliette Greco among many others, became an international anthem for separated lovers and sentimental solitaries. Whatever the genre in which he was writing, Prévert spoke for the forgotten and the dispossessed, and he did so in a discreetly inventive diction. In film, poetry, and song the vices and virtues of ordinary people discovered a distinctive rhythm and coloration, and although Prévert's writing had no explicit political allegiances, its implied politics were clear: art must have no truck with social exclusion, and can remain artful, and in that sense 'high', even if it begins and ends its career among the basement-dwellers of modern society.

A still more remarkable feature of French literature over the last two centuries remains to be mentioned: it has produced its own antidote or counterblast to the industrializing developments that we have described. For all the commercial benefits it enjoys, the novel has itself been a vehicle of critique. Flaubert writes scathingly about the follies of 'industrial art'; Proust tracks the rise and fall of literary reputations, mocking the language of the marketplace as he does so; and Nathalie

Sarraute, in *Les Fruits d'or*, satirizes the paraphernalia of reviews, blurbs, print runs, and prizes that is erected around the lonely efforts of the creative writer. For all the ironic intensity that novelists have brought to this form of social criticism, however, it is among the poets of the period that we find unappeasable indignation and rage. 'La poésie veut quelque chose d'énorme, de barbare et de sauvage' ('Poetry craves something enormous, barbarous and wild'), Diderot had said, at a time when no French poet was likely to rise to the challenge of his slogan. Within a hundred years, however, a certain savagery had come to define the poet's role in society. He was now a visionary, a teller of painful truths, a barbaric voice from beyond the walls of the *polis*. In a phrase made famous by Paul Verlaine, he had become a 'poète maudit'.

This rebellion took a variety of forms. Poets could become difficult in their diction, provocative in their explorations of sexuality, elitist and esoteric in the artistic creeds they professed, or deranged in their quest for new sensations and uncanny states of mind. Far from confining themselves to the discipline of metrical composition, they also wrote prose poems, essays, manifestos, and polemical prefaces to their own works. Their refusal of bourgeois right-mindedness and prudence was so insistent that 'literature' itself became a suspect category. Literature must no longer collude with its own enemies. It must rediscover the *rature*—the cancelling, the crossing out—that its very name harbours. For the later Victor Hugo, poetry was a continuation of the Republican project at the lexical level: hierarchical distinctions between words were as objectionable as those between individuals. For Rimbaud, in *Une Saison en enfer*, poetry could be made from whatever verbal materials came to hand: 'la littérature démodée, latin d'église, livres érotiques sans orthographe' ('out-of-date literature, Church Latin, erotic works with poor spelling'). Obeying what at first may seem an opposite tendency of the poetic imagination, Mallarmé presented the task of the poet as that of purging everyday language of its banality and of restoring its magical power of suggestion. Only when this process of distillation had taken place could poetry assume its highest responsibility, which was that of explaining the world in song. There is, however, no real contradiction between the two attitudes, for in adopting either of them the poet is saying 'no' to social and linguistic consensus, and refusing to offer his works up as merchandise.

Poets in the nineteenth century were the instigators of two major traditions that ran through French literature until the late twentieth. On the one hand, they founded the notion of the artistic avant-garde, and their exemplary gestures of refusal, together with their feverish verbal experimentation, continued to reverberate in the radical art movements of the new century, from Dada and Surrealism to concrete poetry, happenings, and multimedia installations. On the other hand, their works contained a much more inward-looking lesson for literature as a social institution: if literature were to shed its external trappings, and dissociate itself once and for all from trade, entertainment, and transient political affairs, it could become a central source of value in the human sphere. Mallarmé's rallying cries, which had been little heeded in his lifetime, enjoyed an apotheosis after his death: the poet was a new Orpheus; the world existed in order to become a supreme book; and literature existed to exclude and outlast mere world. Echoing through the works of Maurice Blanchot, Raymond Queneau, and Georges Perec, and receiving further endorsement from the theorists of the 1960s and 1970s, these propositions, from having been the basis of a secular religion for Mallarmé himself, began to seem modern, topical indeed, in the second half of the twentieth century. Literature, brought to a peak of exacerbated self-awareness and renamed *texte* or *écriture*, became the site of epistemological enquiry and ethical debate. Its compacted plural meanings were a guarantee of moral seriousness and political rectitude.

Looking back over the literature of the last two hundred years, we see many parallels and continuities. Simone de Beauvoir's *Le deuxième sexe* amplifies the project of female emancipation outlined in 1791 by Olympe de Gouges in her 'Déclaration des droits de la femme et de la citoyenne'. The political eloquence of Charles de Gaulle, even down to its periodic sentence structure, is in direct line of descent from the oratory of the Revolution. And many contemporary aspirants to the Goncourt and other literary prizes are still content to use a broadly Balzacian framework in assembling their fictions. Much has changed, however, and is continuing to change as we write. The idea of a 'masterpiece', for example, has fallen on hard times, as has that of a national literary tradition buttressed by a sequence of unimpeachable 'Pléiade authors'. Over and against an earlier vision of national identity as dependent upon a standardized national language, contemporary literature in French often celebrates diversity—linguistic, ethnic, and cultural. Minority languages, dialects, and sociolects are being called on to inject a new idiomatic energy into literary French. Writers from the former French colonies are becoming influential in metropolitan France. Feminist and gay activists are reaching out to very broad audiences not by employing the serviceable abstractions handed down from earlier generations, but by deriving new literary languages from their specific and local fields of experience.

This denationalization and deregulation of literary culture continues to produce work of outstanding originality and force, but at the same time literature is itself being displaced by the 'new media' and the globalizing enthusiasm that they have brought with them. France now plays a central role in a European economy that is concerned with the enrichment of literary culture only in so far as national literatures are part of an enlarged 'heritage' industry. At a time when information technology is able to offer scholars instantaneous access to the French literature of the past by way of online databases such as *Frantext* and the *Trésor de la langue française*, that literature is becoming less and less prominent on university syllabuses. While computers offer a bulwark against the institutionalized amnesia of the modern literature industry, their effectiveness in this role depends on the continued existence of readers prepared to look beyond the best-sellers and prize-winners of the moment. French literature runs the risk of being available *in toto*, and available to all, while being for practical purposes forgotten by all but a small band of nostalgic devotees.

The Period in Close-Up

In 1793 the minor playwright Philippe Fabre d'Églantine produced a dozen poetic neologisms. Created as the names of the months in the Republican calendar, they were the tribute of a fervent Revolutionary to the new social and political order that had just been inaugurated by the Convention Nationale. Although their period of official service ended in 1805, these products of the literary imagination were to enjoy a long afterlife in French literature and, in certain cases, to pass into international usage. *Pluviôse*, the rainy month, provided Charles Baudelaire with an explosive opening to the first 'Spleen' poem in *Les Fleurs du mal*. *Germinal* became the title of a celebrated novel by Émile Zola, and *Vendémiaire*, the season of the wine-harvest, performed the same service for Guillaume Apollinaire's hymn to the pleasures of drink. *Thermidor* dwindled into a culinary term in the wake of Victorien Sardou's play of that name, and 'Thermidorian' into a cumbersome synonym for 'political moderate', while the misty month continues to travel widely on five continents, thanks to Karl Marx's devastating pamphlet *The Eighteenth Brumaire of Louis Napoleon*.

Looked at in one way, Fabre d'Églantine's twelve-word contribution to the Republican cause will come as no surprise to anyone whose imagination has been seized by the extraordinary events of 1789–99. The Revolution was so momentous in itself, and has had such wide repercussions inside and outside France, that it is easy to think of 'literature' in its narrow modern sense as no more than a background murmur, scarcely audible against the clamour of the public stage. Many minor writers were conscripted as the penmen and penwomen of the new era. They wrote odes for public performance, rough-hewn verses for patriotic songs, and scripts for the pageants, ceremonies, and secular rituals that figured prominently in the daily life of the capital. Politically committed play-writing flourished. Claude Rouget de Lisle rose from obscurity to a fame even more durable and widespread than Fabre's when his 'Chant de guerre pour l'armée du Rhin' was adopted as the national anthem under its new name: 'La Marseillaise'. But this was literary fame of a special sort. It had little to do either with verbal originality or with personal vision. Writers lending their support at this level to the Republican cause were given unique opportunities to be heard and appreciated, but only on condition that they played the role allotted to them by the public bodies of the day. They were called upon to symbolize the Revolution in song, to dramatize the new freedoms it had brought, to stage-manage its festivals, but otherwise expected to remain silent. If writers had bodied forth the new French state only in these ways, the tally of significant works from this period would be meagre indeed.

This is yet another case in which the modern notion of literature as the collective term for fiction, poetry, and drama of high artistic quality proves seriously misleading as a guide to the writings of the past. As soon as we adopt a wider perspective, 'literature' can be seen as a main mover of political events. The two genres often overlooked by modern commentators but having crucial importance in the final decade of the eighteenth century are the pamphlet on the one hand and eloquence or oratory on the other. Both had already reached high-water marks in the seventeenth and earlier eighteenth centuries, but the Revolution gave them an impact and efficacy that they have seldom enjoyed before or since.

Emmanuel-Joseph Siéyès's pamphlet *Qu'est-ce que le Tiers État?*, written immediately before the convocation of the Estates General in 1789, is not only a call to action but a proleptic portrait of what action by and on behalf of the unenfranchised majority of the population might be like:

> Qu'est-ce que le Tiers état?—TOUT
> Qu'a-t-il été jusqu'à présent dans l'ordre politique?—RIEN
> Que demande-t-il?—A ÊTRE QUELQUE CHOSE.
>
> [What is the Third Estate?—EVERYTHING
> What has it been until now in the political sphere?—NOTHING
> What is it asking for?—TO BE SOMETHING]

Throughout, Siéyès's writing is direct, simple, pointed. A far-reaching programme of social change might indeed be implemented to the tune and pulse of successive sentences such as these. Siéyès went on to become the principal drafter of the Rights of Man declaration presented to the National Assembly on 26 August 1789, and, although this celebrated document is a distillation of Enlightenment ideas from a variety of sources and designed to achieve the widest possible consensus, it nevertheless has the stamp of skilled authorship about it. Its rhetoric is that of the pamphleteering tradition, but purged of all ornament. Article VI, for example, holds that the law must be the same for

all citizens—'soit qu'elle protège, soit qu'elle punisse' ('whether it pro-
tects or whether it punishes')—and its rhythm and sentence structure
perform its equalizing political message. Together with the United
States Declaration of Independence, Lincoln's Gettysburg Address,
and certain sections of the Communist Manifesto, it raises modern
political utterance to the level of high art. The answering pamphlet
that the Rights of Man drew from Olympe de Gouges two years later is
altogether less monumental, but this work too—the 'Déclaration des
droits de la femme et de la citoyenne'—has the status of a literary and
political landmark. Indeed its fearless championship of women's rights
still speaks directly to feminist campaigners and a wider public at the
beginning of the twenty-first century.

If printed pamphlets and edicts are a major form of political action
in these years, eloquence, their spoken counterpart, often has the same
defining quality. The orator may feel called on to produce bluster and
verbosity, but in propitious conditions his words too can be a deed.
While the speeches of Mirabeau, Danton, Saint-Just, or Robespierre
have not necessarily been preserved as delivered, and must in some
cases be regarded as archaeological restorations, there can be little real
doubt about the rhetorical skill of their authors. When Danton
announces 'il nous faut de l'audace, encore de l'audace, toujours de
l'audace, et la France est sauvée!' ('we need audacity, still more audacity, always audacity, and France will be saved!') he is unmistakably
seeking a public outcome for his guileful words. Saint-Just and
Robespierre among the Jacobins, while presenting themselves as
abstract theorists of Revolution on certain occasions, readily resort on
others to the denunciation of individuals or entire groups. Then their
speeches are death sentences, performative acts carried out at only one
remove from the executioner's blade. One could say that in matters of
literary invention the initiative has passed, during the Revolution and
the Terror, from those who write for a living to those who write and
speak for a political purpose. The stylistic fingerprints of the latter
group are often difficult to detect, especially as it is their spectacular
public lives and deaths rather than their words that have fed the fantasies of later generations, but the art of eloquence has never had a more
complex grip on a European society. In a battered form, that art is with
us still.

THE ROMANTIC INDIVIDUAL

Few terms familiarly used by historians of literature are as troublesome
as 'Romanticism'. Whether called on to describe a certain mindset or to

place chronological limits around a major artistic movement in early nineteenth-century Europe, the term often has an unhelpful elasticity about it. Some commentators on the case of French Romanticism in particular will enlist Rousseau as its indispensable forebear and be happy to see Symbolism, Surrealism, and numerous more recent artistic creeds as late flowerings of the Romantic temperament. Others will be much more parsimonious, and wish to confine the label 'Romantic' to relatively few authors writing in the period 1810–48. To make matters still more difficult, Romanticism in literature seems to have had a bewildering variety of religious and political bedfellows—conservatives and liberals, Christians and pantheists, royalists and republicans. Sometimes it looks back to a remote past, and sometimes it casts a prophetic gaze into a utopian future. It is narrowly nationalistic in one form and boldly cosmopolitan in another. By 1835, competing definitions of *romantisme* were so common that Alfred de Musset could cast a satirical eye over the whole panoply of them. In the first of his 'Lettres de Dupuis et Cotonet', his mouthpiece Dupuis recounts how Romanticism had been historical in one year, and a matter of introspective intimacy the next, only to re-emerge, shortly after, first as a system of philosophy and political economy, and then as the habit of not shaving and of wearing wide-lapelled waistcoats.

It is possible to be quite precise, however, about certain key elements of Romantic sensibility, and to locate a decisive moment of change in the mid-1790s. While Condorcet, the last of the *philosophes*, was composing his *Esquisse d'un tableau historique des progrès de l'esprit humain* (1794), two gifted younger writers were already beginning to show their mettle: Germaine de Staël, born in 1766, and François-René de Chateaubriand, two years her junior.

Condorcet's theory of knowledge as announced in the opening pages of the *Esquisse* was derived from Locke by way of Condillac, and the paean to the future on which the work ends is a wholesale reapplication of the same theory to the arts and sciences of mankind. The distinctive capacities of the human mind involved the receipt and storage of sense-impressions, and the recombination of those impressions in the distilled form that we refer to as 'ideas'. By way of further advances in mathematics, and the construction of a universal language for the transmission of new knowledge, the range of the mind's combinatory mechanism could be extended indefinitely. At the same time, passion could be moderated by enhanced scientific understanding, and the destructive excesses of passion avoided altogether.

Staël and Chateaubriand, on the other hand, struck a new note. They were both fascinated by the sheer turbulence of human feeling,

by the improbable routes that sexual wishes took in their search for satisfaction, and by the mind's seemingly innate wish to live dangerously.
A Romantic temperament, as they were soon to define it in their essays
and personify it in their fictional heroes and heroines, was subject both
to the lure of the infinite and to the oppressive weight of the everyday.
It veered between exuberance and melancholy, hope and disenchantment, but this self-division of the human mind was a positive as well as
a negative propensity. From inner disequilibrium new knowledge of
an unexpected sort could flow. Impatience, perplexity, and dissatisfac-
tion could bring their own rewards. Suddenly, a new vision of mental
dynamism quite foreign to the heirs of Locke was beginning to take
shape. The perturbations of consciousness were about to acquire their
own prestige. And the instinctual life of human beings began to attract
the attention of writers as an almost autonomous species of literary subject matter, separated for practical purposes from the multi-levelled
life of the social group.

The individual mind—isolated, dramatized, theatricalized—gave
birth to a remarkable crop of fictional works in the years 1800–15.
Staël's *Delphine* and *Corinne*, Chateaubriand's *René* and *Atala*,
Benjamin Constant's *Adolphe*, and Senancour's *Obermann* were all portraits of instinctual desire in action, or retreating from action into guilt,
anxiety, and obsessional brooding. These works employ a variety of
narrative strategies. Staël experimented first with the epistolary form
and then with a third-person narrative having extended first-person
interpolations; Chateaubriand's tales are surrounded by elaborate
framing narratives, while Senancour's work is an almost plotless series
of letters and disquisitions from its forlorn protagonist. Only *Adolphe*
has the character of a substantial, self-explanatory soliloquy, although
even this is framed by an exchange between the supposed publisher and
author of the tale. Yet despite the marked formal differences that these
works display, they find common ground in the attention they pay to
the sheer travail of self-awareness. Constant's hero speaks for an entire
generation when he says of the pain that he will eventually cause his
mistress by leaving her, 'Ne l'éprouvons-nous pas chaque jour en détail
et goutte à goutte, cette douleur?' ('Do we not experience it every day,
in detail, drop by drop—this pain?') Tracing the paths of feeling 'drop
by drop' had become a new literary vocation for prose writers of the
age. The self-analytic individual scanning back and forth between his
or her past, present, and future mental states had brought a new kind of
narrative architecture into being.

Corinne is the most extravagant and the most engagingly diverse of
these works. Its heroine is propelled by amatory enthusiasm and

boundless intellectual curiosity. She is impetuous, quick-witted, and self-determining, but at the same time has a capacity both for reverie in the manner of Rousseau's *promeneur solitaire*, and for ecstatic self-loss before the landscapes and artworks she contemplates. The book is untidy, and its almost free-standing essays on Italian art and literature have a way of upstaging its central story of disappointed love. But as the history of a risk-taking consciousness it has true originality, and points the way towards later works such as Chateaubriand's *Mémoires d'outre-tombe* and Proust's *A la recherche du temps perdu*. Corinne herself is the organizing intelligence on which everything else in the book depends: she absorbs and transfigures the world around her, puts ideas to work on her day-to-day experience, and relishes those moments when, by some inscrutable process of mental combustion, a startling new perspective opens up. She is an intellectual innovator, and a creative critic of the kind that Staël herself was to become in *De l'Allemagne* and *De la littérature*.

If Chateaubriand's memoirs, composed over many years and marked by a constant cross-cutting between time-frames, are the Romantic drama of individual consciousness in its most expansive form, *Obermann* seems at first to have shrunk that drama down to a minimalist shadow-play. 'Je ne vous dis pas ce que je sens, ce que je voudrais, ce que je suis; je ne vois plus mes besoins, à peine je sais mes désirs' ('I am not telling you what I feel, what I should like, what I am; I can no longer discern my own needs; I scarcely know my own desires'): this is the posthumous voice of the ego, speaking from within an obstructed memory of passion. Yet Senancour's narrator has his own virtuosity. Stripped of hope, removed from human relationships, and largely confined to an abstract semi-philosophical diction, he nevertheless reinvents himself, reimagines his own desolation, with sombre relish. Take almost everything else away, and you are still left with the demon of creativity. Sense-impressions and ideas may be few, but the urge to transform the world survives. The Romantic imagination was indeed, as Musset mockingly suggested, to 'rebrand' itself in many seemingly contradictory ways, but at its core there was always a trust in the inventive and shape-changing capacity of the human mind. A Romantic was an introspective who believed himself or herself capable of changing the world.

LITERATURE AND SEXUALITY

The hero of the *roman personnel* is clearly motivated by sex. The plot of *Adolphe* turns upon the cooling of the narrator's sexual ardour, and that of *René* upon the gradual acknowledgement of incestuous passion between a sister and a brother. But, partly for reasons of decorum and partly to safeguard the general moral import of these narratives, little is said in them about the sexual act itself and nothing at all about the physiology of arousal and orgasm. We have to look to a neighbouring and largely clandestine literary tradition to find the sexual interests of the age being pursued under laboratory conditions, as it were. Here, however, in the borderlands between pornographic fantasy and enlightened scientific curiosity, activity was intense. Sexual experiences were endlessly various and strange. They could be catalogued for the reader's benefit either as a shopping list of possible pleasures, or as an elaborate system of classes and sub-classes modelled on a zoological or botanical taxonomy.

A particularly straightforward style of sexual reportage is to be found in *Monsieur Nicolas, ou le cœur humain dévoilé* by Restif de la Bretonne. This huge compendium of reminiscences, assembled in the mid-1770s, is concerned above all else with the serial narration of the protagonist's conquests. The work resembles a blown-up version of Leporello's catalogue aria in Mozart's *Don Giovanni*, but with one telling difference: where Leporello enumerates his master's exploits, Restif is a low-class fellow who brags about his own. Restif deserves a place of honour in any history of European sexuality, for he not only coined the term *érotisme* itself and brought zany charm to the art of erotic fiction, but in numerous tracts and pamphlets he laid out plans for the social management of the sexual appetite. He was a campaigner for sexual freedom within a stable social order, and moved dextrously between prose designed to excite and prose designed to persuade. His limitations, apart from his unstemmable prolixity, have to do with the rigid application of a quantitative measure to sexual performance. Rather in the manner of his older and more celebrated contemporary Giacomo Casanova, whose *Mémoires* were written in French though first published in a German translation, Restif's 'Monsieur Nicolas' keeps a careful record of his partners and the ejaculatory opportunities they afford him. More sex is better than less, and Don Giovanni's *mille e tre* compliant females are the dream of every right-thinking male.

A more complex view of the sexual imperative is to be found in a writer who has become the patron saint of dissident desire, and whose works still represent a *ne plus ultra* of transgressive erotic imagining. At first glance the novels of the marquis de Sade seem to be based on a secularized version of the theological principle which holds that the world, being the product of an omnipotent deity, cannot be more perfect or more fully stocked than it already is. Sade removes the deity

from the scene in favour of a self-creating Nature, and gives the novelist a special responsibility within the natural order: he realizes in his
desire-driven narratives the potential forms of the world, and discovers
new sources of stimulation at every point of the compass. *Les 120
journées de Sodome*, which Sade wrote during his captivity in the
Bastille, certainly has an air of optimism and plenitude about it. The
novel is a festival of stories, loosely modelled on Boccaccio's *Decameron*
and the *Cent Nouvelles nouvelles*, in which a frame narrative encloses a
dizzying profusion of lesser tales, some of them compressed into single
sentences. The whole edifice is introduced as a systematic account of
the human passions given story-book form.

A cue for this project is to be found in Laclos's *Les Liaisons dangereuses*, which had been published two years before Sade took up his
pen. After his seduction of Cécile de Volanges, Valmont announces 'il
n'y a plus que les choses bizarres qui me plaisent' ('it is now only bizarre
things that give me pleasure'). While in Valmont's case 'bizarre things'
are called on to reactivate the jaded appetites of a long-serving liber-
tine, for Sade they are the very sign of a sexual imagination at work.
Sade's libertines are dedicated to exploration and contrivance, and
perversion is their chosen *métier*. This programme has certainly helped
Sade achieve his legendary status among later generations of writers:
he travels ever onwards where others fear to tread; he is an absolutist
among the apostles of desire, and the supreme modern spokesman for
Eros. Yet the imaginative texture of *Les 120 journées*, and of its successor volumes *Justine* and *Juliette*, is much less plural and plentiful than
this posthumous reputation would suggest. In fact, Sade's excremental
fantasies and his scenes of flogging, flaying, piercing, tearing, and
dismemberment soon become an obsessional, self-limiting stock-in-
trade. For Sade, ecstasy lies on the far side of horror and disgust and is
available only to those who are prepared to bring icy resolution and
self-control to their journeys of transgression. The problem, however,
is that disgust quickly loses its power if separated off from other
emotions. It was left to other writers to provide the Sadean vision with
its full complexity, and to psychiatry and psychoanalysis to provide a
theoretical context for *sadism*, the technical term that was derived from
Sade's name within twenty years of his death.

THE NAPOLEONIC LEGEND

Napoléon Bonaparte seized power on 18 Brumaire, An VII (9
November 1799) and so brought the Revolution to an end. Yet this former member of the Jacobin Club continued to further certain aims of

the Revolution throughout his period of personal ascendancy. Self-crowned as Emperor on 2 December 1804, Napoleon I, as he then became, sought popular approval by a bold series of administrative measures at home and military campaigns across Europe. The concentration of power in his own person, and the establishment of an authoritarian apparatus to implement and enforce his wishes, were thought of by Napoleon himself as a providential short cut to the realization of rational and virtuous social goals. Reconciliation between classes, a new sense of citizenship and nationhood, a new legal code and a meritocratic system for training and advancement inside the professions could all have taken a long time to achieve if the task had been left to the still young and unstable democratic institutions of the day. Napoleonic willpower produced rapid results. If there had been trains, they would have run on time.

Napoleon belongs in a history of French literature under a number of separate heads. As a writer, first of all, he deserves a modest place. He was a devoted follower of Rousseau in his early years, and the author of an ambitious 'Discourse on Happiness'. He wrote pamphlets, essays and *contes*, was a prolific correspondent and, during his final exile on Saint Helena, surrounded by followers acting as research assistants and co-authors, he became a historian and memorialist of prodigious energy. The corpus of civil law prepared under Napoleon's direct supervision in the early years of the new century and often referred to as the Code Napoléon, was—and still is—thought of by many people as a masterpiece of clear, succinct literary expression. So much so that Henri Beyle, the imperial diplomat and civil servant who was later to gain fame under the pseudonym Stendhal, claimed to have used the Code as a daily inspiration during the composition of *La Chartreuse de Parme*. A second, indirect, contribution to French literature was made by Napoleon in his capacity as educational reformer: the *lycées*, the elite secondary schools introduced in 1802, were to give a prominent place in their curriculum to the study of literary texts, vernacular as well as classical. And by way of their final-year course in philosophy, they were to provide an introduction to the techniques of critical analysis and argument. Active reading, and the articulation of a coherent response to it, became part of the future professional's basic intellectual training.

By far the richest of Napoleon's legacies to literature, however, is to be found in the works of those fellow writers who, while outstripping him by far in stylistic subtlety, looked to him as an empowering role model. Napoleon, like Louis XIV before him, was the manufacturer of his own mythology, and to this end employed an army of painters, writers, and publicists willing to seek their own glory by praising and emblematizing his. It was as an emblem of will, and prowess, and stubborn persistence in the face of adversity, that his image was to haunt later generations. 'L'Aigle, c'est le génie' ('the Eagle equals genius'), Victor Hugo announced in his *Odes et ballades*, remembering the imperial eagle, and the 'eagle's flight' that had brought Napoleon back from Elba to the mainland in 1815, at the beginning of his final hundred-day adventure. Julien Sorel at the beginning of Stendhal's *Le Rouge et le Noir* sees a bird of prey in the sky above him and interprets it as the call of Napoleonic destiny. 'L'aigle a déjà passé: Napoléon m'appelle' ('The eagle has already flown by: Napoleon summons me'), Gérard de Nerval wrote in an early version of his sonnet 'Horus', finding a modern and public source of support for what until then had been a personal journey back to ancient Egyptian myth.

Yet the legend of Napoleon spoke not merely of a mighty individual will but of an unquenchable thirst for movement, novelty, and diversity. What Napoleon had achieved as a conqueror of foreign lands and as an eager student of the cultures he traversed, the writer could perhaps achieve as a travel diarist, or by the bold, boundary-crossing exercise of his imagination. Hugo's preface to *Les Orientales* ends on a further tribute to the Napoleonic eagle, but not before he has sketched a specifically literary programme of exploration and conquest. The note of exaltation that sounds in Hugo's manifesto was to resonate in numerous other *grands projets* of the nineteenth century. Balzac in the *Comédie humaine* is the 'secretary of society' just as Zola is the chronicler of 'a family under the Second Empire' in *Les Rougon-Macquart*, but in neither case should the modest phrasing deceive us. Both writers, working within the loose format of the novel cycle, are propelled by an imperial sense of mission—to explore the world to its limits, to return with trophies to the writing-table, and, as an essential part of the novel's new drive to inclusiveness, to infuse it with insights gleaned from science, philosophy, and the other arts. A similar quality of Napoleonic exorbitance is to be observed in the career of Jules Michelet who, after voluminous outpourings on the history of the world, France, and the French Revolution, devoted himself in later life to geography and natural history. Birds, insects, mountains, and seas in turn became the protagonists in Michelet's rhapsodic documentary dramas. Whatever existed in the human past or in the natural world could be subdued, and then celebrated, by the all-conquering pen. The charisma of Napoleon for writers and readers in the middle years of the century was such that even his follies, his defeat at Waterloo, and his ignominious last exile could be reprocessed as myth. At such moments he reincarnated the tragic figure of the overreacher. He was an Icarus as well as an eagle. When he suffered, his suffering was exemplary, and contained a promise of rebirth for humankind.

ROMANTICISM IN VERSE

If the inner tumult of the individual became a main preoccupation for prose writers of the first Romantic generation, this did not mean that the language they used was drastically different from that of their eighteenth-century predecessors. The language of *sensibilité* proved durable, and could readily be adapted to the new explorations of inwardness. A similar continuity-in-change is to be seen in the verse of Alphonse de Lamartine, whose first and most famous collection, the *Méditations poétiques* of 1820, not only enjoyed instant popularity but seemed to many of its early readers to define a wholly new kind of lyric poetry. The modern reader is likely to be struck by the familiarity of his diction in this and subsequent volumes rather than by any sense of novelty—linguistic, emotional, or 'philosophical'. Even after the Revolution and the rise and fall of the Napoleonic empire, Lamartine is intent upon emulating his classical and classicizing predecessors.

There are good grounds, however, for thinking of the *Méditations* as a revolutionary work. Its originality lies not in its diction, which is often formulaic and indiscriminately lofty, but in its cadence, its measured recreation of temporal flow:

> Murmure autour de ma nacelle,
> Douce mer dont les flots chéris,
> Ainsi qu'une amante fidèle,
> Jettent une plainte éternelle
> Sur ces poétiques débris.

[Murmur around my skiff, gentle sea whose beloved waves, like a faithful lover, cast an unceasing lament upon these poetic remains.]

Doux, together with its cognates and synonyms, provides these early poems with a continuous refrain. The 'doux tableaux' of 'L'Isolement', the 'doux reflet' and 'doux rayon' of 'Le Soir', and the 'molles clartés' of 'Le Lac' all act as a restraining device, an anxiously applied soft pedal, to prevent any element of the scene from becoming over-intense or flagrant. 'Douce mer' in the above lines, like the 'Murmure' with which the poem begins, has imperative force: the sea should be gentle, and if it finds itself windswept and tempest-tossed the poet expects to be called on as an agent of calm. It was in this spirit that Bizet turned the first three stanzas of the work into a rapturous barcarolle. Yet tranquillity is not the only achievement of the lyric voice in lines like these. Semantic stresses move back and forth between the rhyme-axis and the openings of the line. Material of different logical kinds—observation, reminiscence, simile, value judgement—is compressed into a uniform pattern of metrical units, creating a pattern of zigzags and displaced accents. The 'poétiques débris' are on the one hand the ruins of Pompeii and Herculaneum, for this poem was written on the Bay of Naples, but on the other hand they are a reminder of the transience of poetic art, and of the ways in which death-awareness may infiltrate the poetic voice at work upon its rhymes.

Lamartine's great gift is for short poems having this quality of subdued and bemused animation. Their obsolete language is not a bar to Lamartine's experiments with time-bound human subjectivity, and may indeed be thought of as providing flexible building materials for these. But the flow of Lamartinian time is often stalled when his poetic projects become more ambitious. Indeed the vast Christian epic that he envisaged in the 1830s, two sections of which were completed under the titles *Jocelyn* and *La Chute d'un ange*, takes the reader beyond flow altogether into a world of oceanic stasis. The language that was so well suited to his short lyrical effusions becomes bombastic and vapid as soon as it is pressed into service as a public address system. Lamartine's success as an orator on behalf of liberal causes led to his having a leading role in the provisional government of 1848, but improving oratory in verse couplets was a different matter.

Musset's verse is often more inventive than Lamartine's. The younger poet switches rapidly between tones of voice—slipping sudden sarcasms, for example, into his expressions of nostalgia and regret—and can rebel by way of an indecorous rhyme against the received code of good behaviour for poets. Yet his main talent is of a different order. It is almost that of a stage manager. In the four celebrated *Nuits* that he published between 1835 and 1837 conflicting emotions are shared out between the poet and his muse, and in such a way that each poem becomes a miniature drama built on a pattern of surprise discoveries and reversals of fortune. In *La Nuit de décembre*, the poet-narrator is obsessed by a ghostly pursuer—'Qui me ressemblait comme un frère' ('who was as like me as a brother')—and the work is memorable more for its uncanny plot and its narrative of gradual self-understanding than for its language, which is plain and untextured.

It is clear that these male poets think of themselves as the possessors of a ready-made poetic language and as the holders of a recognized and honourable public office. Even when they speak of their private joys and miseries, they speak on behalf of others. They are exemplary feeling beings, spokesmen for a multitude of less articulate and less theatrically gifted males. Their role requires them not only to speak with authority on intimate matters but to sound like legislators as they do so. Once this sense of vocal self-possession has been secured, their range can be extended to great issues, whether philosophical or political. Alfred de Vigny was a prolific writer in verse but in the long poems collected posthumously as *Les Destinées* he passes more successfully than either of the poets we have just mentioned from a troubled inwardness to the open forum of contemporary debate. Certain subjects, to be sure, cause his otherwise confident verse to falter: railway trains, modern farming methods, and North American colonization, for instance, do not fit happily into his implacable alexandrine. Overall, however, the tone is one of buoyant, civic-minded declamation. This is a man talking to men, in a language with which they are all familiar.

Women's experience does not feature significantly in the work of these poets. And in Vigny's case 'Woman' is a procession of stereotypes often propelled by an undisguised misogyny. It is all the more remarkable, therefore, that this generation of male poets, descended from acclaimed forerunners who were also uniformly male, should have had a great female contemporary. But they did, in the person of Marceline Desbordes-Valmore. She was four years older than Lamartine, published her first collection just before the *Méditations*, and is best known for 'Les Roses de Saadi', written around 1848:

> J'ai voulu ce matin te rapporter des roses;
> Mais j'en avais tant pris dans mes ceintures closes
> Que les nœuds trop serrés n'ont pu les contenir.
>
> Les nœuds ont éclaté. Les roses envolées
> Dans le vent, à la mer s'en sont toutes allées.
> Elles ont suivi l'eau pour ne plus revenir.
>
> La vague en a paru rouge et comme enflammée.
> Ce soir, ma robe encore en est toute embaumée ...
> Respires-en sur moi l'odorant souvenir.

[I wanted, this morning, to bring you roses; but I had collected so many into my closed girdles that the too-tight knots could not contain them. The knots burst. The roses, flying off down the wind, all went away to the sea. They followed the water, no more to come back. The wave seemed red from them, and as if inflamed. This evening, my robe is still full of their rich fragrance ... Breathe from me their sweet-smelling memory.]

This astonishing poem, which freely imitates a passage from the thirteenth-century Persian poet Sadi, is a celebration of the female body. Menstruation here makes its first appearance in French lyric verse, although the roses of the title are gloriously overdetermined:

they flow outwards from the speaker's clothing as a defiant discharge, and return as a fragrance that is also an emblem of insatiable sexual desire. Even in Desbordes-Valmore's earliest published work there is audacity in her disclosure of feeling. Being abandoned by a lover, caring for children, being caught in disturbing fantasies or haunted by traumatic memories, are all transposed into fluid and economical verse. Her diction is formal and colloquial by turns, and she uses its sudden switches not so much to expatiate on feelings as to plot their changing course:

> '—Retournez au monde où l'on aime ...
> Ô mon Sauveur! éteignez-moi!'

> [—Return to a world where people love ... Oh my Lord! Put me out!]

Thus ends her 'Rêve d'une femme', in which the speaker is seduced back into her own past. All retrospective pathways are appealing except the one that leads to youthful love: if I am to become again a love-lamp, the speaker announces, I want to be put out. Desbordes-Valmore not only gives voice to women's experience in the face of an exclusive male club, but achieves a many-voiced complexity that is rarely to be found in the verse of its members.

HISTORY AND PROPHECY

When the Bourbon monarchy was restored in 1814, in the person of Louis XVIII, there began an extraordinary period of intellectual and artistic experiment, and of national stocktaking. Supporters and opponents of the Revolution were in agreement on one thing: that the events of 1789–93 had been a cataclysmic singularity, the aftershocks from which were still being felt. Clearly, lessons were to be learned from the destruction of the *ancien régime* and the installation of the Republican order, but what were they? The sudden rift between epochs was in itself a challenge to historical understanding. Even after an interval of thirty years, the fault-line of the Revolution was still in crucial ways unintelligible to ordinary citizens and to professional students of the past. The new rulers and the liberal opposition urgently needed to know what 1789 meant.

During the Restoration French writers continued to explore the dynamics of the individual mind: lyric poetry, as we have seen, flourished; Madame de Duras, continuing the tradition of the *roman personnel*, wrote *Ourika*, whose first-person narrator was female and black; Maine de Biran, in his *Journal intime*, created a supple abstract prose in which to conduct his journeys to the mental interior; and Joseph

Joubert, in his *Pensées*, provided a bracing lesson in intellectual method. But an ambitious new form of public utterance also sprang into being in these years. This was history-writing with an overt political purpose. Historians stepped forward as the chroniclers of mass movements, of centuries-long European tendencies, and, pre-eminently, of the recent cataclysm itself. Their works were eagerly read as aids to national self-knowledge, and as a modern prose epic in the making.

When the young Chateaubriand published his *Essai sur les révolutions* and *Le Génie du christianisme* he had already given the reading public some idea of what Romantic historiography was to become. Both works skimmed back across the ages with unstemmable rhetorical exuberance. Where the one was a baleful comparative survey of revolutions throughout history, all of which foretold the disaster of 1789, the other was a tribute to the regenerative power of the Christian faith. What revolution had put asunder, the 'genius' of Christianity could reconcile and reunite. The historians who rose to prominence during the Restoration had different political aims, and superior research methods, but they shared Chateaubriand's sense that the present moment offered a unique vantage-point for the historical imagination, and that history was politics by another name. What is more, the magnitude of the task facing historians of this generation required of them verbal invention, narrative skill, and staying power, all on the grand scale. Over and against the *intimiste* concerns of the poets and novelists of the 1820s, the historians wrote monumentally.

In 1823, Adolphe Thiers, destined to become President of the Republic fifty years later, brought out the first volume of his *Histoire de la Révolution française*. A year later François Mignet published his more compact *Histoire de la Révolution française depuis 1789 jusqu'en 1814*. These were to be followed in rapid succession by ambitious historical works from Augustin Thierry, François Guizot, Edgar Quinet, Jules Michelet, and Alexis de Tocqueville. Major differences of emphasis are of course to be seen among these histories. Contemporary political debates and dilemmas are projected back upon an assortment of earlier ages, and the Revolution itself is viewed through a variety of lenses: where Thiers and Mignet, for example, think of the Terror as a transient moment of excess in the working out of the Revolutionary project, Guizot is much more concerned with the discontinuity between 1789 and its bloodstained betrayal four years later. But historians of this generation have a shared belief in the efficacy of their craft. The past is recoverable not as a collection of antiquities, not as the working out of a providential design, but as a dynamic developmental process awaiting its completion. The moment of fulfilment is drawing near, and perspicacious historical writing can speed its coming.

The title of a later work of Mignet's, *La Rivalité de François Ier et de Charles-Quint*, was in due course to appear on the first page of Proust's *A la recherche du temps perdu* as part of the narrator's bedtime reverie. In Proust's hands the *roman personnel* was to become a leviathan, able to swallow French history and historians at a single gulp; the recovery of lost time was a matter for the individual consciousness at work upon its own remembered states. During the Restoration and the early years of the July Monarchy, however, historians rather than novelists were the undisputed masters of the past. They remembered on behalf of the nation, and, by literary labour sometimes even more extensive than Proust's, they brought a national sense of potentiality to birth.

If the Revolution redefined the task of the historian by giving him futures to build, it also encouraged a much more impetuous group of futurologists to declare themselves. These were the utopian social thinkers who also rose to prominence during the Restoration. Where the historians worked by patient deduction and extrapolation from the events of 1789, these thinkers designed new societies and prophesied their imminent arrival. Yet they wrote as they did, and organized their followers as they did, because the Revolution had shown them the way. A new social order and a new secular religion had sprung up a generation earlier, and the miracle could surely be repeated, and on a firmer footing this time. The comte de Saint-Simon published his *Le Nouveau Christianisme* in 1825, Charles Fourier his *Le Nouveau Monde industriel* in 1829 and Auguste Comte the first volume of his *Cours de philosophie positive* in 1830. The writings of all three, like those of Prosper Enfantin, Saint-Simon's main disciple, combine astute analysis of actual social relations with a vein of elaborate fantasy. The origins of modern sociology are to be found here (Comte coined the term), but also a wayward flight from political action as the vehicle of social change. In a way, these writers do not belong to literature at all, even in its extended sense. They are social scientists in one mood, and inventors of experimental communities in another, but in neither are they concerned with the specific powers and complexities of the written word. Even Étienne Cabet, whose *Voyage en Icarie* of 1840 is decidedly a work of prose fiction, is more remarkable for the Icarian communities founded by his followers in the United States than for his literary achievements. Yet the call to action issued by these utopian fantasists continued to echo in French literature for many decades. A tantalizing prospect opened up: perhaps poets could build Icaria by the simple act of writing.

PROSE FICTION PREPARES FOR VICTORY

The 1820s were a period of intense experimentation in prose fiction, and produced their own crop of singular works. Under the inspiration of Walter Scott's historical novels, Vigny returned to the final months of Cardinal Richelieu's life in *Cinq-Mars* and Prosper Mérimée to the St Bartholemew's Day Massacre of 1572 in his *Chronique du règne de Charles IX*. Both authors reanimated and in part reinvented the archival materials on which they drew. The fantastic tale reached an early peak of frenzied inventiveness in Charles Nodier's *Smarra* and *Trilby*, while Jules Janin brought together violence, disabused humour, and narrative self-consciousness in *L'Ane mort et la femme guillotinée*. The early novels of Victor Hugo, culminating in *Le Dernier Jour d'un condamné à mort*, are the most substantial fictional offerings from a single pen, and already display much of the rule-breaking bravado that is to mark the large-scale prose works he produced in mid-career. Stendhal published his *Armance*, together with much occasional writing in a variety of formats. Overall, the final years of the restored Bourbon dynasty, which were presided over by Charles X from 1824 onwards, favoured a certain brisk energizing recalcitrance on the part of artists and intellectuals, but without providing them with any real sense of creative opportunity. Mérimée's finest achievements, in the novellas *Colomba* and *Carmen*, and in a group of incomparable short stories, belong to later decades.

It is never a good idea to overemphasize 'key dates' in the history of literature, or to expect major publishing events to be synchronized with moments of radical political change. We need to pay attention to the slow processes of development that a given literary genre may undergo, to the long periods of apprenticeship that writers may have served before their full individuality becomes visible, and to the encouragement that a new regime may give to mediocre or backward-looking authors. By any standards, however, 1830 was an astonishing year, and the *trois glorieuses*, the July days that brought Louis-Philippe to power, have their counterpart in at least three glories of the French literary tradition (see Figure 15).

The year 1830 sees the tumultuous first performance of Hugo's *Hernani*, to which we shall return, and the publication of Stendhal's *Le Rouge et le Noir* and a group of Balzac's *Scènes de la vie privée*. The novel suddenly seems to change gear. Stendhal and Balzac belong securely to 'world literature', and their influence on other European novelists has been immense. The year 1830 finds them at different career stages: Stendhal's novel marks a high point in his development; Balzac, sixteen

15. *Liberty Leading the People*, by Eugène Delacroix. This celebrated painting commemorates the July Revolution of 1830 and has been made use of, in a variety of formats, during many subsequent political upheavals in France, including those of 1848 and 1968. Delacroix himself was an eyewitness to the events of late July 1830, but guarded in his expressions of sympathy for the insurgents.

years his junior, was still an apprentice and the project of an integrated 'human comedy' was not to be unveiled for more than a decade. Yet the two of them already have much in common. They are both concerned with the tension between individuals and social groups; with politics and sexuality; with mobility between social classes, and the role-play and subterfuge that achieving it demands; with the combined plasticity and rigidity of the ego; with money, power, and fame, and the self-delusions of those who pursue them. Both have learned lessons from a variety of earlier novelists, possess boundless talents for comedy and verbal wit, and value the novel form for its inclusiveness: nothing that is human need be thought of as foreign to the novelist's suddenly enlarged sense of his own role. Add to this their admiration for each other's works and the acclaim they both enjoyed in the middle years of the July Monarchy, and they begin to resemble alternative versions of the same indomitable personality.

STENDHAL AND BALZAC

Yet Stendhal and Balzac are false twins, rather like Haydn and Mozart or Dickens and Thackeray: as soon as we look beneath their shared concerns and certain elements of period style, their differences are striking. Stendhal brings extraordinary grace and dexterity to the organization of his narratives. He values the audacity and quick-wittedness of his heroes and heroines, their willingness to take risks and obey sudden capricious impulses, and creates a speedy, sparkling narrative prose that reflects these qualities of mind. The relationship between Julien Sorel and Mathilde de la Môle in *Le Rouge et le Noir* is a continuous skirmish between self-willed personalities, overseen by a quizzical narrator who is infatuated with each of them in turn. The plot of the novel has an austere tragic design, but the narrative unfolds with comic self-consciousness. Stendhal, having Cervantes, Sterne, and Diderot among his masters, relishes the contrivance, the sheer concoctedness, of fiction while allowing the loves, enthusiasms, and disappointments of his characters to speak out affectingly.

Much has been made of Stendhal's liking for the operatic stage and for the co-presence of farce and pathos that is often to be found there. One way of describing the particular mixture of emotions to be found in his novels would be to call them comic operas in prose. Yet the texture of Stendhal's fiction is more unusual and more complex than this makes it sound. He spins his yarns in such a way that politics, sex, and social behaviour can be woven together in rippling patterns from one moment to the next. At the beginning of the second book of *La Chartreuse de Parme*, for example, Stendhal's analysis of tyranny is multi-layered and mobile. A warrant has been issued for the arrest of Fabrice del Dongo, and Gina, his aunt, is seeking to have it with-drawn. Rather than simply intercede with the lascivious prince de Parme, Gina decides on a dangerous bluff: if the order against Fabrice is not withdrawn, she will exile herself from the court. The prince's desire for Gina increases as his authority over her falters. 'Et que faudrait-il faire pour que madame ne partît point?' ('And what would need to be done to prevent my lady from leaving?'), he asks, suppressing his anger and reminding himself of the 'supreme rank' he holds. Throughout the scene, the tawdry politics of the court are shot through with sensual provocation and threatened violence, and the narrator traces the power-play between characters in a series of rapid verbal touches. Speech, description, and interior monologue are intercut in such a way that the events themselves, as the reader arranges them into a plot-line, are surrounded by echoes and anticipations.

Where Stendhal prizes volatility and speed, in characters as in narrative methods, Balzac often strives for cumulative effects of weight and exhaustiveness. Balzac's various accounts of the architecture of his fictional universe, including the celebrated 'avant-propos' to *La Comédie humaine*, all stress the interdependence of the single works that are its building blocks. Recurring characters and themes give the cycle coherence in the horizontal plane, and stratified levels of enquiry perform the same task vertically. Modern readers are often impatient with these exercises in self-publicity, and with the monarchist and Catholic underpinnings that Balzac claimed he had given the entire edifice. They point to the explosive contradictions that he has installed in his vast scale-model of contemporary French society, and to the enraptured attention he brings to bear on crises, conspiracies, and scandals. There is much to be said for this less comfortable view. The centrally placed chapter of *La Cousine Bette*, originally bearing the title 'Les cinq pères de l'église Marneffe' ('The five fathers of the Marneffe Church'), for example, is a tinder-box of potential disasters. The courtesan Valérie Marneffe is pregnant, and circled about by the possible fathers of her child: five separate stories converge at this moment, and five outcomes are held in a precarious equilibrium. Society, in the view that Balzac bodies forth here, is an unstable compound. The class system is in disarray. Urbanization, industrialization, and colonial expansion are producing a range of unpredictable consequences in Balzac's Paris, and bizarre partnerships in crime. Any novelist appointing himself 'secretary' to a society like this must be prepared to travel widely, and speak in many voices.

There is, however, a doggedness about Balzac's social observation, a relentless sifting of detail, and a willingness to hold forth, that makes him quite unlike any other novelist of the age. Society can be divided into classes and genealogies, and a variety of optical instruments can be used by its chronicler as he inspects these, but wherever and however he looks issues of general import, and incitements to moralizing, rise to meet his gaze. The Balzac novel abhors a vacuum. If, for instance, Rastignac in *Le Père Goriot* is due to dine with Goriot's daughter Delphine, now the wealthy Madame de Nucingen, and appears before his fellow lodgers at the Pension Vauquer in stylish new attire, the episode is laden with portent. The narrator fires off a salvo of aphorisms on the theme of desire intensified by difficulty; various inmates of the lodging-house react briefly to the transfigured Rastignac; and Vautrin launches a fantastical fusillade of his own. 'Une épouse à compartiments', he says of the protagonist's non-existent wife, 'qui va sur l'eau . . . moitié fil, moitié coton, moitié laine' ('A wife with compartments, who travels on water . . . made half of thread, half of cotton, half of wool'). Vautrin parodies the language of advertising, spices his speech with ribaldry, and subjects the female body to a series of distortions. Womankind seen as furniture, compartmentalized, broken down into its components, is part of a verbal pantomime played out between men, but also offers an early glimpse of Vautrin's subversive sexuality. The narrative voice and the Vautrin soliloquy are alike in their insistence and their copiousness. And yet the self-appointed business of the novelist is to keep supplying moral meanings even as his fantasy takes wing and his society inches towards catastrophe. To keep the warring tendencies of his fiction under control, intellectual muscle is required, and Balzac has it in abundance.

A COLOSSUS: VICTOR HUGO

At a culminating moment in Henry James's *The Ambassadors*, the protagonist, Strether, acquires 'seventy blazing volumes' of Victor Hugo's works. The purchase confirms that his seduction by Europe, and by Paris as its cultural epicentre, is now complete. James in 1903 was recapitulating a myth that was already many decades old: the name 'Hugo' had become a talisman, a symbol of literary creativity in its triumphant mode. Hugo connoted voluminousness. Only a volumetric system of measurement could cope with a writer who lived so long and wrote so much. Hugo's career still invites description of this kind. From his turbulent childhood during the Napoleonic wars to the paroxysms of national sentiment and licentious public behaviour that were triggered by his state funeral in 1885, Hugo bestrides and encapsulates his century. He wrote, orated, painted and drew, had opinions on all subjects, recreated in verse the history of humankind, and spoke man to man with the deity. Politically, he was a weathervane: from an early phase of enraged monarchism during the Restoration, he passed to republicanism, to membership of the Assemblée Constituante after the 1848 revolution, to self-imposed exile during the Second Empire, and was an agent of national reconciliation after the defeat of the Paris Commune.

Even if we look simply at Hugo's pronouncements on literature, greatnesses of size, scale, and stature are impossible to avoid. In the lengthy manifesto that he attached to his verse drama *Cromwell* in 1827, he speaks of the Bible, Homer, and Shakespeare as the indispensable forerunners of the new literary epoch he himself enshrines. Dante and Milton serve as harbingers of its epic vision, and Ariosto,

Cervantes, and Rabelais are the supreme comedians of the grotesque from whom the moderns must be prepared to learn. Nature and art are quite distinct, Hugo insists, but it is only in art that nature finds a 'miroir de concentration' ('a concentrating mirror') that is worthy of it. In writing, and particularly in a new, liberated, and fluctuating style of verse composition, the unsubduable energies and changing rhythms of the natural world find voice. The preface to *Cromwell* is a convincing early sketch of the entire Hugo *œuvre*. Its amplitude and exuberance are already here, as is the dynamic interplay between the grotesque and the sublime that was to mark his later work in a variety of genres. The vast appetite and ironclad digestive capacity of the Hugolian artistic ego are already on display.

Yet an emphasis on sheer size is distinctly unhelpful when it comes to the act of reading Hugo today. And it tells us very little about the intense admiration that Hugo's fellow writers continued to extend to him even as he enjoyed unprecedented popular success. A much better approach to Hugo's verse and prose, and to the ingenuity of his verbal art, would involve looking closely at individual stanzas and paragraphs, undistracted by the noise of his reputation and the bulk of his output. For example, in *Notre-Dame de Paris*, the historical novel that Hugo began shortly after *Cromwell*, the hunchback Quasimodo is first seen as an uncanny face staring from the clear central pane of a rose-window. The Parisian populace is about to elect its 'Fools' Pope', and the candidates have passed in procession behind the glass. Hugo's dramatic skill leads him to place Quasimodo's superior misshapenness at the climax of the proceedings, while his verbal skill produces a tiny, clinching lexical drama. Earlier faces were pentagons and hexagons, whereas Quasimodo's boasts a 'nez tétraèdre' ('a tetrahedron of a nose'): he wins the contest because his deformity alone is a three- rather than a two-dimensional affair.

In *Les Travailleurs de la mer*, the prose epic that Hugo wrote during his exile on Guernsey, the struggle between the hero Gilliatt and a giant octopus is described in a sequence of arresting brief utterances, in which learned and colloquial registers converge upon the deadly appetite of the creature: 'Une viscosité qui a une volonté, quoi de plus effroyable! De la glu pétrie de haine' ('viscosity that has willpower, what could be more terrifying! Glue fashioned from hatred'). The force of the passage is again entirely in its detail, and in the sudden swerves of perception and thought that the staccato sentences trace out. At the heart of these grandiose set-pieces an intimacy is taking place, or so the speaking voice of Hugo's prose would suggest: this is thought as it happens, a powerful reflective intelligence at work, and the reader is invited to share its versatile, spasmodic life. Even in *Les Misérables*, which is the most ample and oratorical of Hugo's fictions in prose, this confiding voice is to be heard, establishing a circuit of exchange and fellow feeling between the characters of the novel and a readership already thought of as innumerably large. Jean Valjean, Javert, Marius, and Cosette are different incarnations of everyman and everywoman, but Hugo's narrator speaks of them with particularizing precision as the long tale of their adventures unfolds.

In considering Hugo's thousands of pages of verse we must remember that poetic eloquence for him possessed a self-evident public utility: in his elegies for his dead daughter Léopoldine he speaks on behalf of all bereaved parents, and all other mourners past, present, and future; in the *Châtiments*, his sardonic cry of protest is directed, beyond its immediate political targets, against all tyranny and all social injustice; in 'Ce que dit la bouche d'ombre' he steps forward as a regenerative cosmological force, ever-willing to heal the wounds of humanity and to reconnect the lone individual to the rest of creation. Yet, as in the novels, Hugo's essential gift is for the positioning of complex images within the confident onward flow of his writing:

> Posée au bord du ciel comme une longue scie,
> La ville aux mille toits découpe l'horizon.

[Laid against the sky like a long saw, the town with its thousand rooftops slices the horizon.]

In these lines from the sequence of short poems entitled 'Soleils couchants', the cityscape at evening is seen with sinister exactitude: crocodile fangs had been hanging in the clouds in the poem placed just before this one, and now the rooftops have acquired teeth of their own. The city is solid and sharply delineated, but has a memory of the vaporous sky caught inside it. Often the effect of intensity is produced by fitting the plainest of propositions into a single verse-line, as in

> Elle essuya ses pieds à l'herbe de la rive

[She wiped her feet on the grassy bank]

or

> Ruth songeait et Booz dormait; l'herbe était noire.

[Ruth was dreaming and Booz asleep; the grass was black]

In the first of these, from *Les Contemplations*, the action of foot against grass becomes an erotic provocation, while in the second, from *La Légende des siècles*, an entire pattern of connection between procreative humans and the natural order at large suddenly comes to rest upon two adjoining but disjoined sentences. In all such cases the 'concentrating mirror' that is the entire poem achieves a moment of singular luminosity. Hugo the voluminous, the master of rhetorical amplification, catches transfigurative small-scale perceptions into the weighty flux of his writing.

POETRY AND SOCIETY

Hugo's *Notre-Dame de Paris* caused a widespread revival of interest in the French Middle Ages, but its success was only part of the much more general climate of national retrospection that we have already described. The past was news. The Napoleonic campaigns had been led by a would-be polymathic historian, and the study of ancient cultures had been revitalized by the looted antiquities brought to Paris by the imperial army. Archaeologists, historians, novelists, and poets were caught in a common delirium, a shared sense that the past was newly accessible and available for use. It could be studied empirically or reconstructed by efforts of imagination. All that was needed in either case was a steady hand, and a confident selfhood from which to supervise the operation.

Hugo, as we have seen, was the prototype of the secure self. He contained multitudes, and travelled widely in space and time, but he was always at the helm and the possessor of a hospitable, harmonizing voice. A younger generation of poets who admired him, envied his resourceful diction, and shared his passion for history, were nevertheless to turn French verse in a quite different direction:

> Je suis le ténébreux,—le veuf,—l'inconsolé,
> Le prince d'Aquitaine à la tour abolie:
> Ma seule *étoile* est morte,— et mon luth constellé
> Porte le *soleil* noir de la *mélancolie*.

[I am the darkling one—the widower—the unappeased, the prince of Aquitaine with his tumbledown tower: my sole *star* is dead, and my constellated lute bears the dark *sun* of *Melancholy*.]

Thus opens Nerval's 'El Desdichado', from the sonnet sequence *Les Chimères*. Historical and cultural reminiscences abound. The title is derived from the shield of a dispossessed knight in Scott's *Ivanhoe*; the prince d'Aquitaine is a ghostly medieval ancestor, and the lively symbolic art of heraldry is much in evidence: the narrator is collecting image-fragments for his own escutcheon. Later in the poem he is to pass from historical time into the worlds of romance and folk legend, and to immerse himself finally in Greek myth. But these journeys back take him through an array of personal identities and fantasmal love-objects. The past is not a stable archive, and the poet is not its well-organized administrator. The self is a flickering spectrum of shapes and postures. Sonnet form itself, for all the metrical and phonological regularities that it seems to enforce, dramatizes the discontinuity of the speaking subject. Even in the first stanza, so much concerned with loss and mourning, the poet is both the victim of darkness and its proud proponent.

Nerval in these twelve extraordinary sonnets offers an unaccustomed rallying cry for lyric poets. They can be disconsolate and difficult. They can seize upon gaps, affront good sense, recoil from a salutary public role, exile themselves from society and yet, through their very awkwardness and power of refusal, expect to achieve an enhanced social standing in the eyes of many. Darkness became them. They were the licensed desperadoes that an increasingly comfortable middle class craved. It was Baudelaire, among poets writing in the middle years of the century, who constructed the most complex artistic personality of this kind. Poetic composition, for Baudelaire as for Nerval, was an exercise in pluralizing the self and locating its tension points. If the poetic journey extends far back into the past of European literature, it leads not to a fabled point of origin and unity but to a primary disarray, whether in the tears of Homer's Andromache, the leaking vessel of the Danaids, or the self-torment named in the title of Terence's play *Heautontimorumenos*. If the poet looks outwards from the conflicting desires and rapid mood-swings that are his daily lot, he finds a certain sense of community with the dispossessed of the modern city. Yet beggars, drunkards, prostitutes, prisoners, old people, and immigrants are referred to without condescension or false tenderness in Baudelaire's principal verse collection, *Les Fleurs du Mal*: they are not merely his fellow exiles from a respectable mercantile society, but live their own lives of painful self-division.

In part, the originality of Baudelaire's diction may be seen to flow from this insistence on the composite and unstable character of human subjectivity. He needs a language that can map sudden changes of emotional response. Baudelaire is a writer who can find 'plaisirs furtifs' ('furtive pleasures') inside an innocent paradise, or 'traîtres yeux' ('treacherous eyes') inside a scene of sequestered intimacy, and recreate such discoveries as a series of linguistic shocks. But expressing the matter in such terms does not do justice to the characteristic air of verbal experimentation that Baudelaire's verse possesses. Within a general verse movement that often self-consciously echoes the Racinian alexandrine, improbable word-clusters occur:

Quelle est cette île triste et noire?—C'est Cythère,
Nous dit-on, un pays fameux dans les chansons,
Eldorado banal de tous les vieux garçons.

[Which island is this, so sad and dark?—It is Cythera, we are told, a land made
famous in songs, the commonplace Eldorado of all elderly bachelors.]

For Watteau, in his painted 'Voyages to Cythera', the birthplace of
Aphrodite was already the resort of disabused lovers; for Voltaire, in
Candide, Eldorado was already a derisory fantasy. But Baudelaire gives
two further turns of the screw in a single line: first, the two mythic
landscapes merge into a supercharged banality, and then they are
handed over to aged playboys, the unseemliest spokesmen for sexual
desire.

Baudelaire's language is one in which sense-impressions accumulate
rapidly and different sense-fields interact, but it is also rich in the semi-
technical abstract terms with which the narrator seeks to codify and
interpret the primary materials of his experience. The journey to
Cythera in the end reveals a 'gibet symbolique où pendait mon image'
('a symbolic gibbet from which my own likeness was hanging'), while
a swan lost in the Paris streets becomes a 'myth', an 'image' and an 'allegory', all displayed beneath an 'ironic' sky. The language of criticism
has invaded the traditional language of lyric verse and created a range
of hybrid locutions. Cross-breeding between semantic families has
become a watchword for poets.

When the 16-year-old Rimbaud wrote his own poetic manifesto in
1871, Baudelaire received higher praise than any other predecessor.
The author of *Les Fleurs du Mal* was 'le premier voyant, roi des
poètes, *un vrai Dieu*' ('the foremost seer, the king of poets, *a true
God*'). Many modern readers would endorse this view, and be happy
to proclaim Baudelaire the greatest French poet of them all. But
Rimbaud had a reservation: Baudelaire was too intent on being
'artistic', and too acquiescent towards received literary forms.
Rimbaud's own writing in verse and prose was already more syncopated and abrasive. The poem, for him, brought new worlds into
being image by image, and must be prepared to destroy one world in
order to allow the next its brief moment of radiance. 'Un rayon
blanc, tombant du haut du ciel, anéantit cette comédie' ('a shaft of
white light, falling from the upper skies, annihilates this comedy'),
the narrator of 'Les Ponts' says of his own textual fabrication. The
poet proposes, and himself disposes. The authenticity of his work lies
in the brilliance of its visionary instants and in the impatient turn-
ings of its verbal kaleidoscope, and does not need an additional

machinery of moral debate and adjudication to support it. Yet there is an intense seriousness about Rimbaud, for all the insolent jesting that animates his poetry. His prose poems collected as *Illuminations* and the final verse-poems of his brief career do not point their reader towards themes and issues lying beyond themselves. They are the whole story, the products of a mortal human imagination working alone, in the dark. The poet fashions himself, and is the instrument of his own erasure.

How did it come about that these poets were social outcasts and divided selves yet at the same time the proclaimers of an irrepressible creative potency? If the question is put simply in these terms its answer seems plain enough: powerless individuals were generating a compensatory fantasy about their own importance; a 'revolution in poetic language', as the critic and theorist Julia Kristeva was later to call it, was a desperate recourse for those who had no access to political action proper. The situation in which these poets found themselves was, however, much more involved than this suggests. Baudelaire was at the barricades during February 1848, and again in June. Rimbaud is likely to have been in Paris during the brief lifespan of the Commune in 1871. The cult of novelty that Baudelaire announced in the resounding last phrase of *Les Fleurs du Mal* was to become axiomatic for Rimbaud: to produce new noise, new music, new modes of seeing, feeling, and reasoning, was the true poet's destiny. But this aesthetic credo had taken shape in a social world where rapid change had indeed occurred, and where the language of politics was both visionary and practical. Within the revolutionary tradition inaugurated in 1789 imagined futures were realizable; political regimes rose and fell at the behest of the efficacious word. When a poet laid claim, on behalf of poetry, to a complex intermeshing of thought, speech, and action, he was taking possession of a power-struggle he had witnessed playing itself out on the streets. Poetry could change the existing world, and produce worlds never before seen.

It is in the work of Mallarmé that this view of poetry reaches its paradoxical zenith. 'Devant le papier, l'artiste *se fait*' ('Faced with paper, the artist *creates himself*'), Mallarmé wrote to a friend in the mid-1860s, rejecting the determinism of Hippolyte Taine. Far from being a simple product of 'la race, le milieu, le moment', as Taine had claimed in his *Introduction à l'histoire de la littérature anglaise*, the poet produced himself, syllable by syllable, as he wrote. No human society was able to tell him what he was. Yet later in the same majestic sequence of early letters, Mallarmé was to offer a radically different proposition. Writing was a quest for impersonality, a refusal of clamorous selfhood, and the self-made poet must be prepared to unmake himself thoroughly in order to assume his highest role. He would then no longer be a person but a potentiality of the cosmos, 'une aptitude qu'a l'Univers Spirituel à se voir et à se développer, à travers ce qui fut moi' ('a capacity that the Spiritual World possesses to see itself and develop itself by way of what once was me'). Refusing to be determined by a merely terrestrial milieu, the poet could become an instrument of cognition for the universe itself. This and nothing less was his true milieu, and he was glad to submit to its determinations.

A similar climate of paradox surrounds Mallarmé's practical accounts of the language poets use. On the one hand poetry must be difficult of access, its meanings densely compacted and its music cut across by cacophony. Only in this way can the poet prevent himself from being co-opted into demeaning public service. On the other hand, poetry dreams of making the world intelligible once and for all, and of creating a new sense of community among isolated, deathbound human creatures. In this perspective, its 'difficult' language is a precious intimation of future knowledge and solidarity.

There is no point in understating the perplexity that a poem such as the following can still produce in an unwary reader:

> A la nue accablante tu
> Basse de basalte et de laves
> A même les échos esclaves
> Par une trompe sans vertu
>
> Quel sépulcral naufrage (tu
> Le sais, écume, mais y baves)
> Suprême une entre les épaves
> Abolit le mât dévêtu
>
> Ou cela que furibond faute
> De quelque perdition haute
> Tout l'abîme vain éployé
>
> Dans le si blanc cheveu qui traîne
> Avarement aura noyé
> Le flanc enfant d'une sirène

[Hushed to the crushing cloud | Basalt and lava its form | Even to echoes subdued | By an ineffectual horn | What shipwreck sepulchral has bowed | (You know this, but slobber on, foam) | The mast, supreme in a crowd | Of flotsam and jetsam, though torn | Or will that which in fury defaulted | From some perdition exalted | (The vain abyss outspread) | Have stingily drowned in the swirl | Of a white hair's trailing thread | The flank of a young Siren girl.]

This is one of the modern poems that Tolstoy singled out, in *What is Art?*, as having 'no meaning whatever', and one can readily sympathize with his view. A story of seafaring and shipwreck seems to be present, but in a highly diffracted form. The components do not fit together into a coherent nautical scene, and syntactic ambiguity prevents the watery events that are named from settling into a single causal sequence. Is the *tu* of the first line a second-person pronoun or the past participle of *taire*? Does the siren, at once seen and withdrawn from sight in the last two lines, presage an escape from disaster or disaster itself? Should mariners be listening to siren-songs in the first place? Questions of this kind not only lack straightforward answers, but seem to give the poem its substance. By way of the sound- and sense-echoes that pass back and forth between separate grammatical elements, the poem acquires an unsubduable interrogative texture. Past, present, and future tenses, similarly, are all undecidably in force at the same time. Yet far from being a self-absorbed private utterance, the poem addresses a wide audience on a time-honoured public theme: is there any escape from the deathwards course of human life? Difficult poetic language is replete with possible answers—some encouraging, others not—and in its very busyness and murmur of internal contention aspires to be an agent of social inclusion. Projecting himself beyond the social order, the poet speaks to all who remain inside it and have ears to hear.

We should not leave nineteenth-century poetry, however, without mentioning an astonishing group of writers in whom the adversarial relationship between the poet and the social order reached fever pitch. Most of them lived solitary creative lives, died young, and left behind them works that can easily be seen as singularities or erratic blocks stranded on the very edge of the French literary tradition. Isidore Ducasse, better known as the comte de Lautréamont, in *Les Chants de Maldoror*, Tristan Corbière in *Les Amours jaunes*, and Jules Laforgue in his *Complaintes* and *Derniers vers* are quite unlike each other, and at first reading may not seem to have forebears in common, or forebears at all. Yet each in his eccentric fashion combines lyrical exaltation with truculence, facetiousness, and sarcasm, and in each case this highly unstable amalgam is a legacy from the immediate past. It is also to be found in the work of Paul Verlaine, an older poet who outlived them all. All these brilliant and unsociable writers were descendants of Baudelaire and Hugo, those great enlargers of the tonal and emotional palette of French verse, but for all of them poetry had to be surly and recalcitrant before its positive work of creation or enlargement could begin. For many readers the vehemence directed by these writers against the social group remains the most memorable feature of their works. Saying no to society had never been carried off with a more resourceful combination of bad manners and verbal skill.

WRITING BY WOMEN, 1830–1880

Overall, the middle years of the nineteenth century were not hospitable to the ambitions of female writers. For a majority of women with literary skill the career of professional author was simply not available, and the legal disabilities of women at large were of a kind to thwart their intellectual and artistic creativity. After a period of partial emancipation during the Revolutionary decade, women found themselves actively discriminated against by the Napoleonic Civil Code. In many areas, the law now regarded them as minors, and their subordination to men in such matters as finance, ownership of property, and access to education was deeply ingrained in the institutions of civil society. Women had limited legal rights in the upbringing of their own children; divorce was prohibited from 1816 to 1884; and it was not until the provisional government of de Gaulle at the end of the Second World War that women were finally able to vote in French elections. Against a background of socially accepted misogyny, women were often subjected to caricatural portraiture in works of literature, and until very recently an alarming second-order version of the same tendency was to be found in literary histories of the period. As muses, mistresses, or angels of the hearth, women were confined to the margins of the historical picture. If their writings were discussed at all, they were treated with impatience and condescension. A woman who could write was an oddity, and expected to stand at a respectful distance from the grand thoroughfare along which an endless parade of male talents passed.

It is all the more remarkable, therefore, to find that women in nineteenth-century France could and did write; that they were active in all the main genres; and that certain of their works have a continuing power of imaginative and political provocation. We have already mentioned the distinctive achievements of Staël, Duras, and Desbordes-Valmore, but many others deserve attention and are now beginning to receive it, thanks to 'Des Femmes' and the other feminist publishers who are reprinting their works.

The first of three exemplary figures chosen to illustrate the quality of the writing to be found in this repository of neglected works is Delphine de Girardin, whose contributions to *La Presse* during the July Monarchy have the authority of the finest modern journalism. Girardin possesses the gift of insatiable curiosity, and a prose manner that glitters with delight at each new discovery. She has opinions on everything that modern Paris places in her path, a taste for the uncanny and the paradoxical, and an urbane disrespect for social convention. Her column on modern definitions of womanhood, which appeared in *La Presse* on 12 March 1840, for example, is a virtuoso exercise in proto-feminist critique. 'Woman' no longer exists, Girardin ventures, for she has come apart into an array of separate personages. She is *mère*, *maîtresse*, *ménagère*, and *mégère* ('mother, mistress, housewife, harri-dan'), and wherever one looks in society new definitions abound. Later in this piece, a docile femininity begins to reassert itself, as if the author has suddenly panicked at her own audacity, but the earlier textual display cannot simply be withdrawn: a woman writer had become a polymorph and wished the same good fortune upon her sisters.

An almost exact contemporary of Girardin's was Flora Tristan, in whose writings a very different form of polemical energy is to be found. Tristan was a feminist and a socialist, and the author of *Union ouvrière*, one of the landmark texts in the development of working-class politi-cal awareness in industrialized Europe. Five years before Marx and Engels published their *Communist Manifesto*, Tristan had completed her extraordinary pamphlet and was selling it by subscription, and door to door, all over France. At first glance the most impressive things about the work are those that belong to its public face: its call for soli-darity among workers, the internationalism of its political programme, and the militancy with which Tristan distributed it to its target readers. The work could have been politically efficacious, one senses, even in the absence of verbal invention and a personal style. Yet the peculiar brilliance of the work lies in the shaded background given to each of its main propositions. Tristan knows about the social and psychological forces that can set worker against worker, and writes them in. Similarly, while proclaiming the absolute equality of the sexes, she lays bare the ruses of those who think otherwise about the status of woman: 'On l'a donc élevée pour être une *gentille poupée* et une esclave destinée à *distraire son maître* et à *le servir*' ('She has thus been brought up to be a *sweet-natured doll* and a slave intended to *divert her master* and to *serve him*'). Writing has become a scene in which the struggle of workers and women for emancipation acquires strength and sinew.

The third of these exemplary figures belongs to the later years of the century and is different again both in her politics and in the uses she made of literature. Louise Michel was an anti-authoritarian activist and orator during the 1860s, the author of revolutionary songs, and the celebrated combatant known as the 'Red Virgin' during the Paris Commune. She spent a long period of exile in New Caledonia after the fall of the Commune and devoted herself in later life to the volumes of memoirs for which she is now best remembered. Michel is perhaps only incidentally a writer, and certainly gave more fully of herself at the barricades than on the printed page. Her prose can be slack, repetitious, and incantatory. Yet in her pages on the just war waged by the *communards*, or on the common creatureliness of human beings and animals, writing is a passage towards new modes of feeling and an adventure of the moral imagination.

For all their differences of class and political outlook, Girardin, Tristan, and Michel are alike in their rebellion against repressive stereotypes and in the confidence with which they wield the liberating pen. The age in which they wrote, as we have said, was deeply unconducive to literary activity on the part of women. By 1850 half the female population of France was still illiterate. But all three authors have a quality that sets them apart both from the mass of women who had no access to books and from the conventional female scriveners of the age: they treated literary composition as an experimental workshop in which a new sense of their own womanhood, and of their own multiform humanity, could be forged.

One woman writer towers above all others of the time, however, in the bulk and variety of her output, in her technical prowess and in the free inventiveness with which she endowed the entire literary enterprise. This is Aurore Dupin, an exact contemporary of Girardin's, who, under the pseudonym George Sand, became an international celebrity in her own lifetime and a classic French author soon after. Not the least fascinating feature of her career is the self-possession she displayed under hostile fire from certain fellow writers, including Chateaubriand and Baudelaire, and her conviction that such self-possession, for an artist, involved a perpetual transformation of one's identity. Sand is a novelist, a dramatist, an essayist, an autobiographer, a travel writer, and a voluminous correspondent, and in all these incarnations displays remarkable elasticity both of temperament and of verbal expression. Throughout Sand's writings a vein of utopian fantasy is to be found, and a meliorist vision of the love relationship, but she is also a caustic observer of social and amatory arrangements in their tendency to fall apart.

Even in her earliest novels—*Indiana*, *Valentine*, and *Lélia*—Sand painted remarkable portraits of women as self-determining in their thoughts if not in their social lives. They could love unwisely, suffer at the hands of their partners and of punitive marriage laws, and fall victim to a more general alienation and disenchantment, yet still occupy in the fictional texture the position of central informing consciousness.

Lélia, for example, is knowledgeable and has views. Her mind is a force-field in which the social and political issues of the day can be tracked. The 'rustic' novels of the 1840s—including *La Mare au diable*, *La Petite Fadette*, and *François le champi*—are nowadays Sand's best-known and most approachable works, and often thought of as having a safe, quasi-ethnographic value. Sand herself encouraged this view when she added a long postscript on provincial marriage customs to *La Mare au diable*. Yet what is still surprising in these short works is the candour and energy with which female desire is portrayed, and the reinforcement it receives from the rural landscape. Sand's countryside is a place where the rights of women to pleasure and rewarding work are underwritten by a productive agrarian economy and a benign natural order.

The works that best illustrate this many-levelled empowerment of women are *Consuelo* and its sequel *La Comtesse de Rudolstadt*. This huge diptych unfolds in the middle years of the eighteenth century, and its protagonist, the singer Consuelo, is a pupil of the real-life Neopolitan composer and singing teacher Nicola Porpora (1686–1768). It is a tale of artistic talent rising up spontaneously among the lower orders, and in due course becoming the mainspring of a morally alert and variously creative personality. A good deal of Sand's writing here is of an essayistic kind, as if the accomplishments of her heroine always needed to be bolstered by those of a knowledgeable and well-intentioned narrator, but the novel as a whole is a robust colloquy of ideas and ideologies. At its core lies the talent of women, and the obstacle race that it is obliged to run through male-dominated professional institutions.

The sixth chapter of *Consuelo*, for example, ends on a sustained three-voiced discussion of the singer's merits. Porpora's devotion to musical ability pure and simple is set against an impresario's view that good looks offer better box-office than fine voices; and against both the opinion of Consuelo's young male admirer makes itself heard. 'Mais affectée, mais minaudière, mais insupportable', says Porpora, dismissing the claims of another possible recruit to a new operatic production, 'elle n'a ni âme, ni intelligence' ('But she is affected, simpering and unbearable, and has neither soul nor intelligence'). While it is clear that for Sand soul and intelligence, in music and the other arts, always need to be added to mere executive address, she insists on surveying a whole field of alternative opinions. She has found a narrative method by which female identity can be seen under construction in a criss-cross of male gazes, and with imaginative generosity she espouses the viewpoints even of blackguards and opinionated fools. Women come into being as the creatures of male fear and fantasy, and craven or over-protesting maleness figures prominently in Sand's plot.

Yet in the novel as a whole, and indeed in Sand's massive literary output as a whole, another prouder story is superimposed on these clear-sighted accounts of female subordination. This is the story of women's self-realization. Such a goal can be reached by a number of routes, including those of freely chosen physical labour, craftsmanship, artistry, intellectual endeavour, and love between equals, but in all cases woman herself is the power-source. The Sand heroine has all the energy, adaptability, and capaciousness of mind she needs in order to break free from the restrictions placed upon her by a community of legislating males. To a degree that is extraordinary for France at this time, she creates herself. What is disappointing about Sand's fiction, when these buoyant female characters are looked at from a later age of feminist awareness and action, is that they have no politics to speak of. The realization of their own personhood drives them at speed beyond practical questions of suffrage, education, and legal entitlement. Yet the spectacle of female agency, in the career of author and characters alike, is inspiring to this day. Indeed the emergence of George Sand is one of those seismic events in the history of European thought that helped to make a modern feminist politics possible.

THEATRE IN THE NINETEENTH CENTURY

There is a sharp contrast between French theatre as playgoers of the nineteenth century would have experienced it and the dim memories of it that have passed to later generations. Looked at simply in quantitative terms, the age was prodigious. New plays, often co-written or ghost-written, were manufactured in huge numbers; countless new theatres opened in Paris; and enthusiastic new theatre audiences were discovered. Plays were commodities, and consuming them was a primary form of social display for a newly enfranchised and enriched bourgeoisie. While spoken drama in verse and prose continued to flourish, opera and operetta enjoyed their own long heyday in the middle years of the century.

It is perhaps not surprising that so few of the plays produced at this time should have remained in the modern repertory or survived in print for the benefit of the solitary reader. Such authors as Eugène Scribe, Eugène Labiche, and Georges Feydeau wrote too much, one is tempted to say, and deserve to be remembered only for the handful of works that have continued to find favour with directors and theatre-goers. Labiche's *Un chapeau de paille d'Italie* and *Le Voyage de Monsieur*

Perrichon have had so vigorous an afterlife that it is unnecessary to lament the near-total eclipse of the 170 other comic works he wrote. Besides, there are other forms of survival than that of a continuous production history. Casimir Delavigne's *Les Vêpres siciliennes* survives as Verdi's opera of the same name, *La Dame aux camélias* by the younger Dumas as *La Traviata*, and Maurice Maeterlinck's *Pelléas et Mélisande* as an opera by Debussy, a symphonic poem by Schoenberg, and incidental music by Fauré and Sibelius.

In any case it should not be forgotten that the dramatic text itself is only one element in the composite, multi-dimensional experience of theatre, and that the nineteenth century saw major changes in other elements such as stage design, lighting, and costume. It was not the writers, but Talma, Rachel, Réjane, Sarah Bernhardt, and their fellow great actors who were the theatrical stars of the age. Towards the end of the century theatre directors began to acquire celebrity of their own. André Antoine at the Théâtre Libre, Paul Fort at the Théâtre d'Art, and Aurélien Lugné-Poë at the Théâtre de l'Œuvre all rebelled against the production-line methods of the commercial stage, and by a combination of personal vision and practical-minded leadership created a new kind of artistry. They were the composers of their productions, sculptors moulding and carving their singular creations from the space-time of theatrical performance. They needed writers, of course, but not too many of them and not appearing too prominently on the playbill.

Three figures deserve to be singled out from the multitude of verbal artisans who were writing plays at this time. The first is the hyper-productive Scribe, who was mocked by Hugo, Baudelaire, and many others as a servile flatterer of bourgeois taste. Scribe is best remembered as the pioneer of 'the well-made play', and as the supplier of well-made opera librettos to Auber and Meyerbeer. Scribe's plotting in such works as *Bertrand et Raton* and *Une chaîne* is indeed deft, and his ability to combine a logical order of scenes with a pattern of surprising contrasts and reversals makes him into a formal innovator of considerable power. But Scribe's truly remarkable characteristic is the dramatic urgency and resonance that he imparts to unremarkable lives. Writing in the wake of Diderot and Sedaine, those celebrated practitioners of the *drame bourgeois*, Scribe continues a gradual process of social inclusion: the new professions that an industrialized mercantile society had called into being began to have a voice on the dramatic stage. High drama and a suggestion at least of universal significance could be extracted from the family conflicts and amatory entanglements of plain people. It was Scribe's sense of enlarged possibility for the modern theatre that helped him towards the astonishing European reputation that he eventually enjoyed. Kierkegaard and Ibsen were among his admirers. And it is in the works of the latter that his legacy endures. Modern audiences as they watch *The Master Builder* or *Rosmersholm* are unlikely to be aware that they are witnessing the apotheosis of Scribe's dramatic art. But there can be no doubt that modern Europe's greatest playwright learned many lessons from his industrious predecessor. Ibsen's ennoblement of the bourgeoisie as subject matter for tragedy had been foreshadowed in Scribe's plant-produced domestic dramas.

Scribe was already in mid-career when a short-lived episode in the history of French theatre brought a quite different but equally influential set of dramatic principles to the fore. Romantic drama, as it soon came to be called, was first written and staged in the mid-1820s, but its period of notoriety, beginning with the riotous premiere of Hugo's *Hernani* at the Comédie Française, was the first decade of the July Monarchy. Hugo and Musset are the exemplary figures, although Vigny should not be forgotten, especially as his *Chatterton* illustrates to perfection a dominant imaginative pattern: by recourse to a past epoch the struggles of modern selfhood are thrown into relief. In *Hernani* Hugo travels back to sixteenth-century Spain, and in *Ruy Blas* to the same country a century later. Musset sets his dramatic masterpiece *Lorenzaccio* in Florence in 1537. But while exploiting the fashion for history that we have already described, these authors are overwhelmingly concerned with psychological conflict and with the social constraints that are placed on the self-fashioning of the individual. Ruy Blas, at the beginning of Hugo's play, is at once a free spirit and a prisoner of implacable class divisions. He is a commoner who dares to love a queen, and pronounces the word *laquais* with a tremor of self-disgust:

> Eh bien!—moi, le laquais,—tu m'entends, eh bien! oui,
> Cet homme-là! le roi! je suis jaloux de lui!

[Well!—I, the underling,—well, do you understand me, yes, it is of that very man! the king! that I am jealous.]

Musset's Lorenzo de Médicis, on the other hand, is a nobleman who seeks to use assassination as a tool of social progress. The peculiar complexity of the play lies in the increasing dissoluteness of the protagonist and the gradual waning of his public-spirited resolve. For both dramatists the self is the mainspring of dramatic action. They displace on to the historical past an entirely modern sense of social instability and emotional risk.

In *Lorenzaccio* nineteenth-century France produced one of its few outstanding plays. Many decades were to elapse before Henry Becque's *Les Corbeaux* and Edmond Rostand's *Cyrano de Bergerac* arrived to increase their number to three. Yet the brief flowering of Romantic drama brought a new knowingness to theatrical practice in France. Theatre had been self-aware and self-referring on countless earlier occasions, and these plays of the July Monarchy, with their appearance of historical depth, were in a sense simply adding a time dimension to the familiar picture: European history was a huge cast of characters waiting to be brought back to life as players on the modern stage. What was new about Romantic drama, however, was its lack of concern for historical explanation or narrative logic and the increased attention that it correspondingly paid to individual performative acts. Real or imaginary figures from the European past talk themselves into selfhood, and mutate as their talk changes course. Oaths, declarations, tirades, and whispered subterfuges are their stock-in-trade. The protagonists live from gesture to gesture, and are oddly weightless and characterless in between. The coherence of these plays, which is often striking, comes not from the gradual unfolding of the characters' motives but from the echoes—the dramatic rhymes, one might almost say—that pass between different isolated moments of self-disclosure or self-assertion. This is a gestural drama and its legacies are still with us.

LITERATURE BEFORE THE LAW

The adversarial relationship between writers and the social order became particularly fraught and complicated during the Second Empire. The Emperor, self-appointed to the title of Napoleon III, interfered as readily as his celebrated uncle had in matters of cultural policy. He acted as the patron of bourgeois taste, and was prepared to use the police and the judiciary to protect the population against printed matter deemed offensive. The writers themselves were not only goaded into ever-bolder acts of provocation by the state supervision to which their works were subject, but developed a workaday complicity with the society they professed to despise. Loathing the bourgeoisie became almost a pre-condition for artistic creativity, and writers who were themselves mostly the sons of the professional middle class became fixated on the critique and reversal of its values.

The year 1857 was the *annus horribilis* of this conflict. Gustave Flaubert was an exact contemporary of Baudelaire's, and it was in this year that the two men stood trial for their writings. The prosecution was led in both cases by Ernest Pinard, and the works under scrutiny—

Les Fleurs du Mal and *Madame Bovary*—were exactly those for which each author is now best remembered. Poet and novelist were charged with offences against public morality and religion. In a sense these trials were a simple affront to the Rights of Man. That celebrated document had given a prominent place to the freedom of expression, and although censorship had been reintroduced during the Revolutionary period itself, and extended both under Napoleon and during the Restoration, it was by the 1850s unusual for works of art to come before the courts. Very few charges had been brought during the final decade of the July Monarchy, and 1848 had seen an explicit return to the Enlightenment values codified in the Declaration itself. Seeking to censor literary works, the agents of Napoleon III were behaving with a characteristic illiberal philistinism.

In practical terms, however, the trials did little damage: Flaubert was acquitted; Baudelaire was fined 300 francs and required to remove six poems from his collection. The unwelcome attentions of the prosecutor brought increased sales, and the 'condemned pieces' of *Les Fleurs du Mal* derived an enhanced glamour from that rubric, which continued in use long after the final quashing of the court's verdict in 1949. Moreover, the law having been ranged heavy-footedly against two masterpieces of irony, the scene was now set for the reinforcement of ironic vision that was to preoccupy both writers in their later years.

FLAUBERT'S WAR ON STUPIDITY

In *Madame Bovary* Flaubert found ingenious ways of offending yet still gratifying the bourgeoisie. This is a tale of marriage and adultery in Normandy, and of hypocrisy, stupidity, and cruelty spreading through the fabric of society at large. In this novel, Flaubert perfects a prose style in which two contrary movements of imagination—one of empathy and one of scornful withdrawal—are held in a precarious state of equilibrium. On the one hand his characters and their physical settings are sensuously realized, in interlaced and cross-referring descriptions. Charles Bovary notices oozing moisture on tree-trunks during an early visit to the home of his future wife, and water droplets splashing on to a parasol: 'on entendait les gouttes d'eau, une à une, tomber sur la moire tendue' ('the droplets could be heard falling, one by one, onto the taut fabric'). Later, beads of sweat are visible on Emma's shoulders, and the last drops of curaçao are removed from a glass by her eagerly protruding tongue. Liquid echoes liquid, and everything in these connected scenes acquires intensity from the young couple's awakening desire for each other. Even memories or fantasies can be given a quality of immediacy and bite. On the other hand, a derealizing demon seems also to be at work in Flaubert's prose. After Léon's departure for Rouen, Emma, we are told, suddenly feels bereft of her would-be lover: 'Léon réapparaissait plus grand, plus beau, plus suave, plus vague' ('Léon came back to her larger, more handsome, smoother-mannered, vaguer'). Two voices are sounding at once here, thanks to the 'indirect free style' that Flaubert made his own. The narrator records the progress of a wishful distortion, espousing Emma's viewpoint as she reviews Léon's seductive attributes, but then, with no change in the syntactic pattern, he summons up a quite different value-system: Emma's liking for vagueness is to be her downfall, and is here the subject of a discreet but firm reprimand. Writing having this two-way pull inside it is not of course peculiar to Flaubert, but he deploys it with quite exceptional single-mindedness and guile.

As the tragic design of *Madame Bovary* gradually unfolds, an extraordinary tension builds up inside the texture of the narrative. Derisory human goals and dehumanizing social arrangements are exposed to criticism, yet with endless patience and precision reimagined. They are revived in order to be dispatched again, and the rhythm of their rise and fall is relentless. The manners of the Second Empire, and the sense of public pantomime with which the imperial court invests them, allow Flaubert to reach a vantage-point from which all societies begin to look fraudulent and foolish. Against the alleged baseness and pettifoggery of ordinary lives, he sets the intellectual and aesthetic merits of literary style, and imagines a 'great book about nothing' in which clear thinking and finely tuned verbal expression would join forces for the final battle against *bêtise*.

The fictional works that Flaubert produced in the 1860s and 1870s carry this campaign in a number of new directions. The hateful yet somehow still delicious bourgeoisie of the time had all manner of improbable precursors. In the early history of Christianity, in the lives of the saints and in Carthage after the First Punic War, modern savagery and sensuality could be found in their early draft forms, and Flaubert contemplates these with combined excitement and disgust. The historical novel *Salammbô* in particular has an atmosphere of self-induced mesmerism about it. A worthless past meets a worthless present and the controlling intelligence that oversees their encounter enjoys itself enormously. Even *L'Éducation sentimentale*, which is 'historical' only by a margin of twenty years, draws its strength from an ironic manipulation of the past. The early manhood of the protagonist exists in order to be dismantled, just as the deadly street-battles of 1848 are reduced to comic inconsequentiality. Value resides in the discovery of deficit and the affirmation of loss.

At the time of his death Flaubert was working on a great book about two nobodies, and the torso that was published posthumously as *Bouvard et Pécuchet* is in one light a monument to his lifelong nullifying impulse. From having explored the vicissitudes of the sexual and aggressive instincts in human society, he now turns his corrosive attention to the desire for knowledge. His heroes retire from their lowly jobs to devote themselves to science and the humanities, and stumble into error and delusion at every turn. Yet the Flaubert tone now has forgiveness in it. For example, the fantastic geology and palaeontology that Bouvard and Pécuchet fabricate from their reading of Georges Cuvier, far from being an object lesson in scholarly incompetence, becomes a tender comedy in the lineage of *Don Quixote*. Looking back over the procession of prehistoric epochs, the two knowledge-seekers align themselves with the providential historians of their age: 'C'était comme une féerie en plusieurs actes, ayant l'homme pour apothéose' ('It was like a fairy-pageant in several acts, finding in mankind its apotheosis'). Stupidity is no longer the novelist's satirical target but the prism through which a multifarious world becomes visible. There is nothing to alert the censors in this magical last book. Nothing in it offends public morality and religion, for Flaubert has set his critical sights upon thought itself. From the farcical mishaps that befall the human intellect he has created a festive prose poetry unlike any other, and liberated himself at last from merely bourgeois *bêtise* and *bassesse*.

LITERATURE AND SCIENCE: THE CASE OF 'NATURALISM'

Even as Flaubert was composing his last hyper-ironical fictions, and diluting the category of 'the social' in the process, a group of younger writers were beginning to establish themselves as the conscientious earthbound observers of man and woman in society. With Émile Zola as their standard-bearer, they too were ironists, but they operated in such a way that literary irony began to offer itself as a token of scientific rectitude. Human beings were organisms imprinted with their own evolutionary history, and they happened to gather in groups. The writer who remembered his biology while looking closely at the web of interpersonal relationships, and inserting them into the larger web of economic and class relationships, would discover an inexhaustible play of multiple perspectives. Rearranging these, he could build models of society that were strictly comparable with the explanations offered by the biological sciences, for conflicting forces and elaborate interactive mechanisms were characteristic of both domains. 'Naturalism' in prose fiction, as Zola came to call it, was natural science by an only slightly different name, and a willingness to shift between viewpoints—to think ironically, that is to say—was a sign of its objectivity and disinterestedness.

The particular power of Zola's vision comes not simply from his acquisitive admiration for Claude Bernard's *Introduction à l'étude de la médecine expérimentale* and other scientific essays of the day, but from an outraged sense that literature had been shrinking from its main responsibility. It had stopped telling the truth about the modern French state as experienced by its citizens from day to day. Zola's novels of the 1870s and the essays that he collected as *Le Roman expérimental* in 1880 summoned the consumers of prose fiction to an uncomfortable act of self-examination. The literature they prized had been looking away from the astonishing recent upheavals of the social order. Since the death of Balzac, it had had little of consequence to say about industrialization, or about colonial expansion, the growth of the cities, and the pauperization of the masses. Crime, prostitution, and epidemic disease had been discussed only in a prematurely sanitized form. The follies and misdeeds of the Second Empire had gone largely unrecorded, and the literary imagination had slumbered through the debacle of the Franco-Prussian war. Armed with an observant eye and a miscellaneous array of scientific concepts, Zola ventured forth into this unexplored social landscape.

In one sense Naturalism was simply an opportunistic slogan. When Zola joined forces in 1880 with Guy de Maupassant, Joris-Karl Huysmans, and others to produce a collective volume of stories entitled *Les Soirées de Médan*, the enterprise seemed designed to proclaim and illustrate a coherent new theory of fiction. But although the group clustered around Zola had enemies in common, and much to gain from a display of solidarity, this was a gathering of singular and unclubbable talents. Maupassant and Huysmans were as different from each other as either of them was from Zola himself.

Maupassant's contribution to the Médan volume was 'Boule de suif', and this tale, which launched his career, already contains a complete set of stylistic fingerprints. His writing is crisp and laconic; his plots are studded with tiny descriptive details that bring the 'ordinary vices', as Montaigne called them, of greed, cruelty and hypocrisy into memorable new focus; and, for all the panoramic range and cumulative energy that such novels as *Bel-Ami, Une Vie*, and *Pierre et Jean* possess, Maupassant's genius is for the short story, to the structure of which he gives the air of a mischievous mathematical proof. For Huysmans,

Naturalism was the training ground for one only of his skills. His self-exposure in fiction to poverty, disease, and social rejection was an astringent spiritual exercise, but one that was to make its most complex sense only when other obsessions—mystical, aesthetic, antiquarian, occultist, and lexicographical—began to be given free rein. The fever-ish movement of Huysmans's *A Rebours* and later fiction takes him from abjection to ecstasy and back again, and all in a defiantly anti-natural and unnaturalistic fashion.

When it comes to the powerful creative personality of Zola, how-ever, the term Naturalism still has its uses. Indeed it takes us to the pas-sionate core of his ambitions as a novelist. Science exerted upon him a triple fascination: it was a matter of empirical observation; it involved making inferences and tracing invisible causal pathways; and, supremely, thanks to the recent advances of evolutionary biology, it made sense of human time across the generations. If one important ele-ment of the novelist's task was to go out, notebook in hand, into real human communities, another was to adapt the form of the novel to the suprapersonal causality that modern science saw at work in the life of the human person. Zola's plan for his twenty-volume novel cycle *Les Rougon-Macquart* was drafted to produce saturation coverage of Second Empire France from the social, geographical and historical points of view. The series takes its reader from the *coup d'état* of 1851 to the aftermath of the Franco-Prussian war, from Provence to Paris, from overcrowded tenement to aristocratic salon, and is bound together by recurrent characters that at first glance seem no more than an imitative tribute to those of Balzac. Zola's characters, far from simply recurring, however, are arranged genealogically and often presented as the playthings of an implacable destiny. When Gervaise Macquart descends into drunkenness in *L'Assommoir*, or when her son Jacques Lantier is seized by homicidal frenzy in *La Bête humaine*, they are yielding to a hereditary imperative. Biology has predetermined their deeds and robbed them of all but a fragile illusion of free will.

The 'névrose originelle' ('originating neurosis') of Adelaïde Fouque hangs as a curse over her descendants, Rougons and Macquarts alike, and makes the whole population of the series into a latterday equivalent to the house of Atreus in Greek mythology. Gervaise and Jacques, like Agamemnon, suffer at the hands of their forebears. Zola's adherence to the idea of heredity can easily seem faddish and naïve to modern readers accustomed to thinking of individual human develop-ment as an interplay between nature and nurture. But this and other organizing devices borrowed from contemporary science have real dramatic power when seen in their fictional contexts. At a culminating moment in *Germinal*, for example, the anarchist Souvarine sabotages the central shaft of the coal mine. His action belongs simultaneously to a mechanistic and a mythical world-view: he operates upon equipment that has been named and defined part by part earlier in Zola's narrative, but he does so as a hero seeking vengeance on a malign living creature. He is at once a technician and a dragon-slayer.

Throughout his novels, Zola attends both to the forces that exceed and overshadow the individual human agent and to the impulsive inner world of desire and fantasy in which the action of individuals finds its local origin. Stylistically, his main instrument for achieving this continuous double movement is an idiosyncratic version of free indirect speech. He invents a rampaging narrative voice that absorbs the thoughts and feelings of characters into itself and negotiates with enthusiasm between incompatible points of view, whether social, moral, or political. Far from being the result of a mere infatuation, Zola's recourse to scientific notions can be seen as a powerful shaping impulse at work. His teeming social panorama needed a frame, and in a simplified version of contemporary science he found one. Misappropriated heredity and sensationalized Darwinism brought him closer to the world-view of tragedy than any other French writer of the nineteenth century.

DREYFUS AND AFTER

Zola's *Rougon-Macquart* cycle was already complete, and he was about to publish the final volume of his triptych on Lourdes, Rome, and Paris, when he achieved a new kind of fame as the author of an open letter to Félix Faure, the President of the Republic. This letter, known by its headline as 'J'accuse', appeared in *L'Aurore* on 13 January 1898, and protested with controlled vehemence against a recent miscarriage of justice. Suddenly, the humanitarian vision and moral trenchancy characteristic of Zola's fiction acquired devastating political force. Zola's action marked a watershed in the protracted sequence of events known as the Dreyfus Affair (see Figure 16).

In 1893, the Jewish army captain Alfred Dreyfus had been accused of spying for Germany. He had been court-martialled, found guilty, and sentenced to life imprisonment on Devil's Island. Despite the clear evidence that emerged in 1897 suggesting that Dreyfus had been the victim of a fraud, the original verdict was upheld, to the outrage of Zola and his fellow *dreyfusards*. Dreyfus was retried in 1899, again found guilty, and finally exculpated only in 1906. By the time of 'J'accuse', French public opinion was polarized not simply on a precise question

16. The front page of *L'Aurore*, 1 January 1898, carrying Émile Zola's celebrated open letter ('J'accuse') to the President of the Republic.

of innocence or guilt but on the future destiny of the Republic itself. Broadly speaking, the supporters of the secularizing and socially inclusive reform programme of the Third Republic were on one side, while those of the Catholic Church and the Army, together with an array of monarchists, Bonapartists, and former reactionary insurgents, were on the other. The Affair brought long-standing tensions and hatreds into the open and produced a flood-tide of polemical printed matter. It is an essential factor in any attempt to understand the evolution of politics in modern France, and has left a deep imprint on the history of French literature.

While many novelists, self-appointed as the chroniclers of their time, imported the political struggles surrounding the Affair into their fiction as ready-dramatized subject matter, others were more ambitious and saw here opportunities of a quite different order. Anatole France, for example, in his *L'Île des pingouins*, transposed the campaign against Dreyfus into an exuberant satire on human cruelty, folly, and self-deception. For Proust, who gives the matter a central role in his immense social comedy, the Affair comes to represent the world of opinion as distinct from that of truth and true judgement; his narrator has an exalted sense of his own verbal power and artistic vocation but is detained for long periods in the company of those dunces for whom the name Dreyfus is a spur to empty loquacity. Perhaps the most remarkable attempt to extract a universal message from this astonishing historical episode comes, however, not from a novelist but from Charles Péguy, a poet, dramatist, and pamphleteer. In *Notre jeunesse* and other prose writings he castigates those who have lapsed from their early support for justice pure and unsullied into the daily squalor of practical politics. They had done worse than settle for opinion when truth was at hand, for in their younger years, in the heat of the pro-Dreyfus campaign, they had been touched by a divine flame the simple memory of which should have been enough to protect them from compromise and opportunistic alliance-making later in life. They had had contact with the absolute, yet now willingly consigned themselves to the gutter. For former *dreyfusards* who sacrificed *mystique* to *politique* no words of condemnation were too harsh.

It was in another variety of pamphlet literature, however, that the public rhetoric of the Affair had its most durable and disturbing after-effects. Zola had spoken in 'J'accuse' of 'l'odieux antisémitisme, dont la grande France libérale des droits de l'homme mourra, si elle n'en est pas guérie' ('hateful anti-semitism, from which the great liberal France of the Rights of Man will die, if no cure for it can be found'). But the cure was slow in coming, and anti-Semitic invective now began, in some quarters, to acquire aesthetic credentials. Such writing already had a long history in the post-Revolutionary period, and by the mid-1880s had produced its first best-seller in the form of Édouard Drumont's *La France juive*. This work owed much of its popularity to Drumont's hybridizing, within a single blustering tirade, of three separate themes: Jews were the deicides of Christian tradition, the instigators and upholders of international capitalism, and, by way of the new biologizing racism then gaining currency in France, a colony of invasive organisms. Where Drumont presented himself as a man of action and made no claim to literary sensibility other writers emerging in his wake brought considerable resources of style to bear upon their expressions of hatred and xenophobic alarm. Such writers as Maurice

Barrès, Léon Daudet, and Charles Maurras, the founder of the proto-fascist newspaper *L'Action française*, stepped forward during the Dreyfus years not as tough-talking demagogues but as the proponents of an insinuating form of *belles-lettres* in which the standard anti-Semitic motifs could be elegantly interlaced. This was hate language with a shimmering surface, and its legacies are still apparent in the 1930s: 'la miniscule bête juive ayant fini de mâcher le bulbe du géant américain, le monstre inconscient se jettera sur le colosse russe, également-ment vidé de sa cervelle' ('once the minute Jewish beast has finished munching the medulla of the American giant, that unconscious monster will hurl itself upon the Russian colossus, it too to be emptied of its brains'). Georges Bernanos, writing in these terms in *La Grande Peur des bien-pensants*, his homage to Drumont, seeks both to outwrite an acclaimed predecessor and to modernize his characteristic paranoid fantasy. Bernanos was to be outwritten in his turn by Céline, whose *Bagatelles pour un massacre* bring the anti-Semitic imagination to its point of exorbitance: the hated Jew acts as a trigger for word-play, opulent imagery, and rhythmic experiment. In Céline's prose, murderousness acquires its music. Thirty years after the trials of Alfred Dreyfus, the language of his accusers was again aspiring to the condition of 'literature'.

GIDE AND PROUST

The early years of the new century were a period of extraordinary brilliance in the fields of art, literature, science, and philosophy. Marie Curie was awarded the Nobel prize first for physics and then for chemistry, Sarah Bernhardt continued to be the presiding genius of the French theatre, Gauguin and Cézanne painted their final masterpieces, Debussy and Ravel were composing music of a kind never before heard, and Paris began to exert its magnetic attraction upon numerous artists from outside France. Picasso, Chagall, Modigliani, Gertrude Stein, Falla, Stravinsky, Diaghilev, Nijinsky, and countless others were drawn to a city that, for a timeless moment before the First World War, seemed to have become the international capital of the creative imagination. It is perhaps surprising, therefore, in view of all this clangour and busyness, to find that certain of the most far-reaching changes brought about in prose fiction at this time involved the representation of mental states and internal crises.

By the early nineteen-hundreds, the realist novel had established itself as a monarch among the literary genres. Stendhal, Balzac, Flaubert, and Zola had all been gloriously eccentric figures, but the combined force of their example had given the novel a standardized and easily reproducible format. The novel had a cast of clearly differentiated characters, was narrated for the most part in the third person, contained descriptions, conversations, and scenes of action, and above all, as E. M. Forster was to remark ruefully, it told a story. As its story unfolded a forward-moving chronology was underpinned by a uniform movement from cause to effect. The behaviour of individuals and the pattern of their interactions in society were alike in possessing a causal logic, and the novelist looked to this for guidance in assembling his works. 'Verisimilitude' was his unspoken rule. Remembering a familiar distinction in the history of science, we could say that after a series of violent paradigm-shifts in the history of prose fiction a 'normal novel' had been installed in France, and that the majority of newcomers to the fiction industry were happy to work within its benign, natural-seeming constraints. The prolific Henry Bordeaux might be mentioned as supremely normal in this sense, but dozens of his contemporaries, now largely unread, have a similar place in the aftermath of 'high' realism. Georges Duhamel, Roger Martin du Gard, Jules Romains, and other practitioners of the *roman-fleuve*, though unusual in matters of length, all wrote in accordance with the same accepted formula.

In the early years of the new century, two writers in particular began to question this set of conventions and to rediscover the subversive energies of the novel. Gide and Proust were both experimentalists, for whom the act of storytelling was inveterately strange, ambiguous, and risky, and for both of them the experimental laboratory par excellence was the mind of a self-aware narrator. Far from offering their readers a stable verbal model of the real, three-dimensional, air-filled world, Gide and Proust immersed them in the mobile fabric of self-interested speech. The schemes, follies, and misapprehensions of a narrator's desire-driven intelligence now occupy centre-stage. The novel has become personal and playful once again.

In each of the three short works that Gide termed *récits*— *L'Immoraliste, La Porte étroite*, and *La Symphonie pastorale*—first-person narrative is the vehicle for a delicately calibrated ethical enquiry. Michel, the pleasure-seeking 'immoralist' of Gide's title, for example, seems at first glance the simple spokesman for his own wishes and defender of his own deeds. At either end of the main tale a brief framing narrative sketches viewpoints other than Michel's own, and draws attention to the disturbing complicity that may develop between any artful self-justifier and those he addresses. For the most part, however, the critique of Michel's conduct is woven into his monologue by an art finer than his own. Contemplating the attempts made by human beings to regulate the raw vitality of the natural world, Michel asks: 'Que serait cet effort . . . sans la puissante sauvagerie qu'il domine? Que serait le sauvage élan de cette sève débordante sans l'intelligent effort qui l'endigue et l'amène en riant au luxe?' ('What would this attempt be . . . without the powerful savagery that it masters? What would the savage thrust of this uprising sap be without the effort of intelligence that holds it in check and brings it gaily to its point of luxuriance?'). His hedonistic calculus is fluently and knowledgeably expounded. He uses the rich abstract language of the *moralistes* as skilfully as his counterparts in the other *récits* deploy the moral idiom of the New Testament; and he speaks at such moments with the same blithe matter-of-factness that he shows elsewhere in describing farm machinery, game animals, or the delectable sheen of youthful skin. The narrator stands accused not by ethical counter-arguments but by the largely silent presence of the other characters, who are pressed into the service of his desire and nonchalantly discarded when they can serve it no longer. Gide has constructed a narrative voice that is plausible yet self-incriminating, lucid yet subject to delusion. The strength of each *récit* is in the studied unreliability of its protagonist, and in the fleeting alternative perspectives that open up within his single-minded apologia.

When Gide came to write *Les Faux-Monnayeurs*, the only one of his fictions in prose that he was prepared to call a novel, he again concerned himself with the question of narrative viewpoint. Indeed he contrived a large-scale structure that seems at moments, in its breathtaking pattern of internal echoes and permutations, to be obsessed with the act of narration to the exclusion of all else. The contributions of the overall third-person narrator are interleaved with successive first-person journal entries from Édouard, one of the main characters, who is himself at work upon a novel to be called *Les Faux-Monnayeurs*. The principal narrator soon establishes himself as a character in his own right. He is by turns excited, perplexed, and bored by his own creatures, and skirmishes gracefully with Édouard on the theory of the novel. Édouard, explaining his own views in conversation, seems to want the novel to take its cue from the real world yet still be free from the taint of reality. The narrator intervenes as a wiser fellow practitioner: 'L'illogisme de son propos était flagrant, sautait aux yeux d'une manière pénible. Il apparaissait clairement que, sous son crâne, Édouard abritait deux exigences inconciliables, et qu'il s'usait à les vouloir accorder' ('The illogic of what he propounded was blatant, leapt painfully to the eye. It was clearly evident that Édouard's skull housed two irreconcilable demands and that he was wearing himself out in his effort to harmonize them'). The dazzling insolence of this remark lies not simply in the way one character projects his own illogic and indecision onto another but in Gide's attempt to pre-empt objections to his own book. *Les Faux-Monnayeurs* will triumph in the very flagrancy of its contradictions, he seems to suggest. It will be a farrago of references to an untidy real world, yet at the same time an exquisitely self-referring aesthetic construct rather like Bach's *Art of Fugue*.

Gide was an influential public figure and a campaigner on behalf of what became known, later in the century, as gay rights and gay pride. In part, his authority came from his willingness to speak out on contentious subjects, including politics, religion, and middle-class family life, and to give voice in his fiction and personal writings to dissident forms of sexual desire. Yet the attention he commanded as a spokesman for various causes had to do also with the characteristic rigour of his literary experiments. Gide's narrators are constructions that advertise their own constructedness, fictive beings that announce the inextirpable presence of fiction in human affairs. When such a writer offers a convinced view we are inclined to assume that he has already passed it through the strait gate of self-doubt, and that his new-found certainty has already been fully tested.

The narrator of Proust's *A la recherche du temps perdu* says 'I' in the first sentence of the novel, and continues to say it for three thousand pages. Although this marathon seems impressive in itself, especially when we remember that most earlier exponents of the *roman personnel* had run over very short distances, the major surprise of Proust's novel is to be found in the sheer power of variation that the narrative voice possesses. It absorbs into itself a bewildering array of social, linguistic, and artistic raw materials. It mimics countless other voices, including those of buffoons and charlatans. It contradicts itself with abandon. Now it offers encouraging home truths, and now it spins delusional fantasies. Where Gide creates an elegant criss-cross of perspectives, specified or implied, Proust creates a matted weave of lateral associations, backward glances, and prophecies. Where Gide favours short propositional sentences, Proust allows his sentences to spread and sprout. For Proust the travail of consciousness and the mutability of human selfhood have become the fundamental concerns of the novel, and his typical long sentence enacts them. Proustian syntax becomes a theatre of the time-bound, future-driven human mind.

An extended section of *Le Temps retrouvé*, the final volume of the work, is given over to a theoretical reverie on the powers and limitations of novel form. Like Gide's Édouard, the narrator celebrates the push and pull that the writer experiences between beautiful abstract

ideas on the one hand and the accidents of daily life on the other: 'je sen-
tais se presser en moi une foule de vérités relatives aux passions, aux
caractères, aux mœurs. Leur perception me causait de la joie; pourtant
il me semblait me rappeler que plus d'une entre elles, je l'avais décou-
verte dans la souffrance, d'autres dans de bien médiocres plaisirs' ('I felt
pressure inside me from a host of truths relating to the passions, to
characters, to manners. Perceiving them brought me joy; yet I seemed
to remember that I had discovered more than one of these truths in suffering, and others in pleasures that were paltry indeed'). The true artist
must be prepared to live in no man's land, in the interference-zone
between accident and idea, for this is where artworks of note are born.
What makes the narrator's eloquent commentaries on novels at large
unreliable as an aid to the understanding of this novel in particular is,
however, precisely the preponderance in his remarks of convincing
general ideas. Reading the rest of the novel feels very different from
anything that passages of this kind suggest. The narrator's late theoretical reflections characterize poorly if at all the malice, precision, and
bravado of his earlier social observation.

Making a single acquisitive consciousness into the primary setting
for a long work of fiction raises difficulties at the level of plot. What will
this consciousness do next, the Proust reader begins to ask, what will its
next piece of devilry be? The narrator sweeps aristocrats, bourgeois,
and working people into his festive pageant, strings together jokes,
anecdotes, and quotations, and unleashes data in tumultuous cata-
logues. In Normandy, the coastal railway had many local names: 'on
l'appelait tantôt le *Tortillard* à cause de ses innombrables détours, le
Tacot parce qu'il n'avançait pas, le *Transatlantique* à cause d'une effroyable sirène qu'il possédait pour que se garassent les passants, le
Decauville et le *Funi. . .*' ('people called it the *Corkscrew* because of the
countless detours it took, the *Tacot* because it would not go forward, the
Transatlantic because of the dreadful klaxon that it used to clear
passers-by from its path, the *Decauville* and the *Funi. . .*'). And so the
narrator's philological excursion goes wildly, plotlessly on. From elsewhere in the novel, other journeys echo this one, and other lists of
names have a similar magic. The tension between a linear progression
and an all-at-once associative network is profoundly inscribed in the
book as a whole. But for the moment the narrator's expenditure of
attention is reckless and excessive. He is on holiday from storytelling.
He joyfully dissolves his long-range artistic ambitions into the terminology of trains.

At times the Proustian comedy of consciousness takes on a much
darker colouring. From the collecting of curiosities and the celebration

of diversity, the narrator passes into a ghostly world of absence and loss. His affair with Albertine, on which the entire plot of the novel turns, has a protracted aftermath. After her departure and death, she lives on as a disposition of the narrator's mind, as the inscrutable tendency of his thinking to seek its own defeat. Albertine gives the book the vacant core around which the narrator's soliloquy moves. The later episodes of the novel are still written in a language of extraordinary complexity and inventiveness, but Proust's imagination now feeds on failures of communication between individuals and on the barriers to understanding that the mind seems to erect within itself. During the final tableau of *Le Temps retrouvé* the narrator is at last able to report on a recovered sense of creative opportunity, but the passage towards this moment has been disconsolate and death-haunted. Proust's fictional experiment has led him to explore not simply pleasure but unassuageable pain as a ground of consciousness. The sheer scale and exhaustiveness of this double enquiry makes him unlike any other French novelist of the twentieth century. The vacillating self now has its epic.

LITERATURE AND WAR: 1914–1918

The First World War as experienced by the civilian population finds its way into the closing sections of *A la recherche du temps perdu*, and Proust skilfully integrates into his plot a cataclysm that could not have been anticipated when the first detailed blueprint of the book was laid down. The impact of the war on other writers of note was altogether more direct. Charles Péguy and Alain-Fournier, the author of the celebrated lyrical novel *Le Grand Meaulnes*, were both killed in the field during the early weeks of the conflict. Others saw long periods of active service, survived, and produced novels that to this day stand as moving acts of testimony. Henri Barbusse in *Le Feu*, Roland Dorgelès in *Les Croix de bois*, and Céline in *Voyage au bout de la nuit* all painted memorable pictures of mechanized carnage, and gave voice to the terror and rage of ordinary soldiers caught up in the daily ignominy of the battlefield.

The war provoked a vast literature. In prose and in verse, a multitude of established writers recorded their personal reactions to it, and a significant number of newcomers discovered their literary vocation in the trenches or during the German air raids on Paris. Some of these texts were pro-war rallying cries, others were private expressions of shock or sorrow, and still others were internationalist and pacifist in their sympathies. While Barrès was writing the nationalistic journalism later collected in his compendious *Chronique de la Grande Guerre*, Romain Rolland was appealing for solidarity between German and

French intellectuals in his *Au-dessus de la mêlée*. After the armistice a period of philosophical, moral, and political stock-taking began and in due course produced its own rich crop of essays and treatises.

Few works dating from the war years themselves retained their readership later in the century. The war was a disaster on a previously unimaginable scale, but its apparatus—its bayonets, machine-guns, and shrapnel—had little imaginative resonance, and its conduct was a poor carrier of tragic vision. Much published commentary on the rapidly changing political and military situation in France belonged to the category of occasional literature, and could not be expected to outlast its moment. If there is something approaching a general rule here, however, that rule has a spectacular exception in the person of Guillaume Apollinaire.

Apollinaire served first in the artillery and then in the trenches as an infantryman, and was seriously wounded in 1916. He wrote poetry during each phase of his war career and throughout created works that belonged intimately to military life and yet looked far beyond it. The best-known of his techniques was that of the picture-poem or 'calligram', which allowed the meaning of words to be reinforced—and sometimes skewed or contradicted—by their typographical arrangement on the page. Apollinaire had begun experimenting in this vein before the war started, but found that certain aspects of life under arms suited this 'simultaneist' presentation particularly well. Shells could explode upon the page; sudden changes of military fortune could be translated into pictorial surprises; a multimedia homage could be paid to the dark exhilarations of combat.

But a more radical assimilation of wartime events to Apollinaire's existing artistic practice is to be found in the poems written in free verse or pseudo-biblical *versets*:

> Il y a à minuit des soldats qui scient des planches pour
>   les cercueils
> Il y a des femmes qui demandent du maïs à grands
>   cris devant un Christ sanglant à Mexico
> Il y a le Gulf Stream qui est si tiède et si bienfaisant
> Il y a un cimetière plein de croix à cinq kilomètres.

[There are at midnight soldiers sawing planks for coffins | There are women shouting out for maize in front of a bleeding Christ in Mexico | There is the Gulf Stream, which is so warm and so beneficial | There is a cemetery full of crosses five kilometres away.]

In this poem from *Calligrammes*, entitled 'Il y a', battle has removed all sense of temporal architecture from the poet-narrator's world and all but the sketchiest narrative syntax. What battle now enforces, however, an earlier Apollinairian aesthetic had cultivated with enthusiasm. In 'Zone', the great manifesto-poem that had introduced his pre-war collection *Alcools*, he was already a poet of lurches, switches, and bizarre encounters. The modern world at large came at him that way. A new fluid lyricism had been created by bringing disparate, hard-edged objects together into improbable assemblages. But where references to far-off people and places had previously been the sign of a benevolent jackdaw tendency in modern Western art, they now have a special pathos: the Gulf Stream and the hungry Mexican poor belong to the soldier's kit of memories and can be extinguished at any moment. Warfare imposes a monstrous discontinuity upon the troops but, for as long as they survive, leaves intact a fragile sense of human solidarity. The gaps between the poet's propositions speak of connections lost and precariously regained. The propositions themselves are all understatements. Their broken sequence gives Apollinaire's war poetry the elfin gravity that distinguishes it from everybody else's.

The wry dictum on which 'Il y a' ends summarizes the soldier-poet's current plight, and looks forward to the unsatisfactory aftermath of the war: 'Car on a poussé très loin durant cette guerre l'art de l'invisibilité' ('For people took the art of invisibility very far during this war'). The impersonal artistry of war, spreading as a contagion across the land, has driven massive numbers of human beings underground: those who are invisible for a while in the trenches are soon to be consigned to the definitive invisibility of the grave. But a later disappearing trick remains to be played on them by the practitioners and defenders of high culture. While the nation and its municipalities erect their memorials to the fallen, and devise their ceremonies of remembrance, the book trade becomes forgetful. The war begins to slip from view in the 1920s; it too goes underground. It lives on, however, as a traumatic memory—invisible, unacknowledged, unspeakable, but destined to haunt the work of many later writers.

IN MALLARMÉ'S SHADOW

Mallarmé was by far the most original inheritor of Baudelaire and Hugo. He absorbed the practical lessons of their diction, supercharged their view of poets as the indispensable critics of the social order and, by way of the emphasis he placed on poetic thought as the finest and most demanding thought there was, came to exert huge influence in his turn. His earliest progeny were in the main writers of modest ability. Mallarmé was unfailingly courteous to the young admirers who attended the famous Tuesday receptions he held in his later years, and generous beyond the call of courtesy to the multitude who sent him their slim volumes of verse. These poets—among them Henri de Régnier, Gustave Kahn, and Georges Rodenbach—were impressed above all by the extreme economy that Mallarmé displayed in certain of his shorter works. Poetry could be made, or so they persuaded themselves, from the conventional contents of a middle-class home. A lamp, a curtain, a window, a vase could yield important insights, provided always that the language of the poet was tentative, oblique, and dense with possibility. Mallarmé for these disciples was an indoor poet, and had devised an intricate linguistic machine for the recording of shy intimations and reluctant ideas.

At the same time, Mallarmé's hieratic view of the poet's role in society prompted other writers to come together in groups and publish defiant poetic manifestos. From the launch in 1885 of *La Revue wagnérienne* as the house journal of the Symbolist movement, through to the Unanimism promulgated by Jules Romains and others in the first decade of the new century, poetic schools, systems, and *-isms* abounded, and they all spoke of themselves as the instruments of a world-altering creative power. Romains's credo in *La Vie unanime* was egalitarian and inclusive, and designed to counteract a Symbolism that had begun to founder in its conceited self-regard, but in the very militancy with which Unanimism proclaimed literature as a supreme source of value it resembled its reviled predecessor. Mallarmé, who had himself been far too fastidious to become a member of groupings such as these, created the myth of literature that sustained them all, and that myth, with his unmistakable imprint upon it, survives to this day.

One young writer who attended the *mardis*, and reached his own early maturity under the enabling influence of Mallarmé, went on to become, in the eyes of many, the finest French poet of the twentieth century. This was Paul Valéry, in whom the poetic impulse was accompanied and complicated by a limitless intellectual curiosity. In Valéry's poems, essays, fables, and philosophical dialogues he writes as a public figure and addresses the civilized world at large. Over and against these 'official' compositions, however, sit the twenty-nine volumes of Valéry's *cahiers*, the laboratory records of a lifetime devoted to experimental thinking. These notebooks are to some extent comparable with those of Leonardo da Vinci, Goethe, Kierkegaard, or Walter Benjamin, and Valéry certainly identified himself as knowledge-seeker with the first two authors in this distinguished list.

What makes Valéry's *cahiers* unique is the co-presence within them of two research programmes, each pursued with obsessional intensity.

While the first has to do with the subject matter and problem-solving techniques characteristic of philosophy, mathematics, natural science, and the fine arts, the second is concerned with thinking itself and with the place occupied by thinking beings in the order of nature. This double ambition in a sense simply literalizes Mallarmé's talk of the poet as the Orphic explainer of the Earth. Orpheus now has homework to do. His is the practical task of finding out how minds, variously stimulated, function. We could scarcely be further from the exile of the *poète maudit*. The poet, who a generation ago had been driven beyond the walls of the *polis* for declaiming unpalatable truths, now speaks from within the human community, from its core, its nerve-centre.

The *cahiers* are, among other things, a loose-limbed commentary on Valéry's poetry and have often been used by his critics as exegetical aids. They do not, however, prepare the reader for the drama and the rhetorical virtuosity of the verse, or for the pain and violence that so often appear there. In Valéry's most celebrated poem, *Le Cimetière marin*, for example, the narrator travels from tranquillity to nightmare in a single, long-drawn-out crescendo. At first, sea and sunlight provide the consoling impersonal backcloth to a scene in which the dead lie painlessly in their graves. The large rhythms of nature easily outweigh the small perturbations of human consciousness. But by the mid-point of the poem the terror of death has been rediscovered:

> Chanterez-vous quand serez vaporeuse?
> Allez! Tout fuit! Ma présence est poreuse,
> La sainte impatience meurt aussi!

[Tell me: when thou art vapour, wilt thou sing? | Come, Come! The world is fugitive, my presence | Porous, even divine impatience dies!]

The first of these lines from the dark culminating tableau of the work alludes to La Fontaine's fable 'La Cigale et la Fourmi', and chimes with nearby references to the medieval *danse macabre* and to Hamlet's larking with Yorick's skull in the final act of Shakespeare's play. Everything dissolves, the narrator suggests, including earlier works of literature and the poem you are now reading. *Le Cimetière marin* gives death back its sting. Elsewhere in Valéry's verse images of biting, tearing, and bruising are common. The protagonists of 'La Pythie' and *La Jeune Parque* are racked by intolerable pain. Where Valéry's prose voice is endlessly diplomatic and accommodating, his poetic voice craves contact with destructiveness. As a poet he must be prepared to speak unpalatably, and to reincur the malediction of right-minded people.

This demonic responsibility is discharged with particular relish in 'Ébauche d'un serpent', which revisits the Garden of Eden in search of a poetic persona with teeth. Here, Valéry is of the devil's party, and boasts of it throughout a long catalogue of serpentine slitherings and insinuations. To be a snake, the protagonist announces, is to be a thinker, to live by one's wits, to thrive on multifariousness and unstoppable change. 'Je suis Celui qui modifie', he says, pouring scorn on the unity and uniformity that had figured so prominently in the Creator's original cosmic scheme. The serpent veers between sadness and rage when he remembers his fallen state, but the compensations he enjoys are those of creative thought. Such thought brings two complementary benefits: it transports the individual from mere instinct-driven animality into an excitingly complex mental world, yet allows him to manipulate and intensify the animal appetites to which he nevertheless remains subject. Once bitten, Eve will acquire both knowledge and sensual rapture, to say nothing of their delicious intermingled forms. Throughout, the seductions of thinking are described in self-preening poetic language:

> Dore, langue! dore-lui les
> Plus doux des dits que tu connaisses!
> Allusions, fables, finesses,
> Mille silences ciselés,
> Use de tout ce qui lui nuise

[Gild, tongue! gild for her the sweetest stories that you know—allusions, fables, refinements, a thousand chiselled silences—employ everything that causes her hurt]

The serpent-poet reels off the secrets of his own trade, itemizes the contents of his rhetorical armoury and gloats over their power to hurt. Assonance, alliteration, and internal rhyme give the writing a molten, self-anagrammatizing undertow, as if the cult of metamorphosis so richly celebrated in the argument of the poem had found its way into the ordinary fluctuations of the speaking voice. Yet this is word-play of an aggressive, domineering kind. Valéry has found a way of defending thought and attacking stupidity that is also a sumptuous tribute to individual will bent upon the annihilation of its neighbours.

The American critic Yvor Winters held that only short poems could be great poems, and was slightly embarrassed to find that 'Ébauche d'un serpent' was as long as it was. Nevertheless, Valéry's work was 'the greatest poem which I have ever read, regardless of kind'. When one remembers its penetrating wit, and the sensuous shimmer that Valéry gives to his drama of ideas, this judgement does not seem at all far-fetched. The poem represents, however, a hard-won triumph on Valéry's part over a less admirable quality of his poetic writing elsewhere. This is preciosity, or the tendency to be coyly abstract and conventionally oblique. The adjectives 'pur', 'tendre', and 'saint', for example, often appear as a gratuitous conceptual *appliqué*-work, promising but not delivering a new infusion of philosophical meaning. Valéry's language sometimes goes slack in its anxious striving to be grand. 'Pur' and its cognates occur often in the snake-poem, but there they are energized by the cascading variety of the language that surrounds them. The whole poem has an air of intellectual and linguistic festivity.

DADA AND SURREALISM

'Ébauche d'un serpent' appeared as the lead contribution to the July 1921 issue of *La Nouvelle Revue Française*. For some, including possibly Valéry himself, it would have had its part to play in the continuing work of post-war national reconstruction, for here was a poem that made full use of the lexical and syntactic riches of the French language while observing a time-honoured stringency in matters of metre, rhyme, and strophic form. French and the art of French verse were being rebuilt after the disaster of the war. Violence that had so recently been seen in the clash of armies, was now made internal to artistic creation. And works of high art were expected not just to survive their contact with human aggression but to flourish on the fare.

From the middle years of the war onwards, however, other artists across Europe had been reacting very differently to the catastrophe unfolding around them. Under the banner of Dada—a hobbyhorse in French, but a ready-made fragment of nonsense-speech for a much wider international community—they accused art of complicity with nationalistic war-mongering, and proclaimed art's demise. The dominant personality in this movement was Tristan Tzara, and it was in Zurich that he and his collaborators first began to perform their obsequies for the Western aesthetic outlook. Tzara, a Romanian writing in French in German-speaking Switzerland, quickly became an emblematic supranational figure, and his searing message of revolt was heeded in Berlin, Paris, Barcelona, and New York. Wherever the Dada effect made itself felt a paradox appeared on the scene. Here was an anti-art pantomime from which new and enthralling modes of artistic activity emerged. Dada performances at the Cabaret Voltaire in Zurich were multi-media spectacles, happenings, early draft forms of the performance art that was to be refined and rebrutalized by successive avant-garde movements throughout the twentieth century. Art was lost as a commodity and found again as an event. There was no watertight seal between it and the real world of trousers and trolley-buses. Art could arise anywhere and be made of anything, provided that someone had the madness and decisiveness to make it happen.

When Tzara arrived in Paris early in 1920, he found that the fame of Dada had preceded him. André Breton and Louis Aragon were the editors of the archly misnamed experimental review *Littérature*, Marcel Duchamp had just paid one of his periodic visits from New York, and Francis Picabia, Philippe Soupault, and Paul Éluard were variously active within a broadly Dadaist dispensation. The moustache and beard that Duchamp had added to a reproduction of the Mona Lisa, and the pseudonymous signature that he had placed upon a urinal, had already become talismans of a new beauty. Beauty now resided in gestures rather than in art objects, and in the instant rather than in the slow time of aesthetic delectation. Tzara's arrival did not disappoint the Paris group. Events multiplied. Gesture was rife. A Dada Festival sought to outrage public opinion, and succeeded. Yet even as the air of the French capital rang with explosions of destructive glee from the Dadaists and of civic-minded indignation from their opponents, literature was beginning to reassert itself.

The artistic movement that emerged from Dada, and that Breton in 1924 proclaimed as 'Surrealism', was a systematic attempt to garner up beautiful instants and give them an afterlife. Something of value, some unaccustomed sense of mental potency, had been glimpsed in the nihilistic posturings of those angry young men, and it was now a matter of finding out what this power-source was and exploiting it. While the unconscious mind soon emerged as the answer to this riddle, as the place where beauty, strangeness, desire, and invention all had their point of origin, the best way of harnessing its energies was much less certain. On the one hand special artistic techniques could be devised, whether in painting, film, theatre, or literary composition. In the verbal medium automatic writing seemed to offer a particularly promising route to 'le fonctionnement réel de la pensée' ('the real functioning of thought'), as Breton called it in his first Surrealist Manifesto. On the other hand, success in enlisting the unconscious was perhaps more a matter of changing one's behaviour than of adopting a technique. By wakeful dreaming, hypnosis, self-induced hallucination, or simply by walking the city in a state of wide-open awareness, one could discover a continuous flow of wonders. This hesitation gives the literary works of the Surrealists one of their defining characteristics. This is literature that looks over its own shoulder, and is prepared to dismantle itself at any moment if the real world promises richer rewards. 'Ce qu'il y a d'admirable dans le fantastique' Breton wrote in a footnote to the first Manifesto, 'c'est qu'il n'y a plus de fantastique: il n'y a que le réel' ('the admirable thing in the fantastic is that there is no longer anything fantastic: there is nothing but the real'). The fantastic is both a literary genre and a propensity of the human mind. Sometimes words on a page can procure for writers or readers a sensation of profound interfusion between themselves and the real that surrounds them, but sometimes the same sensation occurs without apparent verbal prompting. In either case the unconscious is at work, transfiguring the daily fabric of the world and creating a close-woven pattern of connections between the desire-driven human perceiver and the objects of his perception. Surrealism is one name among many for this transformative capacity of human desire.

The works produced during the heyday of Surrealist activity are remarkable for the deliberation with which the goal of spontaneous invention is pursued. Breton is a devotee of syntactic complication in *Nadja*, his prose hymn to the uncanny, and Éluard introduces an orderly play of small-scale symmetries and a highly visible overall plot into the headlong effusion that is *Poésie ininterrompue*. Surrealism delights in tensions of this kind, which give the finest of its productions the undecidable beauty that Breton in *L'Amour fou* summarized as 'explosante-fixe, magique-circonstancielle' ('exploding-fixed, magical-circumstantial').

The work that most spectacularly manages to seem at once explosively thrown off and intensively composed is Aragon's *Le Paysan de Paris*. This is the chronicle of a Parisian *flâneur* for whom the city teems with curiosities. Shopping arcades, for example, offer a heady vision of diversity:

Je voudrais savoir quelles nostalgies, quelles cristallisations poétiques, quels châteaux en Espagne, quelles constructions de langueur et d'espoir s'échafaudent dans la tête de l'apprenti, à l'instant qu'au début de sa carrière il se destine à être coiffeur pour dames et commence de se soigner les mains. Enviable sort vulgaire, il dénouera désormais tout le long du jour l'arc-en-ciel de la pudeur des femmes, les chevelures légères, les cheveux-vapeur, ces rideaux charmants de l'alcôve.

[I should like to know what nostalgias, what crystallizations of poetry, what castles in Spain, what edifices of longing and hope are constructed in the head of the apprentice, at the moment when, at the outset of his career, he forms the intention of becoming a ladies' hairdresser and starts to look after his hands. What an enviable destiny it is for the common man, to spend all day long undoing the rainbow of feminine modesty, their lightsome heads of hair, their vaporous hair, those charming bedchamber curtains.]

The bardic rhapsody that begins with these sentences has been triggered by the sight of a ladies' hairdresser. Aragon's narrator imagines
the fantasy world of the apprentice, puts together his own poetic edifice
from conjectural glimpses of someone else's mental construction work,
and retraces the delighted movements of hand through hair. This is a
prose poetry based on shared feelings, and a magical ease of communication between otherwise isolated individuals: your delight becomes
mine, and mine yours. It guards against euphoria, however, by tangling
verbal *trouvailles* in its associative web. 'Cheveux-vapeur', for example,
punning on *chevaux-vapeur* ('horse power'), gives the tenuous tracery
of the customer's locks a sudden locomotive thrust. Aragon knows that
surprise is to be had from language itself as well as from the city streets,
and in *Le Paysan de Paris* and other works from his Surrealist phase
writes with quicksilver brilliance.

It is scarcely necessary to enlist the concept of the unconscious in
describing writing of this kind. Its originality is to be found not in any
one mental zone or system but in the syncopated, flyaway movement
with which it passes from one level to another in what is at once a mind-
scape and a wordscape. Such writing moves from fetish-objects, frozen
desires, towards learned abstractions, passing through all manner of
witticisms and erotic provocations on the way. In prose and in verse the
Surrealists affirm human desire not by harking back, in the manner of
psychoanalysis, to its primal configurations but by looking forward
into its multiform futures.

PROSE FICTION BETWEEN THE WARS

The formal innovations of Gide and Proust had a slow-burning influence on later fiction both in France and internationally, but the immediate impact of those singular writers had less to do with literary form
than with the status of the novelist in society. It became axiomatic that
the house of fiction contained many mansions, that novelists had to be
polymorphous in their sympathies in order to be good at their job, and
that the novel as a genre could make sense of whatever the modern
world placed in its path. Although the protagonists of Gide and Proust
had clearly marked class allegiances and socio-political attitudes, each
writer seemed, in his fictional production overall, to promote a capacious selfhood that had no clear outer limits: in principle at least, fiction
was a means of self-emancipation from the constraints under which
social man and woman laboured.

If for a moment we personify the French novel between the wars,
and think of it as an expanded self of this kind, we can see these years

as ones of triumph. The novel became greedy for new territories, and consolidated its control over those it had acquired in the nineteenth century. Many of the French regions, for example, began to produce their chroniclers. Henri Pourrat set many of his works in the Auvergne, and established himself as a semi-official literary spokesman for his native community. Marcel Aymé played a similar role in the Jura, and Jean Giono in the Basses-Alpes. Catholicism became primary subject matter for fiction, and began to display a distinctive moral and psychological complexity, in the works of François Mauriac and Georges Bernanos. The social world, suffused with political awareness, was amply represented in the works of Louis Guilloux, Paul Nizan, and Aragon, who, though largely repentant for his Surrealist sins by the early 1930s, was still writing with experimental brio in such 'realist' works as *Les Cloches de Bâle* and *Les Beaux Quartiers*. It was in these years too that detective fiction, often patronized as a mere popular genre, came of age. Indeed the works of such writers as Claude Aveline, Pierre Véry, and Pierre Nord installed the modern detective plot so firmly in the national *imaginaire* that it became a template for much experimental fiction in the 1950s and 1960s.

The huge production of fictional matter during the inter-war years is still difficult for observers from later generations to bring into focus. Besides, 'lost' material from the 1920s and 1930s is regularly rediscovered by cultural historians, and this often makes it necessary to revise the larger picture. Something can certainly be done to reduce confusion if we apply such labels as 'the regional novel' or 'the Catholic novel' to the prose literature of this period, although the price to be paid for such simplicity is often very high. If we think of Giono's novels, for example, as a portable distillation of the mountainous south-east of the country, we are likely to limit their range and resonance. In the trilogy *Colline*, *Un de Baumugnes* and *Regain* a local peasantry is mythicized as the life-force incarnate, and a local landscape transformed by an image-bedecked prose into Nature itself. The achievement of Mauriac is similarly understated if excessive emphasis is placed on the Catholic framework of his fiction. In this case one could go much further, and say that such works as *Le Désert de l'amour* and *Thérèse Desqueyroux* demand to be read outside that framework if their implacable tragic design is to be fully appreciated.

Two works published in successive years in the early 1930s deserve to be singled out from this variegated array of inter-war novels. Both of them were instantly acclaimed by literary commentators and the wider reading public, and both take prose fiction in directions that are quite new. The first is Céline's *Voyage au bout de la nuit*, a loosely strung series of adventures in which the first-person narrator, Bardamu, moves from the battlefields of the First World War to Africa, the United States, and the impoverished Paris suburbs. Bardamu is a doctor. He takes sides with the oppressed wherever he goes, and directs a ready flow of bilious invective against generals, colonial administrators, industrial bosses, and other figures of authority. Céline equips Bardamu with an ample diction that is colloquial and learned at the same time, and bathes indifferently in high-flown literary allusion and low-life slang.

After his return to Paris, Bardamu is called upon to tend a young unmarried woman in whom a bungled abortion has produced unstemmable bleeding; he is let into the apartment by the patient's mother:

Elle me laissait m'habituer à la pénombre du couloir, à l'odeur des poireaux pour la soupe, aux papiers des murs, à leurs ramages sots, à sa voix d'étranglée. Enfin, de bafouillages en exclamations, nous parvînmes auprès du lit de la fille, prostrée, la malade, à la dérive.

[She let me get used to the half-light of the corridor, to the smell of leeks for making broth, to the papering on the walls, to their stupid leafy patterns, to her strangulation victim's voice. At last, by way of splutterings and exclamations, we arrived at the bedside of the daughter, prostrated, this ill girl, adrift.]

This is one of many points in the novel where the composite narrative voice develops a self-referential dimension. On the one hand, Bardamu looks outwards to the plight of others—to the mother's shame in the eyes of her neighbours and to the mortal danger threatening the daughter—and empathizingly threads their voices into his. On the other hand, however, his monologue is constantly on the lookout for echoes of itself: the strangled splutterings and exclamations of the one woman and the delirious drift of the other are, for this vocal performer, enviable accomplishments of style.

Céline's *saeva indignatio* is a carrying fluid for all manner of small-scale language games placed end to end. He favours simple syntax. Even his long sentences are additive and enumerative rather than hierarchical in the internal arrangement of their parts. This expostulatory manner, which was to be further radicalized in *Mort à crédit* and the later fiction, forms the basis for an extraordinary experiment in narrative method. Public events, including war, occupation, and imprisonment, do not take place on a public stage and have no continuity or causal logic to them: they are declaimed and exclaimed by a voice, brought into being and extinguished by the imperious babble of a modern minstrel. The chilling feature of this style is that its playful complexity can be made to serve the oppressor as well as the oppressed. From having been, in the early novels, a vehicle for the expression of solidarity between suffering humans it is called on, in the pamphlets already mentioned, to serve sadistic fantasy and hate.

The second of these outstanding novels from the early 1930s is André Malraux's *La Condition humaine*. Unlike Céline, Malraux is concerned with political choice and conflict, and sets out a differentiated cast of characters each representing a distinctive viewpoint. The scene is the aftermath of the Chinese revolution and the seizure of power by Chiang Kai-shek. The plot of the novel traces the betrayal and defeat of the Communist insurgents in Shanghai, and dwells at length on the motives and actions of individuals in this group. Malraux constructs his drama in such a way that discussion, action, and passionate introspection are rapidly intercut. His political agents are thinking beings who lead lives rich in sense-experience.

The anarchist Tchen, for example, is seen in the opening pages of the novel committing a murder, meditating upon it and sensuously embroiled in the forensic detail of the scene. In due course he becomes the officiant in a sacrificial rite: he is now the would-be killer of Chiang Kai-shek and expects to die alongside his victim. Having failed in the assassination attempt and been horrifically wounded, he tries to locate the revolver that will release him from his pain: 'Un policier était tout près. Tchen voulut demander si Chang-Kaï-Shek était mort, mais il voulait cela dans un autre monde; dans ce monde-ci, cette mort même lui était indifférente' ('A policeman was just there. Tchen wanted to ask whether Chiang-Kai-shek was dead, but his wanting belonged to another world; in this world, that death itself was a matter of indifference to him'). The switch from *voulut* to *voulait* inside a single sentence is characteristic of the 'indirect free style' that Malraux uses so liberally in these years. Two kinds of wishing are counterposed: while the first is a self-contained volitional act, the second is a perpetual state of ideological fervour. Even in his last seconds of life, the character is borne along by a transcendent abstract idea.

On occasion, there is an air of empty oratorical uplift about this language, especially when it dwells on such key notions as destiny and fraternal devotion. More often, however, it is used as part of an elaborate anatomy of political motives. Tchen, Kyo, Katow, Gisors, and Clappique each have an individualized mental hinterland, and, by way of his animated abstractions, Malraux specifies the contours of these interior worlds as public events unfold. A new kind of adventure novel is born in *La Condition humaine*, and recreated in *Le Temps du mépris*, on the rise of the Nazis, and *L'Espoir*, on the Spanish Civil War. In each case, the inscrutable dynamism of mass movements and the clash of opposing ideologies are reimagined at grass roots level. Suddenly, it all comes down to a prisoner giving away his cyanide pill, or to a battering-ram moving towards a stout locked door. For Malraux at this stage in his long career, such deeds are ideas in action. If his novels can make a special claim to seriousness in the face of terror and bloodshed, this lies in their ability to dramatize extreme situations and to pinpoint the moments at which thinking switches irreversibly into doing.

THE TWENTIETH CENTURY'S VOLTAIRE: JEAN-PAUL SARTRE

The Sartre who rose to prominence after the Second World War is the very model of the public intellectual, and his achievements already figure in many other histories than those of literature. He was a philosopher, a political scientist, a campaigning journalist, the found-ing editor of *Les Temps modernes*, a supporter of the Front de Libération Nationale in Algeria and of the student uprising of May 1968, a would-be mediator both between Israel and the Arab states and between the opposing superpowers during the Cold War; and in these and countless other activities he gave the act of writing an urgent and provocative role. Within literature, he moved easily between genres. As a novelist and short-story writer who also wrote plays, as an essayist who was also an autobiographer, a literary theorist who was also a screenwriter, Sartre became the Proteus of modern letters. Moreover, he introduced a new kind of life-writing—'existential psychoanalysis'—which, after trial runs devoted to Baudelaire and Jean Genet, reached its apogee in *L'Idiot de la famille*, a 3,000-page speculative biography of Flaubert. Even after his death his intellectual fecundity continued to astonish, as huge previously unsuspected literary and philosophical manuscripts began gradually to enter the public domain.

While it would be foolish to shrink Sartre's wide-ranging intellec-tual activities into a single conceptual model, a relish for snags and paradoxes, or for an initial appearance of these, is to be found through-out his career, and this feature makes his works, early and late, philo-sophical and literary, mutually illuminating to a remarkable degree. Existentialism itself, the philosophical doctrine with which he is most closely associated, has for Sartre a paradox at its core. On the one hand, it offers a radical view of freedom. The individual human subject simply finds himself in the world, thrown into being, and with no world-system and no set of absolute values to appoint him to a place, a direction, or a destiny inside the order of things. He cannot but be free, in the endless procession of self-choosings that his acts represent. On the other hand, he is only contingently there in the world and could as easily not be there at all. Non-conscious being, including that of his own mortal body, hedges him about and hems him in.

L'Être et le Néant, Sartre's major philosophical work, synthesizes arguments from Hegel, Husserl, and Heidegger and ingeniously hybridizes them with the concerns of the French philosophical tradition stemming from Descartes. Repeatedly, Sartre's presentation drives towards moments of fertile discomfort and disequilibrium. Discussing the relationship between *en-soi* and *pour-soi*, between the world of objects and the activities of human consciousness, for example, he announces in a resounding cadence that the *pour-soi*, the very site of freedom, has its own 'facticity', its own existence as mere contingent fact: 'il a le sentiment de son entière gratuité, il se saisit comme étant là *pour rien*, comme étant *de trop*' ('it has the feeling of its complete gratuitousness, is aware of itself as being there *for no reason*, as being *surplus to requirements*'). The following paragraph, reinforcing this claim, then culminates on the inescapable tension that runs through the being of human beings: 'la conscience ne peut en aucun cas s'empêcher d'être et pourtant elle est totalement responsable de son être' ('consciousness cannot in any instance prevent itself from being and yet it is utterly responsible for its own being').

Sartre times his conflicts and crises with dramatic flair in this work. *L'Être et le Néant* is a treatise with a plot, and an argument that looks to all manner of everyday incidents for support. Even in its densest thickets of technical exposition the call of literature is to be heard. Certain elements of Sartre's philosophy are in any case, one suspects, better suited to presentation in fictional form than to the phased unfolding of a conceptual scheme. In *La Nausée*, for example, published before *L'Être et le Néant* but drawing on many of the same materials, the sensation of contingency flows back from the natural world as observed by Roquentin, the first-person narrator, into his observing consciousness, and threatens to engulf it. A theoretical postulate becomes a dramatic scene, and a poem in prose. Sartre gives Roquentin an intense preoccupation with images and in his fictional persona's manipulation of these he returns philosophical enquiry to the viscera and nerve-ends of sentient humankind. What is elsewhere an abstract debate between freedom and its refusal, or between authenticity and bad faith, is here concretized in a public library, a café, or a bed shared by lovers.

La Nausée is a work of psychological penetration and embittered social critique: such are the advantages of doing philosophy impurely and on the sly. It is also, at moments, a splendidly comic work.

Roquentin gloats over the deceased local notables whose portraits line the walls of the Bouville museum, taking particular delight in Olivier Blévigne as painted by Bordurin. The name of the sitter is redolent of nourishing and thirst-quenching produce—olives, wheat, grapes—but this painter, at work in this town, will soon turn him into ordure and mud ('boue'). The bad faith of the bourgeoisie is denounced in Roquentin's tirade and mocked in Sartre's onomastic jest. A philosophical paradigm contrasting authentic being with being that is variously empty, shallow, fraudulent, irresponsible, and delusional has been transposed in *La Nausée* into an unstable fictional texture. The contrast, which seems so straightforward when abstractly formulated, is given a complex sensory content and tracked through an echo-chamber of changing emotions. Roquentin's narrative tone, as it flickers between pain, disgust, anxiety, and merriment, acts almost as a guarantee that philosophy matters to human beings as they live their lives. In this respect at least, the novelist is the teacher and the philosopher his pupil.

In the course of the novel, Roquentin abandons one literary project and toys with another: he will not be the biographer of M. de Rollebon, a shadowy contemporary of Marie-Antoinette, but may instead decide to be a novelist. Moving towards this second option, however, he seems to be in danger of contradicting himself. In a certain light there is little difference between literary composition and historical research: both offer a dubious exit-route from the real time and space of human affairs. Sartre was to live out versions of Roquentin's difficulty in his own later literary career. He despised biography but practised it on a monumental scale. He loathed the bourgeoisie but returned to its pomposities and misdemeanours with rapt fascination. He criticized many artists for their lack of social and political commitment but found convincing evidence of commitment where others found none. Tensions like these are to be found everywhere in his literary output.

When Sartre gave the title *Situations* to the successive volumes of his collected essays, he highlighted one of his own indispensable concepts. The human subject 'fell into being' in a world of material facts, and these included suprapersonal physical forces and social structures. The action of the free and responsible individual was thus unavoidably 'situated', embedded in the rough fabric of a reality that he could never expect to control fully, but it was exactly this ambient pressure of circumstance that gave his choices, his assumptions of responsibility, their grandeur. He had to work with what was at hand and refuse all metaphysical extenuations and escape clauses. In the individual's active adherence to his situation and in his unillusioned effort to create futures within it, lay the kernel of the Sartrean ethics sketched in the lecture *L'Existentialisme est un humanisme* and elaborated in the posthumously published *Cahiers pour une morale*. Living a contradiction became a token of moral and intellectual integrity.

When it comes to the situation of the writer in modern societies, Sartre characteristically has two views, and both are centred on the question of commitment. On the one hand, in *Qu'est-ce que la littérature?*, the committed writer is one who deals in robust communicative prose, and he compares favourably with those who ache after a self-sustaining verbal domain cut off from the ordinary world of speech and action. Poets but not poets alone are given to this cult of the autonomous art object: when we see them at work on words—'les touchant, les tâtant, les palpant' ('touching them, feeling them, fingering them')—we see them moving on our behalf beyond the exigencies of the real. On the other hand, in his long text on Mallarmé and in much of his Flaubert triptych, Sartre comes to see such writers' restless manipulation of the verbal medium as representing an exemplary act of criticism and rebellion. From within language, they wage war on cliché and complacency, and create new varieties of social meaning. They achieve commitment by the very ferocity of their devotion to the inner workings of language. *Engagement* for Sartre comes, therefore, in two guises and at two levels of intensity, and one is tempted, faced with the energy and trenchancy of his writing on both fronts, to say simply that he is right twice over. A more appropriate Sartrean response, however, would be to accept that the onus of deciding between the two views, or of reconciling them, falls upon the individual reader, inescapably situated in his or her turn. No one in modern France has created a richer conceptual field in which to think about the social responsibility of writers and those who read them.

LITERATURE AND WAR: 1939–1945

When German forces invaded northern France in May 1940, at the end of the *drôle de guerre* or 'phoney war', there began a period of social and political upheaval that is without parallel in the post-Revolutionary history of the nation. Many millions of French citizens fled their homes in the face of the German advance, and within a month the French army had been defeated. Two powerful personalities stepped forward to quell public alarm and to restore some sense of national cohesion. These were Marshal Pétain, the hero of Verdun, and Charles de Gaulle, a little-known general who in previous weeks had seen active service in the main battle-zone. Whereas Pétain signed an armistice with the invader, called for a National Revolution, and set about building a new French state that would have at least an appearance of freedom from German authority, de Gaulle broadcast to the nation from London, proclaimed 'La France Libre' and became the de facto leader of the resistance movement inside and outside the country. These visions of a redeemed and reconstructed nationhood were so different, and so violently opposed when they were translated into political action, that the years 1940–4 may justly be thought of as a time of civil war.

There are dangers, however, in adopting a rigidly polarized view of the situation. For the French population at large, daily life was lived not as a clear-cut conflict between collaboration and resistance, but as a series of compromises and short-term survival measures. Acquiescence at one level towards the occupiers, or towards the regime established by Pétain at Vichy, could easily disguise refusal at another. Moral choices were made anxiously, and with an eye to the personal safety of family members and associates. And all the main cultural institutions were caught up in a demoralizing struggle for their own continuation. The press, the theatre, popular entertainment, and the publishing, film, and music industries were all subject to censorship in matters of content and to a variety of practical controls. Literature itself, which had so often been seen as the principle of free speech given material form, was fought over, harried, co-opted to a range of political and military causes, and came to occupy a prominent place in the self-consciousness of the nation. Even for non-readers, literature became a rallying-point.

In one way, the story of literature at this time is a very simple one: during a period of troubled national identity the French literary tradition had acquired an emblematic value; to preserve it was to retain active contact with the past triumphs of French civilization, and the best form of preservation was to add new writing to the existing store of masterpieces. Many writers, including Valéry and Sartre, continued to publish with the mainstream Paris firms, all of whom had been 'Aryanized' by the Nazi authorities. The *Nouvelle Revue Française*, now edited by the collaborationist Pierre Drieu la Rochelle, continued to secure contributions from such figures as Gide, Giono, Aymé, and Montherlant. In many cases, material of an implicitly *résistant* kind could find its way into print unhindered by the censors, who had little aptitude for literary criticism and were unlikely to detect the subtler signs of ironic intent. Much of the writing that was legally published in these years brought off the feat of being anodyne on the surface and subversive underneath. Another group of writers, also part of this simple story, became out and out collaborators with Nazism, presenting themselves in a variety of postures designed to please the occupiers. Céline and Lucien Rebatet were elegists for a lost France and enthusiastic proponents of anti-Semitism; Robert Brasillach eulogized the fascist virtues of strength, manliness, and discipline; Alphonse de Châteaubriant extolled the New Europe that the Third Reich had conjured into being.

The story becomes much more complicated, however, when we consider the large corpus of clandestine writing that appeared during the Occupation. An astonishing range of unofficial news-sheets and magazines were produced, often by local resistance groups. Small presses sprang up, and elaborate distribution networks were established. The most celebrated of these underground publishers was Les Éditions de Minuit, founded by Pierre de Lescure and Jacques Debû-Bridel. The success of their first publication was such that literature soon came to be recognized as a powerful political force both among the resisters themselves and in the general population. The work concerned is the novella *Le Silence de la mer*, written by Jean Bruller under the pseudonym 'Vercors'. What is remarkable about the book is that it achieved its celebrity not by offering a call to arms, or to patriotic fervour, but by setting down a series of ambiguities. The principal characters are an honourable German officer and the French uncle and niece in whose home he has been billetted. The silence of the unwilling hosts is an act of passive protest, but it serves also to isolate their imposed guest as a disturbingly seductive figure. He is a cultivated man, a musician, an admirer of France: 'Ici c'est l'esprit, la pensée subtile et poétique' ('here you find the life of the mind, subtle and poetic thought'). The conflict between Germany and France is restaged as a household tension between charm and sympathy on the one hand and unflagging decency on the other. Everything in the narrative is muted and oblique. Printing and circulating this example of 'subtle thought' under the very eyes of the occupying troops was an act of resistance on behalf of literature itself as well as a defence of the land called 'La France prisonnière' in Vercors's dedication.

French poetry was widely mobilized in both these roles, and reinvigorated in the process. Poems could be published in pocket editions, printed on handbills, dropped from the air, and memorized for further distribution by word of mouth. Lyric poetry in particular, which had such a long previous history of indirect utterance and coded meaning, suddenly became a supple medium for clandestine communication. Ponge, Éluard, Michaux, and Aragon composed major works in this period, and by way of these the occasional poetry of wartime rejoined the mainstream of European literature. Jean Cassou's *Trente-trois sonnets composés au secret*, written in 1941 during the poet's captivity by the Vichy police and published, again by Minuit, much later in the war, are one of the summits of this literature in verse. They combine national retrospection with a rousing defence of an imagination without territorial borders:

> La plaie que, depuis le temps des cerises,
> je garde en mon cœur s'ouvre chaque jour.
> En vain les lilas, les soleils, les brises
> viennent caresser les murs des faubourgs.
>
> Pays des toits bleus et des chansons grises,
> qui saignes sans cesse en robe d'amour,
> explique pourquoi ma vie s'est éprise
> du sanglot rouillé de tes vieilles cours.
>
> Aux fées rencontrées le long du chemin
> je vais racontant Fantine et Cosette.
> L'arbre de l'école, à son tour, répète
>
> une belle histoire où l'on dit: demain ...
> Ah! jaillisse enfin le matin de fête
> où sur les fusils s'abattront les poings!

[The wound that, since the cherry season, I have kept in my heart opens up each day. In vain do lilacs, suns, breezes come to caress the walls of the city districts. Oh country of blue roofs and grey songs, which bleeds endlessly inside its love-gown, explain to me why my life has become enamoured of the rusty sobbing of your ancient courtyards. To the fairies I meet along the way I keep on telling the tale of Fantine and Cosette. The schoolyard tree, in its turn, repeats a fine story in which people say: tomorrow... Ah! may the festival morning at last burst forth in which fists will swoop down upon guns!]

The patriotic allusions brought together here are also a general cry of solidarity with the oppressed. The wound and the spring blossom of the first quatrain are borrowed from Jean-Baptiste Clément's song 'Le Temps des cerises', dear to the *communards* in 1871; Fantine and Cosette, whose story the narrator now recounts, are central characters in Hugo's *Les Misérables*; even the 'chansons grises', imported from Verlaine's 'Art poétique', are associated with the suffering and bloodshed the country is now undergoing. French literature, its verse reprocessed and its tales retold, is at once a local vehicle of resistance and an enduring mouthpiece for the fundamental human freedoms—from hunger, poverty, and terror. The last image of the poem, in which human skin and bone descend upon hard weaponry, speaks at once of this war and all wars, of one imminent act of defiance and of all such acts.

The compromises and complicities that the German occupation imposed on large sections of the French population remained present as a disturbing collective memory in much writing of the post-war years. When in 1947 Simone de Beauvoir gave the title *Pour une morale de l'ambiguïté* to a treatise on existentialist ethics, or when Nathalie Sarraute called her essays on the modern novel *L'Ère du soupçon*, they were remembering a time when ambiguity and suspicion had been political as well as psychological facts. If these concepts were now tools of intellectual enquiry, this was in part because an entire generation of French writers had known them before they became concepts at all, when they were the living medium in which personal choices were made. No work of these years is more deeply marked by this legacy of the Second World War than Albert Camus's *La Chute*, published, like Sarraute's essays, in 1956.

By this time Camus was already widely respected as a novelist, essayist and playwright. He was the author of *L'Étranger* and *La Peste*, both set in his native Algeria, and the founder of the resistance newspaper *Combat*. He was first a friend of Sartre's and then his weightiest moral and political antagonist. In *La Chute* he seems to bracket off much of his earlier teaching. In place of the salutary humanizing 'revolt' against absurdity that he had previously proclaimed, he offers the monologue of a fallen modern consciousness, racked by guilt and self-loathing and addicted to the short-term palliative properties of irony. Camus's protagonist, Jean-Baptiste Clamence, ekes out a life of exile in Amsterdam, interweaving the memory of his own misdeeds with the ills of modern Europe:

Moi, j'habite le quartier juif, ou ce qui s'appelait ainsi jusqu'au moment où nos frères hitlériens y ont fait de la place. Quel lessivage! Soixante-quinze mille juifs déportés ou assassinés, c'est le nettoyage par le vide. J'admire cette application, cette méthodique patience! Quand on n'a plus de caractère, il faut bien se donner une méthode.

[As for me, I live in the Jewish quarter, or in what was known by that name until the moment when our Hitlerian brothers made room there. What a clean-out! Seventy-five thousand Jews deported or killed, that's cleaning by way of the void. I admire such dedication, such methodical patience! When one no longer has character, one really does have to equip oneself with a method.]

Behind one element of the historical record lies another: the deportation and killing of Dutch Jews is a screen behind which the destruction of many tens of thousands of French Jews persists as an indelible memory-trace; and in the rounding-up of those particular men, women, and children the brothers concerned had been not Hitlerians but the French civil authorities and many ordinary citizens. Irony, wit, and debonair social talk are here brought face to face with a monstrous historical fact that leaves them powerless. The narrative undermines itself relentlessly. In creating this narrator, and decking out his name and his narrative with biblical allusions, Camus gave the still-troubled European conscience of the 1950s a down-at-heel mythical grandeur. Jean-Baptiste Clamence was the very embodiment of post-war sensibility now redescribing itself as postlapsarian. He was a Baptist with no saviour in sight, a clamant ego crying in the wilderness, an exemplary sufferer trapped in the hell of the modern metropolis. Born of the Second World War and its immediate aftermath, *La Chute* was also, in its retreat from heroism into anxious immobility, one of the defining novels of the Cold War period and an oblique commentary on the unfolding Algerian crisis.

THE FORTUNES OF THE MODERN NOVEL

From de Gaulle himself downwards, the legacies of the Resistance are to be seen at all levels in modern French culture. Camus's *Combat* appeared as a national daily until 1974, and Les Éditions de Minuit, directed by Jérôme Lindon from 1948 until his recent death, survives to this day. The evolution of Minuit is instructive. It moved from clandestinity under the Occupation to high visibility as the standard-bearer for experimental fiction in modern France. Resistance to an armed enemy from without was gradually transformed into a battle against the traditional novel, now dressed up, for the polemical purposes of the day, as an enemy within. Balzac was often the villain. He was alleged to have wielded fictional representations as a means not just of achieving personal control over the world but of confirming the bourgeoisie as a whole in its controlling and profit-seeking appetites. Although allegations such as these would have seemed plainly off-target to anyone who had read Balzac at length and seen his monumental comic intelligence at work, one can understand how the Minuit authors came to make them. It was largely a matter of tone: Balzac sounded too sure of himself even in his moments of vertigo and madcap exuberance. For Samuel Beckett, Michel Butor, Alain Robbe-Grillet, Claude Simon, Marguerite Duras, and the other members of the team assembled by Lindon in the 1950s, the novel needed to look critically at its own rhetoric, and to remind itself that in a world of continuing colonial warfare and superpower confrontation its powers were limited.

At the beginning of Robbe-Grillet's *Dans le labyrinthe*, published by Minuit in 1959, for example, the rain that was about to descend on Bouville at the end of Sartre's *La Nausée* is continuing to fall, but now on a town that is nameless and depopulated. Later in the same paragraph sunlight and dry dust are also to fall, and before long an even blanket of snow is to cover the scene. In all cases the weather speaks of uniformity and indifference. At first, an affectless neutrality seems to have taken up residence in the house of fiction:

Dehors il neige. Le vent chasse sur l'asphalte sombre du trottoir les fins cristaux secs, qui se déposent après chaque rafale en lignes blanches, parallèles, fourches, spirales, disloquées aussitôt, reprises aussitôt dans les tourbillons chassés au ras du sol, puis figées de nouveau, recomposant de nouvelles spirales, volutes, ondulations fourchues, arabesques mouvantes aussitôt disloquées.

[Outside it is snowing. Across the darkened asphalt of the pavement, the wind chases the fine, dry crystals, which accumulate after each gust in white lines— parallels, forks, spirals—that are soon disarranged, soon caught up in the whirlwinds that flit over the surface of the ground, and then solidified again, to compose new spirals, volutes, forking wave-patterns, animated arabesques that are soon to be disarranged.]

There is more in this description than a moving geometry of snowfall, and more in the sinuous motion of the main sentence than an attempt to imitate the unfolding of a complex meteorological event. What syntax there is provides not a sense of hierarchy but a relentless play of equivalences. The force of the writing is in its thesaurus-like display of lexical alternatives, and its eager enumerative pulse. It sets small grammatical puzzles—'parallèles', adjective or noun?—and solves them; it switches between grammatical classes, between 'fourches' and 'fourchues'; and it allegorizes its own procedures: the changing snow patterns speak of an artful writerly 'recomposition', just as the repeated 'aussitôt' draws attention to the forwards-flung impatience of the sentence itself. Although the fractured plot of *Dans le labyrinthe* tells of lost soldiers and lost battles, Robbe-Grillet's language has an air of victorious self-possession about it. Attention has been diverted from the human personality and towards literature seen as an impersonal combinatorial device. Such writing invites the reader to contemplate the spectacle of unstoppable change, but makes no further promises. There is no suggestion that he might put all that transformational capacity to use in the pursuit of his own chosen goals.

Sarraute is very different from Robbe-Grillet in her primary subject matter. She is concerned with the spasmodic internal life of social men and women; with their fantasies of dominance and self-abasement; with their selfishness, anger, and cruelty; and with the coercive power of social groups. She is a student and a satirist of the desiring mind, and the external world—whether in rain, snow, or sunshine—exists for her only in an already mentalized form. She traces the shifting contours of an always troubled interpersonal space: 'On supputait ... on attendait ... on l'observait ... des yeux cruels, dissimulés partout autour d'elle, épiaient ... bruissements inquiétants, chuchotements' ('They were calculating... they were waiting... they were watching her ... cruel eyes were in disguise everywhere around her, were spying ... worrying rustles, whisperings'). This fragment from *Le Planétarium* contains a thumbnail portrait of the paranoid imagination at work. Other people lie in wait for us everywhere, have designs upon us, fill the world with signs, and always to our detriment. But in writing like this there is little suggestion of pathological excess, or of a remediable ill at large in society. For Sarraute, paranoia together with less extreme mental afflictions such as envy, greed, and snobbery, are worth redramatizing repeatedly because they are systematic and insistent. They are ways of inhabiting the world and of making it intelligible. Sarraute's prose has extraordinary precision: it registers fluctuating intensities of passion in her characters, and seizes clear-headedly on their different degrees of deludedness. Writing like this builds a series of bridges between the aggressive and self-preservative instincts of the human animal on the one hand and its thirst for knowledge on the other. In novel after novel, Sarraute rediscovers the biological underside of human thought processes, and the aspiration towards intellect of squirming organic matter.

While Robbe-Grillet and Sarraute clearly are different in their primary emphases—the one as firmly invested in the surface textures of the external world as the other is in human psychology—they yet have a characteristic in common that marks their work off from much other fiction of the post-war period. These novelists distrust grand schemes and theatrical effects and instead attend fervently to the positioning of individual words and word-groups inside the mobile interlace of their texts. From a volute to an arabesque, or from a rustle to a whisper, they inch their way forwards. They do not favour complex syntax or architectonic plotting. While revelations, recognition scenes, magical enlargements of vision, and sudden switches of narrative direction are certainly all present in their novels, these features are inserted by stealth into the compacted weave of the writing. Robbe-Grillet and Sarraute behave like poets rather than storytellers, that is to say. Novels built in this way can be boldly experimental and, in their rediscovery of lyrical prose, can affirm the continuing importance of artistic vision in an anxious, ambiguous, and suspicious age. But they represent at the same time a determined retreat from the sphere of the human collectivity, and from individual agency within that sphere, as raw material for art. The artist is a self-determining agent when at work on his or her page, but otherwise paralysed on the margins of social, political, and geopolitical life.

The experimental novelists of the 1950s and 1960s are now remembered more for their outstanding individual works—Pinget's *L'Inquisitoire*, for example, Butor's *La Modification*, or Simon's *La Route des Flandres*—than for their membership of a supposed school or tendency. Yet the designation *nouveau roman* was highly successful as a marketing slogan, and together with *nouvelle vague* in film, *nouvelle critique* and *nouvelle philosophie*, gave newness, real or purported, massive cultural prestige. When Philippe Sollers and Jean Ricardou began publishing novels that celebrated themselves as sites of textual production, as adventures in writing, or as places from which the last trace of realistic illusionism had been expelled, the phrase *nouveau nouveau roman* escalated to near-absurdity this branding of fictional works. Even today, this industry-led history of newness makes it difficult to bring a many-faceted literary field into focus. Not only are such individual monuments as Louis Guilloux's *Le Jeu de Patience* or Albert Cohen's *Belle du Seigneur* easily wiped from the historical record, but entire fictional styles or genres can be forgotten.

The post-war years saw, for example, a resurgence of comic writing in prose. The French language, so thoroughly policed by Vichy and the occupiers, was suddenly available again in its variety and inventiveness. Frédéric Dard, often writing under the pseudonym San-Antonio, produced a vast series of low-life detective stories in which plotting and characterization easily give way under pressure from the boisterous language games played by the narrative voice. Slang meets technical terminology in Dard's diction, and ornate periods are shot through with neologisms, jokes, and scurrilous asides. Boris Vian was an inheritor both of Surrealism and of the 'pataphysics', or science of imaginary solutions, invented by Alfred Jarry in the early years of the century. But in such works as *L'Écume des jours* and *L'arrache-cœur* Vian occupied a haunting no man's land between satire and sentiment, between tough-mindedness and whimsicality, and it was his ever-alert linguistic imagination that allowed him to move back and forth between emotional dispositions often thought of as mutually exclusive.

Two figures dominate this fertile landscape of comedy, however, and in both cases experimentation on language is propelled by large philosophical ambition. The first of these is Raymond Queneau, whose career illustrates not only the assimilative powers of literature itself but also the capacity for interdisciplinary dialogue that may lie hidden in the separate fields of art, science, and mathematics. Queneau was a novelist, a poet, an essayist, a campaigner for linguistic reform under the banner of *néo-français*, the editor both of the *Encyclopédie de la Pléiade* and of the influential lectures on Hegel's *Phenomenology* delivered by Alexandre Kojève in the 1930s. Queneau moved between genres and between intellectual conventions with lightly worn omniscience, seeking to revitalize literary French by exposing it to the language of the street, the café, or the fairground. Although he had already written a great deal by the outbreak of war, it was in the postwar period that his verbal and stylistic virtuosity became fully apparent. As language enthusiast Queneau holds two opposite tendencies in perpetual disequilibrium. On the one hand the power of words can be concentrated, and an enriched expressiveness achieved within a concise format, but, on the other, words can run out of control and proliferate throughout the social order. In his *Exercices de style*, for example, a single anecdote is retold in ninety-nine different ways, ranging from laconic to prolix, and from slangy to high-flown. Language seizes on a banal event, fixes it, lays it to rest, but the process is endlessly replayable. Viewpoints multiply, and possible texts stretch to the horizon in all directions. Melancholy is never far away, however, for the power of language thus celebrated often points to a lack of power in the human individual.

Queneau's most extraordinary device for producing this mingled sensation of creativity and desolation is the sonnet sequence *Cent mille milliards de poèmes*. Each line of the ten core poems that constitute the work is printed on a separately movable strip of paper, thereby allowing a very large number of poems—ten to the power of fourteen—to be produced by any reader who has world enough and time. One has only to imagine each of these potential sonnets printed on a single sheet and a thin volume threatens to become intolerably thick.

In 1960, Queneau, together with the mathematician François le Lionnais, founded OULIPO, or the Ouvroir de littérature potentielle, a cerebral boys' club devoted to provocative experiments of this kind. New literary works could be produced either by imposing an arbitrary formal constraint on the emerging products of fantasy, or by submitting an existing literary work to a preordained series of transformations. But in either mode, Oulipian practices were at once playful and alarming. The promise of new meaning was everywhere in the human world, and everywhere threatened to become excessive. It was under the influence of Queneau and the other *Oulipiens* that our second major comedian of language began to embark on his most ambitious work.

This figure was Georges Perec, the author of *La Disparition*, a crime novel from which the letter 'e' is banished, and of *Les Revenentes*, in which that letter stages a comeback and a counter-attack. *La Vie mode d'emploi*, the culminating work of Perec's brief career, is the last 'big book about everything' to have been written in France in the twentieth century. In homage to Joyce's *Ulysses* its action unfolds on a single June day, but two further constraints have been added: everything happens towards eight in the evening, and in a single apartment building. By way of the stories told about its residents, and of the copious associations that any single episode may release, the building becomes a microcosm:

il bourrait à longueur d'années trois navires délabrés de coquillages malais, de mouchoirs philippins, de kimonos de Formose, de chemises indiennes, de vestes népalaises, de fourrures afghanes, de laques cinghalaises, de baromètres de Macao, de jouets de Hong-Kong, et de cent autres marchandises de toutes espèces et de toutes provenances . . .

[for years on end he stuffed three ramshackle ships with Malayan shells, handkerchiefs from the Philippines, kimonos from Formosa, Indian shirts, Nepalese jackets, Afghan furs, lacquerware from Ceylon, barometers from Macao, toys from Hong Kong, and a hundred other products of all kinds and from all places of origin . . .]

This lavish list explodes in the middle of the narrator's description of the Plassaerts, the couple who live on the top floor and trade in Indian artefacts; it refers not to their own dealings, but to those of the neurotic Dutch lawyer who first introduced them to commodities from the Far East. This is one of the numerous points in the novel where Perec seeks to induce a special sort of panic in his reader. He lassoes the world piece by piece into his fictional edifice, and packs every corner with heterogeneous assemblages. But he also announces a combinatorial system that has limitless productive capacity. As we move from the Philippines to Nepal, and from handkerchiefs to jackets, we are embarking on an interminable itinerary. Towards the end, the passage swoons away from precise products and their origins towards a terrifying underlying principle: such pairings can be produced indefinitely, and diversity suppressed by the very mechanism that has been installed to promote it.

La Vie mode d'emploi is a huge compendium of stories, games, gags, and puzzles. As befits a novel of great bulk it takes precautions against monotony: many systems are in play at once; associative strings are knotted together, and then untied and retied tirelessly; oddities are everywhere. Yet inconsolable sadness inhabits the book too. The name of the central character, Percival Bartlebooth, contains echoes of the medieval Grail quest and of Valery Larbaud's cosmopolitan alter ego A. O. Barnabooth, but both are overridden by Bartleby, the eponymous non-hero of Herman Melville's enigmatic story. Perec's character, like Melville's, inhabits a dead letter office. He surrounds himself with undeliverable messages and signs that refuse to signify. We know from Perec's autobiographical writings that he was orphaned by the war, and traumatized by the Holocaust in which his mother was a victim, but even for readers without this knowledge loss speaks plainly in *La Vie mode d'emploi*. The ingenuities of the book, its inclusiveness, and the time-travels that depart from its early evening hour, are all pitched against an encroaching sense of vacancy. This is literary invention at the last ditch and the eleventh hour.

WRITING BY WOMEN IN THE TWENTIETH CENTURY: A LONG REVOLUTION

A new form of literary history is gathering strength as we write, and gradually bringing a large population of previously neglected authors within the purview of French literature. This is the history of writing by women, and its interest lies not so much in the promotion of individual writers to canonical status as in the retrieval from near-oblivion of entire classes of literary production. Over recent centuries, for example, much of what women wrote was published anonymously, pseudonymously, or in collaboration with male writers who were content to see their own names standing alone on title-pages; much of this writing appeared in newspapers, magazines, pamphlets, and other ephemeral formats; and much was not published at all. In letters, diaries, notebooks, legal depositions, handwritten verse collections and family histories, women mobilized the power of the written word without expecting to see themselves in print. Locating, cataloguing, and analysing the material that has survived in these various categories will require a long period of scholarly labour, but the process has begun and remarkable discoveries have already been made. The contribution of women writers to the nineteenth-century theatre industry, for example, or to the Commune, or to life-writing in its many guises, has been reliably mapped and further ambitious investigations are under way.

In the late nineteenth and early twentieth centuries, a good deal of writing by women was of an entirely traditional cast. The novelist who wrote under the pen-name 'Gyp' produced industrial quantities of popular fiction and reactionary political journalism. The poet Marie

Noël published numerous collections in which a discreet Catholic sensibility was moulded to regular verse-form and to a kindly imagery drawn from the natural world. The remarkable feature of these years, however, lies in the right to sexual desire, and to its free expression, that many writers began to claim. Where Noël had occasionally figured herself as waiting, in the manner of Correggio's Io or Bernini's Saint Teresa, for an irresistible divine potency to descend upon her, other writers presented desire as an active principle and themselves as its embodiment.

The poetic narrators of Anna de Noailles, for example, veered between submissiveness and self-assertion, and in the latter mood became not just seekers after their own pleasure but representatives of the life-force itself. The British-born Renée Vivien, similarly, reclaimed lesbianism from the male writers who had so often used it for purposes of titillation, and challenged the moral disapproval behind which their fantasies had sheltered: the desire of woman for woman, in Vivien's verse, had rhythms and fulfilments that were its own, and there was no need to measure these against a set of supposed heterosexual norms. By far the most provocative of these spokeswomen for female sexuality, however, was the novelist Rachilde. Such titles as *Monsieur Vénus* and *La Marquise de Sade*, from the earliest phase of her career, already give a clue to the place that sexual role-reversal was to occupy in her fiction. Rachilde's heroines are taboo-breakers and artists in perversion. The continuing interest of her work has more to do with its transgressive scenarios, and with its militant appropriation of fantasies previously gendered male, than with the quality of her writing, which is for the most part as plain and functional as the standard-issue pornography of the time.

In the work of Colette and Marguerite Yourcenar, however, we find a much broader canvas, a blurring of conventional gender roles, and a confident belief that polymorphous personal identity is a professional requirement for writers. In *Chéri*, for example, Colette brings not just sexual candour but wit and lyricism to a tale of love between an older woman and a younger man, and maintains a complex double perspective throughout: each lover is presented both as an independent self and as a moving image refracted through the prism of the other person's feelings. Yourcenar, a generation younger than Colette, moves with similar boldness on to the terrain of the historical novel, until then explored by few women writers apart from Sand. In her masterpiece, *Mémoires d'Hadrien*, she creates an opulent voice for one of the commanding figures of Roman antiquity. Hadrian was a poet, a philosopher, a cosmopolitan traveller, and a connoisseur of Greek civilization, and in this richly imagined valedictory account of himself he speaks by turns in all these guises, to say nothing of his roles as lover and as commander-in-chief of the imperial armies. Spurred on rather than encumbered by her extensive classical learning, Yourcenar displays ambitions and handles themes that had previously been thought of as the exclusive province of male writers.

Yourcenar's literary works received a special form of public recognition in 1981, when she became the first woman to be elected to the Académie Française. She herself, in her gracious *discours de réception*, drew attention to the extreme lateness of the event and to the long history of injustice that had preceded it:

Ce moi incertain et flottant, cette entité dont j'ai contesté moi-même l'existence, et que je ne sens vraiment délimité que par les quelques ouvrages qu'il m'est arrivé d'écrire, le voici, tel qu'il est, entouré, accompagné d'une troupe invisible de femmes qui auraient dû, peut-être, recevoir beaucoup plus tôt cet honneur, au point que je suis tentée de m'effacer pour laisser passer leurs ombres.

[This uncertain floating self, this entity whose existence I have myself called into question, and that I feel is demarcated only by the handful of works that I have had occasion to write, here it is, such as it is, surrounded, accompanied by an invisible throng of women who ought, perhaps, to have received much earlier this honour, and so much so that I am tempted to absent myself to allow their shades to pass by.]

The dead weight of a centuries-long prejudice is thrown into relief by the two light, insubstantial presences that Yourcenar summons into the chamber: the uncentred writer who achieves selfhood only momentarily, in the fabrications of her pen, and the ghosts of female academicians who never were. The dynamic conservatism of an all-male institution is thus gently mocked. Where men writers have been writers above all, and therefore licensed to be plural and mobile, women writers have been frozen into their womanhood and frozen out of the club.

If the exclusionary practices of the Académie were at last being dismantled, this was not, as Yourcenar with excessive politeness suggests, because its male members had come unaided to see the error of their ways. It was in large part because feminism as a campaigning force had been reborn after the Second World War, and had initiated public debate on women's rights throughout French society.

It was in the aftermath of the Liberation, and within two years of the first French election in which women had had the vote, that Simone de Beauvoir began to write what is still the single most influential work of feminist critique to have been published in the West: *Le deuxième sexe*.

The call to another liberation sounds on every page of the book. It is a tour de force of articulate anger, a long work of polemic in which weightily amassed historical, anthropological, and scientific evidence on the condition of women is given devastating argumentative thrust. Certain aspects of the grand proposition it offers may at first seem strangely self-limiting: its philosophical underpinnings are derived from Sartre's existentialism, the main tenets of which Beauvoir summarizes at the start and revisits throughout, and it contains only glimpses of a feminist political programme. But these seeming limitations conceal real strengths. The existentialist assumption of freedom and responsibility by the situated, time-bound human subject is available on terms of strict equality to women and men alike: 'dare to be free', Beauvoir urges her female readers. And any future politics designed to promote such freedom will need to be based on detailed knowledge of the disabilities that have afflicted women over the centuries. *Le deuxième sexe* is a prolegomenon to political action, and a vigorous catalogue of its potential rewards.

Much of the power of the book derives from the tidal alternation within its argument of amplitude and epigrammatic concision. The range of the historical survey is huge, but each of its phases yields a precise point. Earth goddesses of the ancient world, for example, are first of all conflated into a single archetypal figure and then dispersed across the map:

Capricieuse, luxurieuse, cruelle comme la Nature, à la fois propice et redoutable, elle règne sur toute l'Egéide, sur la Phrygie, la Syrie, l'Anatolie, sur toute l'Asie occidentale. Elle s'appelle Ishtar à Babylone, Astarté chez les peuples sémitiques et chez les Grecs Géa, Rhéa ou Cybèle . . .

[Capricious, lascivious, as cruel as Nature, at once kindly and fearsome, she reigns over the whole of the Aegean, over Phrygia, Syria, Anatolia, over the whole of western Asia. She is called Ishtar in Babylon, Astarte among the Semitic peoples, and among the Greeks Gaia, Rhea or Cybele.]

All that female strength, accumulated or expended, finds its echo in Beauvoir's own prose performance. She hovers over ancient civilizations, measuring the force of their dominant myths in her own writing. But these great female deities are only part of a larger story, and for female emancipation they mark a colossal false dawn. The lives of ordinary women had still been ones of subordination even as myths of Woman seemed to do honour to the entire female sex: 'Terre, Mère, Déesse, elle n'était pas pour l'homme une semblable; c'est *au-delà* du règne humain que sa puissance s'affirmait' ('Earth, Mother, Goddess, she was not a counterpart to men; it was *beyond* the human sphere that her potency declared itself'). Beauvoir's demythologizing intelligence is all the more persuasive for being allied in this way to an adventurous historical imagination: the social conditions in which the myths were produced and perpetuated must be reconstructed, just as the allure of the myths themselves must be re-experienced by the modern observer, if progress towards emancipation is to be made.

A similar feat of imagination is present later in the book, when Beauvoir turns to the lives that modern women live in male-run and still largely misogynistic Western societies. In one sense, the picture is extremely bleak: women are coercively trained from their early years for marriage and motherhood, have inferior legal rights and educational opportunities, are prevented from exercising control over their own fertility, and in the quest for sexual pleasure are the hapless victims of male ignorance and incompetence. But, in another sense, freedom is already within their grasp. The broad rubrics under which much of the discussion is conducted—the adolescent, the lesbian, the married woman, the mother, and so forth—each reveal a spectrum of human possibilities rather than a single essence or an immovable destiny. Beauvoir's catalogue of misfortunes is vast and unwavering, but inside every vignette of women oppressed, dehumanized, and driven to the margins of the socio-political order, is a prophetic image of the free self-choosing to which they are entitled. There are countless return routes from the *au-delà* to which women have been consigned by male institutions, but the return cannot be made by *fiat* or by a spontaneous access of self-awareness by women as a group. It must be initiated by the individual woman acting, in the first instance, on her own behalf and from within her own concrete situation.

What the female agent is doing at such a moment, however, has a much wider significance, for she is affirming the shared humanity of men and women. Beauvoir ends her epoch-making book on the word 'fraternity', imported from the lexicon of the French Republican tradition and given a new frame of reference. Fraternity is now no longer the bond between male citizens and the implicit sign of female exclusion from citizenship and civil rights. It is the bond between men and women brought alive at last to the freedom they hold in common. *Le deuxième sexe* is a celebration of such freedom, and a complex performative utterance. Women must be free to create identities for themselves and project themselves into futures of their own choosing, and Beauvoir's inventive book illustrates its own proposal. It is a kaleidoscopic array of female life-choices, a call to action, and a tireless future-driven journey of self-realization. Although Beauvoir's career had a number of other important strands—she is, for example, a major figure both as a novelist and as an autobiographer—she was never to surpass the sustained brilliance of *Le deuxième sexe*.

The inspirational capacities of Beauvoir's book were recognized only intermittently in the decade after its publication. Modern French feminism in both its reformist and its revolutionary tendencies dated back to the 1790s, and had found expression in numerous women's societies and pressure groups throughout the intervening period. But it was not until the 1960s that either tendency made significant advances. During this period, those who sought to improve the condition of women within the male-dominated Republican order prompted major changes to the laws governing marriage and contraception, while those who thought of that order as inveterately patriarchal and discriminatory were energized by the events of May 1968 into new forms of collective action. It was in the wake of those events that the Mouvement de Libération des Femmes sprang into being, and that the act of writing began to acquire new political urgency for women.

Just as the MLF itself brought attention to bear on the specificity of women's experience, many of the writers associated with the movement proclaimed that writing by women had, or should have, specific textual characteristics. In certain cases *écriture féminine*, as it came to be called, had the primary task of dramatizing the organic life of the human female and of reconnecting the ideas and the fantasies of women to their biological substratum. Annie Leclerc in her *Parole de femme* and Chantal Chawaf in her *Blé de semences*, for example, both position themselves as speaking from within a body that has rhythms, cycles, instincts and pre-programmed chromosomal structures of its own. Their narrators are now alienated from their bodily condition, now ecstatically reabsorbed into it, but in either state the gendered body provides the horizon of expectation against which individual patterns of experience take shape. More strenuous versions of *écriture féminine* are elaborated by Hélène Cixous and Luce Irigaray, both of whom write with surging intellectual ambition. If masculinity is defined as a cult of the phallus then femininity can gather to itself an entire range of virtues. If phallocentrism gives priority to styles of behaviour—including intellectual behaviour— that are linear, goal-directed, homogenizing, and controlling, the feminine is much more than its negative counterpart. It steps forward to represent not just multiplicity, simultaneity, the network of connections inside complex systems, and the sheer unsubduable variety of human wishes, but creativity projecting itself into an open future. Cixous in her essay 'Le rire de la Méduse' and Irigaray in her *Ce sexe qui n'en est pas un* both hold back from Beauvoir's vision of fraternity between the sexes. For both of them sexual difference is a demanding political and philosophical theme, and understanding femininity has a long way to go before the complementarity of feminine and masculine, or the common humanity of both, can be decently reasserted.

The most original woman writer of the later twentieth century is unquestionably Marguerite Duras, and one striking aspect of her achievement is that she raises all the key feminist questions without being detained by them at the level of theory. The literary personality that emerges from her novels, plays, and films is perfectly willing to allow women their individuality, and to look with an unillusioned eye upon the repressive stereotypes under which they are still obliged to live, in France and around the globe, but once the allowance has been made she presses ahead to her own self-transcendence as a female subject. For many of her readers, 'Marguerite Duras', the literary pseudonym, became an emblem of memory and desire in their most intransigent forms, the locus of an extremity, the name given to the divided, death-haunted human subject seen against the broad backcloth of modernity. And Duras's fictional female characters are exemplary in the same way. Aurélia Steiner, Anne-Marie Stretter, and Lol V. Stein are all women projected beyond womanhood. They are interchangeable talismans. In each of them, an insatiable desire speaks its name.

In the later part of her very long career, Duras became a celebrity. Endlessly filmed, photographed, interviewed, and coaxed by her admirers into expansive self-commentary, she became a literary totem, and little that was new or strange entered the picture. Earlier, however, she had brought a remarkable range of themes, motifs, geographical settings, and historical perspectives into her artworks. As a writer and as a film-maker, she had traced numerous criss-crossing itineraries between East and West, and between contemporary Europe and the traumas of the Nazi period. Far from being a myth or a monument, she had been a mobile intersection-point between incommensurable worlds.

This mobility is nowhere more rigorously enforced than in *India Song*, which exists as a film, a play, and a text for silent reading. In each version the ideas of presence, immediacy, and fixity are variously under threat. The anecdotal content of the work involves a commonplace love-triangle, but the participants are seen in perpetual transit. The female protagonist, Anne-Marie Stretter, was the Venetian Anna Maria Guardi earlier in her life, and is dead and buried, in an English cemetery in India, at the time of narration. The males are European diplomats on the move between different postings in Asia. The tale unfolds in flashback; the visible characters do not speak; and the disembodied narrative voices who intone a hearsay account of the affair do so unreliably, changing small details from one repetition to the next. Western dance music is intercut with a chanted Indian lament and with the fourteenth of Beethoven's Diabelli variations. Hunger, poverty, contagious disease, and the rhythms of the sea place an implacable frame around the erotic manoeuvres of a cossetted expatriate community (see Figure 17).

Describing the work in these terms, however, makes it sound rather pedantic—as if a basic lesson on mortality, the mediatedness of desire, and the plasticity of human identity had been transposed into an overemphatic audio-visual display. But Duras is an artist rather than a pedagogue. Everything in *India Song* is, to be sure, mobile and suffused with absence, but these features of the work converge upon the spectator with terrifying tragic force. The mistakes that are present in the voiceover narration place the burden of truth upon the audience: 'ce sont ces légères ERREURS qui prouveront le mieux que SEULS les spectateurs entendent BIEN les conversations privilégiées' ('it is these slight ERRORS that are best able to demonstrate that ONLY the viewers REALLY understand the crucial conversations'). Remarks of this kind in the *India Song* screenplay point towards a general characteristic of Duras's work. She refuses mastery, exults in loss and dispossession, and expects her reader or spectator to follow in her wake. Artistic truth places all comers, writers and readers alike, in a position of extremity. They stand at the edge of the abyss, with no hand-rail or safety-net in sight, and offer themselves up to unappeasable desire. The civil disabilities of women are present in the background of such works as *Moderato cantabile*, *Nathalie Granger*, or *L'Amant*, as is their sexual exploitation by males, but desire itself, for Duras, has no gender. She is a female writer who, in a post-religious age, speaks on behalf of desiring, death-bound humankind at large. If she descends from Staël and Sand in her creative self-assertion as a woman, she descends also from Flaubert and Proust in her unwavering fidelity to the ironies and ambiguities of literary art.

THEATRE IN THE TWENTIETH CENTURY

The extraordinary dynamism of the French stage in the modern period springs from a series of charismatic theatrical personalities rather than from the dramatists who were their contemporaries. Successive generations of directors sought to purge the theatre of its commercialism, open it up to foreign plays and experimental production methods, and extend its reach beyond the capital and beyond the professional middle

17. Delphine Seyrig as Anne-Marie Stretter, with Claude Mann and Didier Flamand, in *India Song* (1974), directed by Marguerite Duras.

class. Four Paris-based directors—Louis Jouvet, Gaston Baty, Charles Dullin, and Georges Pitoëff—joined forces in the inter-war years to proclaim the independent integrity of theatrical art. In the post-war period, Jean Vilar, Roger Planchon, and Ariane Mnouchkine were all powerful democratizers. For each of them theatre belonged to the people and was a collective and collaborative enterprise; it had a responsibility to cross national and class boundaries and be alive to the key socio-political issues of the day.

No career epitomizes the artistic independence of theatre more tellingly than that of the actor-manager Jean-Louis Barrault. This prodigiously talented figure was at once a creative custodian of the classic dramas of the seventeenth and eighteenth centuries, and the sponsor of countless new dramatists. As a vocal performer and stage presence he had unique mesmeric authority, while his role as Baptiste Debureau in Marcel Carné's *Les Enfants du paradis* has given him a firm place in the national iconography of France. His vision of 'total theatre', much influenced by his friend and mentor Antonin Artaud, was widely influential and often had the effect of deflecting attention

from the powers of speech that his acting had done so much to celebrate: speech, and the dramatic text lying behind it, were to be contributors, but no more than that, to a kaleidoscope of ideas and
impressions. Theatre offered a new way of inhabiting space and time,
and of creating fresh points of tension or combustion between the
different sense-fields that each spectator brought to the auditorium.

The case of Artaud himself is especially instructive for anyone seeking to trace the shifting borders between theatre and literature in the
modern age. In the essays collected as *Le Théâtre et son double*, he sets
out a vision of theatre that seems at first to be overridingly concerned
with the materiality of stage performance. Theatre is 'cruel', in
Artaud's celebrated description, because it recreates on a small scale the
brutal play of forces that is to be observed in nature. The spectator is to
be exposed, nerve by nerve, to homeopathic doses of the inhuman
energy that will eventually kill him. This view is propounded, however, not as a detailed lesson in stagecraft but as a sequence of overlapping analogies. Theatre is a plague-attack, a torture chamber, a
shadow-play, a primitive ritual, and while the procession of these com-
parisons seems to sketch out a wordless ideal theatre, a never-never
land of dramatic possibility, it belongs at the same time to a world of
uncompromising textual invention. Artaud's writings on theatre point
their readers away from the printed book yet reassert the primacy of
the written word as they do so. For Artaud the relationship between
performance and text in the theatre needs to be undecidable to be
worth taking seriously, and his theorizing in *Le Théâtre et son double*
has the same quality of deep-lying ambiguity.

Versions of the same ambiguity are to be found elsewhere in the
history of the modern stage. In Paul Claudel's *Le Soulier de satin*, for
example, we encounter a playwright who is in one sense a simple
enthusiast for verbal texture and orotund declamation. These were
the requirements of a firmly held Catholic faith seeking public
expression; a cherished doctrine demanded to be shared with others,
even at the risk of sounding naïvely catechistical. But at the same time
Claudel was a cultural pluralist, eager to learn lessons from Eastern
theatrical traditions, from the opera stage and from the cinema. In
collaboration with Barrault, Claudel succeeded in reshaping his text
towards action and performability. *Le Soulier de satin* is a programmatic account of love between persons seen against a backcloth of
worldwide missionary activity during the Counter-Reformation.
With Barrault at his side, and the spectre of Artaud somewhere in the
distance, Claudel succeeded in creating living theatre from an
unwieldy written text.

Equally remarkable, however, in their attempts to reposition the verbal medium inside the fluid space of stage and auditorium were the proponents of what came to be known, not always helpfully, as the 'theatre of the absurd'. Although Eugène Ionesco, Jean Genet, and Samuel Beckett were often promoted as darlings of the avant-garde, their drama was in fact deeply rooted in the European past. While many playwrights in the middle years of the century—including Jean Giraudoux in *Electre*, Sartre in *Les Mouches*, and Jean Anouilh in *Antigone*—had looked back quizzically to the founding tragic plays of Greek antiquity, the absurdists rediscovered the popular traditions of farce, vaudeville, and the *théâtre de la foire*. Jarry's *Ubu roi* and Roger Vitrac's Surrealist drama *Victor ou les enfants au pouvoir* had already extracted a special form of iconoclasm from the yoking together of two disparate but each long-established theatrical styles. From the encounter between pantomime and well-made drawing-room comedy a scandalous hybrid had in each case been born. In these plays and their successors the language spoken by the characters is at once a complex instrument of expression and the target of an unremitting critique. In Ionesco's *Amédée, ou Comment s'en débarrasser*, for example, the corpse of an apparent murder victim grows across the stage as the action proceeds, while the conversation between a wife and husband competes for the audience's attention. Communicative speech and a dream-like dumb-show are irreconcilably counterposed. Similarly, in Genet's *Le Balcon*, the brothel in which the scene is set becomes a gaudy palace of varieties. The characters, in one perspective, are all talk. They are fantasists who, under the supervision of the proprietress, merely verbalize their desires for domination or bondage. In another perspective, however, Genet's elaborate stage business, with its disguises, stilt-walking, and impromptu plays within the play, is always threatening to supersede mere speech. The characters move beyond verbal self-titillation and become the monsters that their language seems to crave. In cases like these a variegated dramatic diction is challenged and driven awry by an alternative signifying system: that of pantomimic gesture arbitrarily overlaid upon the dialogue.

In the plays of Samuel Beckett this tension achieves a level of intensity that is all the more remarkable for being the product of understatement in both systems. *En attendant Godot* is a play in which meaning is always imminent but perpetually withheld. The two central characters, Vladimir and Estragon, are vaudevillians of a particularly restrained type, prose poets whose preferred language is often bare and monosyllabic. Hamm and Clov, their counterparts in *Fin de partie,* seem at first to be even more impoverished in their expressive means.

They are among the surviving remnant of an obliterated humankind:
the windows of their room give on to a featureless landscape; and the
words they speak often have about them an air of terminal discourage-
ment and regret:

> CLOV. Pourquoi cette comédie, tous les jours?
> HAMM. La routine. On ne sait jamais. (*Un temps.*) Cette nuit j'ai
> vu dans ma poitrine. Il y avait un gros bobo.
> CLOV. Tu as vu ton cœur.
> HAMM. Non, c'était vivant. (*Un temps. Avec angoisse.*) Clov!
> CLOV. Oui.
> HAMM. Qu'est-ce qui se passe?
> CLOV. Quelque chose suit son cours.
>
> [CLOV. Why this play-acting, every day?
> HAMM. Routine. You never know (*Pause.*) Last night I saw
> inside my chest. There was a big pain.
> CLOV. You saw your heart.
> HAMM. No, it was alive (*Pause. Anxiously.*) Clov!
> CLOV. Yes.
> HAMM. What is happening?
> CLOV. Something is following its course.]

The self-referentiality that was already present in *Pathelin* and the
great comic dramas of Molière, Marivaux, and Beaumarchais can
scarcely go further than this. *Fin de partie* is a familiar enough play
about players, but the performances stage-managed by Hamm and
Clov are pitched on the outer margins of the social order and at the limits of intelligibility. What is extraordinary about the play, however, is
that the effects of decor, lighting, and physical action minutely specified
in Beckett's stage directions still allow room for moments of defining
clarity in the text itself. Clov's 'Quelque chose suit son cours' rings out
as incontrovertibly as Edgar's 'Ripeness is all' in the last act of *King
Lear*, and with a similar sense that common wisdom and common language have found each other again in conditions of extremity. Clov has
rediscovered the pitiless causal process of the natural world, in which
human actors have only a momentary and inconspicuous part to play.
His lesson, like Edgar's, is one of endurance, although the 'going hence'
of which Clov speaks is subject to an indefinite delay.

   In the theatre of Beckett, spoken language is jostled, bruised, and at
times incapacitated by stage action, but nevertheless rises to points of
astonishing expressive intensity. Theatrical language has been rescued
from the twin threats of silence and babble, and has rejoined a great
European tradition of stage eloquence. It was this language, finally
freed from the coercions of stagecraft, that reappeared in *Sans* and the

other late prose texts collected as *Têtes-mortes*: 'Gris cendre ciel reflet de la terre reflet du ciel. Air gris sans temps terre ciel confondus même gris que les ruines lointains sans fin' ('Grey ash sky reflection of the earth reflection of the sky. Air grey without time earth sky confused same grey as the ruins distances without end'). In writing like this, the 'lumière grisâtre' ('greyish light') of Beckett's first stage direction in *Fin de partie* has become a cruel grey glare. Devastation had been imagined in that play of the mid-1950s; Hamm and Clov had been inhabitants of the nuclear winter. But in the later writings wintry 'lessness' or 'withoutness' have achieved their definitive form: they are the condition of all thought, the minimal background against which humanity begins to murmur itself towards being. The cross-currents that had previously animated theatrical space are now internal to the literary text. Each sentence in *Sans* invites alternative parsings and scansions. Individual words move between grammatical classes. Word-for-word repetition threatens to take hold, but modulation saves the day. While continuing to write ever more exiguous plays for the stage, Beckett here produced a profoundly moving micro-theatre of the printed page. When we add to his achievements as a dramatist and a prose poet the incomparable tragicomic inventiveness of his novel-trilogy *Molloy*, *Malone meurt*, and *L'Innommable*, Beckett can be seen as one of the supreme literary artists of the twentieth century.

POETRY IN THE LATER TWENTIETH CENTURY

As French poetry emerged from its period of clandestine public service during the German occupation, it quickly began to reassert itself as a recalcitrant and non-aligned social force. Many fine poets who had acquired a distinctive voice long before the outbreak of war—Saint-John Perse, Pierre Reverdy, and Pierre-Jean Jouve, among many others—can be seen moving in new directions in the immediate post-war period. In each case their writing had been profoundly affected by the fall of France, and now drew strength and energy from the removal of the occupiers. Poetry returned to work, but the mood was not simply one of 'business as usual'. The experience of the war, lingering as a deeply imprinted memory-trace, lent urgency and gravity to the task of the poet. From having had local themes, goals, and political allegiances, poetry became more and more explicitly an ontological project, a mode of being. The very act of writing, which until recently may have been carried out in conditions of extreme physical danger, was now presented by many poets as an inherently dangerous philosophical enterprise.

In the work of René Char, for instance, the shift between levels is clearly visible if we compare the *Feuillets d'Hypnos*, written during his service in the *maquis*, with *A une sérénité crispée*, a similar-seeming collection of poetic aphorisms written in the late 1940s. 'Un mètre d'entrailles pour mesurer nos chances' ('A yard of guts to measure our chances'), Char announces in a savage fragment from the earlier work. Later, beyond the range of bombs and bullets, he creates a bloodless scenario in which a lethal power is still astir:

Après l'ultime distorsion, nous sommes parvenus sur la crête de la connaissance. Voici la minute du *considérable danger*: l'extase devant le vide, l'extase neuve devant le vide frais.

[After the last distortion, we reached the crest of knowledge. That was the moment of danger in the extreme: ecstasy before emptiness, a brand-new ecstasy before an emptiness that was fresh.]

A faint residue of Char's native Provençal landscapes is perhaps to be caught in his 'crest', but otherwise the danger named, qualified, and italicized in these peremptory sentences belongs to any human in quest of being. Poetry has become an exemplary act of self-creation, a seizure of knowledge in the face of an ever-encroaching vacancy. Bereft of any value-system external to itself, poetry refers insistently to its own powers and procedures. Rather than look upwards to a transcendent order that would appoint the poet to his place in the world, Char and many others of his generation look across from one moment of knowledge seized or lost to others of the same kind. Their gaze moves from crest to crest in a landscape of their own making.

Among the younger poets whose first notable works were published after the war, this exalted view of poetic composition is widely shared. In the case of Yves Bonnefoy in particular it not only offers a means of engagement with the here and now but takes him on a journey of reconnaissance into the European past. Bonnefoy is a critic, an essayist, and a translator as well as a poet, and in each of these roles he acts as a curator of artistic meaning. His translations of Shakespeare and Yeats combine linguistic precision with recreative exuberance. His art criticism ranges from Byzantium through the High Renaissance to Mondrian, Balthus, and Giacometti, and his literary criticism from the *Chanson de Roland* to Paul Celan. In all cases his emphasis is less on workshop practice or artistic tradition than on the improbability of the creative moment: suddenly, surging up in the real world, a new meaning is born. For Bonnefoy the task of criticism is to model this suddenness in a diction that itself has density and takes risks. If in one sense translator and critic are rescue artists, seeking to preserve precious objects from neglect and ruin, in another sense they are the impetuous shapers of a new future and always likely to give priority to their own verbal act.

Tensions of this kind have a major organizing role in Bonnefoy's verse. There, the personal past and the long vistas of cultural memory are often aligned:

A San Francesco, le soir

... Ainsi le sol était de marbre dans la salle
Obscure, où te mena l'inguérissable espoir.
On eût dit d'une eau calme où de doubles lumières
Portaient au loin les voix des cierges et du soir.

Et pourtant nul vaisseau n'y demandait rivage,
Nul pas n'y troublait plus la quiétude de l'eau.
Ainsi, te dis-je, ainsi de nos autres mirages,
O fastes dans nos cœurs, ô durables flambeaux!

[San Francesco in the evening | ... And so the floor was marble in the dark | Room to which incurable hope had led you. | It might have been calm water where reflected | Lights carried the sounds of candles and evening away. | And yet no ship sought harbour there. No footstep | Troubled the water's stillness any more. | And so it is, I tell you, with our own mirages, | Heart's fun and games, eternal lights!]

In this poem from *Hier régnant désert*, no secure indication of place is given, although we may assume that the Basilica at Assisi, the most celebrated of all the churches dedicated to Saint Francis, is present at least as a memory. Absence, however, is always woven into presence in Bonnefoy's poetry, and losing into having. By way of the stately pun on which the poem turns, the sensation of loss is reinforced: *vaisseau* is at once the nave of a church and a sea-going craft, but neither is here. The superstructure of the building has dissolved into darkness, and the phantom ship that might have replaced it has failed to appear. The marble floor has become a watery expanse on which no foot, human or divine, now walks. Yet for all its references to a vanished Christianity this is a poem not of religious nostalgia but of secular hope. The basilica missing from its own site provides the act of poetry with a setting and a stimulus that are appropriate to it. In all that darkness a this-worldly poetic flame burns brightly and at length.

Although Bonnefoy gives his ontological dramas an air of historical pageantry in poems like this, and in his essays on Italian painting, these dramas are compelling even when dignified cultural reference-points are missing. There is something about the way that personal memory works, and about the variable contours of the speaking voice,

that brings the dialectic of absence and presence into even the most
ordinary of human occasions. And this 'something', for Bonnefoy, is
language. In a philosophical reflection sustained over many decades,
and flowing back and forth between his verse and his prose, he
returns tirelessly to a series of paradoxes on the linguistic envelope
inside which human affairs are conducted. Language gives and takes
away; offers the individual a chance to burrow deep into the textures
of his own experience yet constantly levitates towards a useless universality; allows death to be provisionally mastered yet brings a foretaste of death to the turn of every syllable. For the poet at work, his
chosen medium is, therefore, by turns problem and solution, nightmare and beatitude. The challenge he faces is that of re-entering the
real, re-absorbing himself into it, at the very moment when language
seems to want to move him in the opposite direction. Poetry has the
task of recreating 'le frôlement d'aile de l'existence dans les mots
voués à l'universel' ('the brushing wing-beat of existence inside words
that are destined for universality').

Bonnefoy's poetry of being is threatened and energized, then, by two
kinds of unreality. The first is that of over-investment in the past: the
poet who strives to rebuild San Francesco in words, or noisily celebrates his own acts of memory, may lose his poem in the process. The
second is that of language as it shelves away towards abstractions,
Platonic Ideas, or the first cause: poets should know better than to keep
such company. Bonnefoy is aided in his return to the real by the lesson
of the Surrealists, and in particular by their cult of the poetic image.
Writing in the afterglow of Surrealism, Bonnefoy looks to the image as
a realizing rather than a derealizing force. It brings antithetical states
and incompatible objects together in an unstable intermediate space.
Where Breton had spoken of a supreme point at which contraries
would be reconciled, Bonnefoy speaks of the disruptive coexistence of
those contraries as the very sign that the world has become real again
and that Being has found a place inside it.

Poets of this generation are unembarrassed in their talk of Being,
and happy to run the risk of sounding grandiloquent. Saint-John
Perse spoke for them all in 1960, when, accepting the Nobel prize for
Literature on behalf of poetry itself, he summoned up a language
'où se transmet le mouvement même de l'Être' ('in which the very
motion of Being is transmitted'). Looked at in one way, such a view of
literature could scarcely be more different from the views of the mid-
century experimental novelists who spoke with equal grandeur of the
signifier at play and of the inveterate self-referentiality of any text
worthy of the name. Where the poets seemed to plunge through

language to some wordless existential bedrock, the novelists and their theoretical supporters were trapped in a web of verbal signs, and professed themselves pleased with their condition. Upholders of both views had, however, a common ancestor in the person of Mallarmé. Poets and novelists were alike in thinking of literature as a supreme source of value. Over and against the continuous flow of commodities under capitalism, literature was *le Livre* and could not be traded. It could face down the daily death-fears of the individual and the risk of nuclear apocalypse, for fear and risk were immanent in its creative project. In the end it matters rather little that certain defenders of literature placed their main emphasis on being and its vagaries while others placed theirs on language and its vicissitudes, for both groups brought to literature a readiness to believe, and an incurable hope, at a time when all other belief-systems seemed already to have failed.

BEYOND THE HEXAGON

According to one familiar story, the French language, having been consolidated and codified inside the borders of mainland France, simply emanated outwards as the vehicle of international diplomacy and intellectual debate. Much praised for its elegance, economy, and clarity, and seen as the natural successor of classical Latin when it came to the orderly unfolding of rational argument, French conducted a civilizing mission around the world and fostered enlightened human exchange wherever it went. When the Englishman William Beckford wrote his Arabian tale *Vathek* in French, and when Tolstoy began his *War and Peace* with the words, 'Eh bien, mon prince', they were paying tribute to a language that at all border-crossings had nothing but its genius to declare.

Such a story has a number of serious shortcomings. The specificity of Swiss and Belgian writing in French is absent from it; it says nothing about the ruthlessness with which French was implanted in remote non-European cultures during the years of colonial expansion; and above all it has no place in it for cultural influences converging on metropolitan France from elsewhere. When France is thought of as a receiver rather than a transmitter of such influence its language begins to seem much less stable and homogeneous, and its literature to have a powerful appetite for other civilizations from around the world. Edgar Allan Poe and Walt Whitman, for example, each had a decisive role in the development of modern French poetry, just as Hollywood and the American detective story have left their imprint on much modern fiction. Translation has brought many other literatures into the French mainstream. And when the birthplaces of certain major writers are flagged upon the globe a decidedly non-hexagonal cultural geography begins to emerge. Charles-Marie Leconte de Lisle, for example, the founder of 'Parnassian' poetry in the middle years of the nineteenth century, was born on the Île Bourbon, now Réunion, and his main disciple José-Maria de Heredia was born in Cuba. The poets Lautréamont, Laforgue, and Supervielle were all natives of Montevideo in Uruguay. Tristan Tzara, Eugène Ionesco, and Emil Cioran were born in Romania and wrote their earliest works in Romanian. From Russia came Alexandre Kojève and Nathalie Sarraute; from Lithuania Emmanuel Levinas; from Spain the playwright Fernando Arrabal, the film-maker Luis Buñuel, and Picasso, whose multifarious artistic career included memorable poetic composition in French.

This list could be greatly extended, but even in its short form serves to bring one of the abiding paradoxes of modern French literature into focus. While successive French governments, from Napoleonic times, have sought to impose a legislated uniformity on the national language and the state educational system, Paris has acted as a magnet to exiled artists and writers from elsewhere. While ministers and academicians have encouraged normality in matters of literary expression, and been supported in this endeavour by countless normalizing writers, explosive pressures have built up inside modern literature. The situation is now changing rapidly, as an etiolated English becomes ever more firmly entrenched as the language of international relations and globalized trade. But for much of the twentieth century the cultural prestige of French was unassailable, and based on two seemingly quite disparate features: it was both the international language of rational exchange and the *lingua franca* of artistic revolt.

By far the most complex set of relations between metropolitan France and the wider world beyond Europe are those produced by colonization. This occurred in two waves, widely separated in time: the first took French explorers, traders, and settlers to North America and to the Caribbean in the late sixteenth and early seventeenth centuries, while the second, beginning with the acquisition of Algeria during the July Monarchy, eventually gave France control over vast territories in West and Central Africa, in the Middle East and in Indochina.

The literature of these territories is complex both historically and linguistically, and its principal lines of development are not synchronized with those governing the literature of metropolitan France.

While much French writing produced in Quebec, for example, remained profoundly conservative in tone and outlook until well into the twentieth century, its equivalents in the Caribbean and Africa often prophesied the end of colonial rule and had an atmosphere of insurgency barely held in check. Francophone literature at the present time still has its own range of temporal rhythms, and the gradual process of decolonization begun after the Second World War has had widely different cultural effects from one country to the next. From the point of view of the French language itself there has been two-way enrichment. The written language of the former colonies has been hybridized, lexically and syntactically, with a variety of indigenous languages and this enlarged and revitalized French, when reimported into France, has had numerous creative repercussions. The plasticity, inventiveness, and assimilative power of the national language, already so forcibly proclaimed by domestic literary avant-gardes, has also been reported as news from abroad, and from places as far apart as Martinique, Algeria, and New Caledonia.

Relations between the various literatures now written in French are not simply ones of cooperation and positive reinforcement. Major political differences exist inside *la francophonie*, as do rival writers' organizations and incompatible linguistic ideologies. Strong opposition to the promotion of French as a world language has come from certain former colonies, including Algeria, and the continued production there of literary works in French has often been seen as an insidious form of neo-colonialism. External relations between the international francophone community and its English- and Spanish-speaking neighbours are themselves often troubled, and can create discord even among the most loyal adherents of French as a medium of cross-cultural exchange.

When it comes to the artistic activity of francophone writers, however, the exploitation of cultural difference and political tension has had a fertilizing role. Works as different as *Pluie et vent sur Télumée Miracle* by the Guadeloupean novelist Simone Schwarz-Bart and *La Nuit sacrée* by the Moroccan poet and novelist Tahar Ben Jelloun are alike in the boldness with which they install themselves in their respective intermediate worlds. Antillean folk-narratives in the one case and the syntax and imagery of Arabic poetry in the other are present as a magnetic field in which the normative authority of literary French is subtly called into question. There is nothing programmatic or doctrinaire about works of this kind. They speak of domination and injustice, but they do so in a French that has become again a vehicle for the inclusion and integration of human differences, whether ethnic, social, or linguistic. The emancipatory project of each writer bursts forth in the hybridity and kinetic energy of his or her prose. The language of the colonist has been reclaimed and reinvented by members of the once-colonized community.

This creative estrangement of the French language from its Latin origins has a long history in francophone writing of the twentieth century, and one work above all has come to emblematize the resulting tensions. This is Aimé Césaire's long poem, *Cahier d'un retour au pays natal*. With Léon Damas from French Guiana and Léopold Sedar Senghor from Senegal, Césaire was the instigator of the international *négritude* movement in the 1930s, and the *Cahier* is in a sense its promulgation. At the simplest level it belongs to the genre of 'home thoughts from abroad' and traces an imaginary pathway back to Martinique from the narrator's European exile. Reference is made to the flora and fauna of the island, to its local customs, and to its population at once chattering and mute ('bavarde et muette'). Such imagery, galvanized by Césaire's contact with Surrealism, seems at moments to be turning Martinique into a utopia for modern poets.

Against this affirmative strain in the poem, however, Césaire sets the corrosive memory of slavery. Blacks are not only the victims of their white overlords but, during a long history of enslavement, have come to internalize as a cruel self-destructiveness the hostility of the oppressor:

> l'odeur-du-nègre, ça-fait-pousser-la-canne
> rappelez-vous-le-vieux-dicton:
> battre-un-nègre, c'est le nourrir

[nigger-smell that's-what-makes-cane-grow | remember-the-old-saying: | beat a nigger, and you feed him]

The poet-narrator at such moments becomes a ventriloquist of white attitudes, reviewing with grim relish a parade of familiar stereotypes. His voice contains many voices. Taking advantage of the multiple influences that have shaped Caribbean culture, and the rich linguistic amalgam that is Martinican creole, Césaire turns his poem into an epic display of diversity and difference. The return announced in his title brings him back not to a stable homeland but to a captivating sense of potentiality:

> voici galoper le lambi jusqu'à l'indécision des mornes

[see the conch gallop up to the uncertainty of the morne]

A *lambi* is a large whorled conch shell, and the *mornes* are the hillocks on which shanty settlements were often built. A place of poverty has been enriched; a place of social stagnation has discovered the possibility of speed. But the transforming power of poetic imagination is exercised, in this poem of the mid-1930s, not just on the detail of a remembered Antillean landscape, but on the contemporary European scene, where new persecutions are already under way. Césaire reaches out to mute and oppressed peoples other than his own, and creates a poetic language in which the act of returning is simultaneously a forward movement into a freer future.

A comparably provocative account of exile and return is to be found in Antonine Maillet's *Pélagie-la-Charrette*, which won the Prix Goncourt in 1979. Maillet has become the leading spokesperson for the Acadians, the French native speakers of New Brunswick, Nova Scotia, and Prince Edward Island. These people had been expelled from their lands by the British in 1755, and Maillet's novel tells of their return, at the end of the eighteenth century, from exile in the Carolinas. In her determination and generosity, the eponymous heroine resembles Brecht's Mother Courage and Ma Joad in Steinbeck's *The Grapes of Wrath*. But what makes the work extraordinary is the air of linguistic festivity that surrounds the characters on their long, tempestuous journey home. Narrating the return of a scattered people is at the same time an ingathering of speech-patterns, verb-forms, and specialized terms belonging to a threatened dialect: 'Et les charretons s'en furent aux quatre horizons de la terre de l'ancienne Acadie, poussés par les vents du sud, du suète, du suroît, du noroît, du nordet . . .' ('And the carters had got to the four horizons of the land that had once been Acadia, driven by winds from the south, the sou'east, the sou'west, the nor'west, the nor'east'). The land and the local language of compass-points in which the land is surveyed are brought together by Maillet's narrator in a single act of repossession. The novel is populated with low-life characters who scrape a living from the inhospitable territories they traverse. Their conditions of life may be bare, but the language they speak and the stories they tell are an object-lesson in spontaneous creativity at ground level. Their banter and bravado, their taste for the comical and the grotesque, prove to be contagious: the narrative voice is charmed by the verbal animation of each scene it reports and develops its own Rabelaisian inventiveness and dithyrambic pulse.

Works like those of Césaire and Maillet—and many others of the same kind are to be found in the francophone world outside France—provide a lively critique of the much-vaunted universalism of the French language. In them, standard French is challenged by its own offspring, pluralized, reminded of its own past, and brought into fertile contact with dialects and languages other than itself. At a time when the spirit of Vaugelas and correct usage often seemed to reign even over the works of self-proclaimed avant-gardists in mainland France, francophone writers offered a salutary display of bad manners. They broke the rules; mixed styles; jumped between registers. And while they devoted much particularizing attention to non-standard forms of expression, they nevertheless kept a range of compelling general meanings in their sights. Césaire's Martinique and Maillet's Acadia belong as securely to everyman and everywoman as Balzac's Paris or Dickens's London.

BEYOND THE LITERARY PROFESSION

While we expect professional writers to provide us with a cumulative *défense et illustration* of French literature, and to redefine literature itself by their individual powers of performance, our perspective would be narrow indeed if we confined our attention to this group alone. Much of the most inventive writing produced in France in the twentieth century in fact comes from verbal practitioners whose primary employment lies outside the institutions of literature.

The philosopher Henri Bergson, the mathematician Henri Poincaré and the art historian Henri Focillon are instructive in this regard, and the three have more than a regal forename in common. In such works as *L'Évolution créatrice*, *La Science et l'Hypothèse*, and *Vie des formes* the encounter between the language of literature and the technical lexicon of a major learned discipline is complex and provocative. At first sight, the intellectual traffic seems to be moving in one direction only. Bergson, for example, hybridizes a semi-popular view of Darwinism with his own philosophy of human time and decks out the new conceptual product with literary metaphors that the reading public can be expected to handle with ease. This is evolutionary theory not merely made colourful at the textual level, but given characters and plot. Literature is being enlarged to accommodate the latest scientific and philosophical ideas, and enriched in the process. What is more remarkable about such works, however, is the extent to which they call on devices of rhetoric to vindicate their main propositions. Poincaré's account of creative intuition in the formation of scientific hypotheses, and Focillon's vision of prototypical formal structures migrating across the centuries, are at once argued out in concepts and, in writing of great brilliance, *performed*. The traffic in fact flows in both directions between literature and the 'other' discipline. In each case the author concerned takes us, by way of his writerly display, into his innermost intellectual workshop. The sensation, as unmistakable here as in

Proust or Valéry, is that of witnessing the act of creative thinking as it takes place.

Bergson was awarded the Nobel prize for literature in 1927, and it is not difficult to understand why: literature, in the enlarged sense we have given it from time to time, was his natural habitat. More surprisingly, perhaps, it became the adoptive home of François Jacob and Jacques Monod, who, with André Lwoff, shared the Nobel prize for Physiology and Medicine in 1965. Five years after the award was made, Jacob published *La Logique du vivant* and Monod *Le Hasard et la nécessité*, both of them works of high eloquence and intellectual audacity. Where Monod's book is a review of recent findings in molecular biology and a plea for an 'ethics of knowledge' in natural science, Jacob's is a history of biological thought from the origins to the present, and has the notion of heredity as its multiform protagonist. Who needs the historical novel, one could be forgiven for asking, when a work such as Jacob's is so grand in its chronological reach, so well plotted, so richly stocked with memorable characters and amusing *péripéties*?

Among many other examples of literary imagination flourishing outside the familiar generic confines of 'art' literature, mention should be made of the psychoanalyst Jacques Lacan and the intellectual historian Michel Foucault. Lacan's collected papers, published as *Écrits* in 1966, are as remarkable for their puns, conceits, exacerbated ironies, and fragmentary prose poems as for the cogency of their philosophical propositions. In *Les Mots et les Choses*, published in the same year, Foucault perfected a different form of abstract prose poetry, organized in periodic sentences of great rhythmic variety. It is important of course for the professions of psychoanalysis or intellectual history to cast a sceptical eye on the poetic prowess of such writers, and ask to what extent the success enjoyed by their theories depends on the singularity of their style. Non-professionals will feel entitled to be much more relaxed and may assent to such works as they assent to the fantasticated erudition of Borges, Nabokov, or Calvino. The theorist will be valued by these readers as the contriver of possible worlds, and not expected to pass routine empirical tests. One intellectual discipline, however, has contributed decisively to French literature without raising awkward questions of professional accountability. This is ethnography, and its main contribution has been to the art of the autobiographer.

When the social anthropologist Claude Lévi-Strauss wrote his *Tristes Tropiques* in the mid-1950s, he combined a personal memoir with an ethnographic report on the Indians of the Amazon rainforest. But far from jump-cutting between private and public forms of knowledge, Lévi-Strauss fuses both elements into an elaborate aria of lamentation. He begins by saying that he hates expeditions, and ends by seeking respite from his tiresome fellow humans. In between, the catalogue of their follies, delusions, and self-inflicted miseries has been immense, and incriminating material has been gathered with lofty fair-mindedness from Western and indigenous societies alike. This is autobiography with a slant, borne along on a tide of declamation.

Even more remarkable are the four autobiographical volumes of *La Règle du jeu*, by the ethnographer and museum employee Michel Leiris. Leiris had been a poet and prose writer from an early age, but such activities did not pay his rent. The titles of the individual parts that he composed over thirty-five years—*Biffures, Fourbis, Fibrilles,* and *Frêle bruit*—whisper to each other anagrammatically and speak of fragile or scattered meaning. The whole work is the epic tale of a life spent inside language. Its main episodes range from a childhood mishearing of a phrase from Massenet's *Manon* to a trance-like absorption in the slogans of May 1968. When Manon sings 'Adieu, notre petite table', or when a student rebel paints 'LA VIE VITE' on a wall in the rue Mazet, Leiris stands by as a compulsive glossator. Delectable new worlds are coming into being as language plays its tricks. Sing the mute 'e' in *petite table*, as Manon must, and an unwonted object, a *tetable*, springs into being; introduce a line-break after 'La Vie' and *vite* becomes an adjective, a verb, and an interjection as well as an adverb, and in so doing is transformed into the Open Sesame of the modern age.

The narrative architecture of *La Règle du jeu* is most unusual, in that these cherished moments of semantic intensity are held together not as a developing linear series but as a simultaneous cluster or network. All life-events for Leiris are language-events, nodal points from which meanings radiate outwards. Assembling such events into a book is a matter of allowing each to echo the others, and the whole population of them to become self-regulating. Still more unusual, however, is the Leiris prose style. Early in *Biffures*, for example, the game played between words and music in songs is described in these terms:

Un jeu qui se produit entre l'air et les paroles et tel que celui-là, s'immisçant dans celles-ci, tantôt leur paraît adéquat—apte miraculeusement à en affûter le sens—tantôt mène sa propre partie et ne se mêle à elles que pour en embrouiller le fil ou pour amalgamer en énigmes insolubles rythme, contenu sonore, valeur significative des mots et mélodie.

[A game that occurs between the tune and the words and in such a way that the latter, mingling itself into the former, now seems appropriate to them— miraculously able to sharpen their sense—now goes its own way and involves itself with them only in order to tangle their thread or to amalgamate into insoluble riddles the rhythm, the sound content, the semantic value of words and the melody.]

The suspensions and embeddings of Leiris's syntax recreate for the patient reader the flicker between signifying systems that his text describes. Listening to songs, submitting to the variable pressure of words and melody, produces scansional activity in the hearer, as does highly wrought syntax in readers. Such listening and such reading are akin not simply because they call for many-levelled states of attention but because they allow surprising elucidations to occur against the background of a largely undifferentiated semantic mass. But patience and readiness to ruminate are essential. There is no quick fix.

La Règle du jeu is one of the astonishing books of the twentieth century. That it was written by someone whose main career path lay outside the profession of letters is certainly of interest, especially as it suggests that being a writer, even a part-timer, conferred considerable cultural prestige. Of greater interest, however, is the condition of the literary language that such visitors as Lévi-Strauss and Leiris reveal. By the middle years of the century it was no longer simply a flexible instrument for the expression of ideas and opinions and available to all educated citizens whatever their calling. It was a research laboratory, a philological treasure-house, a repertory of stylistic opportunities. Visitors to it were welcome not as guests bound by the laws of hospitality but as active participants in its experimental programme. The language of literature was driven by a thirst for innovation, and all comers could try their hand at making it new.

THE REVOLUTION REMEMBERED

When France came to celebrate the bicentenary of the French Revolution in 1989 it did so on an appropriately grand scale. Under the presidency of François Mitterrand the momentous events of 1789 were commemorated not simply in oratory and ceremonial but in steel, stone, glass, and reinforced concrete. The openings of the Louvre pyramid, the Opéra-Bastille and the Arche de la Défense were events in their own right, and have left their momentous imprint on the cityscape of Paris. Here was a nation proud enough of its Republican traditions and confident enough of its standing as a world power not to be flustered by these presidential projects. They were at once majestic and amusing, and Mitterrand's personal quest for glory could easily be thought of, as de Gaulle's had been, as a triumph of public-spiritedness: his will was the nation's will concentrated into a single personality. If

France in 1989 paused to replenish its national self-esteem, this was surely no more than it deserved at a time when unquiet memories of the German occupation and the Algerian war still persisted, and when the 'meaning' of the May events in 1968 was still being anxiously sought.

It would no doubt be gratifying to report that writers as well as politicians and planners produced bicentennial *grands projets*, or at least allowed themselves to be amused by the secular cathedrals that were springing up around them. But writers in modern France, as we have already had occasion to note, are a refractory group, and likely to be hostile to social order and its expensive urban emblems. Those who rose to prominence during Mitterrand's presidency, although not lacking in artistic ambition, displayed little interest in enlargements of literary scale or scope. Many of them were quietly making sense of earlier formal innovations, while others were putting literature to work in the service of 'identity politics', as it has come to be known in the United States. The 1980s and 1990s produced no new Balzac, Zola, or Proust. Sartre, like Voltaire, was now dead, and his legacy as a public intellectual was undergoing a long period of decline.

Prose writers made their way back to a variety of topics that had been almost unmentionable during the ascendancy of the new novel and of Structuralist theory. Where novels had previously been thought of as an interplay of signs, or as a textual process, or as adventures in writing, they were now allowed to tell stories again. Where the human subject had previously been a theoretical construct, characterizable above all by reference to its emptiness and mobility, it now became a personality again. In novels and in autobiographical writings the subject was reborn as an organism, a family member, and an actor on the social stage. 'Character' was rediscovered, together with childhood, ageing, and death.

Looked at in one perspective, the final decades of the twentieth century saw the birth of a broadly optimistic and assertive new literature in prose. Storytelling acquired self-conscious swagger and verve in the novels of Daniel Pennac and Jean Echenoz. And life-writing, whether in the form of conventional autobiography or in that of the hybrid genre termed *autofiction* by the critic and novelist Serge Doubrovsky, began to enjoy enormous popular and critical acclaim. The high reputation of Annie Ernaux, for example, rests in considerable part on *La Place* and *Une Femme*, in which her working-class roots, and each of her parents in turn, are elaborately portrayed. Hervé Guibert, in his *A l'ami qui ne m'a pas sauvé la vie*, created one of the most extraordinary works of personal testimony to have emerged from the AIDS crisis.

Guibert, tracing the remorseless encroachments of the disease in his own body, spoke for an entire generation of sufferers. His literary talent had emerged precociously in his early twenties, and, by the time the AIDS diagnosis was confirmed, was fully equipped to meet the challenge of an exorbitant event. Such was the prestige of autobiographical writing by the early 1990s that even Louis Althusser, for so long the impersonal critic of suprapersonal Ideological State Apparatuses, was revealed in his posthumously published *L'Avenir dure longtemps* to have had not just a personal life but a tragic destiny.

Precisely this new emphasis on the first-hand experience of individuals throws into relief, however, one of the limitations of French literary culture in the closing years of the twentieth century. In an alternative perspective, the balance of power can be seen to have shifted decisively from literature to film. When it came to questions of collective responsibility and guilt, the cinema was the privileged instrument of national self-awareness.

Much of the prehistory of cinema belongs to France, being centred on the technical inventions of Louis Lumière and Georges Méliès. It was in the France of the 1920s that an intricate nexus of relations between literature, theatre, and film began to be established: one has only to remember Artaud's performance as Marat in Abel Gance's *Napoléon* to be reminded of just how intricate it sometimes was. And it was in France too that cinema launched one of its most fruitful encounters with the literary canon. In *Les Misérables* as directed by Raymond Bernard, or in Jean Renoir's *Madame Bovary* and *La Bête humaine*, nineteenth-century literature not only reached out to a large popular audience of non-readers but provided devotees of the novels concerned with what amounted to radical critical reinterpretations. This tradition of creative adaptation has continued, by way of Gérard Philippe's successive incarnations of Fabrice del Dongo, Julien Sorel, and Laclos's Valmont, to such remarkable recent films as Jean-Paul Rappenau's *Cyrano de Bergerac* and Raúl Ruiz's *Le Temps retrouvé*. Certain of these works have been so successful in their own terms that it has been possible for large sections of the public to treat the original written text as a mere rough draft, as the unlovely chrysalis from which a fine creature eventually emerges to spread its filmy wings.

In parallel with this symbiosis between film and prose fiction, however, another development was taking place. French cinema was gradually becoming conscious of powers that were its own and at a far remove from the conventions of the printed page. The language of film as handled, say, by Jean Vigo in *Zéro de conduite* or *L'Atalante* had its own grammar and syntax, and it was the rediscovery of these, many years later, by François Truffaut, Jean-Luc Godard, and others that gave the work of the *nouvelle vague* directors its distinctive complexity.

The great film-makers had never been novelists or playwrights in disguise. It was Marcel Carné's understanding of the specificity of the film medium that allowed him to create in *Quai des brumes* and *Le jour se lève* works that are more acutely observed as portraits of French society in the anguished aftermath of the Popular Front than any novels of the period. When we turn our attention to the much longer and still more troubled aftermath of the Second World War, the cinema has again played an essential role, and in ways that literature has for the most part avoided. Louis Malle's *Lacombe Lucien*, for example, explores the mental world of a young wartime collaborator with the Gestapo. And in a sequence of profoundly disturbing documentaries produced in France the destruction of the European Jews became a matter of public record and remembrance. Alain Resnais's *Nuit et brouillard*, Marcel Ophüls's *Le Chagrin et la pitié*, and Claude Lanzmann's *Shoah* all spoke of unspeakable deeds and complicities at a time when literature in prose or verse was still largely silent on the Holocaust. More recently, it is to film rather than to fiction that we are again obliged to turn if we are seeking to understand such complicated social facts as urban poverty, disaffected youth, and tension between ethnic groups. Mathieu Kassovitz's *La Haine* springs to life unrepentantly as film and has few debts either to literature or to social science. Armed with ample tolerance and a hand-held camera, Kassovitz takes the spectator into the closed-off world of the suburban housing development and offers a highly inflected portrait of life as it is lived there. If Zola had been alive today, he is likely to have been a film-maker in this mould rather than a novelist.

It would be wrong to suggest that French literature as a whole has been in retreat in the later years of the Fifth Republic. Across the genres the scene among new writers is animated, and commanding figures from two earlier generations have continued to astonish the reading public work by work. Michel Tournier is the non-aligned writer par excellence: an unashamed high stylist pitting himself against the neutral tones of the new novel, an enthusiast for German metaphysics rather than for the manifold legacies of Saussurean linguistics, a bold imaginer of dissident sexual scenes who rises up against the abstract talk of transgression to which so many of his contemporaries have had recourse. From his first novel *Vendredi ou les limbes du Pacifique* through to *Gaspard, Melchior, Balthasar* and *La Goutte d'or*, Tournier has resisted being stereotyped and writing to a formula. Each work is a free-standing fictional world. Each is lucid in its design and execution, but extravagant in its content.

Within what seems at first to be a self-limiting form of lesbian separatism, Monique Wittig (d. 2003) had a similarly polymorphous and anti-formulaic cast of mind. The witty utopian fantasy of *Les Guérillères* was followed by *Le Corps lesbien*, a violent prose-poetic hymn to the female body, and by *Virgile, non*, which rewrites Dante's *Divine Comedy* as a specifically female trajectory from torment to bliss. Meanwhile in Quebec, the dramatic and novelistic gifts of Michel Tremblay are continuing to find expression in a stream of new publications. Tremblay's first play was *Les Belles-Sœurs*, and from that point onwards he has not only been a bold inventor of dramatic forms but has raised *joual*, the domestic spoken French of Montreal, to an unprecedented level of artistic integrity. This form of popular speech has been derided by some Canadian commentators, but Tremblay cherishes its looseness, its dubious grammaticality, and its ability to absorb and transform words from a variety of seemingly incompatible sources. In his literary work as a whole Tremblay's ear for popular speech, together with the attention he pays to the marginal and the dispossessed in Canadian society, has given him a central cultural authority. For him literature is more plainly a form of social action than for any of his contemporaries in France.

A FINAL NOTE, IN WHICH THE STORY DOES NOT END

The situation of French literature at the beginning of the twenty-first century is therefore one of relatively subdued and dispersed activity. Other cultural practices vie with it for the attention of the public. It contains few dominant personalities. Its energies are expended across many different countries and many different kinds of writing. The authors of today, unlike their counterparts a hundred years ago, seldom think of themselves as the heralds of a new age. Yet the understated mood of the present moment throws into relief certain of the grand continuities that marked this literature from the French Revolution to the death of Sartre in 1980.

Notable among these continuities are the experimentalism to which we have referred on numerous occasions, and the intense concentration of otherwise dissimilar individual authors on questions of language. If the Revolution created a language of nationhood and citizenship, it brought into being at the same time a vehicle for protest against the national institutions and the continuing inequalities of a male-dominated class society. When Hugo wrote his celebrated

'Réponse à un acte d'accusation' he paid tribute to the post-Revolutionary French language as a guarantor of civil liberties, and as a detection device for infringements of them. French had become both the crucible of democracy, and the testing ground for all possible improvements to it.

Countless other writers, as they brought their manipulations of the linguistic medium into the foreground of their works, began to think of literary experiment as having at least an implied political force. When Mallarmé or Proust places a singular new pressure on conventional French syntax, when Queneau invents his *néo-français*, or when Leiris pores over the semantic virtualities of an isolated word, they are all self-consciously changing the way the world looks by altering the internal dispositions of their native tongue. It is scarcely surprising, in a literary tradition like this, that Sartre should have spent so much of his later career trying to understand the efficacy of Flaubert's style, or that Lacan should have taken his distance from Freud by proclaiming an unconscious mind 'structured like a language'.

If French literature of the last two hundred years has the character of a long collaborative linguistic experiment, in which possible worlds, new futures, are summoned up by a newly turned sentence or phrase, it derives from this character both advantages and disadvantages. Among the latter is a sometimes excessive level of what ornithologists studying birdsong know as 'recognition signalling': authors call to each other across literary space, staking out their territorial claims by reference to their near neighbours in the tradition or in the contemporary scene, affirming their membership of this or that species of verbal practitioner. They allude to each other, quote each other, correct, revise, expound, and annotate each other. Literature can become wearisome in its obsessional self-regard. The advantages, however, are striking. Modern French literature, thoroughly ironic and self-aware, hugely freighted with ambiguity, has come to possess, for its admirers in Europe and around the world, an extraordinary symbolic value: it is literature in the purest state available. Those who have an inkling that such a thing as 'absolute literature' might exist could not do better than begin their quest for it in France.

POSTFACE

History has no conclusions, only continuing strands of stories in the making, and literary history is no exception. On the one hand, aesthetic and cultural preferences have finite time-spans and the contours of a whole literary landscape may change from one generation to another, let alone in the course of centuries. On the other, forms, styles, themes, and movements can be remarkably tenacious: poets still write sonnets, dramatists produce plays that recognizably belong to a tradition of European theatre that has lasted for two and a half thousand years, and the much-heralded 'death of the novel' remains a largely abstract concept. Even literary fashions, quintessentially ephemeral, have their afterlives.

Likewise, the stories one can tell about literature are both durable and shifting. Villon and Voltaire, Flaubert and Sartre, remain key players in the history of French literature and are likely to hold their place for a long time to come; yet their status, the roles they play, have been transformed by new readings of their works and of the historical continuum from which those works emerged. Thus, fifty years ago, this short history would not have seemed wholly alien to its readers, but it would also have surprised them. Amid much that was familiar, there would have been for them a constant pulse of strangeness, with many unexpected additions and omissions and some wayward if not outlandish interpretations. In another fifty years, perhaps even in ten, its patterns of foreground and background, of light and shade, are likely to look equally alien or idiosyncratic. The provisional character of a literary history is, however, one of its fascinations, akin in this respect to literature itself with its shifting, chameleon-like textures and images of the world.

We announced in our Preface that our narrative would be resolutely selective, and our treatment of individual periods has indeed highlighted some authors or movements to the detriment of others. At the same time, however, we have cast our net unusually wide, and included many texts that are known today only to a relatively specialist readership. This is because we are convinced that the French literary tradition is remarkable not only for the quality of the major works it encompasses but for the continuity with which such works have been produced over a span of eight centuries and more. For the same reason, we have accorded more space to the earlier periods than other recent literary histories. Although there may be disagreement as to which works are major and which not—the 'canon' is always open to renegotiation—there is no shortage of inspiring works to take over the place of any temporarily demoted from canonical status. In Europe, only English literature displays comparable riches on this sort of time-scale. Even when French has become a language that no one speaks any longer (say in five hundred or a thousand years), it is likely that the great wealth and abundance of its literary artefacts will continue to be decrypted by scholars, if human civilization survives at all, and re-presented in forms that the public of that time, despite its unimaginably different culture, will be able to appreciate, as we appreciate the tragedies of Sophocles or the poetry of Virgil.

One of the defining characteristics of the literary, according to a powerful current of twentieth-century theoretical reflection, is its use of a language that 'defamiliarizes', that makes language itself strange, and with language, the world as we perceive it. Likewise—if more modestly—we hope that this short history, while making available to the present generation a heritage which is in some sense eternally familiar, will also change the angle of perception and promote fresh readings, fresh encounters with the French literary archive.

SUGGESTIONS FOR FURTHER READING

GENERAL

Readers whose curiosity about French literature and its relation to the European heritage has been stimulated by the present volume will find that valuable insights are provided by such classic works on Western literature as Erich Auerbach's *Mimesis. The Representation of Reality in Western Literature* (1946) (trans. Willard J. Trask, Princeton: Princeton University Press, 1953) and Ernst Robert Curtius's *European Literature and the Latin Middle Ages* (1948) (trans. Willard J. Trask, London: Routledge and Kegan Paul, 1979), which situate French literary production in its European context. Further guidance on the literary history of France itself, and much incisive critical discussion, can be found in *A New History of French Literature*, ed. Denis Hollier (Cambridge, Mass., and London: Harvard University Press, 1989) and *The New Oxford Companion to Literature in French*, ed. Peter France (Oxford: Clarendon Press, 1995). Readers who have a good reading knowledge of modern French but wish to find out more about its evolution and its earlier forms can consult Glanville Price, *The French Language. Present and Past* (London: Edward Arnold, 1971), or Wendy Ayres-Bennett, *A History of the French Language through Texts* (London: Routledge, 1996). An indispensable introduction to the historical geography of France is to be found in Fernand Braudel's *L'Identité de la France* (Paris: Arthaud/Flammarion, 1986), which has been translated as *The Identity of France* by Siân Reynolds (London: Collins, 1988). The changing social roles of the writer have been surveyed by John Lough in his *Writer and Public in France: From the Middle Ages to the Present Day* (Oxford: Clarendon Press, 1978); the techniques of verse composition by Clive Scott in his *French Verse-Art* (Cambridge: CUP, 1980) and its remarkable sequence of successor volumes; French theatrical traditions by Alain Viala, Jean-Pierre Bordier, and others in their *Le Théâtre en France, des origines à nos jours* (Paris: Presses Universitaires de France, 1997); the contribution of female authors by Sonya Stephens and others in *A History of Women's Writing in France* (Cambridge: CUP, 2000); and the tradition of 'life-writing' in seminal works by Philippe Lejeune (*Le Pacte autobiographique,* Paris: Seuil, 1975) and Michael Sheringham (*French Autobiography. Devices and Desires*, Oxford: Clarendon Press, 1993).

In the suggestions for further reading that follow we have concentrated, for each of the three periods covered by the present volume, on wide-angle studies rather than on appraisals of individual authors. Scholars of French literature will not need to be reminded, however, that much outstanding critical writing was, until recently, presented in the now unfashionable form of the 'single-author monograph'. Guidance on important works of this kind is to be found in many of the volumes mentioned below.

THE MIDDLE AGES

Given the length and variety of the medieval period, there is no single historical study that covers its social, political, and intellectual background. Maurice Keen's *Chivalry* (New Haven: Yale University Press, 1984) is the broadest and most accessible study of the institutions associated with knighthood. For the early French Middle Ages the works of the major French historians Georges Duby and Jacques Le Goff retain their capacity to inspire. See for example Duby, *Le Chevalier, la dame et le prêtre: le mariage dans la France féodale* (Paris: Hachette, 1981), trans. Barbara Bray as *The Knight, the Lady and the Priest. The Making of Modern Marriage in Medieval* France (Harmondsworth: Penguin, 1985); or Le Goff, *Les Intellectuels au Moyen Age* (Paris: Seuil, 1985), trans. Teresa Lavender as *Intellectuals in the Middle Ages* (Cambridge, Mass., and Oxford: Blackwell, 1993). Another very stimulating book that works between social and intellectual history in the twelfth and thirteenth centuries is Alexander Murray, *Reason and Society in the Middle Ages* (Oxford: Clarendon Press, 1985).

For the later period, Daniel Poirion's *Le Poète et le prince* (Université de Grenoble: Publications de la Faculté des Lettres et Sciences Humaines, 1965), although centred on poetic production, also deals with historical background as does the volume of literary history by the same author, *Le Moyen Age II: 1300–1480* (Paris: Arthaud, 1971). One of the most enduring works on late medieval literature and its background remains the Dutch scholar J. Huizinga's *The Waning of the Middle Ages. A Study of the Forms of Life, Thought and Art in France and the Netherlands in the Fourteenth and Fifteenth Centuries*, trans. F. Hopman (Harmondsworth: Pelican, 1955). For the domain of Occitan, an invaluable introduction is Linda Paterson, *The World of the Troubadours: Medieval Occitan Society ca. 1100–1300* (Cambridge: CUP, 1993).

Still the most challenging overview of medieval literature is Paul Zumthor, *Essai de poétique médiévale* (Paris: Seuil, 1972), trans. Philip E. Bennett as *Toward A Medieval Poetics* (Minneapolis: University of Minnesota Press, 1992). Shorter and less demanding surveys, aimed primarily at a student readership, abound. In English, the best is Simon Gaunt, *Retelling the Tale. An Introduction to French Medieval Literature* (London: Duckworth, 2001); in French, Emmanuèle Baumgartner, *La Littérature française du moyen age* (Paris: Dunod, 1999). Readable and stimulating accounts of medieval literature in relation to the visual arts are provided by Michael Camille in, among other works, *The Gothic Idol. Ideology and Image-making in Medieval Art* (Cambridge: CUP, 1989). Studies of the role of music in medieval literary culture include John Stevens, *Words and Music in the Middle Ages: Song, Narrative, Dance, and Drama* (Cambridge: CUP, 1986) and Christopher Page, *Voices and Instruments of the Middle Ages: Instrumental Practice and Songs in France 1100–1300* (Berkeley: University of California Press, 1986). Page's *The Owl and the Nightingale. Musical Life and Ideas in France 1100–1300* (London: Dent, 1989) moves away from song to musical culture more broadly. Another writer with a broad perspective on medieval literature and culture is Marina Warner; see for example *Alone of all her Sex. The Myth and the Cult of the Virgin Mary* (London: Weidenfeld and Nicolson, 1976) or *Joan of Arc: The Image of Female Heroism* (London: Weidenfeld and Nicolson, 1981). Simon Gaunt and Sarah Kay (eds.), *The Troubadours. An Introduction* (Cambridge: CUP, 1999) presents a useful outline of the literary history of the troubadours, a sampling of critical approaches to their poetry, and pointers to further reading. A similar volume, with a more technical and less literary approach, is F. R. P. Akehurst and Judith M. Davis (eds.), *A Handbook of the Troubadours* (Berkeley: University of California Press, 1995).

Much of the scholarship on medieval literature, whether French or Occitan, is to be found in learned journals and in the introductions to editions of the literary texts. However, there are a number of important monographs that can be recommended to the general as well as the more specialist reader. On the early Middle Ages, R. Howard Bloch, *Medieval French Literature and Law* (Berkeley and Los Angeles: University of California Press, 1977) has been criticized for inaccuracies of detail but nevertheless illuminates conceptual parallels between a wide range of literary texts and the upheavals in contemporary legal practice, where trial by combat or ordeal was giving way to trial by evidence and argument. Another work with broad coverage and a stimulating overall argument is Simon Gaunt, *Gender and Genre in Medieval French Literature*, Cambridge Studies in French 53 (Cambridge: CUP, 1989), which shows how ideas of gender and sexuality are differently constructed in different early medieval genres. It is the genre of romance which has stimulated the most interesting literary studies. Among the landmark studies of this genre are Erich Köhler, *L'Aventure chevaleresque. Idéal et réalité dans le roman courtois* (Paris: Gallimard, 1974), Peter Haidu, *Lion-queue-coupée: l'écart symbolique chez Chrétien de Troyes* (Geneva: Droz, 1972); Robert Hanning, *The Individual in Twelfth-Century Romance* (New Haven: Yale University Press, 1977); Roberta L. Krueger, *Women Readers and the Ideology of Gender in Old French Verse Romance* (Cambridge: CUP, 1993); and Donald Maddox, *Fictions of Identity in Medieval France* (Cambridge: CUP, 2000). Book-length studies of other genres are less common, but on the *chansons de geste* there is Sarah Kay, *The Chansons de geste in the Age of Romance: Political Fictions* (Oxford: Clarendon Press, 1995), and on *fabliaux*, R. Howard Bloch, *The Scandal of the Fabliaux* (Chicago: University of Chicago Press, 1986). An interesting study of debate poetry involving women, which extends into the later Middle Ages, is Helen Solterer, *The Master and Minerva. Disputing Women in French Medieval Culture* (Berkeley: University of California Press, 1995).

Probably the single most influential work of criticism on troubadour poetry, and still worth reading today, is Leo Spitzer, *L'Amour lointain de Jaufre Rudel et le sens de la poésie des troubadours*, University of North Carolina Studies in the Romance Languages and Literatures 5 (Chapel Hill: University of North Carolina Press, 1944). There has been a succession of monographs on the troubadours written by scholars in the United Kingdom: Leslie Topsfield, *Troubadours and Love* (Cambridge: CUP, 1975); Linda M. Paterson, *Troubadours and*

Eloquence (Oxford: OUP, 1975); Simon Gaunt, *Troubadours and Irony* (Cambridge: CUP, 1989); and Sarah Kay, *Subjectivity in Troubadour Poetry* (Cambridge: CUP, 1990). Another stimulating book to have appeared in recent years is Amelia E. van Vleck, *Memory and Re-Creation in Troubadour Lyric* (Berkeley: University of California Press, 1991), which addresses the role of orality and writing in troubadour poetics. The rise of women's and gender studies has fuelled critical interest in the women troubadours and a useful volume of essays devoted to their poetry is William D. Paden (ed.), *The Voice of the Trobairitz* (Philadelphia: University of Pennsylvania Press, 1989).

Two excellent studies encompassing the fourteenth century and the rise of a written culture are Sylvia Huot, *From Song to Book. The Poetics of Writing in Old French Lyric and Lyrical Narrative Poetry* (Ithaca, NY: Cornell University Press, 1987) and Jacqueline Cerquiglini-Toulet, *La Couleur de la mélancholie: La fréquentation des livres au XIVe siècle* (Paris: Hatier, 1993), trans. Lydia Cochrane as *The Color of Melancholy. The Uses of Books in the Fourteenth Century*, foreword by Roger Chartier (Baltimore: The Johns Hopkins University Press, 1997). The former is about the transition from lyric to narrative via the *dit* and the impact which this has on the organization and design of manuscripts; the latter presents the development of a sense of self-conscious authorship in the Middle Ages as a mournful response to the way the world has aged. Peter Ainsworth's *Froissart and the Fabric of History* (Oxford: Clarendon Press, 1990) is a literary reading of Froissart's *Chronique*.

The later medieval lyric has produced a long tradition of scholarly writing, from which we single out two titles for special mention. Paul Zumthor *Le Masque et la lumière: la poétique des grands rhétoriqueurs* remains a groundbreaking study of late medieval to early Renaissance poetry. Jane Taylor, *The Poetry of François Villon: Text and Context* (Cambridge: CUP, 2001), although focused on the famous poet, also provides a wide-ranging study of fifteenth-century poetics.

THE EARLY MODERN PERIOD

A number of outstanding studies by the historians Robin Briggs, Peter Burke, Robert Darnton, and Natalie Zemon Davis provide a sense of the social and cultural context in which early modern French literature was produced: Briggs's *Early Modern France 1560–1715* (Oxford: OUP, 1977), Burke's *Popular Culture in Early Modern Europe* (Aldershot: Wildwood House, 1988) and Davis's *Society and Culture in Early Modern France* (London: Duckworth, 1975) are broad in scope; on particular themes, Davis's *Women on the Margins: Three Seventeenth-Century Lives* (Cambridge, Mass., and London: Harvard University Press, 1995), Burke's *The Fabrication of Louis XIV* (New Haven and London: Yale University Press, 1992), and Darnton's *The Great Cat Massacre and Other Episodes in French Cultural History* (Harmondsworth: Penguin, 1985) are all illuminating and attractively written. Darnton's *The Business of Enlightenment: A Publishing History of the* Encyclopédie *1755–1800*

(Cambridge, Mass.: Harvard University Press, 1979) is more specialized but is a landmark study of a major question.

On the history of ideas and belief, which forms a central strand in the culture of the period, classic studies include Lucien Febvre, *Le Problème de l'incroyance au XVIe siècle: la religion de Rabelais* (Paris: Albin Michel, 1942); R. H. Popkin, *The History of Scepticism from Erasmus to Spinoza* (Berkeley, Los Angeles, and London: University of California Press, 1979); Paul Hazard, *La Crise de la conscience européenne 1680–1715* (Paris: Boivin, 1935) and Peter Gay, *The Enlightenment: An Interpretation*, 2 vols. (London: Wildwood House, 1967, 1973). D. C. Potts, *French Thought since 1600* (London: Methuen, 1974) provides a helpful overview of principal currents of thought.

Another landmark study is Paul Bénichou's *Morales du Grand Siècle* (Paris: Gallimard, 1949), which seminally demonstrates connections between the 'moralists' and the dramatists of the seventeenth century. A number of recent studies of seventeenth-century literature in its sociological aspect have also helped to change perceptions of the 'Grand Siècle': these include Emmanuel Bury, *Littérature et politesse: l'invention de l'honnête homme 1580–1750* (Paris: PUF, 1996); Michael Moriarty, *Taste and Ideology in Seventeenth-Century France* (Cambridge: CUP, 1988); Linda Timmermans, *L'Accès des femmes à la culture (1598–1715)* (Paris: Champion, 1993); and Alain Viala, *Naissance de l'écrivain: sociologie de la littérature à l'âge classique* (Paris: Minuit, 1985).

On poetry in the earlier part of the period, Henri Weber's *La Création poétique au XVIe siècle en France de Maurice Scève à Agrippa d'Aubigné*, 2 vols. (Paris: Nizet, 1956) still provides an impressive panorama; to correct the gender balance, one should add the brilliant comparative study by Ann Rosalind Jones, *The Currency of Eros: Women's Love Lyric in Europe 1540–1620* (Bloomington: Indiana University Press, 1990). Jean Rousset's *La Littérature de l'âge baroque en France* (Paris: Corti, 1954), another classic, focuses mainly on poetry; the term 'baroque' has remained controversial, but Rousset's study played a major role in drawing attention to the much-neglected literature of the early seventeenth century. An exception to our rule excluding studies of individual writers is necessary here: the consummate artistry of La Fontaine is brilliantly captured in Paul Valéry's essay 'Au sujet d'*Adonis*', in *Variété* (Paris: Gallimard, 1924); for a more complete study of the poet and his context, see Marc Fumaroli, *Le Poète et le roi: Jean de La Fontaine en son siècle* (Paris: Éditions de Fallois, 1997).

On the development of the novel and related genres in the later part of the period, the following are especially helpful: Faith E. Beasley, *Revising Memory: Women's Fiction and Memoirs in Seventeenth-Century France* (New Brunswick and London: Rutgers University Press, 1990); Henri Coulet, *Le Roman jusqu'à la Révolution*, 2 vols. (Paris: Armand Colin, 1967–68); English Showalter, *The Evolution of the French Novel 1641–1782* (Princeton: Princeton University Press, 1972); Georges May, *Le Dilemme du roman au XVIIIe siècle: étude sur les rapports du roman et de la critique (1715–1761)* (New Haven: Yale University Press, and Paris: PUF, 1963); and Peter Brooks, *The Novel of Worldliness: Crébillon, Marivaux, Laclos, Stendhal* (Princeton: Princeton University Press, 1969).

The theatre is an enormous terrain. Christian Delmas's *La Tragédie de l'âge classique (1553–1770)* (Paris: Seuil, 1994) and Pierre Larthomas's *Le Théâtre en France au XVIIIe siècle* (Paris: PUF, 1989) both provide useful and attractive surveys. On staging and audiences respectively, see T. E. Lawrenson's *The French Stage in the Seventeenth Century* (Manchester: Manchester University Press, 1957) and John Lough's *Paris Theatre Audiences in the Seventeenth and Eighteenth Centuries* (London: OUP, 1957). Jacques Scherer, *La Dramaturgie classique en France* (Paris: Nizet, 1959) shows how the conventions of seventeenth-century theatre operated in practice, while René Bray's classic study *La Formation de la doctrine classique en France* (Paris: Nizet, 1957) remains a helpful reference study of the complex history of dramatic (and poetic) theory in the same period.

Questions of poetics and rhetoric have been prominent in the revaluation of early modern French literature in the last half-century. Terence Cave's *The Cornucopian Text: Problems of Writing in the French Renaissance* (Oxford: Clarendon Press, 1979), Antoine Compagnon's *La Seconde Main, ou le travail de la citation* (Paris: Seuil, 1979), and Marc Fumaroli's *L'Age de l'éloquence* (Geneva: Droz, 1980) all contributed in their different ways to this shift of emphasis. Grahame Castor's classic study, *Pléiade Poetics* (Cambridge: CUP, 1964), is important not only for sixteenth-century poetic theory but also for the intellectual history of the period. On style, Leo Spitzer's *Essays on Seventeenth-Century French Literature* (attractively translated by David Bellos, Cambridge: CUP, 1983) remains indispensable.

THE MODERN PERIOD

The historical literature on the French Revolution and its aftermath is now vast. William Doyle's *The French Revolution: A Very Short Introduction* (Oxford: OUP, 2001) provides an admirable starting point. A fuller introductory survey is to be found in Simon Schama's *Citizens: a Chronicle of the French Revolution* (London: Penguin, 1989), and more specialized studies are readily available from Norman Hampson, Richard Cobb, Alan Forrest, T. C. W. Blanning, Lynn Hunt and others. Hampson is the author of a remarkable series of political biographies devoted to such central figures as Danton, Robespierre, and Saint-Just. The extraordinary vogue for historical writing in the early nineteenth century is portrayed by Ceri Crossley in his *French Historians and Romanticism* (London and New York: Routledge, 1993). More recent episodes in the political history of France are narrated and discussed in major English-language works by Douglas Johnson, Robert Tombs, H. R. Kedward, and Robert Gildea. A panoramic view of French social history in the modern period is offered by Theodore Zeldin in the two weighty volumes of his *France 1848–1945* (Oxford: OUP, 1973 and 1977). A ground-breaking collective history of French institutions, events, myths, and commemorative acts is to be found in the series of volumes edited by Pierre Nora under the general title *Les Lieux de mémoire* (Paris: Gallimard, 1984–92): *La République, La Nation, Les France*.

The changing social role of the writer in the late eighteenth and early nineteenth centuries has been memorably reconstructed by Paul Bénichou in *Le Sacre de l'écrivain: essai sur l'avènement d'un pouvoir spirituel laïque dans la France moderne* (Paris: Corti, 1985) and its successor volumes. An essential guide to the changing methods of the printing trade, and to their effects both on literary production and on reading habits, has been supplied by J. Smith Allen in his *Popular French Romanticism: Authors, Readers and Books in the Nineteenth Century* (Syracuse, NY: Syracuse University Press, 1981) and *In the Public Eye: a History of Reading in Modern France, 1800–1940* (Princeton: Princeton University Press, 1991).

Outstanding works on prose fiction, and related topics, in the modern period include: Peter Brooks, *Reading for the Plot: Design and Intention in Narrative* (Oxford and New York: OUP, 1984); Christopher Prendergast, *The Order of Mimesis: Balzac, Stendhal, Nerval, Flaubert* (Cambridge: CUP, 1986); David Baguley, *Naturalist Fiction: the Entropic Vision* (Cambridge: CUP, 1990); Shoshana Felman, *La Folie et la chose littéraire* (Paris: Seuil, 1978); Victor Brombert, *The Hidden Reader: Stendhal, Balzac, Hugo, Baudelaire, Flaubert* (Cambridge, Mass., and London: Harvard University Press, 1988); John Cruickshank (ed.), *The Novelist as Philosopher: Studies in Fiction, 1935–60* (London and New York: OUP, 1962); Jean Ricardou, *Pour une théorie du nouveau roman* (Paris: Seuil, 1971); Ann Jefferson, *The Nouveau Roman and the Poetics of Fiction* (Cambridge: CUP, 1980); Colin Davis and Elizabeth Fallaize, *French Fiction in the Mitterrand Years: Memory, Narrative, Desire* (Oxford: OUP, 2000).

The single most compelling account of the development of modern French poetry is still Marcel Raymond's *De Baudelaire au surréalisme* (1940) (Paris: Corti, 1966), which is also available in translation as *From Baudelaire to Surrealism* (London: Peter Owen, 1957). A useful general introduction to the poetry of the period is to be found in the companion volumes *The Appreciation of Modern French Poetry, 1850–1950* and *An Anthology of Modern French Poetry, 1850–1950* by Peter Broome and Graham Chesters (Cambridge: CUP, 1976), while the views of the poets themselves on the creative process have been collected by Robert Gibson in his *Modern French Poets on Poetry* (Cambridge: CUP, 1961). Julia Kristeva's *La Révolution du langage poétique* (Paris: Seuil, 1974) launched a new way of looking at nineteenth-century French poetry as a social act. Among many outstanding studies of surrealism and its forebears, particular mention should be made of Michel Sanouillet's *Dada à Paris* (Paris: Flammarion, 1993) and Sarane Alexandrian's *Le Surréalisme et le rêve* (Paris: Gallimard, 1975).

The general development of French theatre in the nineteenth and twentieth centuries is traced in *Le Théâtre en France, des origines à nos jours* (see above, p. 317). Among major studies of specific periods are: W. D. Howarth, *Sublime and Grotesque: a Study of French Romantic Drama* (London: Harrap, 1975); F. W. J. Hemmings, *The Theatre Industry in Nineteenth-Century France* (Cambridge: CUP, 1993); Martin Esslin, *The Theatre of the Absurd* (Harmondsworth: Penguin, 1968); David Bradby, *Modern French Drama,*

1940–1990 (Cambridge: CUP, 1991). The relationship between literature and painting has been studied by David Scott in his *Pictorialist Poetics: Poetry and the Visual Arts in Nineteenth-Century France* (Cambridge: CUP, 1988) and by the contributors to *Artistic Relations: Literature and the Visual Arts in Nineteenth-Century France* (ed. Peter Collier and Robert Lethbridge, New Haven and London: Yale University Press, 1994). Compelling feminist perspectives on the literature of the period are to be found in: Alison Finch, *Women's Writing in Nineteenth-Century France* (Cambridge: CUP, 2000); Diana Holmes, *French Women's Writing, 1848–1994* (London: Athlone Press, 1996); Margaret Atack and Phil Powrie (eds.), *Contemporary French Fiction by Women: Feminist Perspectives* (Manchester: Manchester University Press, 1990); and Toril Moi, *Sexual/Textual Politics* (London: Methuen, 1985). Belinda Jack provides a lucid overview of French literature from outside France in her *Francophone Literatures: an Introductory Survey* (Oxford: OUP, 1996), while Ginette Vincendeau introduces the tradition of French film in her *Companion to French Cinema* (London: Cassell/ British Film Institute, 1996). The legacies of 1968 are explored by Keith Reader in *The May 1968 Events in France: Reproductions and Interpretations* (Basingstoke: Macmilllan, 1993); *Intellectuals and the Left in France since 1968* (Basingstoke: Macmillan, 1987); and by Margaret Atack in *May 1968 in French Fiction and Film: Rethinking Society, Rethinking Representation* (Oxford: OUP, 1999).

FRENCH LITERATURE IN TRANSLATION

A wide selection of major French texts is now available in translation, in such paperback series as Oxford World's Classics, Penguin Classics and Modern Classics. Many early texts (such as those published in the 'lettres gothiques' series of Livre de poche) are also available in bilingual editions, with facing translations in modern English or modern French. Reading a text in translation is not the ideal way to read it, but may well be preferable to not having read it at all.

SOURCES OF QUOTATIONS

Textes Français (Paris: Firmin-Didot, 1878–1903), vol. I, *ballades* CXXIII and CXXIV.

71–2 Charles d'Orléans, *Poésies*, ed. Pierre Champion, 2 vols., Classiques Français du Moyen Age (Paris: Champion, 1923–4), vol. I, *ballade* VIII.

78 Guillaume de Machaut, *La Fontaine amoureuse*, ed. Jacqueline Cerquiglini, Stock/Moyen Age (Paris: Stock, 1993), ll. 2845–8.

80 Christine de Pizan, *Le Livre du Duc des vrais amans*, ed. Thelma S. Fenster, Medieval and Renaissance Texts and Studies (Binghamton, NY: Center for Medieval and Early Renaissance Studies, 1995), Letter V, 152–4 (p. 176); ll. 39–40 (p. 68).

85 Christine de Pizan, *Le Livre de la Cité des dames*, ed. Earl Jeffrey Richards, trans. Patrizia Caraffi (Rome: Luni, 1997), III. xix (p. 500).

86 *Les Cent Nouvelles nouvelles*, ed. Franklin P. Sweetser, Textes Littéraires Français (Geneva: Droz, 1996), p. 351.

89 Alain Chartier, 'La Belle Dame sans mercy', *The Poetical Works of Alain Chartier*, ed. J. C. Laidlaw (Cambridge: CUP, 1974), l. 780 (p. 359).

92 François Villon, 'Ballade de bonne doctrine', *Le Testament*, ed. Jean Rychner and Albert Henry, Textes Littéraires Français (Geneva: Droz, 1974), ll. 1700–7.

94 Villon, 'Ballade des belles dames de jadis', *Le Testament*, ll. 353–6.

PART II. THE EARLY MODERN PERIOD

100 François Rabelais, *Œuvres complètes*, ed. Mireille Huchon (Paris: Gallimard, Bibliothèque de la Pléiade, 1994), p. 124.

108 Boileau, *Œuvres complètes*, ed. Antoine Adam and Françoise Escal (Paris: Gallimard, Bibliothèque de la Pléiade, 1966), *L'Art poétique*, p. 160.

121 Rabelais, *Œuvres complètes*, p. 149.

123 Rabelais, *Œuvres complètes*, p. 379.

124 Clément Marot, *Œuvres poétiques*, ed. G. Defaux, vol. I (Paris: Classiques Garnier, 1990), pp. 161–2.

126 Maurice Scève, *Délie*, ed. I. D. McFarlane (Cambridge: CUP, 1966), *dizain* 161.

127 Scève, *Délie*, *dizain* 148 and *dizain* 367.

127–8 Pernette Du Guillet, *Rymes* (with Louise Labé, *Œuvres poétiques*), ed. Françoise Charpentier (Paris: Gallimard, Poésie, 1983), no. VIII (p. 38).

128 Louise Labé, *Œuvres complètes*, ed. François Rigolot (Paris: GF-Flammarion, 1986), p. 41.

128–9 Labé, *Œuvres complètes*, sonnet 24.

131 Joachim Du Bellay, *Les Regrets*, ed. J. Joliffe and M.A. Screech (Geneva: Droz, 1966), sonnet 6 and sonnet 1.

132 Ibid., sonnet 31.

132   Pierre de Ronsard, *Œuvres complètes*, ed. Jean Céard, Daniel Ménager et Michel Simonin, vol. I (Paris: Gallimard, Bibliothèque de la Pléiade, 1993), *Second Livre des Sonnets pour Helene*, sonnet 43 (p. 400).

132   Ibid., *Le Second Livre des Amours*, II, sonnet 4 (pp. 254–5).

133   Ibid., *Second Livre des sonnets pour Helene*, sonnet 10 (p. 384; quoted according to the first edition of 1578; see also p. 1383, variants for this sonnet).

134   Agrippa d'Aubigné, *Les Tragiques*, in *Œuvres*, ed. Henri Weber (Paris: Gallimard, Bibliothèque de la Pléiade, 1969), Book II, *Princes*, ll. 77–8 (p. 56).

137   Michel de Montaigne, *Les Essais*, ed. Pierre Villey et V.-L. Saulnier (Paris: PUF, 1965), II. 17, p. 657.

138   Ibid., III.2, p. 806.

140   Théophile de Viau, *Œuvres poétiques*, ed. Guido Saba (Paris: Champion, 1999), vol. I, *Elegie à une Dame*, ll. 71–2, 115–16, 119 (pp. 203, 205).

147   Pierre Corneille, *Œuvres complètes*, ed. Georges Couton, vol. I (Paris: Gallimard, Bibliothèque de la Pléiade, 1980), *Horace*, l. 1319 (p. 887).

148   René Descartes, *Œuvres philosophiques*, ed. Ferdinand Alquié, vol. I (Paris: Garnier, 1963), *Discours de la méthode*, p. 603.

149   Ibid., p. 568.

151   Blaise Pascal, *Œuvres complètes*, ed. Louis Lafuma (Paris: Seuil, l'Intégrale), *Pensées*, no. 780, p. 599, and no. 532, p. 578.

154   Molière, *Œuvres complètes*, ed. Georges Couton (Paris: Gallimard, Bibliothèque de la Pléiade, 1971), vol. II, *Le Misanthrope*, I.1, l. 63 (p. 144).

155   Jean Racine, *Œuvres complètes*, vol. I: *Théâtre—Poésie*, ed. Georges Forestier (Paris: Gallimard, Bibliothèque de la Pléiade, 1999), *Bérénice*, IV.5, ll. 1068–70 (p. 492).

156   Racine, *Œuvres complètes*, *Bérénice*, III.1, l. 736 (p. 480).

156   La Rochefoucauld, *Maximes*, ed. J. Truchet (Paris: Garnier, 1967), p. 7.

156   Molière, *Œuvres complètes*, vol. II, *Dom Juan*, V.2, p. 80.

157   Ibid., vol. I, *L'Impromptu de Versailles*, sc. 1, p. 682.

158–9 Racine, *Œuvres complètes*, *Bérénice*, II.4, ll. 621–4 (p. 476).

159   Bossuet, *Oraisons funèbres*, ed. J. Truchet (Paris: Garnier, 1961), *Oraison funèbre du Prince de Condé*, pp. 407–8.

160   Racine, *Œuvres complètes*, *Athalie*, II.5, ll. 1025–7 (p. 1054).

162   La Bruyère, *Les Caractères*, ed. R. Garapon (Paris: Garnier, 1962), *Des ouvrages de l'esprit*, 1, p. 67.

171   Montesquieu, *Lettres persanes*, ed. Paul Vernière (Paris: Garnier, 1960), Lettre 24, p. 56.

173   Françoise de Graffigny, *Lettres d'une Péruvienne*, ed. Jonathan Mallinson (Oxford: Voltaire Foundation, 2002), p. 222.

174   Voltaire, *Romans et contes*, ed. Frédéric Deloffre et Jacques van den Heuvel (Paris: Gallimard, Bibliothèque de la Pléiade), *Candide*, p. 233.

188 Denis Diderot, *Œuvres romanesques*, ed. H. Bénac (Paris: Garnier, 1962), *Jacques le Fataliste*, p. 528.

189 Jean-Jacques Rousseau, *Œuvres complètes*, vol. III (Paris: Gallimard, Bibliothèque de la Pléiade, 1964), *Discours sur l'origine et les fondements de l'inégalité*, ed. Jean Starobinski, p. 194.

PART III. THE MODERN PERIOD

196 Honoré de Balzac, *Illusions perdues*, ed. Antoine Adam (Paris: Garnier, 1961), p. 14.

205 Denis Diderot, *Œuvres esthétiques,* ed. Paul Vernière (Paris: Garnier, 1959), 'De la poésie dramatique', p. 261.

209 Emmanuel de Siéyès, *Qu'est-ce que le Tiers état?,* ed. Roberto Zapperi (Geneve: Droz, 1970), p. 119.

210 *French Revolution Documents,* I, ed. J. M. Roberts (Oxford: Basil Blackwell, 1966), p. 172.

210 Georges Jacques Danton, *Discours*, ed. André Fribourg (Paris: Hachette, 1910), p. 54 [Assemblée législative, 2 septembre 1792].

212 Benjamin Constant, *Œuvres,* ed. Alfred Roulin (Paris: Gallimard, Bibliothèque de la Pléiade, 1957), pp. 70–1.

213 Étienne Pivert de Senancour, *Obermann*, ed. Jean-Maurice Monnoyer (Paris: Gallimard, Folio, 1984), Lettre LXVIII, p. 391.

215 Choderlos de Laclos, *Œuvres complètes*, ed. Laurent Versini (Paris: Gallimard, Bibliothèque de la Pléiade, 1979), Lettre CX, p. 257.

217 Victor Hugo, *Œuvres poétiques*, vol. I, ed. Pierre Albouy (Paris: Gallimard, Bibliothèque de la Pléiade, 1964), p. 445.

217 Gerard de Nerval, *Œuvres*, ed. Albert Béguin et Jean Richer (Paris: Gallimard, Bibliothèque de la Pléiade, 1952), p. 39.

218 Alphonse de Lamartine, *Œuvres poétiques*, ed. Marius-François Guyard (Paris: Gallimard, Bibliothèque de la Pléiade, 1963), p. 171.

219 Alfred de Musset, *Poésies complètes*, ed. Maurice Allem (Paris: Gallimard, Bibliothèque de la Pléiade, 1957), pp. 310–13.

220 Marceline Desbordes-Valmore, *Poésies* (Paris: Gallimard, Poésie, 1983), p. 181, trans. Alison Finch.

221 Ibid., p. 120.

226 Stendhal, *La Chartreuse de Parme,* in *Romans et nouvelles*, vol. II, ed. Henri Martineau (Paris: Gallimard, Bibliothèque de la Pléiade, 1952), p. 251.

227 Honoré de Balzac, *La Cousine Bette,* ed. Maurice Allem (Paris: Garnier, 1962), p. 239.

228 Balzac, *Le Père Goriot*, ed. Pierre-Georges Castex (Paris: Garnier, 1960), p. 159.

229 Victor Hugo, *Théâtre complet*, vol. I, ed. J.-J. Thierry et Josette Mélèze (Paris: Gallimard, Bibliothèque de la Pléiade, 1963), p. 436.

229 Hugo, *Romans*, vol. III, ed. Henri Guillemin (Paris: Seuil, 1963), p. 140.

229   Ibid., vol. I, ed. Henri Guillemin (Paris: Seuil, 1963), p. 258.

230   Hugo, *Œuvres poétiques*, vol. I, ed. Pierre Albouy (Paris: Gallimard, Bibliothèque de la Pléiade, 1964), p. 787.

230   Ibid., vol. II, ed. Pierre Albouy (Paris: Gallimard, Bibliothèque de la Pléiade, 1967), p. 522.

230   Hugo, *La Légende des siècles*, ed. Jacques Truchet (Paris: Gallimard, Bibliothèque de la Pléiade, 1950), p. 36.

231   Gérard de Nerval, *Œuvres*, ed. Albert Béguin et Jean Richer (Paris: Gallimard, Bibliothèque de la Pléiade, 1952), p. 29.

232   Charles Baudelaire, *Œuvres complètes*, vol. I, ed. Claude Pichois (Paris: Gallimard, Bibliothèque de la Pléiade, 1975), pp. 64 and 53.

233   Ibid., p. 118.

233   Ibid., p. 119.

233   Arthur Rimbaud, *Œuvres*, ed. Suzanne Bernard (Paris: Garnier, 1960), Lettre à Paul Demeny, p. 349.

233   Ibid., p. 273.

234   Stéphane Mallarmé, *Œuvres complètes*, vol. I, ed. Bertrand Marchal (Paris: Gallimard, Bibliothèque de la Pléiade, 1998), Lettre à Eugène Lefébure, p. 669.

234   Hippolyte Taine, *Introduction à l'histoire de la littérature anglaise*, ed. H. B. Charlton (Manchester: Manchester University Press, 1936), p. 39.

235   Mallarmé, *Œuvres complètes*, Lettre à Henri Cazalis, p. 714.

235   Ibid., p. 44, trans. Harry Weinfield.

236   Leo Tolstoy, *What is Art?* and *Essays on Art,* trans. Aylmer Maude (Oxford: OUP, 1930), p. 167.

238   Delphine de Girardin, *Chroniques parisiennes, 1836–1848*, ed. Jean-Louis Vissière (Paris: Des femmes, 1986), p. 243.

238   Flora Tristan, *Union Ouvrière*, ed. Daniel Armogathe et Jacques Grandjonc (Paris: Des femmes, 1986), p. 191.

240   George Sand, *Consuelo. La comtesse de Rudolstadt*, vol. I, ed. Simone Vierne et René Bourgeois (Grenoble: Editions de l'Aurore, 1991), p. 77.

243   Hugo, *Théâtre complet*, vol. I, ed. J.-J. Thierry et Josette Mélèze (Paris: Gallimard, Bibliothèque de la Pléiade, 1963), p. 1520.

245   Gustave Flaubert, *Madame Bovary*, ed. Claudine Gothot-Mersch (Paris: Garnier, 1971), p. 19.

246   Ibid., p. 126.

247   Flaubert, *Bouvard et Pécuchet*, ed. Édouard Maynial (Paris: Garnier, 1965), p. 99.

249   Émile Zola, *Les Rougon-Macquart*, vol. II, ed. Armand Lanoux et Henri Mitterand (Paris: Gallimard, Bibliothèque de la Pléiade, 1961), p. 798 [insert].

252   Zola, *L'Affaire Dreyfus: la vérité en marche,* ed. Colette Becker (Paris: Garnier-Flammarion, 1969), p. 122.

253   Georges Bernanos, *La Grande Peur des bien-pensants: Édouard Drumont* [1931] (Paris: Gallimard, Livre de Poche, 1969), p. 382.

255 André Gide, *L'Immoraliste*, in *Romans*, ed. Yvonne Davet and Jean-Jacques Thierry (Paris: Gallimard, Bibliothèque de la Pléiade, 1958), p. 411.

255 Gide, *Les Faux-Monnayeurs*, in ibid., pp. 1082–3.

257 Marcel Proust, *A la recherche du temps perdu*, vol. IV, ed. Jean-Yves Tadié (Paris: Gallimard, Bibliothèque de la Pléiade, 1989), p. 476.

257 Ibid., vol. III, ed. Jean-Yves Tadié (Paris: Gallimard, Bibliothèque de la Pléiade, 1989), p. 180.

259 Guillaume Apollinaire, *Œuvre poétique,* ed. Marcel Adéma et Michel Décaudin (Paris: Gallimard, Bibliothèque de la Pléiade, 1965), p. 280.

260 Ibid., p. 281.

262 Paul Valéry, *Œuvres*, vol. I, ed. Jean Hytier (Paris: Gallimard, Bibliothèque de la Pléiade, 1957), p. 150, trans. G. D. Martin.

263 Ibid., vol. I, pp. 142–3.

263 Yvor Winters, *The Function of Criticism* (London: Routledge and Kegan Paul, 1962), p. 74.

265 André Breton, *Manifestes du surréalisme* (Paris: Jean-Jacques Pauvert, 1962), p. 40.

266 Ibid., p. 28.

266 Breton, *L'Amour fou* (Paris: Gallimard, 1937), p. 21.

266 Louis Aragon, *Le Paysan de Paris* (Paris: Gallimard, 1926), p. 28.

269 Louis-Ferdinand Céline, *Voyage au bout de la nuit* [1932] (Paris: Gallimard/Folio, 1974), p. 330.

270 André Malraux, *La Condition humaine* [1933] (Paris: Gallimard, 1946), p. 191.

272 Jean-Paul Sartre, *L'Être et le Néant* (Paris: Gallimard, 1943), p. 126.

272 Ibid., p. 127.

274 Jean-Paul Sartre, *Qu'est-ce que la littérature?* (Paris: Gallimard, 1948), p. 65.

276 Vercors, *Le Silence de la mer* [1942] *et autres récits* (Paris: Albin Michel, 1951), p. 33.

277 Jean Cassou, *Trente-trois sonnets composés au secret* [1944] (Paris: Mercure de France, 1962), pp. 49–50.

278 Albert Camus, *La Chute* (Paris: Gallimard, 1956), p. 16.

280 Alain Robbe-Grillet, *Dans le labyrinthe* (Paris: Minuit, 1959), p. 11.

281 Nathalie Sarraute, *Œuvres romanesques*, ed. Jean-Yves Tadié (Paris: Gallimard, Bibliothèque de la Pléiade, 1996), p. 467.

284 Georges Perec, *La Vie mode d'emploi* (Paris: Hachette, 1978), p. 318.

287 Marguerite Yourcenar, *Discours de réception à l'Académie française* (Paris: Gallimard, 1981), p. 10.

288 Simone de Beauvoir, *Le deuxième sexe* (Paris: Gallimard, 1949), p. 90.

288 Ibid., p. 91.

292 Marguerite Duras, *India Song. Texte, théâtre, film* (Paris: Gallimard, 1973), p. 57.

296 Samuel Beckett, *Fin de partie* (Paris: Minuit, 1957), p. 49.

297   Beckett, *Têtes-mortes* (Paris: Minuit, 1972), pp. 73–4.
298   René Char, *Poèmes et prose choisis* (Paris: Gallimard, 1957), p. 42.
298   Ibid., p. 233.
299   Yves Bonnefoy, *Poèmes* (Paris: Gallimard, Poésie, 1982), p. 126, trans. Anthony Rudolf.
300   Bonnefoy, *L'Improbable et autres essais* (Paris: Gallimard, Folio/essais, 1992), p. 117.
300   Saint-John Perse, *Œuvres complètes* (Paris: Gallimard, Bibliothèque de la Pléiade), p. 444.
304   Aimé Césaire, *The Collected Poetry*, ed. and trans. Clayton Eshleman and Annette Smith (Berkeley, Los Angeles, London: University of California Press, 1983), p. 58.
304   Césaire, *The Collected Poetry*, p. 72.
305   Antonine Maillet, *Pélagie-la-Charrette* (Paris: Grasset, 1979), p. 279.
308   Michel Leiris, *Biffures (La Règle du jeu*, vol. I, 1948) (Paris: Gallimard, 1975), p. 20.
308   Leiris, *Frêle bruit (La Règle du jeu*, vol. IV) (Paris: Gallimard, 1976), pp. 166–7.
308   Leiris, *Biffures*, p. 18.

INDEX

In addition to identifying substantive mentions of people, works, and topics, this index provides the dates (where known) of French writers and works discussed in this book. For most authors dates are those of birth and death, but for some medieval writers they mark the period (indicated by *fl.*) during which they were presumed to be active. Works are indexed under the names of their authors wherever possible. Unless otherwise indicated the dates of works are those of publication, except for early medieval works where they are those of assumed composition, and for early modern plays where they are those of first performance.